Food in the Fast Lane

Beta Sigma Phi

Beta Sigma Phi

Food in the Fast Lane

EDITORIAL STAFF

Managing Editor	Mary Jane Blount
Executive Editor	Debbie Seigenthaler
Project Managers	Georgia Brazil, Mary Cummings
Editors	Ashlee Brown, Christie Carlucci Jane Hinshaw, Linda Jones Charlene Sproles, Mary Wilson
Associate Editors	Tracy Barrett, Judy Jackson Carolyn King, Rachel Lawson Debbie Van Mol
Typographers	Pam Newsome Sara Anglin, Jessie Anglin
Award Selection Judges	Bill Ross Mary Jane Blount Charlene Sproles

Cover Photograph: Courtesy of the Hershey Foods Corporation; Page 1: Courtesy of the Michigan Asparagus Advisory Board, Corning, Inc., and Wish-Bone® Italian Dressings; Page 2: Courtesy of the Hershey Foods Corporation

© Favorite Recipes® Press, A Division of Heritage House, Inc. MCMLXII
    P.O. Box 305141, Nashville, Tennessee 37230

ISBN: 0-87197-346-4
Library of Congress Number: 92-23181

Manufactured in the United States of America
First Printing 1992
Second Printing 1992

Recipes for photographs are on pages 24–26.

Contents

Beta Sigma Phi

Linda Rostenberg

Dear Beta Sigma Phis:

If there's one thing we sisters have in common besides sorority, it's that we're all BUSY! Luckily, many of you have spared a few minutes from your packed schedules to send us some recipes that are quick to make and delicious—and the result is our newest Beta Sigma Phi cookbook:

Food in the Fast Lane

Personally, I love the concept. What's better than a dish that takes minutes to make, tastes great, and impresses everybody? People like me who are generally allergic to kitchens are gonna love this book!

You'll find some *quick and easy craft projects* in this book, too. As usual, we've awarded *prizes in various food categories*; these 'best-of-the-best' recipes are specially marked in the book with the ❖ symbol.

I think the Beta Sigma Phi *Food in the Fast Lane* cookbook is going to be my favorite resource when I need to throw dinner together quickly and well—which is just about daily! And won't this book make a wonderful *holiday gift* for another busy Beta Sigma Phi, or an inept bachelor, or a new-to-the-kitchen newlywed?

It's the perfect present for a busy person—brought to you by Beta Sigma Phis—the best cooks on earth, and the busiest ones!

Yours in Beta Sigma Phi,

Linda Rostenberg

Linda Rostenberg
Beta Sigma Phi International
Executive Committee

Menu Magic

With the demands of family, jobs, volunteer work and managing households, entertaining may become something we still love but never seem to find the time for. But if you, like most of us, have put off entertaining at home because you're too busy, we've got some great ideas to help you have *fun* in the fast lane. Welcoming friends and family need not be an elaborate affair requiring days of preparation and hours in a hot kitchen, nor do you need to spend a fortune. We've put together menus, recipes and preparation hints from Beta Sigma Phi members around the country for reunion dinners, superbowl parties and mystery dinners, as well as lifesavers like thirty-minute suppers, elegant last-minute luncheons and easy brunches. Shazam! We've even got holiday feasts to delight your guests and leave you with time to enjoy them too.

Try-Something-New Chapter Social

Custard Chicken Loaf
Sliced Baked Potatoes
Three-Bean and Rice Casserole
Black Olive Salad — Easy Pepper Salad
Rhubarb Butter Crunch
Chart House Mud Pie

Each member of our chapter chose to bring to our social an easy recipe she had never tried. We enjoyed all of the dishes. This menu represents just some of the choices.

Laureate Xi
Coos Bay, North Bend, Oregon

CUSTARD CHICKEN LOAF

1 loaf stale bread, cubed	1/2 teaspoon pepper
3 tablespoons cream	5 cups chopped cooked
3 tablespoons melted	chicken
butter or margarine	3/4 cup all-purpose flour
2 tablespoons chopped	1/2 cup melted butter
onion	4 cups chicken broth
1/4 cup chopped celery	6 eggs, slightly beaten
1/2 teaspoon poultry	Buttered dry bread
seasoning	crumbs
1 teaspoon salt	

Preheat oven to 325 degrees. Combine first 8 ingredients in bowl; mix well. Spread in greased 9-by-13-inch baking dish. Top with chicken. Blend flour into 1/2 cup butter in double boiler. Stir in chicken broth. Cook until thickened, stirring constantly. Stir a small amount of hot mixture into eggs; stir eggs into hot mixture. Spoon over chicken. Top with bread crumbs. Bake until bubbly and set. Yield: 12 servings.

Juanita Carlsen

SLICED BAKED POTATOES

4 medium baking	1/4 cup shredded
potatoes	Cheddar cheese
1 teaspoon salt	1 1/2 tablespoons grated
3 tablespoons melted	Parmesan cheese
butter or margarine	
2 to 3 teaspoons	
chopped fresh parsley,	
chives, thyme or dill	

Preheat oven to 425 degrees. Cut potatoes into thin slices, cutting to but not through bottom. Place in baking pan. Sprinkle with salt; drizzle with butter. Sprinkle with choice of herbs. Bake for 50 minutes or until tender. Sprinkle with cheeses. Bake until cheeses melt. Yield: 4 servings.

Donna Bird

THREE-BEAN AND RICE CASSEROLE

1 16-ounce can kidney	1 16-ounce can stewed
beans	tomatoes
1 16-ounce can	1 4-ounce can chopped
garbanzo beans	green chilies, drained
1 16-ounce can black	3 cups water
beans	1 10-ounce package
1 medium onion,	frozen peas, thawed
chopped	1/2 cup pimento-stuffed
2 tablespoons vegetable	green olives
oil	
2 cups uncooked long	
grain rice	

Preheat oven to 375 degrees. Rinse and drain beans. Sauté onion in oil in Dutch oven until tender. Add rice. Cook until opaque. Add beans, tomatoes, green chilies and water. Bring to a boil. Bake, covered, for 30 minutes. Stir in peas and olives. Bake for 15 minutes longer. Yield: 12 servings.

Hazel Clay

BLACK OLIVE SALAD

2 large tomatoes,	2 4-ounce cans
chopped	chopped black olives,
1 large bunch green	drained
onions, chopped	1/2 cup vegetable oil
1 8-ounce jar picante	1 teaspoon garlic salt
sauce	

Combine tomatoes, green onions, picante sauce, olives, oil and garlic salt in bowl; mix well. Marinate in refrigerator for up to 24 hours. Yield: 6 servings.

Linda Martin

EASY PEPPER SALAD

1 red bell pepper	1/2 cup olive oil
1 green bell pepper	1 teaspoon minced garlic
1 yellow bell pepper	Salt and pepper to taste

Place peppers on rack in broiler pan. Broil until skin is blackened. Place in plastic bag. Let stand for 15 minutes. Peel peppers; cut into 2-inch squares. Combine with olive oil, garlic, salt and pepper in bowl. Marinate in refrigerator. Yield: 6 to 8 servings.

Gloria Golder

RHUBARB BUTTER CRUNCH

3 cups chopped fresh or
   frozen rhubarb
1 cup sugar
3 tablespoons
   all-purpose flour
1 cup oats

1 cup packed light
   brown sugar
1½ cups all-purpose
   flour
½ cup butter
½ cup margarine

Preheat oven to 350 degrees. Mix rhubarb with sugar
and 3 tablespoons flour in 9-by-9-inch baking pan.
Mix oats, brown sugar and 1½ cups flour in bowl.
Cut in butter and margarine until crumbly. Sprinkle
over rhubarb. Bake for 40 minutes. May double
rhubarb for 9-by-13-inch pan, leaving topping ingredients the same. Yield: 12 servings.

Muriel Brainurd

CHART HOUSE MUD PIE

½ package chocolate
   wafers, crushed
¼ cup melted butter or
   margarine
1 gallon coffee ice
   cream

1½ cups hot fudge
   sauce
Whipped cream
Chopped nuts

Mix wafer crumbs with butter in bowl. Press over
bottom and side of 9-inch pie plate to form crust.
Spread with ice cream. Freeze until firm. Let stand at
room temperature for 15 minutes. Serve with hot
fudge sauce, whipped cream and nuts.
Yield: 8 servings.

Juanita Carlsen

Quick Elegant Luncheon

Deviled Eggs
Chicken Salad-Stuffed
Tomatoes
Melon Slices
Blueberry Muffins
Rice Cream Pie

*This is one of my favorite summer menus for a
light, yet filling luncheon. The pie recipe is
special because it was my grandmother's favorite
dessert.*

Susan McDonald, Xi Alpha Omega
Story, Wyoming

DEVILED EGGS

6 hard-cooked eggs
1 tablespoon Dijon
   mustard
2 tablespoons
   mayonnaise-type
   salad dressing

⅛ teaspoon sugar
⅛ teaspoon onion
   powder
⅛ teaspoon salt
Paprika to taste

Slice eggs lengthwise. Remove yolks to bowl and
mash. Add next 5 ingredients; mix well. Spoon into
egg whites. Sprinkle with paprika. Chill, covered,
until serving time. Yield: 6 servings.

CHICKEN SALAD-STUFFED TOMATOES

6 tomatoes
Chopped walnuts
Margarine
3 cups chopped cooked
   chicken
1 cup chopped celery
½ cup chopped green
   onions

¾ cup sliced grapes
1 teaspoon salt
1 teaspoon pepper
½ cup mayonnaise
½ cup mayonnaise-
   type salad dressing
2 teaspoons lemon juice

Slice tomatoes into 6 wedges, cutting to but not
through bottom. Invert onto plate. Chill in refrigerator. Sauté walnuts in margarine in skillet until
golden brown. Mix next 6 ingredients in bowl. Add
mixture of mayonnaise, salad dressing and lemon
juice; mix gently. Scoop into tomatoes on serving
plates. Top with walnuts. Yield: 6 servings.

BLUEBERRY MUFFINS

1⅓ cups all-purpose
   flour
1 cup oats
¼ cup packed light
   brown sugar
1 tablespoon baking
   powder
½ teaspoon cinnamon

½ teaspoon salt
   (optional)
1 cup skim milk
1 egg, beaten
3 tablespoons vegetable
   oil
1 cup fresh or frozen
   blueberries

Preheat oven to 425 degrees. Mix dry ingredients in
bowl. Combine milk, egg and oil in small bowl. Add
to dry ingredients; mix just until moistened. Fold in
blueberries. Spoon into paper-lined muffin cups.
Bake for 20 to 25 minutes or until golden brown.
Yield: 12 to 15 servings.

RICE CREAM PIE

½ cup peanut butter
½ cup light corn syrup
2 cups crisp rice cereal

½ gallon vanilla ice
   cream or ice milk,
   softened

Blend peanut butter and corn syrup in bowl. Stir in
cereal. Press into deep-dish pie plate to form crust.
Spoon ice cream into prepared pie plate. Freeze for
1½ hours or longer. Cut into squares with knife
dipped in warm water. Yield: 6 to 8 servings.

Heart-Healthy Dinner

Grilled Lamb Chops
Barbecued Potatoes
Au Gratin Scallions
Jelly Muffins
English Trifle

This menu is a result of my husband's recent heart surgery. We are finding that we can still enjoy good food on a heart-healthy diet.

Lou Alexander, Xi Xi Rho
Arlington, Texas

GRILLED LAMB CHOPS

2 lamb chops, trimmed
1 tablespoon olive oil
1/4 teaspoon pepper
1/2 teaspoon salt or
  herbs to taste

Sprinkle lamb chops with olive oil and pepper. Grill over hot coals for 3½ to 4 minutes on each side or until done to taste. Sprinkle with salt or herbs. Yield: 2 servings.

BARBECUED POTATOES

2 large potatoes
1 tablespoon melted
  margarine
1 tablespoon honey
1/8 teaspoon pepper
2 teaspoons chili
  powder
1/4 teaspoon garlic
  powder

Preheat oven to 425 degrees. Cut potatoes into thin slices; place in baking pan sprayed with nonstick cooking spray. Combine remaining ingredients in bowl; mix well. Spread evenly over potatoes. Bake for 15 to 20 minutes or until tender. Yield: 2 servings.

AU GRATIN SCALLIONS

2 bunches scallions
1/2 cup skim milk
1 slice white bread,
  crumbled
2 tablespoons grated
  Parmesan cheese
1/2 teaspoon salt
1/4 teaspoon pepper

Preheat oven to 450 degrees. Cook scallions in boiling water to cover in saucepan for 5 minutes; drain. Place in baking dish. Pour milk over scallions. Combine crumbled bread, Parmesan cheese, salt and pepper in bowl; mix well. Sprinkle over scallions. Bake for 10 minutes. Yield: 2 servings.

JELLY MUFFINS

2 cups all-purpose flour
1 tablespoon baking
  powder
2 tablespoons sugar
1 teaspoon salt
2 egg whites
1/3 cup corn oil
1¼ cups skim milk
2 tablespoons jelly or
  jam
2 tablespoons sugar

Preheat oven to 425 degrees. Sift first 4 dry ingredients into bowl; make well in center. Add egg whites, oil and milk; mix just until moistened. Fill greased muffin cups 2/3 full. Drop 1/2 teaspoon jelly into center of each muffin. Sprinkle each with 1/2 teaspoon sugar. Bake for 22 minutes. Yield: 1 dozen.

ENGLISH TRIFLE

1 large angel food cake
1 large package vanilla
  instant pudding mix
2½ cups skim milk
1 8-ounce jar
  raspberry preserves
1/4 cup sherry
1 21-ounce can light
  cherry pie filling
8 ounces light whipped
  topping

Cut cake into cubes. Combine pudding mix with milk in bowl; mix until smooth. Layer cake cubes, preserves, sherry, pudding mixture and pie filling 1/2 at a time in trifle bowl. Top with whipped topping. Chill, covered, until serving time. Yield: 12 servings.

St. Patty's Green Potluck

Artichoke Dip — Chips
Chilies Rellenos José — Tortellini Salad
Oriental Chicken Salad
Green Bean Casserole
Irish Potato Salad — Watergate Salad
Broccoli and Grape Salad
Layered Pea Salad — Coleslaw
Fruit Plate
Green Upside-Down Pineapple Cake

See Index for similar recipes.

At this St. Patrick's Day potluck dinner, everyone brought green food and wore green clothes. The clothes had been exchanged at the previous meeting in plain green bags and each member had to wear what had been provided.

Noreen Bruns, Preceptor Beta Sigma
Aurora, Colorado

CHILIES RELLENOS JOSÉ

1 26-ounce can whole green chilies	1/4 cup all-purpose flour
1 pound Monterey Jack cheese, cut into strips	5 eggs
	1 1/4 cups milk
8 ounces Cheddar cheese, shredded	1/2 teaspoon salt
	Tabasco sauce, paprika and pepper to taste

Preheat oven to 350 degrees. Split 1 side of peppers; discard seed and rinse. Place 1 strip of cheese in each chili; fold over to enclose cheese. Layer peppers and shredded cheese 1/2 at a time in greased 7-by-13-inch baking dish. Beat flour gradually into eggs in bowl. Add milk, salt, Tabasco sauce, paprika and pepper; mix well. Pour over layers. Bake for 45 minutes or until knife inserted in center comes out clean. Yield: 10 to 12 servings.

Adrienne Morris

TORTELLINI SALAD

1 9-ounce package spinach and cheese tortellini	1/2 cup ranch salad dressing
2 cups frozen mixed broccoli, carrot and cauliflower	1/2 teaspoon Italian seasoning
	1/4 cup grated Parmesan cheese

Cook pasta using package directions. Drain over vegetables in colander. Combine vegetables, pasta and salad dressing in bowl; mix well. Add Italian seasoning and cheese; toss to mix well. Chill until serving time. Yield: 10 to 12 servings.

Pat Rohach

GREEN BEAN CASSEROLE

2 29-ounce cans French-style green beans	1 10-ounce can cream of mushroom soup
1 8-ounce can mushrooms	Salt and pepper to taste
1 7-ounce can sliced water chestnuts	1 6- to 8-ounce package frozen onion rings

Preheat oven to 350 degrees. Drain beans, mushrooms and water chestnuts. Combine with soup, salt and pepper in bowl; mix well. Spoon into 2-quart baking dish. Bake for 30 minutes. Top with onion rings. Bake for 15 minutes or until onions are crisp. Yield: 10 to 12 servings.

Marianne Funk

BROCCOLI AND GRAPE SALAD

2 stalks broccoli, chopped	1 cup raisins
2 stalks celery, chopped	1 cup mayonnaise
3 green onions, chopped	1 tablespoon vinegar
1 1/2 cups seedless green grapes	2/3 cup sugar
	8 ounces bacon, crisp-fried, crumbled

Combine vegetables, grapes and raisins in bowl; mix well. Add mixture of mayonnaise, vinegar and sugar; mix well. Top with bacon; toss lightly. Yield: 10 to 12 servings.

Sondra West

Relaxed Reunion Dinner

Oven-Fried Oysters
Baked Potatoes — Cheese Sauce
Stir-Fried Asparagus
Tossed Green Salad
Five-Minute Cheesecake
Wine — Coffee

See Index for similar recipes.

This is a dinner we shared with childhood friends from Alabama.

Iva Mintonye, Laureate Zeta
Coquille, Oregon

OVEN-FRIED OYSTERS

2 small jars oysters	3 tablespoons cornmeal
1/2 cup margarine	1/2 teaspoon paprika
3/4 cup baking mix	1/4 teaspoon pepper
1/2 teaspoon garlic powder	2 eggs, beaten

Preheat oven to 425 degrees. Drain oysters and pat dry. Melt margarine in oil-lined 10-by-15-inch baking pan. Mix dry ingredients in shallow dish. Dip oysters into eggs; coat with dry ingredients. Arrange in margarine in prepared pan, turning to coat well. Bake for 15 minutes or until cooked through. Yield: 4 servings.

FIVE-MINUTE CHEESECAKE

8 ounces cream cheese, softened	1 graham cracker pie shell
8 ounces sour cream	1 21-ounce can cherry pie filling
1/4 cup milk	
1 large package vanilla instant pudding mix	

Process cream cheese, sour cream and milk in blender until smooth. Combine with pudding mix in bowl; mix well. Spoon into pie shell. Spread pie filling evenly over top. Chill until serving time. Yield: 6 servings.

Thanksgiving Dinner

Pumpkin Soup
Vegetables in Mustard Vinaigrette
Turkey and Dressing
Creamy Potatoes
Buttered Brussels Sprouts
Mincemeat Tarts
Cranberry Cordial — Coffee

See Index for similar recipes.

Members of our Chapter cooked and served Thanksgiving Dinner for ourselves and our husbands. We made a festive occasion of it, with beautifully decorated tables and fall flowers.

Franke Mae Woods, Preceptor Eta Alpha
Merced, California

PUMPKIN SOUP

For a different presentation, serve this in a hollowed-out pumpkin which has been heated at 350 degrees for 20 minutes.

6 cups chicken broth	1/2 teaspoon salt
2 to 3 cups peeled cubed pumpkin	5 peppercorns
1 cup thinly sliced onion	1/2 cup whipping cream, warmed
1 clove of garlic, minced	1 teaspoon chopped parsley
1/2 teaspoon thyme	

Combine first 7 ingredients in saucepan. Bring to a boil. Simmer for 20 minutes. Remove and reserve 1/2 cup pumpkin mixture. Simmer remaining mixture for 20 minutes longer. Purée 2 cups of the mixture at a time in blender or food processor. Combine in saucepan. Simmer until heated through. Stir in cream and reserved pumpkin mixture. Garnish with parsley. Yield: 8 servings.

VEGETABLES IN MUSTARD VINAIGRETTE

Flowerets of 1 head cauliflower	1/3 cup tarragon or Japanese rice vinegar
Flowerets of 1 head broccoli	1 cup olive oil
1 1/3 pounds asparagus	1 shallot, minced
1 pound green beans	Salt and freshly ground pepper to taste
5 1/3 ounces snow peas	Chopped herbs such as parsley, tarragon, chervil or dill
1 pound carrots, cut into sticks	
1/3 cup Dijon mustard	

Blanch and chill vegetables. Whisk mustard and vinegar in bowl. Add oil gradually, whisking constantly. Add shallot, seasonings and herbs. Serve over vegetables. Yield: 8 servings.

TURKEY AND DRESSING

Soak the raisins overnight in 1/2 cup Cognac for this recipe.

2 cups chopped onions	1 15-ounce can chestnuts, drained, chopped
2 cloves of garlic, minced	1 tablespoon sage
1/2 cup butter or margarine	2 teaspoons marjoram
1 pound pork sausage	1 teaspoon thyme
1/2 cup chopped shallots	1/4 teaspoon ground cloves
1 1/2 cups chopped tart apples	2 teaspoons salt
1 cup chopped celery	1/8 teaspoon cayenne pepper
1 recipe corn bread, crumbled	1 teaspoon pepper
1/2 cup raisins	2 eggs
1/2 cup chopped parsley	1 16-pound turkey

Sauté onions and garlic in butter in large skillet over medium heat for 5 minutes or until tender. Add sausage and shallots. Cook for 10 minutes or until sausage is crumbly and brown. Stir in apples and celery. Cook for 10 minutes or until tender; drain. Combine with corn bread, raisins, parsley, chestnuts and seasonings in bowl; mix well. Add eggs; toss lightly. Stuff into turkey. Roast using directions for turkey. Yield: 8 to 12 servings.

CREAMY POTATOES

2 1/2 pounds Russet potatoes, peeled, cooked	Salt to taste
	1/2 teaspoon pepper
1/4 cup butter or margarine	1 tablespoon chopped chives
3 ounces cream cheese, softened	3/4 cup (about) milk
	Butter or margarine
	Paprika to taste

Mash potatoes with 1/4 cup butter, cream cheese, salt, pepper and chives in bowl until smooth. Add enough milk to make of desired consistency. Spoon into baking dish. Dot with additional butter; sprinkle with paprika. Bake for 1 hour. May store in airtight container in refrigerator for up to 2 weeks. Yield: 8 servings.

CRANBERRY CORDIAL

1 1/2 cups cranberries	1 bottle of sauvignon blanc
1 1/2 cups sugar	

Combine cranberries with sugar in bowl; mix until sugar dissolves. Add wine; mix well. Pour into bottles; seal. Let stand in cool place for 22 days or longer. Strain into glasses. Yield: 8 servings.

New Year's Eve Dinner

Honey-Baked Ham
Green Beans with Bleu Cheese
and Walnuts
Parslied Carrots
Gourmet Potatoes
Rolls — Butter
Chocolate Cake with Raspberries
Chardonnay

See Index for similar recipes.

This menu was served to four couples at a birthday dinner party. The guests were classmates and friends of fifty years. The toast was made with champagne from New Mexico where the friendships began.

Betty Seale, Xi Omicron Lambda
Blythe, California

GREEN BEANS WITH BLEU CHEESE AND WALNUTS

2 pounds tender green beans	3 cups toasted walnut halves
8 slices bacon	Freshly ground pepper to taste
8 ounces bleu cheese, crumbled	

Simmer green beans in water in saucepan just until tender-crisp; drain. Rinse and drain again. Cut bacon into 1/4-inch wide strips. Fry in skillet until crisp; remove to drain. Add beans to bacon drippings in skillet. Cook over medium heat until heated through, stirring to coat well. Add bleu cheese; toss until cheese begins to melt. Sprinkle with walnuts and pepper. Top with bacon. Serve immediately. Yield: 8 servings.

GOURMET POTATOES

2 cups shredded sharp cheese	1/4 teaspoon pepper
1/4 cup butter or margarine	6 medium potatoes, cooked, cooled
1 1/2 cups sour cream	2 tablespoons butter or margarine
1/3 cup grated onion	Paprika to taste
1 teaspoon salt	

Preheat oven to 350 degrees. Melt cheese with 1/4 cup butter in saucepan. Stir in sour cream, onion and seasonings; remove from heat. Shred potatoes into cheese mixture; mix well. Spoon into greased 2-quart baking dish. Dot with 2 tablespoons butter; sprinkle with paprika. Bake for 30 minutes. Yield: 8 servings.

Progressive Dinner Appetizer Course

Broccoli Soup
Cheese
Crackers
Cranberry Punch

I served this to fifty people before we went to a family Christmas Eve buffet supper. I served the soup in Christmas mugs and the punch from a crystal punch bowl.

Mary Chino, Laureate Lambda
Ogden, Utah

BROCCOLI SOUP

3/4 cup chopped onion	6 cups milk
2 pounds fresh broccoli, chopped	1/2 teaspoon garlic powder
3 cups water	1/2 teaspoon salt
3 14-ounce cans chicken broth	1/4 teaspoon pepper
3 10-ounce cans cream of potato soup	1/4 cup all-purpose flour
	1 cup water

Cook onion and broccoli in 3 cups water in large saucepan until tender; drain. Add chicken broth and potato soup. Simmer for 15 minutes. Add milk, garlic powder, salt and pepper. Simmer for 20 minutes. Stir in mixture of flour and 1 cup water. Simmer until thickened, stirring occasionally. Yield: 20 servings.

CRANBERRY PUNCH

1 gallon cranberry-apple juice	1 quart orange juice

Combine cranberry-apple juice and orange juice in large container; mix well. Chill until serving time. Pour into punch bowl. Garnish with cranberries coated with egg white and sugar. Tie red ribbon around ladle. Yield: 20 cups.

Thirty-Minute Special Dinner

Tyrolean Veal Scallopini
White Pasta with Butter and Olive Oil
Sicilian Green Salad
Fresh Fruit with Wine

During the Christmas holidays, I found a message on my answering machine at 5:30 that my husband was bringing two business associates to dinner at 6:30. This was the meal I chose on such short notice and by 6:30 it was ready. When my guests arrived, however, they turned out to be my best friend and her husband, who were home for the holidays. It was a beautiful surprise for me and a terrific dinner for everyone.

Bridgette Ross, Laureate Alpha Pi
Elyria, Ohio

TYROLEAN VEAL SCALLOPINI

4 very thin slices boiled ham	1 egg
4 thin veal scallops	1/4 teaspoon oregano
4 teaspoons prepared mustard	1/2 teaspoon salt
1 teaspoon thyme	1/2 cup dry bread crumbs
2 thin slices Swiss cheese	1/2 cup vegetable oil

Layer 1 slice of ham on each veal scallop. Spread ham with mustard; sprinkle with thyme. Cut cheese slices into halves. Place 1/2 cheese slice on top. Roll veal to enclose filling; secure with wooden pick. Beat egg with oregano and salt in shallow dish. Dip veal rolls in egg mixture; coat with bread crumbs. Sauté in hot oil in skillet for 10 minutes or until golden brown on all sides. Yield: 4 servings.

WHITE PASTA WITH BUTTER AND OLIVE OIL

1 16-ounce package thin spaghetti	2 tablespoons olive oil
2 tablespoons butter or margarine	Garlic powder, salt and pepper to taste
1 teaspoon chopped parsley	Grated Parmesan cheese to taste

Cook pasta using package directions; drain but do not rinse. Combine with next 6 ingredients in bowl; toss to mix well. Top with cheese. Yield: 4 servings.

SICILIAN GREEN SALAD

1 head Romaine lettuce, torn	1/4 cup orange juice
1 2-ounce can sliced black olives, drained	2 teaspoons red wine vinegar
2 oranges, peeled, thinly sliced	1/4 cup olive oil
	1/4 teaspoon paprika
	1/2 teaspoon salt

Combine lettuce, olives and oranges in salad bowl. Combine remaining ingredients in small bowl; mix well. Add to salad; toss lightly. Yield: 4 servings.

FRESH FRUIT WITH WINE

1 cup strawberry halves	1 cup Port
1 cup grapes	1/2 cup sugar
1 cup sliced banana	1/4 teaspoon nutmeg
1 cup cantaloupe cubes	8 ounces whipped topping
1 cup pineapple chunks in syrup	

Combine fruit, wine, sugar and nutmeg in bowl; mix well. Chill until serving time. Spoon into serving dishes. Top with whipped topping. Yield: 4 servings.

Lucky New Year's Day Dinner

Baked Coca-Cola Ham
Black-Eyed Peas — Collard Greens
Sliced Tomatoes
Chow Chow — Watermelon Rind Pickle
Corn Bread

See Index for similar recipes.

This is a Southern menu to bring good luck during the coming year. For the black-eyed pea dish, I drain a can of black-eyed peas, add 1/2 cup chopped onion and 1 cup water, and simmer until heated through. The easy corn bread recipe is on the package of self-rising cornmeal.

Mimi Davis, Gamma Tau
Clinton, Mississippi

BAKED COCA-COLA HAM

1 6 to 9-pound ham	1/2 to 1 can Coca-Cola

Preheat oven to 325 degrees. Place ham in baking pan. Pour Coca-Cola over ham. Bake using directions on ham or for 20 minutes per pound. Yield: 12 servings.

COLLARD GREENS

1 bunch collard greens	1 tablespoon salt
2 or 3 slices bacon	1/2 teaspoon pepper

Wash greens well, discarding stems. Combine with bacon, salt and pepper in pressure cooker. Add water to just cover. Cook using manufacturer's directions for 8 minutes. Yield: 6 servings.

Lazy Summertime Supper

Salad-by-Committee
French Bread
Watermelon Wedges
White Wine

We enjoyed this supper on our screened porch nestled in the trees with good friends and a family of gray foxes that came to eat from a pan of food we put down. The hostess makes the dressing portion of this salad and each guest brings an ingredient or two.

Mary Wrobel, Xi Beta Alpha
Madison, Alabama

SALAD-BY-COMMITTEE

2 6-ounce jars marinated artichoke hearts	1 pound chopped cooked ham
1 cup vegetable oil	2 cups cherry tomatoes
1/3 cup red wine vinegar	1 cup sliced radishes
1 teaspoon sugar	1 cup sliced cucumber
1/2 teaspoon garlic powder	1 each green bell pepper, red bell pepper and yellow bell pepper, cut into strips
1/2 teaspoon dry mustard	
1/2 teaspoon salt	1/2 cup sliced black olives
1/2 teaspoon pepper	1 small purple onion, sliced into rings
8 ounces fresh mushrooms, sliced	2 avocados, chopped
3 heads iceberg lettuce, torn	3 hard-cooked eggs, sliced
1 pound chopped cooked chicken	1 pound bacon, crisp-fried, crumbled
1 pound chopped cooked roast beef	

Drain and chop artichokes, reserving marinade. Combine reserved marinade with next 7 ingredients in bowl; mix well. Add artichokes and mushrooms.

Chill, covered, in refrigerator. Combine lettuce with meats, vegetables and avocados in large bowl. Add artichoke mixture; toss gently. Arrange egg slices around edge; sprinkle with bacon. Yield: 18 servings.

Working Wife's Treat

Lamb Chops
Broiled Zucchini — Broiled Tomatoes
Tossed Salad — Italian Dressing
Dinner Rolls — Wine

This is the dinner that my husband sometimes makes for me when I have had a hard day. It takes about 15 or 20 minutes to prepare—just enough time to sip a glass of wine and put my feet up.

Sharon Ouwerkerk, Xi Theta Xi
Wooster, Ohio

LAMB CHOPS

2 lamb chops	Salt and pepper to taste
Oregano to taste	

Place lamb chops on rack in broiler pan; sprinkle with oregano. Broil 3 inches from heat source for 6 minutes on each side. Sprinkle with salt and pepper. Yield: 2 servings.

BROILED ZUCCHINI

2 small zucchini	Salt and pepper to taste
Melted butter or margarine	

Cut off ends of zucchini; cut into halves lengthwise. Place cut sides down on rack in broiler pan. Broil for 6 minutes. Turn zucchini cut sides up. Brush with butter. Broil for 6 minutes longer. Season with salt and pepper. Yield: 2 servings.

BROILED TOMATOES

1 large tomato	Rosemary, salt and pepper to taste
Melted butter or margarine	

Cut off stem end of tomato. Cut small opening in blossom end. Cut into halves. Place cut sides up on rack in broiler pan. Brush with melted butter. Sprinkle with rosemary, salt and pepper. Broil for 6 minutes. Yield: 2 servings.

Swift Super Bowl Party

Artichoke Dip — Chili Bean Dip
Chips — Fresh Tomato Salsa
Marinated Mushrooms
Fresh Vegetables — Mexican Fruitcake
Mexican Hot Chocolate — Quick Sangria

This traditional party of our chapter always features Mexican food; many dishes have been the same year after year, for as long as 30 years in some cases.

Dorothy W. Adams, Laureate Iota
Shreveport, Louisiana

ARTICHOKE DIP

1 4-ounce can chopped green chilies
1 cup grated Parmesan cheese
1 cup fat-free mayonnaise
1 14-ounce can artichoke hearts, drained
6 to 12 drops of hot sauce, or to taste
Tortilla chips

Preheat oven to 350 degrees. Combine undrained chilies, cheese, mayonnaise and artichokes in bowl; mix well. Spoon into lightly greased 1-quart baking dish. Bake for 15 to 20 minutes or until heated through. Sprinkle with hot sauce. Serve with chips. Yield: 6 to 8 servings.

CHILI BEAN DIP

1 16-ounce can refried beans
1 16-ounce can chili
1 16-ounce can tomatoes with green chilies
4 to 8 ounces process cheese, chopped
6 to 8 green onions, chopped
Hot tortilla chips

Mix first 5 ingredients in bowl. Spoon into shallow dish. Serve with chips. Yield: 10 to 12 servings.

FRESH TOMATO SALSA

5 medium tomatoes, chopped
1/3 cup tomato sauce
1/4 cup finely chopped purple onion
2 small jalapeño peppers, seeded, minced
3 cloves of garlic, minced
2 tablespoons lime juice
2 tablespoons minced cilantro or parsley
1 tablespoon chopped fresh oregano or 1 teaspoon dried oregano
1 teaspoon salt

Mix all ingredients in bowl gently. Chill until serving time. Serve over toasted French bread, with tortilla chips or with fish or chicken. Yield: 10 to 12 servings.

MARINATED MUSHROOMS

2 pounds fresh large mushrooms
5 7-ounce cans green chili salsa
1 teaspoon salt
1 5-ounce jar pimento-stuffed olives
Chopped fresh cilantro or parsley

Mix mushrooms with salsa, salt and olives in bowl. Marinate, covered, in refrigerator overnight. Sprinkle with cilantro. Yield: 20 to 24 servings.

MEXICAN FRUITCAKE

2 cups all-purpose flour
2 cups sugar
2 teaspoons baking soda
2 eggs
1 20-ounce can crushed pineapple
8 ounces cream cheese, softened
1/2 cup margarine, softened
2 cups confectioners' sugar
1 teaspoon vanilla extract
1 cup broken pecans

Preheat oven to 350 degrees. Mix flour, sugar, baking soda, eggs and pineapple in bowl. Spoon into ungreased 10-by-12-inch cake pan. Bake for 45 minutes. Remove to wire rack to cool. Combine next 4 ingredients in bowl; mix until smooth. Spread over cake; sprinkle with pecans. Yield: 10 to 12 servings.

MEXICAN HOT CHOCOLATE

1 1/2 cups water
3 1-ounce squares unsweetened chocolate
1/2 cup sugar
3 tablespoons instant coffee
1 teaspoon cinnamon
1/2 teaspoon nutmeg
1/4 teaspoon salt
4 cups milk
Whipped cream

Combine first 7 ingredients in large saucepan. Bring to a boil over medium heat, stirring occasionally; reduce heat. Simmer for 4 minutes, stirring constantly. Stir in milk. Cook until heated through. Beat for 1 minute or until foamy. Serve with whipped cream. Yield: 8 servings.

QUICK SANGRIA

1 33-ounce bottle of rosé, chilled
1 33-ounce bottle of Burgundy, chilled
2 12-ounce cans frozen pink lemonade concentrate, thawed
Juice of 2 limes
2 33-ounce bottles of club soda, chilled
1 lemon, thinly sliced
1 lime, thinly sliced
1 orange, thinly sliced

Combine wines and fruit juices in large pitcher; mix well. Add club soda; mix gently. Add sliced fruit. Serve over ice. Yield: 25 servings.

Dinner at Grandmother's

Fettucini with
Tomato-Basil Sauce
Green Beans with Oregano
Bread
Texas Tea Cakes
Red Wine

This was a meal I loved at my grandmother's house when I was a child. Now it is a favorite of my children.

Sandra Malone, Preceptor Mu Phi
Houston, Texas

FETTUCINI WITH TOMATO-BASIL SAUCE

1/4 cup chopped onion	1/2 teaspoon pepper
1 clove of garlic, minced	12 ounces fettucini,
1/4 cup olive oil	cooked, drained
1 28-ounce can peeled	Freshly grated
tomatoes, chopped	Parmesan cheese
6 fresh basil leaves,	Chopped fresh basil and
chopped	chives
1 teaspoon salt	

Sauté onion and garlic in olive oil in skillet. Add undrained tomatoes, 6 basil leaves, salt and pepper. Simmer, covered, for 20 minutes. Combine with fettucini in bowl; toss to mix well. Top with Parmesan cheese and additional fresh basil and chives. Yield: 4 servings.

GREEN BEANS WITH OREGANO

3 cups chopped fresh	4 ounces fresh
green beans	mushrooms
4 slices bacon, crisp-	1/2 envelope onion soup
fried, crumbled	mix
1 10-ounce can cream	1/4 teaspoon oregano
of mushroom soup	

Cook beans in water to cover in saucepan just until tender-crisp; drain. Combine with half the bacon, mushroom soup, mushrooms, onion soup mix and oregano in bowl; mix well. Chill for 24 hours. Preheat oven to 350 degrees. Spoon bean mixture into baking dish. Bake for 35 minutes. Top with remaining bacon. Yield: 4 servings.

TEXAS TEA CAKES

1 cup butter, softened	4 cups plus 3
1 cup plus 1 tablespoon	tablespoons sifted
sugar	all-purpose flour
2 eggs	1 teaspoon baking
4 teaspoons vanilla	powder
extract	1/2 teaspoon salt

Preheat oven to 350 degrees. Cream butter and sugar in mixer bowl until light and fluffy. Beat in eggs 1 at a time. Add vanilla. Sift in flour, baking powder and salt; mix well. Roll between sheets of waxed paper sprayed with nonstick cooking spray and floured. Cut out with cookie cutter in shape of Texas. Place on cookie sheet. Bake for 8 to 10 minutes or until golden brown. Cool on wire rack. Yield: 4 dozen.

Casual Supper

Grape and Cantaloupe Medley
Bacon-Cheese Delights
Seasoned French Fries
Kahlua Parfaits

See Index for similar recipes.

This is a quick and easy supper to prepare and serve to casual groups such as the softball board meeting or a card party. The parfaits are made with scoops of French vanilla ice cream, a drizzle of Kahlua and hot fudge sauce, whipped cream and cherry. Top with a small drizzle of additional Kahlua.

Linda Gizienski, Xi Alpha
Coventry, Rhode Island

BACON-CHEESE DELIGHTS

8 slices bacon	1 cup chopped green bell
4 slices American cheese	pepper
2 tomatoes, sliced	1 cup chopped onion
4 slices bread, lightly	Salt and pepper to taste
toasted	

Preheat oven or toaster oven to 425 degrees. Fry bacon until almost crisp; remove from skillet. Layer cheese slices and tomato slices on toasted bread. Sprinkle with green pepper, onion, salt and pepper. Top each with 2 slices bacon. Place on baking sheet. Bake for 8 minutes or until bacon is crisp. Cut into smaller pieces. Yield: 4 servings.

Easy Family Birthday Dinner

Spaghetti Pie
Buttered Corn
Tossed Green Salad
Garlic Breadsticks
Pear and Pudding Dessert

See Index for similar recipes.

We have several birthdays in February and March, so we combine them all into one birthday dinner. This is an easy menu that everyone in the family can help with.

Claudia M. Long, Kappa Kappa
Meriden, Kansas

SPAGHETTI PIE

1 pound ground beef	1 12-ounce package
1/4 cup chopped celery	spaghetti, cooked
1 30-ounce jar extra-	2 eggs
chunky spaghetti sauce	1/2 teaspoon garlic salt
with onion and garlic	1/2 cup grated Parmesan
1 2-ounce jar sliced	cheese
mushrooms, drained	

Preheat oven to 375 degrees. Brown ground beef with celery in saucepan, stirring until ground beef is crumbly; drain. Stir in spaghetti sauce and mushrooms. Simmer for 15 minutes. Combine spaghetti, eggs, garlic salt and half the cheese in bowl; toss lightly. Spoon into greased 10-inch pie plate, pressing over bottom and sides of plate to form crust. Spoon ground beef into prepared plate; sprinkle with remaining cheese. Bake for 25 to 30 minutes or until heated through. Let stand for 5 minutes before serving. Yield: 6 servings.

PEAR AND PUDDING DESSERT

1 16-ounce can pear	Cinnamon to taste
halves	
Milk	
1 6-ounce package	
chocolate instant	
pudding mix	

Drain pears, reserving juice. Cut pears into halves. Add enough milk to reserved juice to measure 3 cups. Combine milk mixture with pudding mix in bowl; mix well. Spoon into serving dishes. Top with pears; sprinkle with cinnamon. Yield: 6 servings.

Rate-the-Recipe Dinner

Fresh Vegetables
Dill Dip
Sweet and Sour Cocktail Meatballs
Lemon Chicken
Zucchini Bread
Fruit Sauce

See Index for similar recipes.

I prepared this menu when I was hostess for the Sorority. For the program, I provided each member with a sheet to rate the recipes for submission to this year's cookbook. This was the result of the meeting and dinner.

B. J. McKenzie, Xi Gamma Xi
Beverly, West Virginia

LEMON CHICKEN

2 pounds chicken breast	1/4 cup fresh lemon juice
filets	1 clove of garlic, crushed
2 tablespoons corn oil	Freshly ground pepper
or melted margarine	to taste

Preheat oven to 350 degrees. Cut chicken into bite-sized pieces; rinse and pat dry. Arrange in shallow 10-inch baking dish. Combine oil, lemon juice, garlic and pepper in bowl; mix well. Pour over chicken. Bake until chicken is tender, basting occasionally. Yield: 6 servings.

FRUIT SAUCE

1 cup pineapple juice	2 tablespoons
1/2 cup sugar	all-purpose flour
1 tablespoon margarine	1 cup whipping cream
1 egg, beaten	

Combine pineapple juice, sugar, margarine, egg and flour in saucepan; mix well. Cook over medium heat until thickened and smooth, stirring constantly. Cool completely. Whip cream in chilled bowl until soft peaks form. Fold into cooked mixture. Serve with zucchini bread or as dip with fresh fruit. Yield: 2 cups.

Fast Fall Luncheon

Smoked Chicken Salad
Red Onion Soup with Apple Cider
Parker House Rolls
Chocolate Chip-Pecan Pie
White Zinfandel — Coffee

See Index for similar recipes.

I enjoy this menu because most of the preparations can be done the night before and sometimes make the rolls from a recipe that can be refrigerated.

Diane Heyman, Mu Theta
Paxton, Illinois

SMOKED CHICKEN SALAD

3 tablespoons balsamic vinegar	Boston and Bibb lettuce, torn
1 teaspoon fresh basil	Watercress
1 teaspoon fresh marjoram	1 pound smoked chicken
1/2 cup extra-virgin olive oil	Sections of 1 large pink grapefruit
Salt to taste	1 avocado, peeled, sliced
Freshly ground pepper to taste	2 tablespoons sunflower seed or toasted pine nuts

Process first 6 ingredients in food processor until smooth. Combine with greens in plastic bag; shake to coat. Arrange greens, chicken, grapefruit and avocado on serving plate. Drizzle with remaining dressing; sprinkle with sunflower seed. Yield: 6 servings.

RED ONION SOUP WITH APPLE CIDER

1 1/4 pounds red onions, thinly sliced	1/2 cup dry white wine
2 tablespoons butter or margarine	1/2 cup apple cider
	1 bay leaf
2 tablespoons all-purpose flour	1 1/2 teaspoons thyme
1 teaspoon minced garlic	Salt and pepper to taste
3 cups canned beef broth	6 1/2-inch slices French bread
3 cups chicken broth	2 cups shredded Swiss cheese

Sauté onions in butter in large saucepan over medium heat until golden brown. Add flour. Cook for 2 minutes, stirring constantly. Add garlic. Cook for 1 minute. Add broths, wine, apple cider and bay leaf. Bring to a boil; skim surface. Stir in thyme. Simmer for 40 minutes. Season with salt and pepper. Preheat broiler. Place bread on baking sheet; sprinkle with cheese. Broil just until cheese melts. Ladle soup into serving bowls, discarding bay leaf. Top with slice of bread. Yield: 6 servings.

CHOCOLATE CHIP-PECAN PIE

2 eggs, at room temperature	1 cup chopped pecans, lightly toasted
1 cup sugar	1 tablespoon bourbon
1/2 cup all-purpose flour	1 teaspoon vanilla extract
1/2 cup melted butter or margarine, cooled	1 unbaked 9-inch pie shell
1 cup semisweet chocolate chips	Whipped cream

Beat eggs at high speed in mixer bowl until thickened and lemon-colored. Beat in sugar gradually. Beat in flour and butter at low speed. Stir in next 4 ingredients. Spoon into pie shell. Bake for 40 minutes or until golden. Serve with whipped cream. Yield: 8 servings.

Diane Johnson

Summer Salad Supper

Pasta Salad — Fruit Salad
Yogurt Dressing — Green Salad
Tea — Kool-Aid

See Index for similar recipes.

This is a light salad supper to enjoy in the summer.

Gail Lincoln, Omega
Baton Rouge, Louisiana

PASTA SALAD

1 8-ounce package spiral pasta, cooked	1/4 cup chopped green or black olives
2 hard-cooked eggs, chopped	1/2 cup mayonnaise
8 ounces imitation crab meat	1 tablespoon spicy mustard
3 green onions, chopped	1 tablespoon olive juice

Combine all ingredients in bowl; mix well. Chill until serving time. Yield: 4 servings.

YOGURT DRESSING

1 cup plain yogurt	1 tablespoon vanilla extract
1 cup whipped topping	

Combine all ingredients in bowl; mix well. Serve with salad of fresh fruit such as bananas, strawberries, seedless grapes and pineapple. Yield: 2 cups.

Dinner for Two

Steak Bonne Femme
Steamed New Potatoes
Glazed Carrots
Fruit-Cream Parfait

I prepared this menu for a very quiet dinner with my husband.

Joanne Metcalfe, Preceptor Epsilon Omega
Alton, Illinois

STEAK BONNE FEMME

½ large red onion, *thinly sliced into rings*	*1½ teaspoons corn oil*
10 medium mushrooms, *sliced*	*2 6-ounce top sirloin* *steaks, ¾ inch thick*
½ clove of garlic, *minced*	*2 tablespoons beef broth*
1½ teaspoons butter or *margarine*	*Salt and freshly ground* *pepper to taste*

Warm ovenproof platter in 200-degree oven. Sauté onion, mushrooms and garlic in butter and oil in large skillet until tender. Increase heat. Sauté until onions are brown and juices have evaporated. Remove with slotted spoon. Add steaks and additional butter and oil if necessary. Cook for 3 to 4 minutes on each side for rare. Remove to warm platter. Add broth to skillet, stirring to deglaze. Cook until liquid is reduced to desired consistency; reduce heat. Add onion mixture. Cook until heated through. Season with salt and pepper. Spoon over steaks. Yield: 2 servings.

STEAMED NEW POTATOES

6 to 8 small unpeeled *new potatoes*	*Minced parsley*

Cut potatoes into thin slices. Place in steamer basket over boiling water in saucepan. Steam for 15 minutes or until tender. Sprinkle with parsley. May steam carrots for Glazed Carrots at same time. Yield: 2 servings.

GLAZED CARROTS

4 or 5 medium carrots	*1½ teaspoons honey*
3 tablespoons butter or *margarine*	*1½ teaspoons grated* *orange rind*

Peel carrots and cut into 3-inch sticks. Place in steamer basket over boiling water in saucepan. Steam for 15 minutes or until tender. Combine with butter, honey and orange rind in small saucepan. Cook until glazed. May steam with new potatoes if desired. Yield: 2 servings.

FRUIT-CREAM PARFAIT

4 ounces cream cheese, *softened*	*Grated rind of ½* *orange and ½ lemon*
½ cup whipping cream	*1¼ cups sliced fresh or* *frozen fruit*
2 tablespoons *confectioners' sugar*	*Whipped cream*
½ to 1 teaspoon lemon *juice*	*Chopped nuts*

Beat cream cheese and ½ cup whipping cream at high speed in mixer bowl until fluffy. Add confectioners' sugar, lemon juice and rinds; beat at low speed until smooth. Spoon half the mixture into 2 wine glasses. Top with half the fruit and remaining whipped mixture. Freeze for 10 to 15 minutes. Top with remaining fruit, additional whipped cream and chopped nuts. Yield: 2 servings.

Garage Sale Supper

Potato-Cheese Soup
Coleslaw
Aunt Gertie's Corn Bread
Lemon Cheesecake

I always serve this menu to the members at the annual chapter garage sale at my house. The dessert may change, but the rest of the menu is a tradition.

Joy LeMasters, Laureate Alpha Chi
Beaumont, Texas

POTATO-CHEESE SOUP

8 large potatoes	*8 ounces Velveeta cheese,* *chopped*
2 medium onions	*6 cups milk*
3 stalks celery	*¼ teaspoon seasoned* *salt*
4 cups water	
3 tablespoons instant *chicken bouillon*	*Cayenne pepper to taste*

Peel and chop vegetables. Combine with water and bouillon in saucepan or pressure cooker. Cook until tender; remove from heat. Mash vegetables with potato masher. Stir in remaining ingredients. Cook just until heated through. Yield: 12 to 15 servings.

COLESLAW

8 cups shredded cabbage	3 tablespoons sugar
2 cups shredded carrots	2 tablespoons Dijon
5 tablespoons cider	mustard
vinegar	1½ cups mayonnaise

Combine cabbage and carrots in large bowl. Mix remaining ingredients in small bowl. Add to slaw; mix well. Yield: 10 to 12 servings.

AUNT GERTIE'S CORN BREAD

1 cup cornmeal	¼ teaspoon baking soda
⅓ cup all-purpose flour	1 cup buttermilk
1 tablespoon sugar	¼ cup corn oil
2 teaspoons baking	2 eggs, beaten
powder	

Preheat oven to 400 degrees. Mix dry ingredients in bowl. Stir in buttermilk, oil and eggs. Spoon into greased 9-by-9-inch baking pan. Bake for 25 to 30 minutes or until golden brown. Yield: 9 servings.

LEMON CHEESECAKE

1 recipe graham cracker	1 cup sugar
pie crust	1 12-ounce can
1 3-ounce package	evaporated milk,
lemon gelatin	chilled
8 ounces cream cheese,	Juice and grated rind of
softened	1 lemon

Line 9-by-13-inch dish with graham cracker mixture. Dissolve gelatin in boiling water in bowl; cool. Beat cream cheese and sugar in mixer bowl until light and fluffy. Add to gelatin; mix well. Whip chilled evaporated milk with lemon juice and lemon rind in mixer bowl until soft peaks form. Fold in gelatin mixture. Spoon into prepared dish. Chill until set.
Yield: 12 to 15 servings.

Annual Officers' Dinner

Avocado Chicken — Rice Pilaf
Orange-Spinach Salad
Hot Rolls — Wine

At this annual occasion, officers of the sorority prepare a meal for all the members. This dinner begins a year of good food, good friends and good recipes to share.

Nancy Sickles, Xi Epsilon
Port Huron, Michigan

AVOCADO CHICKEN

12 chicken breast filets	12 avocado slices
All-purpose flour	12 ½-inch tomato
Eggs, beaten	slices
Seasoned bread	12 boiled ham slices
crumbs	12 Swiss cheese slices
Margarine	

Preheat oven to 350 degrees. Rinse chicken and pat dry. Pound flat with meat mallet. Coat with flour, dip in eggs and coat with bread crumbs. Sauté in margarine in skillet until golden brown. Place in baking dish. Layer avocado, tomato and ham over chicken. Bake for 25 minutes. Add cheese. Bake for 5 minutes longer. Yield: 12 servings.

Coe Fix

RICE PILAF

1½ cups chopped onion	2 envelopes chicken
2 cups chopped celery	noodle soup mix
2 cups uncooked rice	2 teaspoons salt
½ cup butter or	½ teaspoon each thyme,
margarine	sage and pepper
5 cups water	

Sauté onion, celery and rice in butter in saucepan until rice is golden brown. Stir in water, soup mix, salt, thyme, sage and pepper. Simmer, covered, for 15 minutes or until rice is tender and liquid is absorbed. Yield: 12 servings.

Lea Gourlay

ORANGE-SPINACH SALAD

¾ cup mayonnaise	2 tablespoons chopped
2 tablespoons honey	green bell pepper
1 tablespoon lemon juice	2 tablespoons chopped
1 tablespoon caraway	pimento
seed	1 11-ounce can
10 ounces fresh spinach,	mandarin oranges,
torn	drained
1 head iceberg lettuce,	1 cucumber, sliced
torn	
2 tablespoons chopped	
onion	

Combine mayonnaise, honey, lemon juice and caraway seed in bowl; mix well. Combine spinach, lettuce, onion, green pepper, pimento, mandarin oranges and cucumber in large salad bowl. Add salad dressing; toss to mix well. Yield: 12 servings.

Ginny Zimmer

The crisp, refreshing taste of a slightly chilled dry Chablis, Montrachet, or a full-bodied California Chardonnay wine complements the flavor of chicken.

Quick Dinner for Eight to Twelve

Chicken-Asparagus Casserole
Spring Salad — French Rolls
Jo-Jo's — White Wine — Coffee

See Index for similar recipes.

The casserole for this menu can be prepared in advance and even men like it.

Jo Anna R. Hamilton, Xi Epsilon Alpha
Muskogee, Oklahoma

CHICKEN-ASPARAGUS CASSEROLE

2 16-ounce cans asparagus spears, drained	1 10-ounce can cream of celery soup
3½ cups chopped cooked chicken	¾ cup mayonnaise
1 7-ounce can water chestnuts, drained, thinly sliced	1 5-ounce can evaporated milk
½ cup toasted almonds	½ cup white wine
	¾ cup grated Parmesan cheese

Preheat oven to 350 degrees. Arrange asparagus in 9-by-13-inch baking dish sprayed with nonstick cooking spray. Layer chicken, water chestnuts and almonds in prepared dish. Mix next 4 ingredients in bowl. Spoon over layers; top with cheese. Bake for 20 to 25 minutes or until bubbly. Yield: 8 to 12 servings.

SPRING SALAD

2 tablespoons margarine	2 11-ounce cans mandarin oranges, drained
⅓ cup sugar	
⅛ teaspoon nutmeg	
¾ cup English walnuts, broken	1 small purple onion, thinly sliced
1 head red leaf lettuce, torn	⅓ cup poppy seed salad dressing
1 bunch spinach, torn	

Combine first 3 ingredients in skillet. Heat until margarine is bubbly. Add walnuts. Cook until toasted, stirring to coat well. Combine lettuce and spinach with oranges and onion in salad bowl. Add walnuts and salad dressing; toss lightly. Yield: 8 to 12 servings.

JO-JO'S

3 egg whites	1 cup sugar
½ teaspoon baking powder	1 cup broken nuts
	25 crackers, crushed

Beat egg whites in mixer bowl until soft peaks form. Add baking powder and sugar, beating until stiff. Fold in nuts and cracker crumbs. Drop by spoonfuls onto baking sheet sprayed with nonstick cooking spray. Bake for 15 minutes. Cool for 5 minutes. Cool on wire rack. Yield: 3 dozen.

Saturday Morning Brunch

Citrus Sparkling Champagne
Orange Juice
Sausage and Apple Rings
Scrambled Egg Casserole
Orange-Zested Grits
Fresh Fruit Salad
Caramel-Nut Ring
Blueberry Crumb Muffins
Cream Cheese Danish Bars
Coffee — Tea

This brunch honored our council's Woman of the Year along with other chapters' Woman of the Year. It was served buffet-style at the lake home of one of our members.

Linda Necrason, Xi Nu Alpha
Winter Park, Florida

CITRUS SPARKLING CHAMPAGNE

6 cups cold water	1 6-ounce can frozen lemonade concentrate, thawed
1 12-ounce can frozen orange juice concentrate, thawed	
	1 fifth of Champagne

Combine first 3 ingredients in large pitcher. Chill for 12 hours. Add Champagne; mix gently. Serve from pitcher or punch bowl. Yield: 8 servings.

SAUSAGE AND APPLE RINGS

24 ounces pork sausage	¼ cup butter or margarine
4 large cooking apples, cored	¼ cup chopped fresh parsley
⅔ cup sugar	
1 teaspoon cinnamon	

Shape sausage into patties ¼ inch thick and 3½ inches in diameter. Cook in 12-inch skillet over medium heat for 10 to 15 minutes or until brown on both sides. Remove to warm plate; drain and wipe skillet. Cut ends off of apples; cut each apple into 3 slices. Coat with mixture of sugar and cinnamon. Brown a few at a time in butter in skillet, turning frequently and sprinkling with remaining cinnamon-sugar. Place on sausage patties. Top with parsley. Yield: 12 servings.

SCRAMBLED EGG CASSEROLE

2½ tablespoons all-purpose flour	3 tablespoons melted butter or margarine
2 tablespoons melted butter or margarine	12 eggs, beaten
2 cups milk	½ teaspoon salt
½ teaspoon salt	½ teaspoon pepper
¼ teaspoon pepper	1 4-ounce can sliced mushrooms, drained
8 ounces cream cheese, cubed	2¼ cups bread crumbs
¼ cup chopped green onions	½ cup melted butter or margarine
	¼ teaspoon paprika

Blend flour into 2 tablespoons butter in heavy saucepan. Cook for 1 minute. Add milk gradually. Cook over medium heat until thickened, stirring constantly. Add ½ teaspoon salt, ¼ teaspoon pepper and cream cheese; mix until smooth. Remove from heat. Sauté green onions in 3 tablespoons butter in large skillet. Add eggs, ½ teaspoon salt and ½ teaspoon pepper. Cook until soft-set, stirring frequently. Add mushrooms and cheese sauce. Spoon into greased 9-by-13-inch baking dish. Toss bread crumbs with ½ cup melted butter. Spread over casserole; sprinkle with paprika. Chill, covered, overnight. Preheat oven to 350 degrees. Bake for 30 minutes or until heated through. Yield: 12 servings.

ORANGE-ZESTED GRITS

1 cup uncooked quick-cooking grits	1 teaspoon grated orange rind
1 teaspoon salt	1 cup orange juice
3 cups boiling water	4 eggs, beaten
¼ cup butter or margarine	2 tablespoons brown sugar

Preheat oven to 350 degrees. Stir grits into salted boiling water in saucepan. Cook over medium heat for 3 minutes, stirring constantly; remove from heat. Add next 4 ingredients; mix well. Spoon into greased 1½-quart baking dish. Sprinkle with brown sugar. Bake for 45 minutes or until knife inserted in center comes out clean. Yield: 8 to 12 servings.

CARAMEL-NUT RING

½ cup melted butter or margarine	2 tablespoons water
½ cup chopped pecans	2 8-ounce cans crescent dinner rolls
1 cup packed light brown sugar	

Preheat oven to 350 degrees. Brush bottom and side of 12-cup bundt pan with 2 tablespoons melted butter. Sprinkle with 3 tablespoons pecans. Combine remaining butter with remaining pecans, brown sugar and water in saucepan. Bring to a boil, stirring occasionally. Remove roll dough from can in rolls; do not separate. Cut each roll into 16 slices. Arrange half the slices in overlapping layer in prepared bundt pan. Pour half the sauce over slices. Repeat layers. Bake for 25 to 30 minutes or until golden brown. Cool in pan for 3 minutes. Invert onto serving plate. Yield: 8 to 12 servings.

BLUEBERRY CRUMB MUFFINS

¼ cup butter or margarine, softened	1 teaspoon vanilla extract
⅓ cup sugar	1½ cups fresh blueberries
1 egg	½ cup sugar
2⅓ cups all-purpose flour	⅓ cup all-purpose flour
4 teaspoons baking powder	½ teaspoon cinnamon
½ teaspoon salt	¼ cup butter or margarine, softened
1 cup milk	

Preheat oven to 375 degrees. Cream ¼ cup butter and ⅓ cup sugar in mixer bowl until light and fluffy. Beat in egg. Add sifted mixture of 2⅓ cups flour, baking powder and salt alternately with milk, mixing well after each addition. Stir in vanilla and blueberries. Fill greased muffin cups ⅔ full. Mix ½ cup sugar, ⅓ cup flour and cinnamon in bowl. Cut in ¼ cup butter until crumbly. Sprinkle over muffin batter. Bake for 25 to 30 minutes or until golden brown. Yield: 1½ dozen.

CREAM CHEESE DANISH BARS

16 ounces cream cheese, softened	1 egg yolk
¾ cup sugar	2 8-ounce cans crescent dinner rolls
2 tablespoons lemon juice	1 egg white
1 teaspoon vanilla extract	1 teaspoon water
	½ cup slivered almonds

Preheat oven to 350 degrees. Beat cream cheese and sugar in mixer bowl until light. Add lemon juice, vanilla and egg yolk; mix until fluffy. Unroll roll dough. Place 1 can dough in 9-by-13-inch baking pan; press perforations to seal. Spread with cream cheese mixture. Top with remaining roll dough; press perforations to seal. Brush with mixture of egg white and water; sprinkle with almonds. Bake for 30 minutes. Cool in pan for 20 minutes. Cut into 1-by-2-inch bars. Yield: 4 dozen.

Easy Company Dinner

Chicken and Rice
Onion Casserole — Turnip Casserole
Coleslaw

See Index for similiar recipes.

This menu takes a little more time to prepare, but it can all be done in advance and the casseroles baked while you entertain guests.

Betty Byatt, Laureate Upsilon
Stratford, Ontario, Canada

CHICKEN AND RICE

6 chicken breast filets	1 10-ounce can cream
1 cup uncooked rice	of mushroom soup
1 envelope onion soup	1 soup can water
mix	

Preheat oven to 300 degrees. Rinse chicken; pat dry. Layer rice and chicken in baking pan. Pour mixture of soup mix, soup and water over layers. Bake, tightly covered with foil, for 3 hours. Yield: 6 servings.

ONION CASSEROLE

12 small onions	1/4 cup almonds
1 tablespoon butter or	1/3 cup shredded
margarine	Cheddar cheese
1 10-ounce can cream	1/3 cup dry bread crumbs
of mushroom soup	

Preheat oven to 350 degrees. Cook onions in water to cover in saucepan just until tender; drain. Arrange in greased 1-quart baking dish. Dot with butter. Combine soup and almonds in bowl; mix well. Spread over onions. Top with cheese and bread crumbs. Bake for 30 minutes. Yield: 6 servings.

TURNIP CASSEROLE

2 or 3 turnips, peeled,	1/2 teaspoon pepper
chopped	1 cup bread crumbs
1 cup applesauce	2 teaspoons melted
4 teaspoons sugar	butter or margarine
1 tablespoon salt	

Preheat oven to 350 degrees. Cook turnips in water in saucepan until tender; drain. Mash with applesauce, sugar, salt and pepper in bowl. Spoon into baking dish. Top with mixture of bread crumbs and melted butter. Bake for 30 to 50 minutes or until heated through. Yield: 6 servings.

Summer Dessert Party

Chocoberry-Yogurt Refresher
Chocolate-Citrus Cooler
Double-Decker Cereal Treats
Apricot Snacking Bars
Vanilla Chip Trail Mix
Peanut Butter and Jelly
Thumbprint Cookies
Chocolate Ice Crispy Pie

Gather your friends for a sweet-tooth extravaganza on the patio or by the pool. It would, of course, be just as good at any time of the year.

Hershey Foods Corporation

CHOCOBERRY-YOGURT REFRESHER

8 ounces strawberry	3 tablespoons Hershey's
yogurt	chocolate syrup
1 cup chilled milk	2 tablespoons light corn
1/2 cup sliced fresh	syrup
strawberries	

Combine all ingredients in blender container; process until smooth. Serve over crushed ice. Yield: 3 servings.

Photograph for this recipe is on the Cover.

CHOCOLATE-CITRUS COOLER

1 1/2 cups chilled milk	3 tablespoons Hershey's
1/4 cup thawed frozen	chocolate syrup
orange juice	1 scoop vanilla ice
concentrate	cream

Combine all ingredients in blender container; process until smooth. Pour over crushed ice. Top with additional ice cream. Yield: 8 servings.

Photograph for this recipe is on the Cover.

DOUBLE-DECKER CEREAL TREATS

2 cups Reese's peanut	1 teaspoon vanilla
butter chips	extract
2 tablespoons vegetable	2 cups light corn syrup
oil	1 1/3 cups packed light
1 teaspoon vanilla	brown sugar
extract	12 cups crisp rice cereal
2 cups Hershey's	
semisweet chocolate	
chips	

Line 10-by-15-inch pan with foil. Combine peanut butter chips, oil and 1 teaspoon vanilla in bowl. Combine chocolate chips and 1 teaspoon vanilla in second bowl. Bring corn syrup and brown sugar to a boil in large saucepan over medium heat, stirring constantly. Add half the mixture to each bowl of chips, stirring until smooth. Stir 6 cups cereal into each mixture immediately. Spread peanut butter mixture into prepared pan. Spread chocolate mixture over top. Cool completely; cut into bars. Store in airtight container. May microwave corn syrup mixture on High for 5 to 6 minutes, stirring every minute until mixture boils if preferred. Yield: 6 dozen.

Photograph for this recipe is on page 2.

APRICOT SNACKING BARS

1 cup boiling water	1/4 teaspoon salt
1 6-ounce package dried apricots, cut into 1/4-inch pieces	1 cup all-purpose flour
	11/3 cups Hershey's vanilla milk chips
1/2 cup margarine, softened	1/3 cup wheat germ
1/3 cup sugar	2 tablespoons all-purpose flour
1/4 cup packed light brown sugar	2 tablespoons honey
1 teaspoon vanilla extract	1 egg white
	1/2 teaspoon shortening
1/4 teaspoon baking soda	1/3 cup Hershey's vanilla milk chips

Preheat oven to 350 degrees. Stir boiling water into apricots in small bowl. Let stand, covered, for 5 minutes; drain. Cream margarine, sugar and brown sugar in mixer bowl until light and fluffy. Blend in vanilla. Add baking soda, salt and 1 cup flour; mix well. Add 11/3 cups vanilla milk chips. Press evenly into 8-by-8-inch baking pan. Spread apricots over top. Combine wheat germ, 2 tablespoons flour, honey and egg white in small bowl; mix until crumbly. Sprinkle over apricots. Bake for 30 minutes or until light brown. Cool on wire rack. Combine shortening and 1/3 cup vanilla milk chips in glass bowl. Microwave on High for 30 seconds; stir. Microwave at 15 second-intervals until chips are melted. Drizzle from tines of fork over top of baked layer; let stand until firm. Cut into squares. Yield: 16 servings.

Photograph for this recipe is on page 2.

VANILLA CHIP TRAIL MIX

1/2 cup melted margarine	4 cups bite-sized crisp wheat cereal squares
2 tablespoons Hershey's baking cocoa	1 cup slivered almonds
2 tablespoons sugar	1 cup golden raisins
4 cups toasted oat cereal rings	12/3 cups Hershey's vanilla milk chips

Preheat oven to 250 degrees. Stir margarine, cocoa and sugar together in bowl. Mix cereals and almonds in large bowl. Add margarine mixture; toss to coat well. Pour into 9-by-13-inch baking pan. Bake for 1 hour, stirring every 15 minutes. Cool completely. Stir in raisins and vanilla milk chips. Store in airtight container in cool dry place. Yield: 111/2 cups.

Photograph for this recipe is on page 2.

PEANUT BUTTER AND JELLY THUMBPRINT COOKIES

1 cup margarine, softened	1 teaspoon baking powder
13/4 cups packed light brown sugar	11/2 cups quick-cooking oats
2 eggs	11/2 cups Hershey's peanut butter chips
2 teaspoons vanilla extract	3/4 cup jelly or preserves
3 cups all-purpose flour	1/2 cup Hershey's peanut butter chips
1 teaspoon salt	

Cream margarine and brown sugar in mixer bowl until light and fluffy. Beat in eggs and vanilla. Add mixture of flour, salt and baking powder; mix well. Stir in oats and 11/2 cups peanut butter chips. Chill, covered, for several hours or until firm. Preheat oven to 400 degrees. Shape cookie dough into 1-inch balls; place on ungreased cookie sheet. Press thumb gently into center of each cookie. Bake for 7 to 9 minutes or until light brown. Cool slightly on cookie sheet. Press indentations again if desired. Remove to wire rack to cool completely. Fill centers with jelly. Garnish with 1/2 cup peanut butter chips. Yield: 5 dozen.

Photograph for this recipe is on page 2.

CHOCOLATE ICE CRISPY PIE

1/2 cup Hershey's chocolate syrup	2 cups crisp rice cereal
1/3 cup Hershey's semisweet chocolate chips	1/4 cup sour cream
	1 quart favorite ice cream, softened

Mix chocolate syrup and chocolate chips in medium glass bowl. Microwave on High for 45 seconds or until hot; stir until smooth. Reserve 1/4 cup mixture. Combine remaining chocolate mixture with cereal in bowl, stirring to coat well. Press over bottom and side of buttered 8-inch pie plate with back of spoon. Freeze for 15 to 20 minutes or until firm. Combine reserved chocolate mixture with sour cream in bowl; mix well. Spoon half the ice cream into pie shell. Drizzle with half the sour cream mixture. Repeat layers. Freeze until serving time. Yield: 6 servings.

Photograph for this recipe is on page 2.

Relaxing Brunch

Cream of Asparagus Soup
Shrimp Potpie
Bibb Salad with Citrus Dressing
Cherry and Apple Phyllo Crunch
Lemon-Ginger Tea

This menu, simple enough to enjoy at a relaxing get-together with friends, is spiced up with some special touches.

Michigan Asparagus Advisory Board
Corning, Inc.
Wish-Bone® Italian Dressings

CREAM OF ASPARAGUS SOUP

2 15-ounce cans asparagus spears, drained	3 cups chicken broth
1¼ cups chopped onions	¾ cup light cream
⅓ cup Wish-Bone® Italian Dressing	Nutmeg and white pepper to taste

Cut off and reserve asparagus tips. Cook onions in salad dressing in medium saucepan over medium heat for 3 minutes or until tender, stirring occasionally. Add chicken broth and asparagus stalks. Bring to a boil; reduce heat. Simmer, covered, for 3 minutes, stirring occasionally. Purée ½ at a time in blender. Combine with asparagus tips in saucepan. Stir in cream, nutmeg and pepper. Cook just until heated through; do not boil. Yield: 6 servings.

Photograph for this recipe is on page 1.

SHRIMP POTPIE

⅓ cup finely chopped onion	1 teaspoon Worcestershire sauce
⅓ cup finely chopped carrot	½ teaspoon thyme
¼ cup finely chopped celery	1 pound peeled shrimp, cooked
⅓ cup Wish-Bone® Italian Dressing	1 15-ounce can cut asparagus, drained
⅓ cup all-purpose flour	1 15-ounce package refrigerator pastry for 2 pie shells
¾ cup chicken broth	
¾ cup light cream	1 egg
1 cup shredded Cheddar cheese	1 teaspoon water

Preheat oven to 400 degrees. Cook onion, carrot and celery in salad dressing in medium saucepan over medium-high heat for 4 minutes or until tender, stirring occasionally. Stir in flour. Add broth gradually. Cook for 2 minutes or until thickened, stirring constantly. Stir in next 4 ingredients. Combine with shrimp and asparagus in large bowl; mix gently. Line 10-inch Corning Ware quiche pan with 1 pastry. Add shrimp mixture. Top with remaining pastry. Seal and flute edges; cut vents. Brush with mixture of egg and water. Bake for 35 minutes or until golden brown. Let stand for 10 minutes. Yield: 6 servings.

Photograph for this recipe is on page 1.

BIBB SALAD WITH CITRUS DRESSING

1 medium head Bibb lettuce, torn	½ cup Wish-Bone® Herbal Italian Dressing
Sections of 2 oranges	
1 medium red onion, sliced into rings	2 teaspoons honey
½ teaspoon Dijon mustard	½ teaspoon grated lemon rind

Combine lettuce, oranges and onion in large bowl. Chill in refrigerator. Blend mustard, salad dressing, honey and lemon rind in small bowl. Add to salad at serving time; toss to mix well. Yield: 6 servings.

Photograph for this recipe is on page 1.

CHERRY AND APPLE PHYLLO CRUNCH

1 21-ounce can cherry pie filling	½ cup chopped walnuts
3 cups chopped peeled apples	¼ teaspoon cinnamon
	3 sheets phyllo dough
2 tablespoons black raspberry or black currant liqueur	2 tablespoons melted butter or margarine

Preheat oven to 375 degrees. Combine next 5 ingredients in bowl; mix well. Spoon into Corning Ware 1½-quart open casserole. Unfold phyllo dough and cover with waxed paper and damp cloth. Brush 1 sheet at a time with melted butter, layering on work surface. Tear layers into irregular 3-inch pieces. Arrange over cherry mixture. Bake for 25 minutes or until apples are tender. Yield: 6 servings.

Photograph for this recipe is on page 1.

LEMON-GINGER TEA

2 tablespoons chopped gingerroot	2 quarts cold water
3 ¾-by-1½-inch strips lemon peel	6 Lipton tea bags
	¾ cup sugar
	¼ cup lemon juice

Combine gingerroot, lemon peel and water in medium saucepan. Bring to a boil; remove from heat. Add tea bags. Steep, covered, for 5 minutes. Strain into saucepan. Stir in sugar and lemon juice. Serve hot or over ice. Yield: 6 servings.

Photograph for this recipe is on page 1.

Crafty Crafts

What is it about cooking and crafts that
makes them go hand in hand so naturally?
Perhaps it has to do with the pleasure we
derive from knowing that we've put a little
bit of ourselves into those things we make by
hand, whether it's a cake or a collage. If setting
aside time to cook is difficult for most of us,
trying to budget time for crafts, especially
around the holidays, is even harder. That's why
we think you'll especially appreciate the
thoughtful craft ideas that follow. While we've
put together a number of innovative, charming
ideas for gifts and such, nearly all these projects
are inexpensive, easy and, most importantly,
quick to do. They range from shoelace
bows for your teenager's sneakers to adorable
Christmas tree decorations that can be
adapted for table settings and party favors.
Who says handmade has to be hard?

T-Shirt Blouse

Do you want a dressy blouse but don't want to spend a fortune for it? Here's just the one for you. With a purchased collar and a man's T-shirt, you can whip this up in an hour or so.

MATERIALS

Purchased Battenburg lace collar
Long sleeve white T-shirt
1¾ yards (⅛-inch wide) white satin ribbon

DIRECTIONS

☐ With wrong sides together, pin collar to neck of T-shirt matching shoulder seams.

☐ Trim excess T-shirt material so T-shirt neck is even with collar.

☐ Sew using ¼-inch seam allowance. Clip seams.

☐ Topstitch ⅛ inch from neck edge.

☐ Cut ribbon into 6 pieces; 4 to measure 12 inches and 2 to measure 7 inches.

☐ Mark the 4 corners of the collar on the T-shirt.

☐ Fold ribbon piece in half and tack at T-shirt mark.

☐ Thread ribbon through holes in collar and tie each in a bow.

☐ Make a bow from each 7-inch ribbon piece.

☐ Tack 1 bow to each sleeve cuff.

Polka-Dot Shoelace Bows

Shoelace bows are all the rage. Little girls and big girls alike will love them.

MATERIALS

18 inches (7/8-inch wide) black polka-dot grosgrain ribbon
18 inches (7/8-inch wide) red polka-dot grosgrain ribbon
6 inches (3/8-inch wide) red grosgrain ribbon
4 clothespins
1 pair (26-inch) white shoelaces
2 (5/8-inch diameter) 4-hole buttons

DIRECTIONS

☐ Cut black polka-dot ribbon into 2 equal pieces.

☐ Cut red polka-dot ribbon into 2 equal pieces.

☐ Cut red ribbon into 2 equal pieces.

☐ Make a bow with 13/4-inch loops from 1 black polka-dot and 1 red polka-dot ribbon piece. Hold each loop in place with a clothespin.

☐ Wrap 1 red ribbon piece tightly around center of bow leaving excess ribbon at bottom of bow. Stitch in place.

☐ Form small loop with excess red ribbon. Stitch in place. (Bow will slide on shoelace.)

☐ Hand sew button to top center of red ribbon.

☐ Repeat procedure for remaining shoelace bow.

Buttons and Buttons Barrette

Wouldn't you love to have a small gift as a special surprise for a little girl that has been especially good. This barrette will take you only minutes to make and we're sure you'll get a giant hug from the recipient.

MATERIALS

Buttons of various sizes and shapes
Hot glue gun
1 (3-inch) spring-clasp hair barrette

DIRECTIONS

☐ Randomly glue buttons to barrette creating multiple layers.

Victorian Collage

*Create an heirloom collage for a special family
member by gathering such vintage items as
family photographs, Grandmother's hairpin,
Mother's lace handkerchief and a lock of
hair from the youngest family member.*

MATERIALS

Suede-covered matboard
Dried flowers
Beads, buttons, lace and ribbon
Old photographs and mementos

DIRECTIONS

☐ Cut mat to desired size.

☐ Arrange mementos, dried flowers, photographs,
beads, buttons and lace as desired.

☐ Frame as desired and cover front of collage with
clear glass.

Fabric Frame

Do you have a favorite poster that needs framing but custom framing does not fit into your budget? You can be your own custom framer with only a few supplies and a little time. Give a friend's room (or even your own) a custom-finished look that complements or copies other patterns in that room.

MATERIALS

Dry mounted poster (Dry mounting available at any frame shop.)

¼-inch foam core (size to be 2 to 3 inches larger all around than poster)

Fabric (size to be 3 inches larger all around than foam core)

Fabric glue

Spray adhesive

Piping or cording (length determined by measuring circumference of poster)

DIRECTIONS

☐ Center foam core on wrong side of fabric.

☐ Stretch fabric to back of foam core, mitering corners for a smooth fit.

☐ Glue fabric to back of foam core with fabric glue, keeping fabric taut and grain of fabric straight. Let dry.

☐ Glue poster to front of fabric-covered base with spray adhesive. Let dry.

☐ Glue piping or cording around edge of poster with fabric glue. Let dry.

Christmas Napkins and Napkin Rings

Set a pretty country Christmas table with these charming napkins and napkin rings. Appliquéing scrap fabric pieces onto purchased napkins make this a quick afternoon project.

MATERIALS

Scraps of red, brown, green print and red print fabrics
4 purchased muslin napkins
24 inches (¼-inch wide) red satin ribbon
Red acrylic spray paint
4 heart-shaped wooden pieces
Hot glue gun
4   (2-inch diameter) grapevine wreaths

DIRECTIONS

☐ Cut 4 tree shapes from green print fabric using pattern. Cut 4 hearts from red fabric using pattern. Cut 4 tree bases from brown fabric using pattern. Cut small squares from red print fabric for packages.

☐ Position tree and package appliqués on napkins.

☐ Set sewing machine for appliqué. Using satin stitch, appliqué pieces in the following order: tree, tree base, heart, packages. (Use green thread to appliqué tree. Use brown thread to appliqué tree base. Use red thread to appliqué heart and Christmas packages.)

☐ Cut satin ribbon into twelve 2-inch pieces. Tie each piece into a bow and hand stitch to top of each package.

☐ Spray hearts with paint. Let dry.

☐ Glue a heart to each grapevine wreath.

Cut 4 for napkin rings

Cut 4 from red fabric

Cut 4 from green print fabric

Cut 4 from brown fabric

Counter Top Tree

*Edible decorations do double duty—they look
great and taste delicious. Tie decorated
doughnuts, bagels or cookies to a dowel tree
and use as a kitchen decoration.*

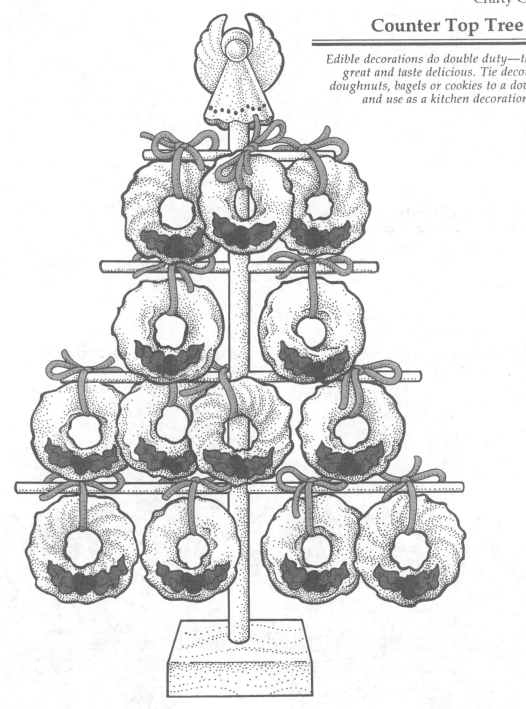

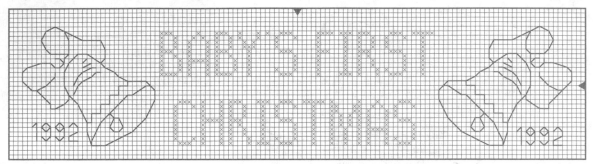

Baby's First Christmas Bib

A child's first Christmas is always a special one. "Decorate" a favorite infant with this colorful bib. It is sure to become a treasure to pass from generation to generation.

MATERIALS

1 red baby bib with 14-count Aida cloth insert
1 embroidery needle
DMC® Embroidery Floss = 8m skeins
 (1 skein each): Blanc White

DIRECTIONS

☐ Mark center of cross-stitch fabric both ways with long running stitch using needle and thread.

☐ Work cross-stitch according to chart and color key, beginning at intersection of arrows on chart to ensure proper placement of fabric.

Backstitch bells and numbers in DMC Blanc White

⊞ DMC Blanc White

☐ Each square on chart represents 1 fabric thread. Use 2 strands of floss for cross-stitch and 1 strand of floss for backstitch.

☐ Press finished work.

Sensational Centerpiece

You needn't spend a lot of money or time to create a simple yet elegant centerpiece. Use a wicker tray and an assortment of votive candles, greenery and Spanish moss for a smashing arrangement.

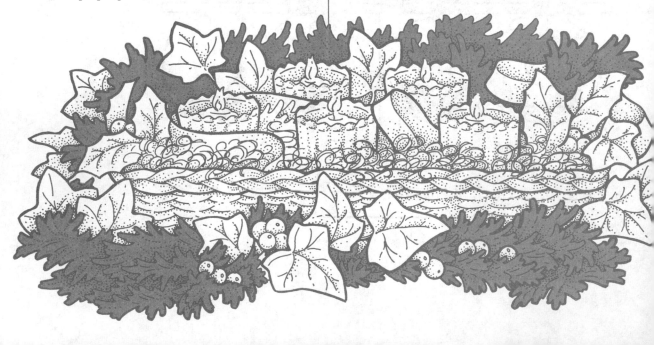

MATERIALS

Spanish moss
Wicker tray
Crystal votive candleholders
Assorted greenery and holly berries
Red votive candles

DIRECTIONS

☐ Place a layer of Spanish moss on bottom of tray.

☐ Arrange candleholders, greenery, and holly berries over Spanish moss.

☐ Place votive candles in candleholders.

Decorative Luminaries

Set a pretty table and help the environment by recycling tin cans into charming luminaries.

MATERIALS

Clean, dry, empty fruit or vegetable can
Tin snips
Hammer
Nail
Enamel spray paint
Plate
Votive candle
Fresh fruits and greenery

DIRECTIONS

☐ Cut diagonal and straight lines into can using tin snips. Refer to drawing for placement.

☐ Use a hammer and nail to punch hole designs into can.

☐ Press down on can until it has the desired shape.

☐ Spray can with enamel spray paint. Let dry.

☐ Place luminary in center of table. Place candle in center of luminary. Decorate around luminary with fresh fruits and greenery.

Tooth Pillow

Make life a little easier for the tooth fairy. Place "lost" tooth in this handy little pocket, hide it under the pillow, and the next morning the tooth fairy will have replaced the tooth with cash. (No more searching for a tiny tooth in the middle of the night.) The tooth fairy will love you for it.

MATERIALS

Scraps of muslin and print fabrics
Permanent markers

DIRECTIONS

☐ Cut 2 of pattern piece A from muslin fabric.

☐ Cut 2 of pattern piece B from print fabric.

☐ Cut 1 of pattern piece C from print fabric.

☐ With right sides together, pin 1 of pattern piece A to 1 of pattern piece B. Sew using 1/4-inch seam allowance. Repeat with remaining fabric pieces.

☐ Pin pocket to front of pillow as indicated on pattern. With right sides together, pin front to back. Sew using 1/4-inch seam allowance, leaving small opening for turning.

☐ Clip curves and turn. Sew opening closed.

☐ Draw face with permanent marker as indicated.

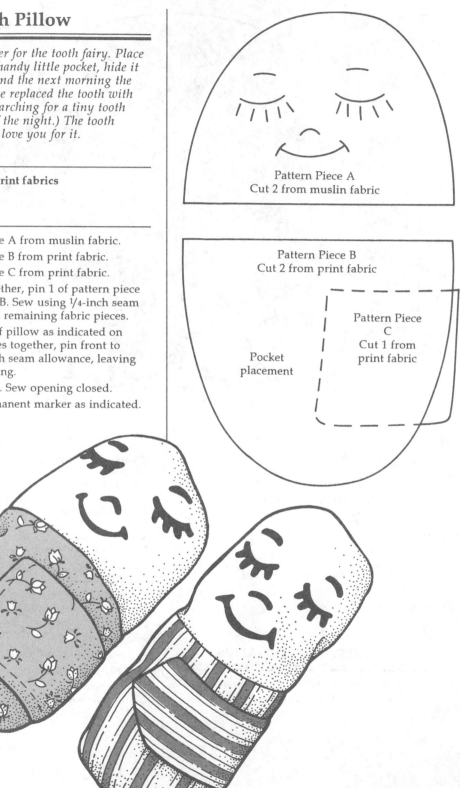

Pattern Piece A
Cut 2 from muslin fabric

Pattern Piece B
Cut 2 from print fabric

Pattern Piece C
Cut 1 from print fabric

Pocket placement

Handmade Stationery

Children will enjoy making these cards as much as loved ones will enjoy receiving them. Variations on color and design are as boundless as your child's imagination.

MATERIALS

1 (12-by-9-inch) piece green construction paper
1 (5½-by-7-inch) piece red construction paper
Craft glue
Photocopy of favorite family photograph

DIRECTIONS

☐ Fold green construction paper in half to form card.

☐ Glue red construction paper to front of card.

☐ Glue photocopy of photograph to center of red construction paper.

☐ Write message on inside of card.

Spectacular Table Decorations

Glue cookie cutters into unusual table decorations. Continue the theme with napkin holders and place cards for guests to take home as mementos.

Christmas Light Earrings

If you have a friend that likes flashy things (or maybe you do yourself?) then we have just the thing for you. These earrings will be the perfect accent for your Christmas outfit and is sure to be a conversation piece.

MATERIALS

17 inches (¼-inch wide) gold metal ribbon
1 red Christmas light
2   (1½-inch diameter) bells
Hot glue gun
2 clip-on earring backs
1 green Christmas light

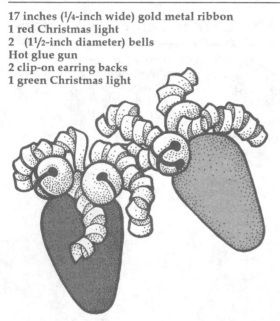

DIRECTIONS

☐ Cut gold metal ribbon into 4 pieces; 2 pieces to measure 6 inches in length and 2 pieces to measure 2½ inches in length.

☐ Wrap 6-inch metal ribbon piece around red Christmas light and twist to secure.

☐ Wrap 2½-inch metal ribbon around twisted portion to secure.

☐ Thread bell through 1 metal ribbon and center over twisted pieces.

☐ Wrap each ribbon piece around a pencil to curl.

☐ Glue Christmas light to earring back.

☐ Repeat procedure for green Christmas light.

Bundles of Bows

If you sometimes feel "all thumbs" when it comes to making bows then here's some ideas that are sure to please you.

PETAL BOW

☐ Use short, leftover ends of ribbon to create flower blossoms.

☐ Taper ends and press together in center. Wrap center with string and knot (Figures 1 and 2).

☐ Glue bright holly berry, pearl bead or colored sequin to center for a nice finishing touch (Figure 3).

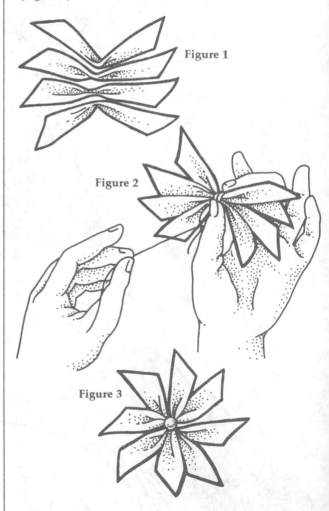

Figure 1

Figure 2

Figure 3

CIRCLE BOW

□ Hold end of ribbon firmly between thumb and forefinger. Make a series of circular loops, each larger than the one before (Figure 4).

□ Fasten with a strip of tape (Figure 5).

□ This bow may be used alone or several small ones may be grouped together and tied to the package at different angles.

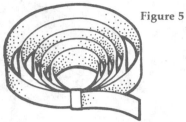

Figure 5

Figure 4

PERFECT BOW

□ Add a touch of elegance to your Christmas tree by tying 1¼-inch wide gold mesh ribbon into bows directly onto the tree branches.

□ Take a length of ribbon and hold one end in your right hand and one end in your left hand. Form a loop on each end. Cross the loops one over the other; tie loops into knot and pull tight.

□ You'll have a perfect bow.

Beribboned Table Setting

If you can tie a bow, you can set a romantic table. Beribbon the chair, napkins, pomanders and anything else that strikes your fancy.

Holiday Double-Dip

For a holiday double-dip,
"favor" your guests with these
delightful holiday decorations
to enjoy a second time at home.

Goody Baskets

No time to cook? Assemble the ingredients
for a homemade dish in a small basket,
along with the accessories and,
of course, the recipe.

Snacks in a Snap

You know that feeling. The neighbors who dropped by to return the borrowed camping gear seem to be settled on the sofa for the evening. Your teenager has just brought half his soccer team home for a quick fill-up. You suddenly remember that it's your turn to bring the appetizer for the supper club meeting in two hours. No, a bowl of chips is not the only hope in these situations. Whether you need instant goodies for an impromptu party or fancy treats that can be made ahead, you'll find them here. We've included easy appetizers, dips, spreads, and delicious munchies you can keep in the refrigerator or the cookie jar, both for everyday use and for elegant offerings your guests will be sure you slaved over. But Shhh—that's your secret.

EASY BEEFY CHEESE BALL

1 tablespoon dried
 onion flakes
2 tablespoons cold water
2 tablespoons
 mayonnaise-type
 salad dressing
1 teaspoon sugar

8 ounces cream cheese,
 softened
1 2½-ounce jar dried
 beef, chopped
½ cup chopped walnuts
 or pecans
 Crackers

Mix onion flakes with water in small bowl. Let stand for 15 minutes. Combine next 4 ingredients in bowl; mix well. Add onion flakes; mix well. Chill, covered, for 2 hours or longer. Shape into ball; roll in chopped nuts. Serve with crackers. Yield: 8 servings.

Peggy Evoniuk, Xi Alpha Delta
Sand Springs, Oklahoma

EASY BEEF AND OLIVE CHEESE BALL

16 ounces cream cheese,
 softened
1 2-ounce jar green
 olives, drained,
 chopped
3 tablespoons
 Worcestershire sauce

1 2-ounce package
 dried beef, finely
 chopped
1 tablespoon garlic salt
 Chopped nuts (optional)
 Crackers

Combine first 5 ingredients in bowl; mix well. Shape into ball; roll in nuts. Serve with crackers.
Yield: 12 servings.

Della Wooddell, Kappa Xi
Platte City, Missouri

QUICK-AND-EASY CHEESE BALL

16 ounces cream cheese,
 softened
2 tablespoons chopped
 green olives
1 cup small curd
 cottage cheese
2 teaspoons grated
 onion

2 teaspoons
 Worcestershire sauce
3 or 4 dashes of hot
 sauce
12 ounces dried beef,
 finely chopped
 Crackers

Mix first 6 ingredients in bowl. Add half the beef; mix well. Shape into ball; chill. Roll in remaining beef. Serve with crackers. Yield: 10 to 12 servings.

Margaret Sanders, Xi Epsilon Nu
Cape Girardeau, Missouri

ZESTY CHEESE BALL

12 ounces cream cheese,
 softened
1 2-ounce jar dried
 beef, finely chopped

1 8-ounce bottle of
 creamy Italian dressing
 Finely chopped pecans
 Crackers

Mix first 3 ingredients in bowl. Chill until firm. Shape into ball; roll in pecans. Serve with crackers. Yield: 8 servings.

Joyce Shaffer, Preceptor Alpha Gamma
Stone Mountain, Georgia

SMITHFIELD HAM-CHEESE BALL

8 ounces cream cheese,
 softened
1 2½-ounce can
 deviled Smithfield
 ham

½ cup chopped pecans
¼ cup red or green
 pepper jelly

Combine cream cheese and deviled ham in bowl; mix well with fork. Shape into ball. Chill, wrapped in plastic wrap, overnight. Roll in pecans; place on serving plate. Heat jelly in saucepan. Spoon over cheese ball. Yield: 15 servings.

Bettina V. Joyner, Gamma Tau
Carrollton, Virginia

HOLIDAY CHEESE BALL

16 ounces cream cheese,
 softened
1 8-ounce can crushed
 pineapple, drained
2 tablespoons chopped
 onion

¼ cup chopped green
 bell pepper
1 teaspoon salt
2 cups chopped pecans
 Pineapple slices,
 cherries and parsley

Combine cream cheese and pineapple in bowl; mix well. Add onion, green pepper, salt and half the pecans; mix well. Shape into 1 or 2 balls; roll in remaining pecans. Garnish with pineapple slices, cherries and parsley. Yield: 16 servings.

Phyllis Johnson, Preceptor Iota
Tampa, Florida

PIMENTO CHEESE BALL

8 ounces cream cheese,
 softened
1 5-ounce jar pimento
 cheese spread
1 5-ounce jar Old
 English cheese spread

2 tablespoons minced
 onion
2 tablespoons minced
 parsley
1 cup chopped nuts
 Crackers

Combine cream cheese, cheese spreads, onion and parsley in bowl; mix well. Shape into ball; roll in nuts. Chill, wrapped with plastic wrap, for 1 hour. Serve with crackers. Yield: 12 servings.

Jessie Neier, Xi Epsilon Psi
Terre Haute, Indiana

BRAUNSCHWEIGER PARTY LOG

3 ounces cream cheese,
 softened
1 8-ounce roll
 braunschweiger

3 ounces real bacon bits
 Crackers or rye bread

Beat cream cheese in bowl until light. Remove wrapping carefully from braunschweiger. Frost with cream cheese; roll in bacon bits. Chill in refrigerator. Serve with crackers or rye bread. Yield: 8 servings.

Beatrice G. Busko, Laureate Gamma
Great Falls, Montana

DONNA SUE'S CHICKEN BALL

8 ounces cream cheese, softened
1 6-ounce can chunk chicken
1 stalk celery, chopped
1 small white onion, chopped
Garlic salt to taste
1 large jar bacon bits
Crackers

Combine cream cheese with celery, onion and garlic salt in bowl; mix well. Shape into ball; roll in bacon bits. Chill overnight. Serve with crackers. Yield: 12 servings.

Sylvia Fabrizi, Preceptor Alpha Chi
Pittsburgh, Pennsylvania

CRAB BALL

This was a hit at a Super Bowl Party.

8 ounces cream cheese, softened
2 teaspoons chopped chives (optional)
1/4 teaspoon garlic powder or garlic salt
1/4 teaspoon salt
6 ounces frozen or canned crab meat, drained
1/2 cup chopped pecans
Crackers or fresh vegetables

Combine cream cheese, chives, garlic powder and salt in bowl; mix well. Fold in crab meat. Shape into ball or log; roll in pecans. Serve with crackers or fresh vegetables. Yield: 8 servings.

Vickie Booker, Xi Gamma Delta
Cartersville, Georgia

OYSTER LOG

1 4-ounce can smoked oysters, drained
Garlic powder to taste
1/2 teaspoon onion flakes
8 ounces cream cheese, softened
Sliced green and black olives
Paprika to taste
Crackers

Combine oysters, garlic powder and onion flakes in bowl; mix well. Roll cream cheese to rectangle between waxed paper; remove top sheet of waxed paper. Spread with oyster mixture. Roll as for jelly roll to enclose filling. Place on serving dish. Garnish with olives and paprika. Serve with crackers. Yield: 8 servings.

Emma Irene Powell, Laureate Alpha Lambda
Grants Pass, Oregon

SALMON PARTY BALL

1 16-ounce can red salmon, drained, flaked
8 ounces light cream cheese, softened
1 tablespoon finely chopped onion
1 tablespoon lemon juice
1/4 teaspoon liquid smoke
1/4 teaspoon salt
1/3 cup finely chopped walnuts or pecans
1/4 cup parsley flakes
Crackers

Combine salmon with next 5 ingredients in bowl; mix well. Shape into ball. Chill, covered, for 8 hours. Coat with mixture of walnuts and parsley flakes. Serve with crackers. May spoon into bowl and sprinkle with walnuts and parsley to serve as dip. Yield: 16 servings.

Beverley Delbridge, Alpha Tau
Exeter, Ontario, Canada

PARTY SALMON LOG

1 16-ounce can salmon, drained
8 ounces cream cheese, softened
1 tablespoon lemon juice
2 teaspoons grated onion
1 teaspoon horseradish
1/4 teaspoon salt
1/2 cup chopped pecans or walnuts
3 tablespoons chopped parsley
Crackers

Flake salmon into bowl, discarding skin and bones. Add next 5 ingredients; mix well. Chill for several hours. Shape into log. Roll in mixture of pecans and parsley. Serve with crackers. Yield: 16 servings.

Stephanie Reid, Eta Mu
Marietta, Georgia

FANTASTIC ARTICHOKE DIP

1 6-ounce jar marinated artichokes, drained
1 15-ounce can artichokes, drained
1 3-ounce can chopped chilies, drained
6 tablespoons mayonnaise
1 1/2 cups shredded extra sharp Cheddar cheese
Tortilla chips

Preheat oven to 350 degrees. Chop marinated artichokes and artichokes. Combine with chilies in round glass pie plate; mix well. Spread mayonnaise over top of mixture. Sprinkle with cheese to cover. Bake for 15 minutes. Serve with tortilla chips. Yield: 8 servings.

Robin Gibeson, Xi Pi Gamma
Santa Rosa, California

GUACAMOLE DIP

2 soft avocados, mashed
1 tablespoon lemon juice
1/4 teaspoon garlic powder
Salt to taste
1/4 cup chopped onion
1/2 cup chopped tomato
1/4 cup chopped green bell pepper

Combine avocados, lemon juice, garlic powder and salt in bowl; mix well. Stir in onion, tomato and green pepper. Spoon into serving dish. Yield: 4 to 6 servings.

Rose Giron, Xi Epsilon Theta
Pueblo West, Colorado

RED BEANS AND BACON DIP

This is different and ready in a very short time.

3 slices bacon, chopped	1 cup sour cream
1 8-ounce can red kidney beans, drained	1/4 teaspoon salt
	1/8 teaspoon garlic powder
1 tablespoon chopped green bell pepper	1/8 teaspoon pepper
1 teaspoon dried minced onion	Tortilla chips

Place bacon in 1½-quart microwave-safe casserole. Microwave, covered, with paper towel, on High for 3 to 4 minutes or until crisp, stirring after 2 minutes. Stir in beans, mashing with fork. Microwave, covered, for 2 to 3 minutes or until hot. Stir in green pepper, minced onion, sour cream, salt, garlic powder and pepper. Microwave, covered, for 1 minute or until of serving temperature. Serve with tortilla chips. Yield: 1½ cups.

Mary Jo Bent, Master Epsilon
Kansas City, Missouri

BEER CHEESE DIP

I have served this many times as a snack during football games.

1 16-ounce jar Cheese Whiz	1 teaspoon Worcestershire sauce
4 ounces beer	2 round loaves rye bread
1 teaspoon minced garlic	

Combine Cheese Whiz, beer, garlic and Worcestershire sauce in bowl; mix well. Cut top from 1 loaf bread. Remove center carefully leaving 2-inch shell. Pour mixture into shell. Cut remaining loaf bread into bite-sized pieces. Place shell and bread pieces on serving dish. Yield: 20 to 30 servings.

Kathy Streitz, Alpha Epsilon
Robbinsdale, Minnesota

BLEU CHEESE DIP

8 ounces bleu cheese, mashed	1 clove of garlic, minced
1 cup mayonnaise	1 teaspoon sugar
1/2 cup sour cream	2 tablespoons chopped scallions
1 teaspoon lemon juice	

Combine all ingredients in bowl; mix well. Yield: 30 to 40 servings.

Esther Sullivan
Centerville, Virginia

Linda Kay Collins, Xi Alpha Kappa, Mason City, Iowa, has made her Dip Quick! in a hotel room at Beta Sigma Phi conventions. Melt 12 ounces sliced Velveeta cheese and add one 10-ounce can chili without beans. Keep hot in slow cooker for dipping nacho chips.

HOT BROCCOLI DIP

2 4-ounce cans mushroom stems and pieces, drained	2 10-ounce packages frozen chopped broccoli, thawed, drained
1/2 cup chopped onion	1/2 cup slivered almonds
1/4 cup margarine	1/2 teaspoon garlic powder
2 10-ounce cans cream of mushroom soup	1 teaspoon Worcestershire sauce
2 5-ounce jars process cheese spread	3 or 4 drops hot pepper sauce
8 ounces process cheese food, cut into cubes	Chips or crackers

Sauté mushrooms and onion in margarine in large skillet for 3 minutes or until onion is clear. Add soup, cheese spread and cheese cubes. Cook until mixture is smooth and bubbly, stirring constantly. Add broccoli, almonds, garlic powder, Worcestershire sauce and hot pepper sauce. Simmer for 10 minutes, stirring occasionally. Pour into serving bowl. Serve with chips or crackers. Yield: 100 servings.

Becky Geary, Xi Phi Beta
Richmond, Texas

CHEDDAR-ONION DIP

1 10-ounce can Cheddar cheese soup	1 small container French onion dip
1 cup shredded sharp Cheddar cheese	Pepper to taste
1/2 teaspoon dry mustard	1 loaf French bread

Combine soup, cheese, mustard, dip, and pepper in saucepan; mix well. Cook until cheese is melted, stirring frequently. Pour into fondue pot. Cut French bread into bite-sized pieces. Serve with dip. Yield: 30 to 40 servings.

Vicki Brashears, Xi Omicron
Frostburg, Maryland

CHEESE FONDUE

1½ to 2 pounds ground beef	1 16-ounce can tomatoes, drained
1 small onion, chopped	1 10-ounce can golden mushroom soup
1 pound Velveeta cheese, cubed	2 mild jalapeño peppers, chopped
1 5-ounce jar Old English cheese spread	Tortilla chips
Garlic salt to taste	

Brown ground beef with onion in skillet, stirring until ground beef is crumbly; drain. Add Velveeta cheese, cheese spread, garlic salt, tomatoes, soup and jalapeño peppers. Simmer until cheese melts, stirring frequently. Serve with tortilla chips. May also be made in microwave. Yield: 20 to 30 servings.

Diana Jackson, Mu Kappa
Ellinwood, Kansas

CHEESY VEGETABLE DIP

8 ounces cream cheese, softened
1 5-ounce jar Roka Bleu cheese spread, softened
1 5-ounce jar Old English cheese spread, softened
1½ teaspoon grated onion
1 teaspoon Worcestershire sauce
Chopped nuts or parsley
Carrot and celery sticks or crackers

Combine cheeses in mixer bowl; beat well. Add onion and Worcestershire sauce; mix well. Chill until serving time. Serve with carrot and celery sticks or crackers. May shape into ball and roll in chopped nuts or parsley. Yield: 20 to 30 servings.

Donna M. Snyder, Xi Eta Xi
Edinboro, Pennsylvania

CHILI CON QUESO

1 10-ounce can Cheddar cheese soup
1 4-ounce can chopped green chilies
½ cup salsa or picante sauce
1 tomato, chopped
Tortilla chips

Combine soup, green chilies, salsa and tomato in saucepan. Cook over low heat until heated through, stirring constantly. Serve warm with tortilla chips. Yield: 6 servings.

Carol J. Wilson, Laureate Alpha Epsilon
Hays, Kansas

CLAM DIP JOLLY ROGER

2 cups sour cream
1 6-ounce can clams, minced
1 tablespoon Worcestershire sauce
2 teaspoons lemon juice
½ teaspoon thyme
¼ teaspoon MSG
¼ teaspoon salt
¼ teaspoon pepper

Combine sour cream and clams with half the liquid in mixer bowl. Add remaining ingredients; beat at low speed until doubled in volume. Chill until serving time. Yield: 4 cups.

Kay M. Bennett, Xi Beta
Charlotte, North Carolina

CORNED BEEF DIP

24 ounces cream cheese, softened
¼ cup onion flakes
5 tablespoons sour cream
8 ounces corned beef, thinly sliced
2 packages onion bagels

Combine cream cheese, minced onion, sour cream and corned beef in bowl; mix well. Cut bagels into bite-sized pieces. Serve with dip. May use one 12-ounce can corned beef. Yield: 30 to 40 servings.

Alice Laporte
Harrow, Ontario, Canada

HOT CRAB DIP

This is a recipe of my aunt's that I use whenever I need a good easy dish to take to a get-together.

16 ounces cream cheese, softened
1 cup sour cream
¼ cup mayonnaise
Juice of ½ lemon
1 teaspoon dry mustard
Onion or garlic salt to taste
1 cup shredded sharp Cheddar cheese
1 pound cooked crab meat
Crackers

Preheat oven to 325 degrees. Combine cream cheese, sour cream, mayonnaise, lemon juice, mustard, onion salt and ½ of the cheese in bowl. Spoon into 1½-quart casserole; mix well. Stir in crab meat. Sprinkle with remaining ½ cup cheese. Bake for 35 minutes. Serve with favorite crackers. Yield: 30 to 40 servings.

Barbi G. Davis, Lambda
Bland, Virginia

CRAB DIP POLYNESIAN

1 7-ounce can crab meat, drained
1 cup coconut
1 cup mayonnaise-type salad dressing
1 cup sour cream
¼ cup chopped onion
¼ teaspoon curry powder
2 tablespoons chopped parsley
1 2-ounce can sliced mushrooms, drained

Combine all ingredients in bowl; mix well. Chill until serving time. Yield: 3 to 3½ cups.

Emma van Os, Laureate Alpha Omega
Seattle, Washington

CRAWFISH DIP

2 large onions, finely chopped
2 stalks of celery, finely chopped
1 large green bell pepper, finely chopped
1 jalapeño pepper, finely chopped
1 bunch parsley, finely chopped
1 bunch green onions, finely chopped
½ cup margarine
1 pound crawfish tails, chopped
1 pound whole crawfish tails
2 10-ounce cans cream of mushroom soup
Salt and pepper to taste
Crackers or chips

Sauté chopped onions, celery, green pepper, jalapeño pepper, parsley and green onions in margarine in large skillet for 10 minutes. Add crawfish tails and soup. Cook for 15 minutes, stirring frequently. Add salt and pepper. Serve with crackers or chips. May also serve as a main dish over rice or spaghetti. Yield: 40 to 50 servings.

Enola B. Kilchrist, Xi Alpha Zeta
Rayne, Louisiana

LOBSTER DIP

This vegetable dip is always everyone's favorite. Make sure you bring copies of the recipe to the party, as it will definitely be a request.

1 11-ounce package frozen lobster, thawed	1½ cups mayonnaise
8 ounces cream cheese, softened	1 small onion, finely chopped
1 teaspoon sweet pickle relish	Pinch of sugar
	Assorted vegetables

Drain lobster. Process in food processor or blender until finely chopped. Combine lobster and cream cheese in bowl; mix well. Add relish, mayonnaise, onion and sugar; mix well. Serve with julienned vegetables. Yield: 12 to 15 servings.

Betty Quinn, Nu
Hampton, New Brunswick, Canada

MOM'S MEATBALLS AND CHEESE DIP

2 pounds ground beef	1 teaspoon meat tenderizer
4 eggs	1 pound Velveeta cheese, chopped
8 ounces crackers, crushed	1 10-ounce can Ro-Tel tomatoes
½ white onion, finely chopped	
¼ cup chili powder	

Preheat oven to 350 degrees. Combine ground beef, eggs, crackers, onion, chili powder and meat tenderizer in bowl; mix well. Shape into small balls; place on baking pan. Bake for 10 to 12 minutes or until light brown; drain. Melt cheese in saucepan over low heat. Add tomatoes; mix well. Heat to serving temperature. Pour into chafing dish. Serve with meatballs. Yield: 16 to 20 servings.

Lisa Orbin, Phi Gamma
Macon, Missouri

KEVIN'S FAVORITE MEXICAN DIP

8 ounces cream cheese, softened	2 tomatoes, chopped
1 cup Mexican sour cream	4 ounces longhorn Cheddar cheese, shredded
1 green bell pepper, chopped	4 ounces Monterey Jack cheese, shredded
¼ to ½ cup chopped onion	Tortilla chips

Combine cream cheese and sour cream in bowl; mix well. Add next 5 ingredients; mix well. Serve with tortilla chips. May be served immediately or chilled for several hours. Yield: 20 to 30 servings.

Kimberly Beard, Lambda Epsilon
Ankeny, Iowa

MUSHROOM DIP

2 6-ounce cans sliced mushrooms, drained	1 10-ounce can cream of mushroom soup
2 medium onions, chopped	¼ cup dry sherry
¼ cup butter or margarine	1 package Melba rounds

Sauté mushrooms and onions in butter in skillet. Add soup gradually, stirring constantly. Heat to serving temperature. Add sherry; mix well. Pour into chafing dish. Serve hot with Melba rounds. Yield: 12 to 15 servings.

Ann Abney, Xi Alpha Kappa
La Fayette, Georgia

NACHO DIP

This recipe was a hit at the sorority meeting at my house; my husband and friends ask for it all the time.

8 ounces cream cheese, softened	1 bunch green onions, finely chopped
1 15-ounce can chili with beans	2 cups shredded Cheddar cheese
1 4-ounce can chopped green chilies	

Preheat oven to 350 degrees. Layer all ingredients in the order listed in 9-by-13-inch casserole. Bake for 20 minutes. Yield: 10 to 12 servings.

Becky Stephens, Zeta Beta
Parkersburg, West Virginia

PEPPERONI DIP

I was introduced to this recipe by a new neighbor. What a good way to make a friend.

8 ounces cream cheese, softened	1½ tablespoon dried minced onion
½ cup sour cream	2 teaspoons chopped chives
3 ounces pepperoni, chopped	½ cup chopped pecans
1 4-ounce can chopped green chilies	Tortilla chips

Combine cream cheese and sour cream in bowl; mix well. Add pepperoni, undrained green chilies, minced onion and chives; mix well. Spoon into 1-quart baking dish; sprinkle with pecans. Bake for 20 minutes or until puffy and edges are bubbly. Serve hot with tortilla chips. May substitute ⅔ cup chopped salami for pepperoni. Yield: 8 to 10 servings.

Merle Gabriel, Xi Alpha Phi
Millersville, Maryland

AMARETTO DIP

We served this at our recent Mexican Fiesta. It is very refreshing after spicy foods.

8 ounces cream cheese, softened	2 tablespoons whipping cream
1 cup ricotta cheese	1/4 cup Amaretto liqueur
1/2 cup sugar	Assorted fresh fruit
2 egg yolks	

Combine first 6 ingredients in blender container. Process just until mixed. Chill until serving time. Serve with apples, pears, pineapple, strawberries and or oranges. Yield: 12 to 15 servings.

Dianne Wilson, Xi Beta Chi
Mississauga, Ontario, Canada

APPLE FRUIT DIP

16 ounces whipped topping	1 14-ounce can sweetened condensed milk
1 3-ounce can frozen pink lemonade, thawed	Sliced apples

Combine whipped topping, pink lemonade and condensed milk in bowl; mix well. Serve with sliced apples. Yield: 2 cups.

Devon Borton, Gamma Pi
Hutchinson, Kansas

CARAMEL APPLE DIP

8 ounces cream cheese, softened	1 teaspoon vanilla extract
1/2 cup packed brown sugar	Cinnamon to taste
1/4 cup honey	Sliced apples

Combine first 5 ingredients in bowl; beat well. Chill until serving time. Serve with sliced apples. May serve cold or warm in microwave.
Yield: 6 to 8 servings.

JoEllen Stremel, Theta Chi
Dodge City, Kansas

❖ CREAMY CARAMEL FRUIT DIP

8 ounces cream cheese, softened	2 teaspoons lemon juice
3/4 cup packed brown sugar	1 cup milk
1 cup sour cream	1 4-ounce package vanilla instant pudding mix
2 teaspoons vanilla extract	Assorted fresh fruit

Combine cream cheese and brown sugar in mixer bowl; beat well. Add next 5 ingredients, beating well after each addition. Chill until serving time. Serve with assorted fruit for dipping. Yield: 16 to 20 servings.

Debbie Braun, Xi Delta Omicron
Hutchinson, Kansas

FRUIT DIP

1 4-ounce package vanilla instant pudding mix	2 or 3 tablespoons Amaretto or brandy
1 cup milk	Assorted fresh fruit
8 ounces whipped topping	

Combine pudding mix and milk in mixer bowl; beat well. Fold in whipped topping and Amaretto. Chill until serving time. Serve with assorted fruit for dipping. Yield: 8 to 10 servings.

Shelley Jersak, Alpha Delta
Swan River, Manitoba, Canada

ORANGE FRUIT DIP

I served this with 12 different fresh fruits to my chapter sisters at a meeting and they just loved it.

1 cup plain yogurt	1/2 teaspoon grated orange rind
3 tablespoons confectioners' sugar	2 teaspoons orange juice

Combine yogurt and confectioners' sugar in mixer bowl; beat well. Add orange rind and juice; mix well. Pour into serving bowl. Chill until serving time. Yield: 4 to 6 servings.

Marlene J. Weber, Preceptor Eta
Yorkton, Saskatchewan, Canada

SMOOTHIE FRUITEE DIP

1 4-ounce package vanilla instant pudding mix	2 cups sour cream
	Assorted fresh fruit

Combine pudding mix and sour cream in bowl; beat well. Chill until serving time. Serve with assorted fresh fruit to dip. Yield: 8 to 10 servings.

Peggy Brim, Epsilon Epsilon
Brooksville, Florida

CARROT SPREAD

Great to serve at meetings. The girls enjoy it and I always go home with an empty bowl.

8 ounces cream cheese, softened	1 4-ounce can chopped green chilies, drained
1 cup grated carrot	1/4 teaspoon Beau Monde seasoning
2 teaspoons chopped pimento	Party bread or crackers
1/2 cup shredded cheese	

Combine cream cheese, carrot, pimento, cheese, chilies and seasoning in bowl; mix well. Serve on party bread or crackers. Yield: 3 cups.

Tori Baca, Xi Psi Beta
Beeville, Texas

FRUITY CHEESE SPREAD

16 ounces cream cheese, softened	1/4 cup chopped nuts
1 3-ounce package any flavor gelatin	Assorted fresh fruit and crackers

Beat cream cheese in mixer bowl until light. Add gelatin; beat well. Shape into 5-inch ball. Cover with plastic wrap; chill until firm. Press chopped nuts over surface of cheese ball. Serve with fruit and crackers. Yield: 2 cups.

Carole Nevins, Preceptor Beta Kappa
Monrovia, California

JULIE'S CHEESE SPREAD

This may be prepared ahead of time and refrigerated overnight.

8 ounces cream cheese, softened	1 clove of garlic, minced
1/2 cup butter or margarine, softened	1 teaspoon Worcestershire sauce
3 tablespoons chopped fresh parsley	3 tablespoons chopped onion
1 teaspoon garlic powder	1 teaspoon seasoned salt
	1/4 teaspoon pepper
	Crackers

Combine first 9 ingredients in mixer bowl. Beat until light and fluffy. Chill until firm. Let stand at room temperature 30 minutes before serving. Serve with crackers. Yield: 1 1/2 cups.

Bev Wilson, Beta Theta Chi
Mt. Brydges, Ontario, Canada

CHICKEN SALAD SPREAD

2 5-ounce cans breast of chicken, drained	2 tablespoons chopped onion
1/2 cup chopped celery	1/2 cup mayonnaise
1/4 cup chopped green olives	Toasted bread rounds or unsalted crackers
1/4 cup chopped walnuts	

Combine first 6 ingredients in bowl; mix well. Chill in refrigerator. Serve on toasted bread rounds or unsalted crackers. Yield: 10 to 12 servings.

Marlys Montz, Preceptor Alpha Epsilon
Marshalltown, Iowa

❖ LAYERED CURRIED CHICKEN

16 ounces cream cheese, softened	2/3 cup raisins
2 cups cottage cheese	2/3 cup flaked coconut
1/2 cup sour cream	2 cups chopped cooked chicken
4 teaspoons curry powder	1 cup chopped salted peanuts
1 10-ounce jar chutney	1/4 cup chopped green onions
2/3 cup chopped green onions	Crackers

Combine first 4 ingredients in bowl; beat well. Spread in 9-by-13-inch dish. Spoon chutney over top. Sprinkle with mixture of 2/3 cup green onions, raisins and coconut. Top with chicken. Garnish with chopped peanuts and 1/4 cup green onions. Serve with crackers. Yield: 20 to 30 servings.

Donna Fraser, Xi Zeta
Calgary, Alberta, Canada

HAM SPREAD

2 6-ounce cans flaked ham	1 tablespoon minced onion
8 ounces cream cheese, softened	1/4 teaspoon dry mustard
1/4 cup mayonnaise	Crackers
2 tablespoons parsley	

Combine first 6 ingredients in mixer bowl. Beat at medium speed until is smooth. Chill, covered, until firm. Serve with crackers. Yield: 2 1/2 cups.

Trish Caswell, Xi Alpha Epsilon
Whitecourt, Alberta, Canada

HEARTS-OF-PALM SPREAD

1 14-ounce can hearts of palm, drained, chopped	1/2 cup grated Parmesan cheese
1 cup shredded mozzarella cheese	1/4 cup sour cream
3/4 cup mayonnaise	2 tablespoons minced green onions
	Crackers

Preheat oven to 350 degrees. Combine first 6 ingredients in large bowl; mix well. Spoon into 9-inch quiche dish. Bake for 20 minutes or until bubbly. Serve with crackers. May microwave, loosely covered, in glass dish on Medium for 7 to 8 minutes, stirring once. Yield: 2 cups.

Charlotte J. Zeiller, Xi Mu Nu
Dunnellon, Florida

RAISIN-ALMOND DELIGHT

1/2 cup butter or margarine, softened	1/4 cup cold water
12 ounces cream cheese, softened	1/2 cup golden raisins
1/2 cup sour cream	1 cup toasted slivered almonds
1/2 cup sugar	Grated rind of 2 lemons
1 envelope unflavored gelatin	Crackers

Cream butter, cream cheese and sour cream in mixer bowl until light and fluffy. Add sugar; beat well. Soften gelatin in water; add to creamed mixture. Stir in raisins, almonds and lemon rind. Spoon into 1-quart mold; chill. Invert onto serving platter. Serve with crackers. Yield: 35 servings.

Hazel M. Moffett, Preceptor Chi
Chestertown, Maryland

HEARTY-SMARTY CREAM CHEESE

3 tablespoons dry
mustard
1 8-ounce jar
pineapple sundae
topping or pineapple
jam
1 8-ounce jar apple
jelly

2 tablespoons prepared
horseradish
1 tablespoon freshly
ground pepper
Cream cheese
Crackers

Combine first 5 ingredients in large bowl; mix well.
Pour over softened cream cheese on serving plate.
Serve with crackers. May prepare sauce and store in
airtight container for up to 2 months. Yield: 2 1/3 cups.

Arlene Parks
Valentine, Nebraska

MUSHROOM SPREAD

1/2 cup butter or
margarine, softened
8 ounces cream cheese,
softened
1 egg, beaten

1 6-ounce can chopped
mushrooms, drained
Garlic powder to taste
French bread

Preheat oven to 350 degrees. Cream butter and cream
cheese in mixer bowl until light and fluffy. Add egg,
mushrooms and garlic powder; beat well. Spread on
thin slices of French bread; place on baking sheet.
Bake for 15 minutes. Yield: 2 cups.

Brenda Keith, Chi Phi
Vandenberg Air Force Base, California

NACHO SPREAD

1 4-ounce can tiny
shrimp, drained
1/4 cup chopped green
onions
1 to 2 tablespoons
chopped green chilies

1/4 cup mayonnaise
30 to 40 round nacho or
tortilla chips
1 1/2 cups shredded
Cheddar cheese

Combine first 4 ingredients in bowl; mix well.
Spread over chips. Sprinkle with cheese. Arrange in
circle on microwave-safe plate. Microwave on
Medium-High for 1 to 2 minutes or until cheese melts.
Yield: 6 to 8 servings.

Vivian Curle, Preceptor Pi
Kindersley, Saskatchewan, Canada

REUBEN SPREAD

*I made this recipe for the first time for our sorority
Christmas auction.*

1 cup shredded Swiss
cheese
1 cup shredded
American cheese
8 ounces deli corned
beef, chopped

1 cup mayonnaise
1 16-ounce can
sauerkraut, drained,
chopped
Bagel chips and party
rye bread

Preheat oven to 350 degrees. Combine first 5 ingredients in large bowl; mix well. Spoon into
8-by-12-inch baking dish. Bake for 30 minutes. Serve
with bagel chips and party rye bread. Yield: 6 cups.

Pat Case, Epsilon Gamma
Pikeville, Kentucky

SALMON SPREAD

1 15-ounce can
salmon, drained,
flaked
1 tablespoon lemon juice
8 ounces cream cheese,
softened

2 teaspoons grated
onion
1/4 teaspoon salt
1/2 cup chopped pecans
Crackers or toast

Combine salmon, lemon juice, cream cheese, onion
and salt in bowl; mix well. Chill in refrigerator until
firm. Shape mixture into 2 balls. Roll in chopped
pecans. Chill on serving plate until serving time.
Serve with crackers or toast. Yield: 6 servings.

Karen Massingham, Zeta Gamma
Port Hardy, British Columbia, Canada

SEAFOOD SPREAD

2 cups (scant) sour
cream
8 ounces cream cheese,
softened
1 6-ounce can shrimp,
drained, chopped
1 6-ounce can
crab meat, drained,
flaked
1 8-ounce jar seafood
cocktail sauce

1 green bell pepper,
chopped
1 red bell pepper,
chopped
2 tomatoes, chopped
2 cups (scant) shredded
mozzarella cheese
Crackers, nacho chips
or bread

Beat sour cream and cream cheese in mixer bowl
until light and fluffy. Spread in 10-by-15-inch shallow dish. Combine shrimp, crab meat and cocktail
sauce in bowl; mix well. Spoon over creamed mixture. Sprinkle with green and red peppers and
tomatoes; top with mozzarella cheese. Serve with
crackers, nacho chips or bread. Yield: 11 cups.

Lynda Wray, Preceptor Alpha
Whitehorse, Yukon, Canada

SESAME CHEESE SPREAD

This is one of the fastest hors d'oeuvres you can make.

8 ounces cream cheese
1 tablespoon toasted
sesame seed

1 tablespoon soy sauce
Crackers and Melba
toast

Place cream cheese in small shallow serving dish.
Pierce several times with wooden pick. Sprinkle with
sesame seed. Pour soy sauce over top. Serve with
crackers or Melba toast. Yield: 6 servings.

Susan Martin, Xi Theta
Belleville, Ontario, Canada

QUICK BACON-CHEESE ROLLS

1 8-count can crescent
  rolls
3 ounces cream cheese,
  softened
2 tablespoons milk

4 slices crisp-fried
  bacon, crumbled
2 tablespoons chopped
  onion

Preheat oven to 350 degrees. Separate roll dough into 4 rectangles, pressing perforations to seal. Beat cream cheese and milk in small bowl until smooth. Stir in bacon and onion. Spread over rectangle; roll up to enclose filling. Cut each roll into four 1-inch pieces. Arrange on baking sheet. Bake for 12 minutes or until golden brown. Yield: 16 servings.

Janet Gosack, Xi Beta Kappa
Salmon, Idaho

BACON STIXS

5 slices bacon, cut into
  halves lengthwise
10 thin breadsticks

1/2 cup grated Parmesan
  cheese

Wrap bacon slices diagonally around breadsticks. Coat with cheese. Arrange on microwave-safe baking dish lined with paper towels. Microwave on High for 4 1/2 to 6 minutes or until bacon is cooked through. Roll in remaining cheese. Yield: 10 servings.

Lila Couch, Xi Gamma Sigma
Toccoa, Georgia

BLACK SNO-BALLS

8 ounces cream cheese,
  softened
1 6-ounce can pitted
  black olives, drained

2 cups dried minced
  onion, toasted
1/2 grapefruit

Pat out small portion of cream cheese; wrap around olive. Roll in minced onion. Skewer with wooden picks. Cover grapefruit with foil. Arrange olives in grapefruit. Yield: 6 servings.

Marilyn M. Dixon, Xi Alpha Lambda
Warner Robins, Georgia

"BOAT" BREAD

1/2 cup butter or
  margarine, softened
1 cup mayonnaise
1 cup shredded Cheddar,
  Monterey Jack, Swiss
  or mozzarella cheese

Garlic powder, Italian
  seasoning and dried
  minced onion to taste
1 large loaf Italian
  bread, sliced
  lengthwise

Preheat broiler. Mix first 3 ingredients in bowl. Stir in seasonings. Spread over cut sides of bread. Place on baking sheet. Broil 5 inches from heat source for 5 minutes or until bubbly and light brown. Slice to serve. Yield: 24 to 30 servings.

Sue Ellen Bartlett, Gamma Lambda
Annapolis, Maryland

PICKLE BREAD

8 ounces cream cheese,
  softened
1 envelope ranch
  salad dressing
  mix

1 large loaf French
  bread, sliced lengthwise
1 16-ounce jar whole
  dill pickles, sliced
  lengthwise

Beat cream cheese with salad dressing mix in bowl until smooth. Spread over cut sides of bread. Layer sliced pickles on bread. Slice to serve. Yield: 12 servings.

Wendy Wendtland, Epsilon Alpha
Fond du Lac, Wisconsin

PRETZEL-RING BREAD

1 11-ounce can
  breadsticks
1 egg, beaten
Caraway or sesame
  seed or coarse salt

1 cup sour cream
2 tablespoons Dijon
  mustard

Preheat oven to 350 degrees. Separate breadsticks into 8 portions; unroll. Shape each portion into 15-inch rope; arrange into pretzel shape. Place on greased 13-inch baking pan with sides touching. Brush with beaten egg; sprinkle with caraway seed. Bake for 18 minutes; cool for 5 minutes. Combine sour cream and mustard in bowl; mix well. Place dip in center of serving plate surrounded by pretzels. Yield: 8 servings.

Marie Umbriac, Preceptor Alpha Upsilon
Tamaqua, Pennsylvania

❖ REUBEN LOAF

3 1/4 cups all-purpose
  flour
1 tablespoon sugar
1 teaspoon salt
1 envelope yeast
1 cup hot water
1 tablespoon margarine,
  softened

1/4 cup Thousand Island
  salad dressing
4 slices Swiss cheese
1 6-ounce package
  thinly sliced beef
1 8-ounce can
  sauerkraut, drained
1 egg white, beaten

Preheat oven to 400 degrees. Combine 2 1/4 cups flour, sugar, salt and yeast in bowl; mix well. Stir in water, margarine and enough remaining flour to make soft dough. Knead for 4 minutes on lightly floured surface. Roll to 10-by-14-inch rectangle. Place on lightly greased baking sheet. Spread with salad dressing. Layer cheese, beef and sauerkraut on dough. Fold up sides, sealing edge to enclose filling. Brush with egg white. Cut slits in top. Bake for 25 minutes or until golden brown. Cut into slices to serve. Yield: 6 servings.

Suzanne Mansell, Kappa Sigma
Richmond, Missouri

SOOOOO GOOOOOD SWEETIES

2 8-count cans crescent rolls	1 teaspoon vanilla extract
16 ounces cream cheese, softened	1 egg white, beaten
1 cup sugar	Milk
1 egg yolk	Confectioners' sugar

Preheat oven to 350 degrees. Unroll 1 can crescent roll dough; press into ungreased 8-by-12-inch baking dish, sealing perforations. Beat cream cheese, sugar, egg yolk and vanilla in bowl until smooth. Spread over dough. Unroll remaining dough, sealing perforations. Place over filling. Brush with egg white. Bake for 30 minutes; cool slightly. Mix milk and confectioners' sugar in small bowl, stirring until of desired consistency. Spread over top. Cut into squares to serve. Yield: 16 servings.

Leona Kardas, Preceptor Pi
Glendale, Arizona

SWEET CRESCENT SNIPS

1 8-count can crescent rolls	Chopped nuts, flaked coconut or sesame seed
1/3 cup melted margarine	Fruit or honey dip

Preheat oven to 375 degrees. Separate crescent rolls into 8 triangles. Dip in margarine. Coat with chopped nuts, coconut or sesame seed. Arrange on baking sheet. Cut each triangle into 6 smaller triangles; separate. Bake for 12 to 15 minutes or until golden brown. Serve with fruit or honey dip. May use chopped pecans, peanuts, almonds or walnuts. Yield: 32 servings.

Mildred L. Neel, Laureate Gamma Alpha
Venice, Florida

BAKED CREAM CHEESE

I received raves on this at a recent sorority meeting. Everyone thought I'd slaved over it but it's a breeze.

1 8-count can crescent rolls	8 ounces cream cheese
1 1/2 teaspoons fresh minced dillweed	1 egg yolk, beaten
	Fresh whole dill sprigs

Preheat oven to 350 degrees. Roll out crescent roll dough on lightly floured surface to form 4-by-12-inch rectangle, pressing perforations to seal. Press minced dillweed gently onto top of cream cheese. Place coated side down on dough. Fold up sides to enclose cheese. Bake for 20 to 22 minutes or until golden brown. Garnish with fresh dill sprigs. May substitute 1/2 teaspoon dried dillweed for fresh dillweed. Yield: 16 servings.

Patsy Thoss, Zeta Nu
Monroeville, Alabama

GOLDEN BRIE

2 tablespoons butter or margarine	1/4 cup golden raisins
1/4 cup slivered almonds	2 tablespoons dry sherry
2 tablespoons light brown sugar	8 ounces Brie cheese
	French bread or crackers

Microwave butter in 9-inch glass pie plate on High for 30 seconds or until melted. Add almonds, tossing to coat. Microwave for 3 to 4 minutes or until almonds are light brown, stirring once. Stir in brown sugar, raisins and sherry. Microwave for 1 minute; stir. Place cheese in center of microwave-safe serving dish. Spoon sauce over top. Microwave for 45 to 60 seconds or until heated through. Serve with French bread or crackers. May substitute 1 tablespoon water for sherry. Yield: 8 servings.

Eileen B. Brice, Preceptor Chi
Chestertown, Maryland

SAVORY TOASTED CHEESE

*The original recipe for this comes from **The Closet of Sir Kenelme Digby Opened** published in 1669 in London.*

2 tablespoons butter or margarine	2 10-ounce packages frozen chopped broccoli, thawed
3 ounces Brie cheese	4 slices crisp-fried bacon, crumbled
4 ounces cream cheese	

Preheat oven to 350 degrees. Combine butter and cheeses in small saucepan. Cook over low heat until melted, stirring frequently. Place broccoli in greased 2-quart baking dish. Sprinkle with crumbled bacon. Spread evenly with cheese mixture. Bake for 20 to 30 minutes or until golden brown and bubbly. Yield: 8 servings.

Sharyne Graham, Preceptor Alpha Nu
Newport, North Carolina

CHEESE BREAD SQUARES

1 cup margarine	3/4 teaspoon garlic salt
2 5-ounce jars Old English cheese spread	3/4 teaspoon Tabasco sauce
Worcestershire sauce to taste	1 teaspoon dillweed
3/4 teaspoon onion powder	1 loaf French bread, sliced lengthwise

Preheat oven to 350 degrees. Place margarine and cheese in glass bowl. Microwave for 1 minute or until melted; stir. Add Worcestershire sauce, onion powder, garlic salt, Tabasco sauce and dillweed; mix well. Spread mixture evenly over bread. Place on baking sheet. Bake for 10 to 15 minutes or until golden brown. Cut into squares to serve. Yield: 24 servings.

Holly Crowell, Zeta Kappa
Red Oak, Iowa

CHEESE WELLINGTON

1 8-count can crescent rolls	Crackers
1 12-ounce block Monterey Jack cheese	Fruit

Preheat oven to 350 degrees. Press crescent roll dough into large rectangle, sealing perforations. Place cheese in middle of dough. Fold up edges to enclose cheese. Place in nonstick baking dish. Bake for 20 to 30 minutes or until golden brown. Serve with crackers and fruit. Yield: 12 servings.

Catherine McLeod Chitty, Beta Phi
Winston-Salem, North Carolina

FRIED MOZZARELLA

16 ounces mozzarella cheese	Vegetable oil
2 eggs, slightly beaten	1 cup meatless spaghetti sauce
1 to 1½ cups Italian-seasoned bread crumbs	

Cut cheese into ½-by-3-inch sticks. Dip in egg; coat with bread crumbs. Fry one at a time in hot oil in skillet; drain. Serve with spaghetti sauce as dip. Yield: 4 to 6 servings.

Kay Skov, Alpha Phi
The Dalles, Oregon

TOASTED CHEESE MUFFINS

8 ounces Cheddar cheese, shredded	2 eggs, beaten
½ cup butter or margarine, softened	1 teaspoon each garlic salt and onion salt
	8 English muffins, split

Preheat oven to 400 degrees. Combine cheese, butter, eggs, garlic salt and onion salt in bowl; mix well. Spread on muffin halves. Arrange on baking sheet. Bake for 10 minutes or until light brown. Yield: 16 servings.

G. Marion Van Istendal, Epsilon Master
Hollywood, Florida

CURRIED CHICKEN ROUNDS

This is a great finger food for little folks.

1 5-ounce can chunk chicken	1 teaspoon lemon juice
½ cup shredded cheese	¼ teaspoon curry powder
1 8-ounce can water chestnuts, drained, chopped	Pepper to taste
¼ cup mayonnaise	1 8-ounce can flakey rolls
2 tablespoons chopped onion	3 tablespoons chutney

Preheat oven to 350 degrees. Combine chicken, cheese, water chestnuts, mayonnaise, onion, lemon juice, curry powder and pepper in bowl; mix well.

Separate each roll into 3 portions. Arrange on baking sheet. Spread with 2 teaspoons chicken mixture and ¼ teaspoon chutney. Bake for 10 minutes or until golden brown. Yield: 36 servings.

Ruthanne Huber, Xi Beta
Lincoln, Nebraska

PARTY CHICKEN LIVERS

2 pounds chicken livers, cut into halves	¼ cup finely chopped onion
1½ teaspoons salt	¼ cup cooking sherry
¼ cup butter or margarine	½ teaspoon hot pepper sauce

Sprinkle chicken livers with salt. Sauté in butter in skillet until brown. Remove to warm platter. Cook onion in drippings in skillet until tender. Add sherry and pepper sauce, stirring to deglaze skillet. Return chicken livers to skillet. Cook for 10 minutes or until done to taste. Yield: 12 to 16 servings.

Sharon Johns, Preceptor Delta Psi
Queen City, Missouri

RUMAKI

A wonderful appetizer for small dinner parties; serve with wine and cheese.

1 pound chicken livers, cut into halves	8 slices bacon, cut into halves
1 6-ounce can whole or sliced water chestnuts, drained	Vegetable oil

Roll chicken livers and water chestnuts in bacon, securing with wooden picks. Fry in a small amount of oil in skillet until bacon is crisp. May also broil in oven. Yield: 4 servings.

Karla Woodard, Theta
Rozet, Wyoming

CHILI-CHEESE CUBES

8 eggs, beaten	3 cups shredded Monterey Jack cheese
½ cup all-purpose flour	2 4-ounce cans green chilies, drained, seeded, chopped
1 teaspoon baking powder	
¾ teaspoon salt	
1½ cups cottage cheese	

Preheat oven to 350 degrees. Beat eggs with flour, baking powder and salt in bowl. Add cottage cheese, Monterey Jack cheese and chilies; mix well. Spoon into greased 9-by-13-inch baking pan. Bake for 40 minutes. Let stand for 10 minutes. Cut into small squares to serve. Yield: 3 to 4 dozen.

Marcia Kirby, Preceptor Epsilon Omega
East Alton, Illinois

CHILI FUDGE

16 ounces Cheddar
cheese, shredded
16 ounces mozzarella
cheese, shredded

4 eggs, beaten
1 8-ounce jar picante
sauce
Crackers

Preheat oven to 350 degrees. Sprinkle cheeses into 9-by-12-inch nonstick baking pan. Beat eggs and picante sauce in bowl. Pour over cheeses. Bake for 30 to 40 minutes. Cut into bite-sized portions. Serve with crackers. Yield: 10 servings.

Georgie Sinner
Aurora, Nebraska

CRAB MEAT PUFFS

1 5-ounce jar Old
English cheese spread
1/2 cup margarine,
softened
1 6-ounce can crab
meat, drained, flaked

1/2 teaspoon seasoned
salt
1 1/2 tablespoons
mayonnaise
Garlic salt to taste
6 English muffins, split

Preheat oven to 350 degrees. Combine cheese, margarine, crab meat, seasoned salt, mayonnaise and garlic salt in bowl; mix well. Spread on muffins; arrange on baking sheet. Bake for 15 minutes. Cut into quarters to serve. Yield: 48 servings.

Sue Wisler, Zeta Phi
Bryan, Ohio

CRABBY TOMATO BAGELS

4 ounces light cream
cheese, softened
2 tablespoons grated
Parmesan cheese
3 tablespoons light
mayonnaise

1 teaspoon lemon juice
1/2 cup crab meat
2 large tomatoes,
peeled, sliced
4 bagels, split

Preheat broiler. Beat cream cheese with Parmesan cheese, mayonnaise and lemon juice in bowl until smooth. Mix in crab meat. Place 1 slice tomato on each bagel half. Spread with crab mixture. Arrange in broiler pan. Broil 6 inches from heat source until golden brown. May cut into halves or quarters to serve. Yield: 16 to 32 servings.

Jo B. Teel, Xi Beta Epsilon
Clanton, Alabama

CRAB-SHRIMP NACHOS

1 6-ounce can crab
meat, drained, flaked
1 6-ounce can small
shrimp, drained
2 to 3 tablespoons
mayonnaise
Cayenne pepper to taste

2 cups shredded mixed
Cheddar and Colby
cheeses
1 12-ounce package
tortilla chips
Sliced black olives

Preheat oven to 350 degrees. Combine crab meat and shrimp with enough mayonnaise to hold mixture together. Stir in cayenne pepper and cheeses. Spread on tortilla chips. Place on baking sheet. Bake for 10 minutes or until cheese is melted. Top with sliced olives. Yield: 15 servings.

Karen Fleming, Preceptor Alpha Beta
Montgomery, Alabama

CUCUMBER ROUNDS

1 envelope Italian salad
dressing mix
8 ounces cream cheese,
softened

1 loaf sliced cocktail
bread
Cucumber slices
Dillweed to taste

Combine salad dressing mix and cream cheese in bowl; mix well. Spread mixture on bread slices. Top with cucumber slices; sprinkle with dill. Yield: 40 servings.

Johanne Kingston, Xi
Lebanon, New Hampshire

TUNA IN-A-CUCUMBER

1 7-ounce can tuna,
drained
3 ounces cream cheese,
softened
1 tablespoon
mayonnaise
1 tablespoon lemon juice

1/2 teaspoon salt
(optional)
1/4 teaspoon pepper
1 tablespoon pickle
relish
3 medium cucumbers
Crackers

Combine tuna, cream cheese, mayonnaise, lemon juice, salt, pepper and relish in bowl; mix well. Chill in refrigerator. Core cucumbers to remove seed, leaving 1/4-inch shell. Stuff tuna mixture into cucumbers; chill. Slice cucumbers; place on serving plate. Serve with crackers. Yield: 20 servings.

Paulette Klaja, Preceptor Alpha Chi
Pittsburgh, Pennsylvania

FRESH FRUIT COCKTAIL SAUCE

8 ounces cream cheese,
softened
1/4 cup sugar, syrup or
honey

Orange juice
Fresh fruit

Beat cream cheese and sugar in bowl until light and fluffy. Stir in enough orange juice to make of desired consistency. Serve over mixed fresh fruit, such as grapes, orange sections, pineapple chunks, sliced bananas, sliced strawberries, sliced pears, raspberries or blueberries. Yield: 2 cups sauce.

Norma W. Conner, Laureate Gamma
Fayetteville, Arkansas

HAM ROLLS

3/4 cup melted butter or margarine
3 tablespoons poppy seed
3 tablespoons prepared mustard
1 medium onion, grated

3 24-count packages party rolls, cut into halves
1 pound baked Virginia ham, chopped
16 ounces Swiss cheese, shredded

Preheat oven to 350 degrees. Combine melted butter, poppy seed, mustard and onion in small bowl; mix well. Brush both halves of rolls with mixture. Combine ham and cheese in bowl. Spoon onto bottom halves of rolls; replace tops. Arrange on baking sheet. Bake for 15 minutes or until cheese is melted. May reheat in microwave. Yield: 36 (2-roll) servings.

Delores Gayle Duff, Preceptor Alpha Upsilon
Lenoir City, Tennessee

SPELDONNAS

12 prepared dinner rolls, cut into halves
Thinly sliced ham
Thinly sliced Swiss cheese

1/2 cup butter or margarine, softened
1/4 cup minced onion
1/4 cup prepared mustard
1 tablespoon poppy seed

Preheat oven to 350 degrees. Place generous amount of ham and cheese on bottom half of each roll. Combine butter, onion, mustard and poppy seed in small bowl; mix well. Spread on top half of each roll. Place on bottoms. Wrap each roll in foil; place on baking sheet. Bake for 20 minutes. Yield: 12 servings.

Sharon Carlile, Xi Delta Epsilon
Zillah, Washington

HOLIDAY CORNUCOPIAS

I prepare these each year at Thanksgiving. The kids really love them!

20 slices white bread
2 tablespoons melted butter or margarine
3 ounces cream cheese, softened
3 tablespoons minced onion

1 1/2 teaspoons prepared horseradish, drained
1 4-ounce can deviled ham
1/8 teaspoon celery seed
Salt and pepper to taste
Fresh parsley

Preheat oven to 350 degrees. Cut 20 circles from bread slices with 3-inch round cookie cutter. Flatten with rolling pin. Brush both sides with melted butter. Roll up to form cornucopias; secure with wooden picks. Arrange on baking sheet. Bake for 12 minutes. Combine cream cheese, onion, horseradish, deviled ham, celery seed, salt and pepper in bowl; mix well. Place 1 teaspoon mixture in each cornucopia. Garnish with fresh parsley. Yield: 20 servings.

Julie Jones, Mu Omicron
Broken Arrow, Oklahoma

HOT PUFFS

1/2 cup mayonnaise
1/4 cup chopped onion
2 tablespoons chopped parsley

24 butter crackers
6 slices cheese, cut into quarters

Preheat broiler. Combine mayonnaise, onion and parsley in bowl; mix well. Spread over crackers. Top with cheese. Arrange on baking sheet. Broil 5 inches from heat source for 3 minutes or until cheese melts. Yield: 24 servings.

Barbara Whelan, Xi Alpha
Beaconsfield, Quebec, Canada

BARBECUE MEATBALLS

1 1/2 cups fine bread crumbs
2 onions, finely minced
1 clove of garlic, minced
1 teaspoon paprika
1/2 teaspoon each salt and pepper
3 tablespoons canola oil

2 pounds very lean ground beef
1 15-ounce bottle of catsup
1 7-ounce bottle of chili sauce
1/2 cup packed dark brown sugar

Preheat oven to 350 degrees. Combine bread crumbs, onions, garlic, paprika, salt and pepper in bowl; mix well. Add oil and ground beef; mix well. Shape into bite-sized meatballs. Arrange on baking sheet. Bake for 30 to 45 minutes or until browned, turning once. Place in chafing dish. Combine catsup, chili sauce and sugar in saucepan; mix well. Bring to a boil, stirring frequently. Pour over meatballs. Serve with wooden picks. Yield: 20 to 40 servings.

Carol Frances Astop, Xi Alpha Iota
Calgary, Alberta, Canada

SNACK MEATBALLS

1 6-ounce can evaporated milk
2 teaspoons Worcestershire sauce
1 envelope onion soup mix

1 pound ground beef
1 tablespoon Worcestershire sauce
2 cups catsup
3/4 cup packed dark brown sugar

Preheat broiler. Mix evaporated milk, 2 teaspoons Worcestershire sauce and soup mix in bowl; let stand for 5 minutes. Add ground beef; mix well. Shape by tablespoonfuls into balls. Place on rack in broiler pan. Broil 5 inches from heat source for 10 to 12 minutes or until brown. Do not turn. Combine remaining 1 tablespoon Worcestershire sauce, catsup and brown sugar in saucepan; mix well. Cook until heated through, stirring frequently. Add meatballs. Cook until heated through. May be frozen and reheated. Yield: 8 servings.

Wilma Romero, Xi Gamma Omicron
Colorado Springs, Colorado

SWEET AND SOUR MEATBALLS

2 pounds sausage
1/4 cup Italian-seasoned
  bread crumbs
1 cup grape jelly
2/3 cup prepared mustard

Mix sausage and bread crumbs in bowl. Shape mixture into bite-sized balls. Place in microwave-safe baking dish. Microwave a few at a time on High for 5 minutes; drain. Combine grape jelly and mustard in saucepan. Cook over low heat until smooth, stirring constantly. Add meatballs to sauce. Simmer for 30 minutes longer. Serve in chafing dish.
Yield: 20 servings.

Joan Maddock, Xi Lambda Iota
Lompoc, California

THE BEST STUFFED MUSHROOMS

Only minutes to prepare and cook!

3/4 cup bread crumbs
1/2 cup melted butter or
  margarine
1 clove of garlic, pressed
1/4 cup sweet vermouth
1 tablespoon chopped
  parsley
Salt and pepper to
  taste
10 to 12 large fresh
  mushroom caps
2 tablespoons butter or
  margarine

Toss bread crumbs with melted butter in bowl. Add garlic, vermouth, parsley, salt and pepper; mix well. Spoon mixture into mushroom caps. Sauté in 2 tablespoons butter in skillet for 5 to 7 minutes or until tender. Serve hot or cold. Yield: 4 servings.

Linda Gizienski, Xi Alpha
Coventry, Rhode Island

BEEF-STUFFED MUSHROOM CAPS

Our teen-aged son makes these and serves them to us before a special dinner at home. They can be made hours ahead and popped in the oven before guests arrive.

4 ounces ground beef
1/4 teaspoon garlic salt
Salt and pepper to taste
24 large fresh
  mushroom caps
1/4 green bell pepper,
  finely chopped
4 ounces mozzarella
  cheese, shredded

Preheat oven to 400 degrees. Brown ground beef with garlic salt, salt and pepper in skillet, stirring until ground beef is crumbly; drain. Spoon mixture into mushroom caps. Top with mixture of green pepper and cheese. Sprinkle with additional garlic salt. Place on baking sheet. Bake for 7 to 10 minutes or until cheese is bubbly and light brown. Serve hot.
Yield: 6 servings.

Dorothy V. Connolly, Preceptor Gamma Kappa
Merritt, British Columbia, Canada

STUFFED MUSHROOM CAPS

1 pound fresh
  mushrooms
1/4 cup finely chopped
  onion
1/4 cup finely chopped
  ham
8 butter crackers,
  crushed
1/4 cup melted butter or
  margarine
1/4 cup grated Parmesan
  cheese
Salt amd pepper to taste
Minced garlic and
  parsley to taste
2 tablespoons olive oil

Preheat oven to 350 degrees. Remove stems from mushrooms; set aside caps. Mince stems. Add to onion, ham and crushed crackers in bowl; mix well. Stir in 2 tablespoons butter and 2 tablespoons Parmesan cheese. Add seasonings to taste. Spoon mixture into mushroom caps. Sprinkle with remaining Parmesan cheese. Place in 8-by-10-inch baking dish coated with olive oil. Bake for 10 minutes. Drizzle with remaining butter. Bake for 10 to 15 minutes longer or until brown. Yield: 6 servings.

Connie Hester, Alpha Rho Iota
Burnet, Texas

OLIVE-CHEESE PUFFS

1/2 cup butter or
  margarine
1 cup water
1 cup all-purpose flour
4 eggs
2/3 cup chopped black
  olives
1/2 cup shredded
  American cheese

Preheat oven to 375 degrees. Bring butter and water to a boil in saucepan over low heat. Add flour, beating until mixture forms ball and leaves side of pan; remove from heat. Beat in eggs 1 at a time. Stir in olives and cheese. Drop by teaspoonfuls 2 inches apart onto greased baking sheet. Bake for 15 to 20 minutes or until golden brown. Yield: 6 dozen.

Donnis Helbourg, Alpha Lambda
Atlantic, Iowa

OLIVE NIPS

1/2 cup all-purpose flour
1/8 teaspoon dry
  mustard
1/4 teaspoon salt
1 cup shredded sharp
  Cheddar cheese
1 teaspoon milk
2 to 3 tablespoons
  minced onion
3 tablespoons melted
  butter or margarine
1 or 2 drops of Tabasco
  sauce
25 olives

Preheat oven to 400 degrees. Mix flour, dry mustard, salt and cheese in bowl. Add milk, onion, butter and Tabasco sauce; mix well. Shape into balls around olives, covering completely. Place on baking sheet. Bake for 10 to 12 minutes or until golden brown. Yield: 25 servings.

Betty J. Buckles, Laureate Phi
Phoenix, Arizona

YUMMY ONION PUFFS

The onion and butter mixture used in the recipe is also good on vegetables or baked potatoes.

1 envelope onion soup
   mix
1 cup butter or
   margarine, softened

1 8-ounce can biscuits

Preheat oven to 400 degrees. Mix soup mix and butter in medium bowl. Cut each biscuit into quarters; arrange on ungreased baking sheet. Top with butter mixture. Bake for 8 minutes or until golden brown. Yield: 40 servings.

Jody Prokupek, Xi Epsilon Rho
Sturgis, Michigan

PEPPERONI PINWHEELS

1 8-ounce can crescent
   rolls
1 3½-ounce package
   sliced pepperoni

2 ounces mozzarella
   cheese, shredded
1 cup pizza sauce

Preheat oven to 350 degrees. Separate roll dough into 4 rectangles; press perforations to seal. Place 8 slices pepperoni on each rectangle; sprinkle with cheese. Roll up each rectangle from narrow side to enclose filling; seal edges. Cut each roll into 4 slices; pinch dough together on 1 side of each slice to seal. Place sealed side down on ungreased baking sheet. Bake for 18 to 20 minutes or until golden brown. Heat pizza sauce in saucepan or microwave. Serve with pinwheels. Yield: 16 servings.

Carol Duncan, Kappa Xi
Platte City, Missouri

ITALIAN PINWHEELS

1 3½-ounce package
   pepperoni, chopped
1 cup shredded
   mozzarella cheese
1 teaspoon oregano

1 egg, beaten
½ 6-ounce can tomato
   paste
2 8-ounce cans crescent
   rolls

Preheat oven to 375 degrees. Mix first 5 ingredients in bowl. Separate roll dough into 8 rectangles; press perforations to seal. Spread with pepperoni mixture. Roll up rectangles from narrow side to enclose filling. Cut each roll into 6 slices. Place cut side down on ungreased baking sheet. Bake for 12 minutes. Yield: 48 servings.

Connie George, Laureate Gamma Sigma
Bellflower, California

Delores Liptak, Preceptor Kappa, Syracuse, New York, makes Cocktail Franks by heating 10 ounces elderberry jam, 4 ounces mustard and 2 pounds franks cut into 1-inch pieces in slow cooker on High for 10 minutes and Low for 45 minutes.

FRIED PITA BREAD

You can make your own Cajun seasoning with a mixture of 3 tablespoons salt, 2 teaspoons red pepper and 1 teaspoon garlic powder.

1 or 2 packages pita
   bread rounds

Oil for frying
Cajun seasoning to taste

Cut pita bread into bite-sized pieces. Fry in hot oil in skillet until crisp; drain on paper towel. Shake with seasoning in bag to coat well. Yield: 6 to 12 servings.

Pat Huval, Zeta Kappa
Breaux Bridge, Louisiana

PITA BREAD CRISPS

10 pita bread rounds
1¼ cups mayonnaise
½ cup grated Parmesan
   cheese

⅓ cup onion flakes
Garlic salt and parsley
   flakes to taste

Preheat oven to 350 degrees. Split pita bread rounds into halves. Combine mayonnaise, cheese and onion flakes in bowl; mix well. Spread onto pita rounds; cut into serving pieces. Place on baking sheet. Sprinkle with garlic salt and parsley flakes. Bake for 10 to 12 minutes or until golden brown. Yield: 10 servings.

Helen L. Smith, Preceptor Beta Eta
Troy, Michigan

PITA APPETIZERS

1 10-ounce package
   frozen chopped
   spinach, cooked,
   well drained
1 cup sour cream
1 cup mayonnaise
3 green onions, finely
   chopped

1 envelope vegetable
   soup mix
1 7-ounce can water
   chestnuts, drained,
   chopped
1 package small pita
   bread rounds

Combine spinach and next 5 ingredients in bowl; mix well. Spread on pita rounds just before serving. Yield: 20 servings.

Heather Bellamy, Xi Alpha Theta
Medicine Hat, Alberta, Canada

ARTICHOKE PIZZA

2 8-ounce cans crescent
   rolls
1 14-ounce can
   artichoke hearts,
   drained, chopped

½ cup mayonnaise
¾ cup shredded
   mozzarella cheese
¾ cup grated Parmesan
   cheese

Preheat oven to 375 degrees. Place roll dough in 9-by-13-inch baking pan; press perforations to seal. Bake using package directions. Combine artichokes with remaining ingredients in bowl; mix well. Spread over baked layer. Bake for 15 minutes longer.

Let stand for 5 minutes; cut into squares.
Yield: 4 to 6 servings.

Lyn Patterson, Beta Omega
La Cygne, Kansas

CONFETTI BITES

2 8-ounce cans crescent
rolls
16 ounces cream cheese,
softened
3 tablespoons
mayonnaise-type
salad dressing
1/2 teaspoon basil
1/4 teaspoon garlic
powder
Chopped fresh
vegetables
Salad seasoning to taste

Preheat oven to 350 degrees. Press roll dough into 10-by-15-inch baking pan, sealing perforations. Bake for 12 to 15 minutes or until golden brown. Cool to room temperature. Combine cream cheese with salad dressing, basil and garlic powder in bowl; mix well. Spread over baked layer. Top with vegetables; sprinkle with salad seasoning. Cut into squares. Yield: 36 servings.

Elnora Marie Teed, Iota Kappa
Livonia, New York

MINIATURE CURRIED PIZZAS

2 cups shredded
Cheddar cheese
1 cup chopped green
onions
3/4 cup mayonnaise
1 cup chopped black
olives
1 teaspoon curry powder
8 English muffins, split

Preheat oven to 350 degrees. Mix first 5 ingredients in bowl. Spread on muffins. Place on foil-lined baking sheet. Bake for 10 to 15 minutes or until cheese melts. Cut into quarters. Yield: 8 servings.

Bernice James, Preceptor Beta Phi
White Rock, British Columbia, Canada

GREEK-STYLE PIZZA

2 medium onions, sliced
2 medium green bell
peppers, cut into strips
1 cup Italian salad
dressing
1 12-ounce can
crescent rolls
2 medium tomatoes,
thinly sliced
1 cup sliced black olives
12 to 16 ounces feta
cheese

Preheat oven to 375 degrees. Mix onions and green pepper with salad dressing in bowl. Marinate in refrigerator for 2 hours to overnight; drain. Press roll dough onto baking pan or pizza pan, sealing perforations and turning up edge. Bake for 11 to 13 minutes or until golden brown. Cool to room temperature. Layer tomatoes, onion, green peppers and olives in order listed over baked layer. Crumble cheese over layers. Bake for 5 to 8 minutes or broil for 2 to 3

minutes or until light brown. Cut into serving pieces. Yield: 20 servings.

Debi Perry, Alpha Tau
Clarksville, Tennessee

MINIATURE PIZZAS

1 pound mild Cheddar
cheese, shredded
1 pound bacon, crisp-
fried, crumbled
1 10-ounce bottle of
chili sauce
1 tablespoon honey
12 English muffins, split

Preheat broiler. Combine cheese, bacon, chili sauce and honey in bowl; mix well. Spread on muffins; place on baking sheet. Broil for 5 minutes or until cheese is bubbly. Yield: 24 servings.

Patsy A. Weatherdon, Xi Nu
Salisbury, New Brunswick, Canada

PIZZA CUPS

12 ounces ground beef
1 16-ounce can tomato
paste
1 tablespoon minced
onion
1/2 teaspoon salt
1 teaspoon Italian
seasoning
1 10-ounce can biscuits
1/2 to 3/4 cup shredded
mozzarella cheese

Preheat oven to 400 degrees. Brown ground beef in skillet, stirring until crumbly; drain. Stir in tomato paste, onion and seasonings. Cook over low heat for 5 minutes, stirring frequently. Press 1 biscuit over bottom and side of each muffin cup. Spoon ground beef mixture into prepared muffin cups. Sprinkle with cheese. Bake for 12 minutes or until golden brown. Yield: 12 servings.

Stella Zawko, Theta Master
Belton, Missouri

VEGETABLE PIZZA

2 cans crescent rolls
1 envelope ranch or
bacon salad dressing
mix
8 ounces cream cheese,
softened
1 cup mayonnaise
1 teaspoon dillweed
Chopped vegetables
such as cauliflower,
broccoli, carrots, celery,
green onions, cucumber,
tomatoes, mushrooms,
green pepper or olives
Shredded Cheddar
cheese

Preheat oven using roll can directions. Press roll dough into 11-by-15-inch baking pan or large pizza pan, sealing perforations. Bake using package directions. Cool to room temperature. Combine salad dressing mix, cream cheese, mayonnaise and dillweed in bowl; mix well. Spread over baked layer. Top with vegetables of choice; sprinkle with cheese. Cut into serving pieces. Yield: 24 servings.

Brenda Clarke, Xi Eta
Newcastle, Wyoming

FAST QUICHE PLEASERS

Cut these quiches into larger pieces for a quick and easy lunch dish.

1 can crescent rolls	3/4 cup milk
4 long slices Swiss cheese	4 slices bacon, crisp-fried, crumbled
3 eggs, slightly beaten	1 tablespoon parsley flakes
1 tablespoon onion flakes	

Preheat oven to 425 degrees. Separate roll dough into 4 rectangles. Press 2 rectangles over bottom and 1 inch up sides of each of 2 oiled and floured 8-by-8-inch baking pans; seal edges and perforations. Layer cheese slices over dough. Combine eggs, onion and milk in bowl; whisk until smooth. Pour into prepared pans. Sprinkle with bacon and parsley. Bake for 15 to 18 minutes or until set. Cool for 5 minutes. Cut into 2-inch squares. Yield: 32 servings.

Dorothy Holbrook, Preceptor Epsilon Kappa
Winter Park, Florida

TERIYAKI SALMON STRIPS

3 pounds salmon filets, skin removed	1 teaspoon crushed chili pepper
1 cup soy sauce	1 teaspoon lemon pepper
1/2 cup white wine	1 teaspoon parsley flakes or Italian seasoning
1/2 cup packed light brown sugar	
Juice of 1 lemon	1 tablespoon finely chopped ginger
1 small onion, chopped	
1 tablespoon crushed garlic	1 teaspoon coarsely ground black pepper
1 tablespoon chopped seeded jalapeño pepper	Oil for frying
	Dill dip

Cut salmon into 1/2-inch strips. Combine next 12 ingredients in shallow dish; mix well. Add salmon; coat well. Marinate for 15 minutes; drain. Fry salmon strips in oil in skillet until brown; drain. Serve with dill dip. Yield: 12 servings.

Gayle Rhodes, Xi Chi
Port Alberni, British Columbia, Canada

CREAM CHEESE-BACON BARS

12 slices white bread	1 tablespoon milk
3 ounces cream cheese, softened	1 teaspoon horseradish
4 slices bacon, crisp-fried, crumbled	1/2 teaspoon Worcestershire sauce

Trim crusts from bread. Combine remaining ingredients in bowl; mix well. Spread on half the bread slices; top with remaining bread. Cut each sandwich into thirds. Yield: 18 servings.

Linda Suber, Xi Alpha Mu
Rocky Mount, North Carolina

PECAN-CREAM CHEESE SANDWICHES

16 slices white, whole wheat or rye bread	3 tablespoons finely chopped onion
1/4 cup butter or margarine, softened	3 hard-cooked eggs, finely chopped
8 ounces cream cheese, softened	3 tablespoons chili sauce
2/3 cup finely chopped pecans	3 tablespoons chopped green bell pepper

Spread 1 side of bread slices lightly with butter. Combine remaining ingredients in bowl; mix well. Spread on half the bread slices; top with remaining bread. Yield: 8 servings.

Virginia Caywood, Preceptor Beta Omega
Ft. Worth, Texas

HOT HERO SANDWICHES

1 loaf French bread	1 4-ounce jar chopped mushrooms, drained
16 ounces Cheddar cheese, shredded	1/2 cup vegetable oil
1 4-ounce can chopped black olives	2 8-ounce cans tomato sauce
1 onion, chopped	Oregano to taste

Preheat broiler to 350 to 400 degrees. Slice French bread. Combine remaining ingredients in bowl; mix well. Spread on French bread; place on baking sheet. Broil just until bubbly. Yield: 12 servings.

Margery A. Marsh, Laureate Nu
Englewood, Colorado

DEEP-FRIED MOZZARELLA SANDWICHES

8 slices bread	All-purpose flour
4 slices mozzarella cheese	1 egg
	Oil for deep frying

Trim crusts from bread. Place 1 slice of cheese between 2 pieces of bread to make 4 sandwiches. Coat with flour. Beat egg in shallow dish. Dip sandwiches in egg, coating completely. Deep-fry in hot oil until golden brown. Serve hot. Yield: 4 servings.

Sherrill Lloyd, Nu Chi
Napa, California

SOUR CREAM-HAM SANDWICH SPREAD

2 5-ounce cans chunk ham	1 cup sour cream
1 tablespoon (heaping) mayonnaise	1 teaspoon onion juice
	36 to 48 slices bread

Flake ham into bowl. Stir in mayonnaise, sour cream and onion juice in bowl. Trim crusts from bread. Spread half the bread slices lightly with ham mixture; top with remaining bread. Cut each sandwich into quarters. Yield: 72 to 96 small sandwiches.

Virginia Ainsworth, Xi Alpha Omega
Bogalusa, Louisiana

FILLED HARD ROLLS

12 hard rolls	6 green onions, chopped
1 pound cheese, shredded	1 cup chopped cooked
1 4-ounce can chopped	ham
black olives	Tabasco sauce, garlic
1 8-ounce can tomato	powder and pepper to
sauce	taste

Preheat oven to 300 degrees. Cut rolls into halves horizontally. Remove part of centers. Combine remaining ingredients in bowl; mix well. Spoon onto roll bottoms; replace tops. Wrap in foil; place on baking sheet. Bake for 30 minutes or until cheese melts. Yield: 12 servings.

Charlotte Green, Laureate Gamma
Pocatello, Idaho

SPANISH ROLLS

1 pound ground beef	1 4-ounce can chopped
1 pound Cheddar	black olives
cheese, shredded	1 8-ounce can tomato
2 small onions, chopped	sauce
1 clove of garlic, finely	2 packages small French
chopped	rolls or 1 package
2 4-ounce cans	large French rolls
chopped green chilies	

Preheat oven to 325 degrees. Brown ground beef in skillet, stirring until crumbly; drain. Combine with next 6 ingredients in bowl; mix well. Cut ends from rolls; scoop out centers. Fill with ground beef mixture; wrap in foil. Let stand for 30 minutes or longer. Place rolls on baking sheet. Bake for 1 hour. Yield: 24 servings.

Dawn Roney, Xi Alpha Theta
West Jordan, Utah

APPETIZER WIENERS

1 10-ounce jar	3 1-pound packages
blackberry preserves	wieners
1 6-ounce jar prepared	
mustard	

Heat preserves and mustard in saucepan, stirring to mix well. Cut wieners into bite-sizes pieces. Add to sauce. Cook until heated through. Serve from chafing dish. May serve cooked wieners on wooden picks with sauce for dipping. Yield: 30 servings.

Ruth Pullen, Laureate Alpha Omicron
Eastlake, Colorado

GLAZED LITTLE SAUSAGE SMOKIES

1 pound bacon	1½ cups packed light
1 package little smokies	brown sugar
sausages	

Preheat oven to 350 degrees. Cut each bacon slice into thirds. Wrap 1 piece around each sausage; secure with wooden pick. Place in 9-by-13-inch baking dish; sprinkle with brown sugar. Bake for 45 minutes. Yield: 12 servings.

Martha Kirby, Preceptor Gamma Iota
Little York, Illinois

HOT DOG APPETIZERS

1 envelope brown gravy	1 package hot dogs
mix	½ cup apple jelly
½ cup cold water	2 tablespoons catsup

Blend gravy mix and water in skillet. Cut hot dogs into bite-sized pieces. Add to skillet with jelly and catsup. Simmer until jelly is melted and hot dogs are heated through. Yield: 8 to 10 servings.

Judy Edwards, Alpha Zeta
Lebanon, Oregon

SAUSAGE-APPLE BALLS

1 pound sausage	½ cup chopped walnuts
2 cups baking mix	½ teaspoon apple pie
1 cup raisins, chopped	spice
1 cup grated apple	

Preheat oven to 350 degrees. Combine sausage, baking mix, raisins, apple, walnuts and apple pie spice in bowl; mix well. Shape into 1-inch balls; place on baking sheet. Bake for 20 minutes or until light brown. Yield: 12 servings.

Julie Rothe, Alpha Tau
Lafayette, Indiana

SAUSAGE BALLS

1 pound sausage	2½ cup baking mix
8 ounces sharp Cheddar	Worcestershire sauce
cheese, shredded	and hot sauce to taste

Preheat oven to 375 degrees. Combine sausage, cheese, baking mix, Worcestershire sauce and hot sauce in bowl; mix well. Shape into 1 to 2-inch balls; place on baking sheet. Bake for 20 minutes or until golden brown. Yield: 36 servings.

Michelle Kiser, Theta Theta
Coffeyville, Kansas

SAUSAGE AND CHEESE BALLS

These are easy to make in advance and store in the freezer. Thaw for 30 minutes and bake as directed.

3 cups baking mix	12 ounces Cheddar
1 pound hot sausage	cheese, shredded

Preheat oven to 400 to 425 degrees. Combine all ingredients in bowl; mix well. Shape into small balls; place on baking sheet. Bake for 15 to 18 minutes or until golden brown. Yield: 10 to 15 servings.

Darlene D. Dorsch, Preceptor Theta
Virginia Beach, Virginia

SAUSAGE-CHEESE ROLLS

2 pounds pork sausage
2 pounds Velveeta
  cheese, chopped
1 pound mild Cheddar
  cheese, chopped
1 pound sharp Cheddar
  cheese, chopped
1 10-ounce can Ro-Tel
  tomatoes
1 4-ounce can chopped
  green chilies

Brown sausage in skillet, stirring until crumbly; drain. Melt cheeses in double boiler, stirring to mix well. Combine sausage, cheeses, tomatoes and chilies in bowl; mix well. Spread in lightly buttered 9-by-13-inch dish. Chill for 1 hour. Slice lengthwise into 4 to 6 strips. Shape into rolls. Wrap in foil. Chill until serving time or freeze until needed. Yield: 4 to 6 rolls.

Ingrid Lea, Xi Omicron Eta
Deer Park, Texas

BAYOU SHRIMP

5 pounds medium shrimp,
  peeled, deveined
1 bag shrimp and crab
  boil seasoning
2 12-ounce cans beer or
  3 cups water
1 teaspoon salt
1 tablespoon Tabasco
  sauce
1 tablespoon
  Worcestershire sauce
1/2 teaspoon garlic
  powder
3 tablespoons fresh
  lemon or lime juice
Pepper to taste
1 cup melted unsalted
  butter or margarine

Preheat oven to 350 degrees. Place shrimp in baking dish. Bring seasoning bag to a boil in beer in large saucepan. Add salt, Tabasco sauce, Worcestershire sauce, garlic powder, lemon juice and pepper. Simmer for 10 minutes. Pour over shrimp. Drizzle with butter. Bake for 15 minutes. Yield: 20 servings.

Mary Ann Kientz, Alpha Lambda
Aurora, Colorado

HOT SPINACH BALLS

These appetizers may be frozen and placed directly in the oven to bake.

2 10-ounce packages
  frozen chopped
  spinach, cooked,
  well drained
2 cups stove-top stuffing
  mix
1 cup grated Parmesan
  cheese
6 eggs, beaten
3/4 cup (or less) butter
  or margarine, softened
1 tablespoon garlic salt
1/2 teaspoon each MSG,
  thyme and pepper

Preheat oven to 350 degrees. Combine all ingredients in bowl; mix well. Shape by tablespoonfuls into balls; place on baking sheet. Bake for 10 to 15 minutes or until golden brown. Yield: 20 servings.

Sonia L. Sholter, Alpha Pi
Lloydminster, Alberta, Canada

SPINACH BROWNIES

1 cup all-purpose flour
1 teaspoon baking
  powder
1 teaspoon salt
2 eggs, beaten
1 cup milk
1/4 cup melted margarine
1/2 cup chopped onion
1 pound Cheddar
  cheese, shredded
1 10-ounce package
  frozen chopped
  spinach, drained

Preheat oven to 350 degrees. Sift flour, baking powder and salt into bowl. Beat eggs with milk and margarine in small bowl. Add to dry ingredients; mix well. Stir in onion, cheese and spinach. Spoon into greased 9-by-13-inch baking dish. Bake for 40 minutes. Cut into squares. Serve warm. Yield: 15 servings.

Marie Stephenson, Preceptor Alpha Eta
Chattanooga, Tennessee

TACO TARTLETS

1 pound lean ground beef
2 tablespoons taco
  seasoning mix
2 tablespoons ice water
1 cup sour cream
2 tablespoons taco sauce
1 2-ounce can chopped
  black olives, drained
1 cup shredded Cheddar
  cheese
3/4 cup crushed tortilla
  chips (optional)

Preheat oven to 425 degrees. Combine ground beef, taco seasoning mix and water in bowl; mix well with hands. Press over bottoms and sides of 30 miniature muffin cups. Mix sour cream, taco sauce and olives in bowl. Spoon into prepared muffin cups; sprinkle with cheese and chips. Bake for 12 minutes or until tests done. Loosen from muffin cups with fork or knife. Serve immediately. Yield: 30 servings.

Cindi Sweedler, Xi Theta Lambda
Williams, Iowa

TOMATO BITES

1 3-ounce can smoked
  oysters
1 pint cherry tomatoes

Drain oysters and pat dry. Slice tomatoes almost into halves. Place 1 oyster in center of each tomato; secure with wooden picks. Yield: 20 servings.

Jody Gallup, Beta Xi
Burlington, Ontario, Canada

POMIDORO ECELLENTE

This is better if the spread marinates in the refrigerator overnight. We serve it at a special meal after our "Ladies Pasta" 5-pin bowling tournament.

2 large firm tomatoes,
  chopped, drained
1 medium onion, finely
  chopped
1 clove of garlic, crushed
1/4 teaspoon sweet basil
Salt and pepper to taste
Toasted 3-inch Italian
  bread rounds

Combine tomatoes, onion, garlic, basil, salt and pepper in bowl; mix well. Serve on bread rounds. Yield: 8 servings.

Olga J. Kirk, Preceptor Beta Eta
Blacksburg, Virginia

TORTILLA ROLLS

8 ounces cream cheese, softened
1 4-ounce can chopped black olives, drained
1 4-ounce can chopped green chilies, drained
Tabasco sauce to taste
12 flour tortillas

Combine cream cheese, olives, green chilies and Tabasco sauce in bowl; mix well. Spread on tortillas. Roll to enclose filling. Cut into 1 inch slices. Chill or serve immediately. Yield: 12 servings.

Patricia Taylor, Xi Eta Xi
Garden Grove, California

CARAMEL CRACKERS

2 10-ounce packages miniature butter crackers
1 cup roasted peanuts or pecans
1 cup sugar
1/2 cup butter or margarine
1/2 cup light corn syrup
1 teaspoon baking soda
1 teaspoon vanilla extract

Preheat oven to 250 degrees. Combine butter crackers and peanuts in buttered 9-by-13-inch baking dish. Bring sugar, butter and corn syrup to a boil in saucepan; remove from heat. Stir in baking soda and vanilla. Pour over crackers and peanuts; mix well. Bake for 45 minutes to 1 hour, stirring every 15 minutes. Spread on waxed paper; let stand until cool. Break into small pieces. Store in airtight container. Yield: 16 servings.

Shirley Grudzinski, Preceptor Kappa
Grand Island, Nebraska
Ginny Mross, Alpha Chi Chi
Pleasanton, Texas

SNACKERS

My children prefer these snacks to potato chips.

1/3 to 1/2 cup vegetable oil
1 envelope green garden salad dressing mix
1/4 teaspoon dillweed
1 10-ounce package miniature butter crackers

Combine first 3 ingredients in medium bowl; mix well. Add crackers; toss to mix well. Spread on baking sheet. Let stand for 10 minutes. Store in airtight containers. Yield: 8 servings.

Marilyn Cumming
Oakville, Ontario, Canada

PUFFED CRACKERS

60 crackers
1/2 cup melted butter
Seasonings such as sesame or poppy seed, garlic powder or salt

Preheat oven to 400 degrees. Place 5 crackers at a time in ice water in bowl; let stand for 30 seconds. Remove carefully with slotted spoon. Place in single layer on buttered baking sheet. Drizzle with butter, covering completely. Sprinkle with seasoning of choice or leave unseasoned. Bake for 12 to 15 minutes or until puffed and golden brown. Reduce oven temperature to 300 degrees. Bake for 15 minutes longer. Remove to wire rack to cool. Store in airtight container. Yield: 60 servings.

Owen Whitlock, Alpha Epsilon Beta
Seabrook, Texas

CRACKER SNACK

60 butter crackers
1 cup sweetened condensed milk
8 ounces dates, chopped
1 cup chopped nuts

Preheat oven to 350 degrees. Arrange crackers on baking sheet. Combine condensed milk and dates in double boiler. Cook until thickened, stirring constantly; remove from heat. Stir in nuts. Spoon 1 teaspoon mixture onto each cracker. Bake for 1 minute. Cool on wire rack. Yield: 60 servings.

Irene M. Crist, Laureate Alpha Delta
Des Moines, Iowa

SWEET DREAMS

12 crackers
1/4 cup peanut butter
12 large marshmallows

Preheat broiler. Spread each cracker with peanut butter; top with marshmallow. Place on baking sheet. Broil just until marshmallow melts. Yield: 12 servings.

Tammye Stahler, Beta Alpha
Mena, Arkansas

SWEDISH NUTS

1 pound pecan halves
2 egg whites
1 cup sugar
Salt to taste
1/2 cup margarine

Preheat oven to 325 degrees. Spread pecan halves on baking sheet. Toast for 10 minutes. Beat egg whites in mixer bowl until stiff peaks form. Beat in sugar and salt. Fold in pecan halves. Melt margarine in 9-by-11-inch baking pan. Spread pecan mixture evenly in margarine. Bake for 30 minutes, stirring every 10 minutes. Yield: 6 to 8 servings.

Dorinda Todaro, Preceptor Delta Delta
Sanford, Florida

TOASTED BUTTER PECANS

1 pound pecan halves
1 tablespoon seasoned
  salt

¼ cup butter or
  margarine, cut into 4
  pieces

Place pecan halves in 1½-quart baking dish. Sprinkle with seasoned salt; dot with butter. Microwave on High for 7 to 8 minutes, stirring halfway through baking time. Yield: 8 servings.

Helen Grace Young, Laureate Epsilon
McComb, Mississippi

SWEET WALNUTS

2 egg whites
½ cup melted margarine

1 cup sugar
1 pound walnuts

Preheat oven to 350 degrees. Beat egg whites with margarine in mixer bowl until stiff peaks form. Add sugar gradually, beating constantly. Fold in walnuts. Spread in 9-by-13-inch baking dish. Bake for 30 minutes, stirring every 10 minutes. Yield: 8 servings.

Margaret Beech, Xi Eta Eta
North Huntingdon, Pennsylvania

CINNAMON POPCORN

¼ cup butter or
  margarine
¼ cup packed light
  brown sugar

¼ cup popcorn, popped
Cinnamon to taste
Nuts or raisins
  (optional)

Microwave butter and brown sugar on High in glass bowl for 45 to 60 seconds or until butter melts. Pour over popcorn in bowl. Add cinnamon; toss to coat well. May add nuts or raisins if desired. Yield: 3 to 4 servings.

Cori Amundrud, Alpha Psi
Coronach, Saskatchewan, Canada

PARTY POPCORN

I made these for card night and it was so popular I never got out of the kitchen, making batch after batch.

¼ cup butter or
  margarine
1 10-ounce package
  marshmallows

½ cup peanut butter
10 cups popped popcorn
½ cup sunflower seed
1 cup nuts

Melt butter in 3-quart saucepan. Add marshmallows and peanut butter. Cook until melted; remove from heat. Combine with popcorn, sunflower seed and nuts in bowl; mix to coat well. Shape into balls; place in paper liners. May add popsicle sticks if desired or spread in 9-by-13-inch dish and decorate with raisins, sprinkles or candies. Yield: 20 to 25 servings.

Sandra Collins
Lakeside, Arizona

PEANUT BUTTER POPCORN

1 bag microwave
  popcorn
½ cup sugar
½ cup light corn syrup

½ cup peanut butter
½ teaspoon vanilla
  extract

Microwave popcorn using package directions. Bring sugar and corn syrup to a rolling boil in saucepan; remove from heat. Stir in peanut butter and vanilla. Pour over hot popcorn in bowl; mix well. Yield: 8 servings.

Brenda Freepons, Delta Omega
Prosser, Washington

POPCORN BALLS

1 cup light corn
  syrup
½ cup sugar

1 3-ounce package
  fruit-flavored gelatin
9 cups popped popcorn

Bring corn syrup and sugar to a boil in saucepan over medium heat. Stir in gelatin until dissolved. Pour over popcorn in bowl; mix well. Shape into balls. Let stand on waxed paper until cool. Yield: 9 servings.

Lynda Miller, Kappa Gamma
Eldridge, Iowa

CARAMEL CORN

Do not use a bag made of recycled material for this recipe or for any recipe prepared in the microwave.

1 cup packed light
  brown sugar
¼ cup light corn syrup
½ cup margarine
Salt to taste

½ teaspoon baking soda
4 to 5 quarts popped
  popcorn
1 cup dry-roasted
  peanuts (optional)

Combine brown sugar, corn syrup, margarine and salt in 2-quart glass bowl. Microwave on High until mixture comes to a boil; stir to mix well. Microwave for 2 minutes longer. Stir in baking soda. Combine with popcorn and peanuts in large bag. Close bag and shake to mix well. Microwave on High for 3 minutes, shaking after 1½ minutes. Spread on baking sheet to cool. Yield: 20 servings.

Karen Hagerman, Xi Delta Psi
Erie, Pennsylvania
JoAnn M. Norton, Xi Phi
Hot Springs, South Dakota

PRETZEL SNACK

½ envelope ranch salad
  dressing mix
½ bottle of Orville
  Redenbacher's
  popcorn oil

1 tablespoon dillweed
1 12-ounce package
  large pretzels, broken

Preheat oven to 200 degrees. Combine salad dressing mix, oil and dillweed in bowl; mix well. Pour over pretzels in large baking pan. Bake for 1 hour, stirring every 15 minutes. Yield: 12 servings.

Sylvia Cornell, Alpha Gamma
Mt. Vernon, Ohio

CEREAL MIX WITH WHITE CHOCOLATE

1 pound white chocolate	2 cups dry-roasted
3 cups Cheerios	peanuts
3 cups rice Chex	2 cups "M & M's"
3 cups corn Chex	Chocolate Candies
2 cups pretzel sticks	

Melt white chocolate in double boiler. Pour over mixture of remaining ingredients in bowl; mix to coat well. Spread on waxed paper. Let stand until cool. Break into small pieces. Yield: 15 servings.

C. K. Vugteveen, Kappa
Sioux City, Iowa

SWEET-TOOTH CHEX MIX

1 12-ounce package Crispix	2 16-ounce cans mixed nuts
1 12-ounce package rice Chex	2 1/2 cups dark corn syrup
1 12-ounce package corn Chex	2 1/2 cups sugar
2 8-ounce packages pretzels	1 pound margarine
	4 teaspoons vanilla extract
2 4-ounce packages sunflower seed	

Combine cereals, pretzels, sunflower seed and nuts in 2 large bowls. Bring corn syrup, sugar and margarine to a boil in saucepan. Boil for 2 minutes. Stir in vanilla. Pour over cereal mixture in bowls; mix to coat well. Spread on waxed paper to cool. May adjust ingredients to suit individual tastes. Yield: 25 servings.

Michelle Noble, Eta
Winnemucca, Nevada

PARTY MIX

1 cup corn oil	1 16-ounce package
2 teaspoons dillweed	thin cheese wheat
2 teaspoons lemon pepper	crackers
1 envelope ranch salad dressing mix	1 12-ounce package pretzels
1 16-ounce package cheese crackers	

Combine first 4 ingredients in small bowl; mix well. Pour over mixture of crackers and pretzels in large glass bowl; toss to coat well. Microwave on High for 5 minutes, stirring after 3 minutes. Cool to room temperature. Store in airtight container. Yield: 15 servings.

Nancy Eads, Omega Mu
Ridgeway, Missouri

QUICK SNACK MIX

2 or 3 packages of your favorite miniature crackers such as butter crackers, sun-toasted wheats, Triscuits, etc.	1 to 1 1/2 pounds Gardetto's Snak-Ens Deluxe Snack Mix
1 8-ounce package pretzels	1 11-ounce can cashews or salted peanuts

Combine all ingredients in large airtight container; mix well. Yield: 25 servings.

Joyce Mattes, Preceptor Gamma Xi
Kalona, Iowa

SECONDS-FROM-A-SNACK

This only takes seconds to make, and everyone will want seconds. It is great to share as gifts in holiday tins or to take in the car when travelling.

16 ounces "M & M's" Plain Chocolate Candies	4 ounces raisins
	1 8-ounce package pretzel sticks
16 ounces "M & M's" Peanut Chocolate Candies	1 12-ounce package Chex cereal
4 ounces sesame sticks	8 ounces white yogurt-covered small pretzels

Combine first 6 ingredients in bowl; mix well. Spoon into airtight container; top with pretzels. Serve with scoop. Yield: 20 servings.

Lynn Marie Desmond, Zeta Lambda
Toledo, Ohio

SNACK MIX

1 12-ounce package Do-Dads	1 16-ounce package "M & M's" Peanut Chocolate Candies
1 8-ounce package pretzels	1 16-ounce can mixed nuts
1 16-ounce package chocolate-covered raisins	1 12-ounce package cheese-flavored fish crackers
1 16-ounce package "M & M's" Plain Chocolate Candies	Sunflower seed to taste

Combine all ingredients in large bowl; mix well. Store in airtight container. Yield: 20 servings.

Peggy Carey, Preceptor Gamma Lambda
Grand Blanc, Michigan

Shelley Kirkpatrick, Phi Psi, Regina, Saskatchewan, Canada, makes Tangy Cheese Toast by combining equal amounts each of shredded Cheddar and Swiss cheese with 1 finely chopped green onion and mayonnaise to moisten. Spread on French bread slices and bake in preheated 400-degree oven for 20 minutes.

TRASH

1 cup butter or
  margarine
1 8-ounce jar peanut
  butter
2 cups semisweet
  chocolate chips
1 16-ounce package
  rice Chex
1 8-ounce package
  dates, chopped

1 15-ounce package
  raisins
1 16-ounce jar dry-
  roasted unsalted
  peanuts
2 1-pound packages
  confectioners' sugar

Melt first 3 ingredients in saucepan, stirring to mix
well. Pour over mixture of cereal, dates, raisins and
peanuts in bowl; mix well. Combine with
confectioners' sugar in large trash bag; shake to coat
well. Store in airtight container. Yield: 20 servings.

Ellie Iversen
Cary, North Carolina

LAMBDA SANGRIA

We like to serve this punch at our annual Salad Supper.

1 1-liter bottle white,
  red or rosé wine
1 12-ounce can frozen
  5-Alive juice
  concentrate

1 2-liter bottle ginger
  ale
Sliced oranges, lemons
  or limes

Combine first 3 ingredients in large punch bowl; mix
well. Garnish with sliced oranges, lemons or limes.
Add ice and serve. Yield: 20 servings.

Patricia Taylor, Lambda
Bluefield, West Virginia

APPLE-CINNAMON CREAM LIQUEUR

*The first time I served this I was in a new town with
new friends during the holiday season. I now serve it
every year during the holidays.*

1 14-ounce can
  sweetened condensed
  milk
1 cup apple schnapps

1 cup whipping cream
4 eggs
1/2 teaspoon cinnamon

Combine all ingredients in blender container.
Process until well mixed. Serve over ice. May store
tightly covered in refrigerator for 1 month. Stir
before serving. Yield: 8 (1/2-cup) servings.

Terry Eagy, Zeta Tau
Othello, Washington

---

*Billie J. Morris, Preceptor Mu Chi, Ozona, Texas, prepares
a Tea Syrup which keeps in the refrigerator for months and
when added to water to make tea of desired strength, always
tastes freshly brewed. Bring 3 cups water, 1/2 cup loose tea
and 1/2 teaspoon baking soda to a boil. Strain over sugar,
stirring until sugar dissolves.*

VANILLA CONFECTION COFFEE

1 teaspoon light corn
  syrup
1/4 to 1/2 teaspoon
  vanilla extract

Hot coffee
1 can whipped cream

Combine corn syrup and vanilla in coffee mug. Pour
in hot coffee, stirring to mix. Top with dollop of
whipped cream. Yield: 1 serving.

Debi Siwinski, Zeta Chi
Monticello, Indiana

MOCK CHAMPAGNE

1 cup sugar
1 cup water
2 1/4 cups grapefruit juice

1 cup orange juice
3/4 cup grenadine syrup
3 quarts ginger ale

Combine sugar and water in saucepan. Bring to a
boil, stirring frequently. Remove from heat. Cool
slightly. Add juices and grenadine syrup; mix well.
Chill until serving time. Add ginger ale just before
serving. Yield: 16 servings.

Linda Werkheiser, Beta Chi
St. Joseph, Illinois

STRAWBERRY DAIQUIRI

1 6-ounce can frozen
  lemonade concentrate
1 6-ounce juice can rum
14 ice cubes

1 10-ounce package
  frozen strawberries,
  partially thawed

Combine all ingredients in blender container.
Process until puréed. Pour in daiquiri glasses.
Yield: 6 to 8 servings.

Jo Anne Hoffer, Preceptor Zeta Phi
Sunnyvale, California

HOLIDAY EGGNOG

12 large eggs
1 1/2 cups sugar
1/2 teaspoon salt
2 quarts milk
2 tablespoons vanilla
  extract

1 cup brandy (optional)
1 teaspoon nutmeg
2 cups whipping cream,
  whipped
Nutmeg to taste

Combine eggs, sugar and salt in heavy saucepan;
mix well. Add 1 quart milk gradually, beating well.
Cook over low heat, 170 to 175 degrees on candy
thermometer, for 25 minutes or until mixture thickens and coats a spoon, stirring constantly. Do not
boil. Pour custard into large bowl. Add remaining 1
quart milk, vanilla, brandy and 1 teaspoon nutmeg.
Chill until serving time. Fold in whipped cream.
Pour into chilled punch bowl. Garnish with additional nutmeg. Custard may be made early in the day
and stored in refrigerator. Yield: 32 (1/2-cup) servings.

Nina J. Brannon, Laureate Beta Tau
Fort Walton Beach, Florida

HOT BUTTERED RUM

This was served at one of our sorority meetings and brings warm memories of gatherings with sorority sisters.

1 pound butter
1 1-pound package
  light brown sugar
1 1-pound package
  dark brown sugar
2 teaspoons cinnamon
2 teaspoons nutmeg
1 quart vanilla ice
  cream, softened
Light rum
Whipped topping
Cinnamon sticks

Combine butter, light and dark brown sugar, cinnamon and nutmeg in mixer bowl; beat until light and fluffy. Stir in ice cream. Pour into freezer container. Freeze, covered. Thaw slightly before serving. Combine 3 tablespoons butter mixture and 1 jigger rum in large mug. Pour in boiling water until filled, stirring well. Top with whipped topping. Serve with cinnamon stick stirrer. Unused butter mixture may be refrozen. Yield: 25 servings.

Sandra LeFevre, Preceptor Kappa Phi
Waco, Texas

KIWI-YOGURT SMOOTHIE

This was given to me by a friend who is always looking for low-calorie recipes.

2 kiwifruit, sliced
1 banana
1/4 cup plain low-fat
  yogurt
3 ice cubes
2 large strawberries

Combine kiwifruit, banana, yogurt and ice cubes in blender container. Process until puréed. Pour into 2 glasses. Garnish with strawberries. Yield: 2 servings.

T. Ann Kerschner, Laureate Alpha Tau
McPherson, Kansas

SPEEDY MARGARITAS

1 6-ounce can frozen
  limeade concentrate
1 6-ounce juice can
  Tequilla
1/2 12-ounce can beer
Ice cubes
Salt

Combine limeade concentrate, Tequilla, beer and ice cubes in blender container. Process until ice is chopped and mixture is foamy. Dip glass rims into water; dip into salt to coat. Pour Margaritas into glasses. Yield: 4 to 6 servings.

Amy Berthold, Zeta Tau
Warrensburg, Missouri

QUICK ORANGE JULIETTE

1 6-ounce can frozen
  orange juice
  concentrate
1 cup milk
1/2 cup water
1/3 cup sugar
Ice cubes

Combine all ingredients in blender container. Process until well mixed. Pour into glasses. Yield: 4 servings.

Georgiann Trenholm, Laureate Alpha Delta
Gresham, Oregon

ORANGE JULIUS

This is a favorite with children. Overnight guests ask for it each morning.

1 6-ounce can frozen
  orange juice
  concentrate
1 cup milk
1 cup water
1 teaspoon vanilla
  extract
1/2 cup sugar
Ice cubes

Combine all ingredients in blender container. Process for 30 seconds. Yield: 4 servings.

Teresa James, Delta Upsilon
Olean, Missouri

APPLE PUNCH

1 46-ounce can
  pineapple juice
1 12-ounce can frozen
  apple juice
  concentrate
1 12-ounce can frozen
  orange juice
  concentrate
3 1-liter bottles ginger
  ale

Combine juices in freezer container; mix well. Freeze for 2 days. Place mixture in punch bowl. Add ginger ale 1 hour before serving. Yield: 20 servings.

Marynelle Bassford, Laureate Phi
Arlington, Virginia

CHAMPAGNE PUNCH

1/3 cup lemon juice
1/4 cup sugar
2 bottles champagne
1 pint ginger ale
1 10-ounce package
  frozen strawberries

Combine all ingredients in large punch bowl. Stir gently to mix. Yield: 30 to 40 servings.

Betty Cutting, Laureate Delta Tau
Amarillo, Texas

CHAMPAGNE-SHERBET PUNCH

This simple recipe is delicious, refreshing and light. It looks pretty without adding garnishes.

2 bottles champagne,
  chilled
1 bottle Sauterne,
  chilled
1/2 gallon lime, lemon or
  raspberry sherbet
1 2-liter bottle ginger
  ale, chilled

Combine champagne and Sauterne in punch bowl. Add sherbet, stirring gently to mix. Pour in ginger ale. Yield: 25 servings.

Shiela Shallcross, Delta
Arlington, Texas

COFFEE PUNCH

3/4 cup instant coffee
2 cups sugar
2 cups water
6 12-ounce cans
   evaporated milk,
   chilled

1/2 gallon vanilla ice
   cream
2 quarts club soda,
   chilled

Combine instant coffee, sugar and water in punch bowl; mix well. Add evaporated milk and ice cream, stirring gently to mix. Pour in club soda. Yield: 30 servings.

Isabelle Bahan, Eta Rho
Mandeville, Louisiana

SPARKLING PUNCH

1 12-ounce can frozen
   lemonade concentrate
1 12-ounce can frozen
   orange juice
   concentrate
1 46-ounce can
   unsweetened pineapple
   juice

1 liter club soda,
   chilled
Sliced oranges
Maraschino cherries

Add water to frozen juices using package directions. Combine juice mixtures and pineapple juice in freezer container; mix well. Freeze. Combine juice mixture and club soda in punch bowl 30 minutes to 1 hour before serving. Garnish with sliced oranges and maraschino cherries. Yield: 24 to 30 servings.

Tammy Goebel, Zeta Phi
Bryan, Ohio

SANGRITA

2 green onions, minced
1 jalapeño pepper, minced
1 tablespoon sugar
1/2 teaspoon salt
1/2 cup orange juice,
   chilled

4 cups tomato juice,
   chilled
1/3 cup lime juice, chilled
1 cup Tequila
Lime wedges

Combine green onions, jalapeño pepper, sugar and salt in punch bowl; mix well. Add juices; mix well. Stir in Tequila. Ladle into punch cups. Garnish with lime wedges. Yield: 8 to 10 servings.

Joanne Watts, Preceptor Lambda
Waterloo, Ontario, Canada

ALMOND TEA

1 gallon hot tea
1 6-ounce can frozen
   orange juice
   concentrate
1 6-ounce can frozen
   lemonade concentrate

2 teaspoons vanilla
   extract
1 tablespoon almond
   extract
1 1/2 cups sugar

Combine hot tea, orange juice concentrate, lemonade concentrate, flavorings and sugar in saucepan; mix

well. Heat to serving temperature. May also be served cold. May substitute 1 1/2 cups lemon juice for frozen lemonade and 1 cup instant orange-flavored breakfast drink for orange juice. Yield: 10 to 15 servings.

Marjorie Duckworth, Pi Eta
McQueeney, Texas

VELVET HAMMER

1 quart vanilla ice
   cream
2 tablespoons coffee
   liqueur

2 tablespoons dark rum
Chocolate-covered
   coffee beans

Combine ice cream, liqueur and rum in blender container. Process until smooth. Pour into freezer container. Freeze, covered, until firm. Spoon into brandy snifters or glass dessert bowls. Garnish each with 1 chocolate-covered coffee bean. Yield: 4 to 6 servings.

Janice Porter, Xi Psi
North Vancouver, British Columbia, Canada

WHISKEY SOURS

1 6-ounce can frozen
   lemonade concentrate
1 6-ounce lemonade
   can 7-Up

1 6-ounce lemonade
   can rye whiskey
6 ice cubes
1 egg

Combine all ingredients in blender container. Process on High for 30 seconds. Pour into tall glasses. Yield: 4 servings.

Brenda Legge, Lambda Alpha
Welland, Ontario, Canada

BANANA WINE COOLERS

1 medium bottle
   Lambrusco
1/2 bottle cream of
   banana liqueur
2 12-ounce cans 7-Up

1 6-ounce can frozen
   orange juice
   concentrate
Orange or lemon slices

Combine all ingredients in large pitcher; mix well. Serve over ice in large glasses. Garnish with orange or lemon slices. Yield: 6 servings.

Lynn Schaffarzick, Beta Alpha
Kemmerer, Wyoming

WINE COOLERS

2 cups orange juice
1 6-ounce can frozen
   lemonade concentrate
1 cup Triple Sec

1 liter club soda, chilled
1 cup apricot nectar
White wine

Combine orange juice, lemonade, liqueur, club soda and apricot nectar in large pitcher; mix well. Add enough white wine to measure 1 gallon. Yield: 16 servings.

Melinda Atha, Epsilon Gamma
El Dorado, Arkansas

Swift Soups

Just the word "soup" evokes thoughts of
long hours of chopping, stirring, and of slow
simmering. And hours of kitchen cleanup.
Now, admittedly, homemade soup is one of the
delights of the table, whether for family or
guests. But the time involved can be
daunting—unless you try the "soups for-
the-overscheduled" we've collected here.
You'll be delighted at the variety and quality
of the soups you have created, ranging from
cool summer appetizers to hearty winter main
dishes. Most can be put together in just a few
minutes from ingredients you can keep stocked
in the pantry. If homemade soup is something
you've given up on, now is a good time to put it
back in your repertory. You'll find these recipes
real godsends on those days when time is hard
to come by—but big appetites aren't.

BEEF AND TORTELLINI SOUP

I use ground deer sausage and spinach tortellini in this soup. I serve it with breadsticks or hard rolls for a complete meal or as an appetizer for Italian meals.

1 pound ground beef	1 19-ounce package
1 10-ounce can onion	dry or fresh tortellini
soup	1 teaspoon basil
1 28-ounce can	3½ cups water
tomatoes in purée	1 or 2 14-ounce cans
1 9-ounce package	beef broth
frozen green beans	

Brown ground beef in heavy 5-quart saucepan for 10 minutes, stirring until crumbly; drain. Add soup, tomatoes, green beans, tortellini, basil, water and beef broth. Bring to a boil; reduce heat to medium. Cook for 15 minutes or until tortellini is tender. Add zucchini if desired. Cook just until tender. Yield: 6 to 8 servings.

Beth Swanson, Xi Alpha Gamma
Rock Springs, Wyoming

SPEEDY BORSCH

1 pound ground beef	½ teaspoon garlic
6 cups water	flakes
1 6-ounce can tomato	2 tablespoons lemon
paste	juice
2 cups shredded cabbage	Salt to taste
1 cup chopped potato	¼ teaspoon pepper
¼ cup instant minced	1 16-ounce can diced
onion	beets
2 teaspoons dillseed	Sour cream

Brown ground beef in large saucepan, stirring until crumbly; drain. Add water, tomato paste, cabbage, potato, onion, dillseed, garlic flakes, lemon juice, salt and pepper; mix well. Bring to a boil; reduce heat. Simmer, covered, for 5 minutes or until potatoes are tender. Add undrained beets. Simmer, covered, for 2 minutes or until heated through. Serve with sour cream. Yield: 6 to 8 servings.

Dora Kelly, Xi Alpha Phi
Campbell River, British Columbia, Canada

CHEESY BEEF AND VEGETABLE SOUP

1 pound ground beef	¼ teaspoon basil
1 medium onion,	¼ teaspoon salt
chopped	⅛ teaspoon pepper
1 package cheeseburger-	1 10-ounce package
macaroni Hamburger	frozen mixed
Helper	vegetables, thawed
1 16-ounce can whole	
tomatoes	

Brown ground beef with onion in saucepan, stirring until ground beef is crumbly; drain. Stir in sauce packet from Hamburger Helper, tomatoes, basil, salt and pepper; stir to break up tomatoes. Bring to a boil;

reduce heat. Simmer for 10 minutes. Stir in macaroni from Hamburger Helper and mixed vegetables. Simmer, covered, for 10 minutes or until macaroni is tender. Yield: 4 servings.

Konda Cooper, Xi Delta Beta
York, Nebraska

CLEAN-THE-REFRIGERATOR SOUP

Use your imagination and beef or leftover roast or steak and any leftover vegetables you have in the refrigerator.

1 pound ground beef	Leftover vegetables
1 or 2 16-ounce cans	such as that small
tomatoes	dish of whole kernel
2 medium potatoes	corn, 2 limp celery
unpeeled, chopped	stalks, carrot sticks,
1 cup uncooked	½ green bell pepper,
macaroni or	baked potato, coleslaw
spaghetti	or sliced onions

Brown ground beef in large saucepan, stirring until crumbly; drain. Add tomatoes, chopped potatoes and macaroni. Add whatever leftovers you have in the refrigerator. Cook until ingredients are tender. Yield: 10 to 12 servings.

Joan Moreland, Preceptor Alpha Omega
Oklahoma City, Oklahoma

SOUTHWEST SOUP

2 pounds ground beef	2 10-ounce cans
1 large onion, chopped	minestrone soup
3 16-ounce cans ranch-	1 16-ounce can beef
style beans	broth
1 10-ounce can Ro-Tel	Shredded cheese
tomatoes with green	Corn bread
chilies	

Brown ground beef with onion in saucepan, stirring until ground beef is crumbly; drain. Add beans, tomatoes, soup and beef broth; mix well. Simmer for 45 minutes. Serve with shredded cheese and corn bread. Yield: 8 to 10 servings.

Holly Bryan, Xi Tau Nu
Wink, Texas

SOUTH DAKOTA SPECIAL

2 pounds ground beef	1 15-ounce can pinto
2 large onions, sliced	beans, drained
1 green bell pepper,	1 15-ounce can kidney
sliced	beans, drained
1 17-ounce can cream-	1 tablespoon
style corn	Worcestershire sauce
1 17-ounce can whole	1 tablespoon chili
kernel corn, drained	powder
1 28-ounce can whole	French rolls
tomatoes	Bleu cheese spread

Brown ground beef in saucepan, stirring until crumbly. Add onions and green pepper. Sauté until onions are tender, stirring occasionally; drain. Add corn, tomatoes, beans, Worcestershire sauce and chili powder; mix well. Bring to a boil; reduce heat. Simmer for 20 minutes. Serve with French rolls and bleu cheese spread. Yield: 8 servings.

Susan Rector, Zeta Zeta
Port Orchard, Washington

TACO SOUP

2 pounds lean ground beef	2 20-ounce cans pinto beans or jalapeño pinto beans
1 medium onion, chopped	2 20-ounce cans Mexican-style stewed tomatoes
1 1-ounce envelope taco seasoning mix	
1 1-ounce envelope ranch salad dressing mix	1 4-ounce can chopped green chilies
2 20-ounce cans whole kernel corn	1 or 2 teaspoons garlic powder
	Shredded cheese

Brown ground beef with onion in skillet, stirring until ground beef is crumbly; drain. Stir in taco seasoning mix and salad dressing mix. Combine with corn, beans, tomatoes, green chilies and garlic powder in slow cooker; mix well. Cook on Low for 2 hours or longer. Top servings with cheese. May add cayenne pepper, jalapeño pepper or additional chili pepper for spicier soup. Yield: 8 to 10 servings.

Mary Rice, Iota Mu
Nacogdoches, Texas

TACO SALAD SOUP

8 ounces ground beef	1½ cups water
¼ cup chopped onion	2 tablespoons taco seasoning mix
1 16-ounce can kidney beans, chili beans or pinto beans	1 avocado, chopped
1 16-ounce can stewed tomatoes, chopped	1 cup shredded Cheddar cheese
1 8-ounce can tomato sauce	1 cup sour cream
	Corn chips

Brown ground beef with onion in large saucepan, stirring until ground beef is crumbly; drain. Add beans, tomatoes, tomato sauce, water and seasoning mix; mix well. Simmer for 15 minutes. Top servings with avocado, cheese, sour cream and corn chips. Yield: 4 to 6 servings.

Sharon Walker, Zeta
Ketchikan, Alaska

BEEFY V-8 SOUP

1 pound ground beef	1 10-ounce can cream of celery soup
1 onion, chopped	
1 46-ounce can V-8 juice	1 16-ounce package frozen mixed vegetables

Brown ground beef with onion in heavy saucepan, stirring until ground beef is crumbly; drain. Add V-8 juice, soup and mixed vegetables; mix well. Simmer for 45 minutes or until vegetables are tender. Yield: 6 servings.

Connie Eaton, Xi Zeta
Chadron, Nebraska

VEGETABLE AND MEATBALL SOUP

4 cups canned tomatoes	4 teaspoons salt
½ cup chopped celery	1½ pounds lean ground beef
2 cups sliced carrots	
5 medium potatoes, peeled, chopped	2 eggs
1 large onion, chopped	⅓ cup cracker crumbs
6 cups water	2 tablespoons milk
1 teaspoon sugar	2 teaspoons seasoned salt
2 teaspoons chopped parsley	Pepper to taste
2 teaspoons oregano	2 16-ounce cans green or wax beans
2 teaspoons basil	
3 bay leaves	1 12-ounce can whole kernel corn or 1 cup frozen corn
2 teaspoons seasoned pepper	

Combine tomatoes, celery, carrots, potatoes, onion, water, sugar, parsley, oregano, basil, bay leaves, seasoned pepper and salt in large heavy saucepan. Bring to a boil. Combine ground beef, eggs, cracker crumbs, milk, seasoned salt and pepper to taste in bowl; mix well. Shape into 1-inch balls. Drop into boiling soup. Simmer for 20 minutes. Add beans and corn. Simmer for 10 minutes longer. Discard bay leaves. Yield: 10 servings.

Denise LaPalme, Xi Delta Lambda
Windsor, Ontario, Canada

DUMP CHILI

I won first place in a chili cook-off with this recipe and was actually embarrassed at how much easier it was than the other entries.

1 12-ounce can roast beef in gravy	1 8-ounce jar chunky salsa
1 15-ounce can chili beans	1 tablespoon chili powder
1 4-ounce can chopped green chilies	½ teaspoon cumin

Combine all ingredients in large saucepan; mix well. Cook until heated through. May substitute canned chicken for beef. Yield: 4 to 6 servings.

Priscilla Culkowski, Xi Omicron
Alexandria, Virginia

Norene M. Fossick, Alpha Master, Nashville, Tennessee, makes Easy Bean and Tomato Soup by combining a 16-ounce can undrained tomatoes, ½ cup ground cooked ham and a 24-ounce jar Great Northern beans. Heat in microwave.

QUICK-FIX CHILI

This recipe won first place at our sorority 1992 Super Bowl chili cook-off. I stir it up quickly on the stove top and keep it warm in a slow cooker for easy serving.

1 pound lean ground beef	1 envelope chili
1 16-ounce can	seasoning mix
tomatoes, chopped	1 envelope onion soup
2 15-ounce cans red	mix
kidney beans	1/4 teaspoon each
1 10-ounce can	cumin, cayenne pepper
tomatoes with green	and black pepper
chilies	(optional)
1 1/2 cups water	

Brown ground beef in large saucepan, stirring until crumbly; drain. Add remaining ingredients. Bring to a boil; reduce heat. Simmer for 10 minutes. Yield: 8 servings.

Mary Bradshaw, Xi Alpha
Omaha, Nebraska

CAULIFLOWER AND HAM CHOWDER

1 cup chopped celery	1/4 cup water
2 cups sliced cauliflower	2 tablespoons
1 14-ounce can chicken	cornstarch
broth	2 cups chopped cooked
1 cup evaporated milk	ham
1 10-ounce can cream	1/2 cup shredded cheese
of potato soup	

Cook celery and cauliflower in chicken broth in saucepan for 10 minutes. Stir in evaporated milk and potato soup. Blend water and cornstarch in small bowl. Stir into soup with ham. Cook until thickened, stirring constantly. Add cheese. Simmer until cheese melts. Yield: 6 servings.

Joyce Reeves, Theta Master
Grandview, Missouri

HAM AND CHEESE CHOWDER

2 cups thawed frozen	2 1/2 cups water
hashed brown	2 cups chopped cooked
potatoes	ham
1 1/2 cups thinly sliced	1 17-ounce can cream-
carrots	style corn
1/2 cup chopped green	1 11-ounce Cheddar
bell pepper	cheese soup
1/4 cup chopped red bell	1/2 cup water
pepper	White pepper to taste

Combine potatoes, carrots, bell peppers and water in heavy saucepan. Bring to a boil; reduce heat. Simmer, covered, for 15 minutes or until vegetables are tender. Add remaining ingredients; mix well. Cook until heated through, stirring frequently. Yield: 8 servings.

Joan Kranz
Smithfield, Virginia

CHEESY HAM CHOWDER

1 6-ounce package au	1 to 2 cups chopped
gratin potato mix	cooked ham
4 cups water	1 teaspoon caraway
2 cups chopped cabbage	seed (optional)
1 cup chopped carrot	1 cup milk

Combine potatoes and seasoning packet with water, cabbage, carrot, ham and caraway seed in large saucepan; mix well. Simmer, covered, for 15 to 20 minutes or until potatoes are tender. Add milk. Simmer, uncovered, for 5 minutes longer. Yield: 6 servings.

Sally Kitchen, Laureate Gamma
Owosso, Michigan

CHEESY HAM AND BROCCOLI SOUP

8 ounces broccoli,	6 tablespoons melted
chopped	butter or margarine
2 tablespoons chopped	8 ounces cooked ham,
onion	chopped
6 cups chicken stock	8 ounces Swiss cheese,
2 cups milk	shredded
1 cup cream	
6 tablespoons	
all-purpose flour	

Simmer broccoli and onion in chicken stock in medium saucepan for 1 hour. Bring milk and cream to a simmer in small saucepan. Blend flour into butter in small saucepan. Cook for 2 minutes or until light brown. Add to soup, mixing well. Add heated milk mixture; mix well. Simmer for 10 minutes; reduce heat. Stir in ham and cheese. Cook until cheese melts. Yield: 8 servings.

Janet Dougherty, Xi Beta Alpha
Appleton, Wisconsin

❖ ITALIAN SAUSAGE CHILI

12 ounces hot or mild	1 4-ounce can chopped
Italian sausage	mild green chilies
1 small onion, chopped	1/4 teaspoon oregano
1 tablespoon chili	8 ounces sour cream
powder	3/4 cup shredded
2 16-ounce cans black-	Cheddar or Monterey
eyed beans	Jack cheese
1 12-ounce can light	
beer	

Remove casing from sausage. Brown with onion and chili powder in 4-quart saucepan, stirring until crumbly; drain. Add undrained beans, beer, green chilies and oregano; mix well. Bring to a boil over high heat; reduce heat. Simmer for 15 minutes, stirring occasionally. Top servings with sour cream and cheese. Yield: 6 servings.

Barbara Osborn, Xi Sigma
Holtville, California

GERMAN SAUSAGE CHOWDER

1 pound cooked bratwurst, cut into 1/2-inch pieces	Pepper to taste
	4 cups shredded cabbage
2 cups chopped peeled potatoes	3 cups milk
	3 tablespoons all-purpose flour
1/2 cup chopped onion	1 cup shredded Swiss cheese
2 cups water	
1 1/2 teaspoons salt	Chopped parsley

Bring first 6 ingredients to a boil in large heavy saucepan; reduce heat. Simmer, covered, for 20 minutes or until potatoes are nearly tender. Stir in cabbage. Simmer for 10 minutes or until vegetables are tender. Stir in 2 1/2 cups milk. Blend remaining 1/2 cup milk with flour in bowl. Stir into soup. Cook until thickened, stirring constantly. Stir in cheese until melted. Garnish with parsley. Yield: 6 servings.

Cynthia L. Thomas, Alpha Tau
Orono, Maine

KIELBASA-BEAN SOUP

1 medium potato, peeled, chopped	3 cups water
	8 ounces kielbasa, thinly sliced
2 carrots, sliced	
1 medium onion, chopped	1 10-ounce can bean and bacon soup
1/2 cup chopped celery	

Bring vegetables and water to a boil in large saucepan; reduce heat. Simmer for 10 minutes or until vegetables are tender. Add sausage and soup; mix well. Cook until heated through. Yield: 4 servings.

Ella Leinwebber, Laureate Alpha Iota
Spokane, Washington

REUBEN SOUP

2 1/2 pounds kielbasa, sliced	2 14-ounce cans beef broth
2 tablespoons melted butter or margarine	1 cup dry vermouth
	2 teaspoons caraway seed
1 32-ounce can sauerkraut, drained, rinsed	2 bay leaves

Brown sausage lightly in butter in 5 to 6-quart saucepan. Add remaining ingredients; mix well. Bring to a boil; reduce heat. Simmer until serving time. Remove bay leaves. Serve with French bread and salad with Thousand Island Dressing. Yield: 6 servings.

Julie Gibson, Xi Gamma Beta
Centreville, Virginia

Shirley Horton, Laureate Epsilon Psi, Stockton, California, combines 1 can tomato soup and 1 soup can milk with 3 tablespoons peanut butter and heats to make Sooper-Dooper Tomato Soup.

WINTER WARM-UP

1 10-ounce can cream of mushroom soup	3 soup cans water
	1 5-ounce can Vienna sausage, sliced, or
1 10-ounce can green pea soup	1 5-ounce can shrimp

Combine soups in 2-quart saucepan; mix well. Stir in water gradually. Add Vienna sausage. Cook until heated through, stirring frequently. Serve with crackers or breadsticks. Yield: 6 to 8 servings.

Anne M. Copeland, Xi Kappa Omicron
Kimberling City, Missouri

CHICKEN-CHEESE SOUP

4 chicken breasts	Garlic powder, salt and pepper to taste
2 chicken bouillon cubes	
1 cup chopped carrot	1/2 cup uncooked rice
1 cup chopped onion	16 ounces Mexican-style or plain Velveeta cheese, chopped
1 cup chopped green bell pepper	

Rinse chicken and pat dry. Cook in water to cover in saucepan until tender. Remove and chop chicken, reserving broth. Add bouillon, vegetables and seasonings to broth. Simmer for 20 minutes. Add rice and chicken. Simmer for 20 minutes or until rice is tender. Stir in cheese until melted. Yield: 8 servings.

Carla Pearson, Omicron Delta
McPherson, Kansas

COLD CHICKEN AND CUCUMBER SOUP

1 10-ounce can cream of chicken soup	3/4 cup cold water
	1/3 cup seeded, finely chopped cucumber
1/3 cup sour cream	
3/4 cup vegetable juice cocktail	1/4 teaspoon rosemary

Combine soup and sour cream in bowl; mix until smooth. Stir in remaining ingredients. Chill for 3 hours. Serve in chilled bowls. Yield: 3 to 4 servings.

Jeanne Gordon, Xi Zeta Omicron
Trenton, Ontario, Canada

CHICKEN-NOODLE SOUP

2 5-ounce cans chunky chicken	1 medium potato, peeled, sliced
8 cups water	3 tablespoons chicken-flavored soup base
1/2 cup sliced carrot	
1/2 cup sliced celery	6 ounces uncooked noodles
1 small onion, chopped	

Combine chicken, water, carrot, celery, onion, potato and soup base in large saucepan; mix well. Cook until vegetables are tender. Stir in noodles. Cook for 15 minutes longer. Serve with fresh-baked bread. Yield: 6 to 8 servings.

Susan Rector, Beta Iota
Omaha, Nebraska

CHICKEN-RICE SOUP WITH VEGETABLES

6 ounces chicken breast
  filets
1 teaspoon corn oil
3 cups water
1 14-ounce can chicken
  broth
1 10-ounce package
  frozen mixed vegetables
1 tablespoon chopped
  parsley
1 cup uncooked instant
  brown rice

Cut chicken into bite-sized pieces. Rinse and pat dry. Sauté in oil in 2-quart saucepan until light brown. Add water, chicken broth and vegetables. Bring to a boil. Stir in parsley and rice. Bring to a boil; reduce heat. Simmer, covered, for 5 minutes. Remove from heat; let stand for 5 minutes. Yield: 6 to 8 servings.

Colleen Abar, Laureate Delta
Grand Forks, North Dakota

CHICKEN-TORTELLINI SOUP

2 cups chopped cooked
  chicken
3 14-ounce cans
  chicken broth
1 cup sliced carrot
1/4 cup chopped onion
  (optional)
1 cup chopped celery
1/2 cup grated Parmesan
  cheese
1/2 teaspoon thyme
1/4 teaspoon oregano
1 16-ounce package
  frozen cheese tortellini

Combine chicken, chicken broth, vegetables, cheese and herbs in 4-quart saucepan. Cook over medium heat for 10 minutes or until carrots and celery are tender. Add pasta. Cook for 10 minutes longer. Yield: 8 servings.

Marsha Cunningham, Alpha Eta
Williamsport, Pennsylvania

❖ MEXICAN CHICKEN-CORN SOUP

3 1/2 cups fresh or frozen
  corn
1 cup chicken broth
1/4 cup melted butter or
  margarine
2 cups chopped cooked
  chicken
1 clove of garlic,
  chopped
1 teaspoon cumin
2 cups milk
1 4-ounce can chopped
  green chilies
3 dashes of Tabasco sauce
1 cup shredded plain or
  jalapeño Monterey
  Jack cheese
Tortilla chips
Chopped tomatoes,
  olives, sour cream,
  chopped green onions
  and salsa

Process corn and chicken broth in blender until smooth. Combine with butter, chicken, garlic and cumin in saucepan; mix well. Simmer for 5 minutes, stirring constantly. Stir in milk. Heat to the boiling point; reduce heat. Stir in green chilies, Tabasco sauce and cheese. Simmer until heated through. Ladle over tortilla chips in serving bowls. Top with tomatoes, olives, sour cream, green onions and salsa. Yield: 8 servings.

Karla Wilkinson, Xi Alpha Omega
Story, Wyoming

MONTEREY CHICKEN SOUP

2 cups milk
1 10-ounce can cream
  of chicken soup
2 cups chopped cooked
  chicken or 1 6-ounce
  can chicken
1/4 cup chopped onion
2 tablespoons chopped
  green bell pepper
2 tablespoons chopped
  pimento
Salt to taste
4 slices bacon, crisp-
  fried, crumbled
1 cup shredded
  Monterey Jack cheese
Paprika to taste

Combine milk, soup, chicken, onion, green pepper, pimento, salt and half the bacon in saucepan. Cook until heated through. Stir in cheese until melted. Top servings with remaining bacon and paprika. Yield: 4 to 5 servings.

Pat Windholz, Xi Beta Omicron
Hays, Kansas

MULLIGATAWNY SOUP

1/2 cup chopped onion
1 medium carrot,
  chopped
2 stalks celery,
  chopped
1/4 cup butter or
  margarine
1 1/2 tablespoons
  all-purpose flour
2 teaspoons curry
  powder
4 packets low-salt
  chicken bouillon
4 cups boiling water
1/2 cup chopped cooked
  chicken
1 Granny Smith apple,
  peeled, chopped
1/2 cup cooked rice
1/8 teaspoon thyme
1/4 teaspoon pepper
1/2 cup hot cream

Sauté onion, carrot and celery in butter in skillet. Stir in flour and curry powder. Cook for several minutes. Dissolve chicken bouillon in boiling water in saucepan. Add sautéed mixture; mix well. Simmer for 30 minutes. Add chicken, apple, rice, thyme and pepper. Simmer for 15 minutes. Stir in hot cream just before serving. Yield: 6 servings.

Agnes Jackson, Preceptor Alpha Mu
Tsawwassen, British Columbia, Canada

QUICK HOMEMADE CHICKEN SOUP

I include a loaf of homemade bread or rolls when I take this soup to a sorority sister who is under the weather.

2 10-ounce cans
  chicken broth
3 cups water
3/4 teaspoon thyme,
  dill or tarragon
1/8 teaspoon pepper
3 4-ounce chicken
  breast filets
2 medium carrots,
  sliced
1 medium parsnip, sliced
1 medium turnip,
  peeled, cut into
  1/2-inch pieces
1 medium onion,
  chopped
1 or 2 cloves of garlic,
  minced
1 cup ruffled egg noodles
Parsley sprigs

Bring broth, water, thyme, and pepper to a boil in large saucepan. Rinse chicken and pat dry. Add

chicken, vegetables and garlic to soup. Bring to a boil; reduce heat. Simmer for 10 to 20 minutes or until chicken is tender. Remove and shred chicken. Add noodles to soup. Simmer for 8 to 10 minutes or until noodles are tender. Stir in chicken. Cook until heated through. Garnish with parsley.
Yield: 6 to 10 servings.

Colleen LeBlanc, Xi Gamma
Fredericton, New Brunswick, Canada

SPEEDY WHITE CHILI

1 large white onion, chopped	1 4-ounce can chopped green chilies
1 tablespoon vegetable oil	1 tablespoon garlic salt
1 10-ounce can chicken broth	2 1/2 teaspoons cumin
2 5-ounce cans chicken, drained	2 teaspoons oregano
	2 1/2 teaspoons coriander
2 15-ounce cans Great Northern beans	1/2 teaspoon cayenne pepper

Sauté onion in oil in large saucepan until tender. Add chicken broth, chicken, beans, green chilies, garlic salt, cumin, oregano, coriander and cayenne pepper; mix well. Bring to a boil; reduce heat. Simmer for 15 to 20 minutes or until heated through. May store in airtight container in refrigerator.
Yield: 8 to 10 servings.

Becky Brown, Zeta Beta
Omaha, Nebraska

WHITE CHILI

2 medium onions, chopped	2 48-ounce jars Great Northern beans
1 tablespoon corn oil	5 cups canned chicken broth
4 cloves of garlic, minced	1 12-ounce can light beer
2 4-ounce cans chopped green chilies	4 cups chopped cooked chicken breasts
2 teaspoons cumin	1 1/2 cups shredded Monterey Jack cheese
1 1/2 teaspoons oregano	
1/4 teaspoon ground cloves	Sour cream
1/4 teaspoon cayenne pepper	Salsa

Sauté onions in oil in large saucepan until tender. Stir in garlic, green chilies, cumin, oregano, cloves and cayenne pepper. Sauté for 2 minutes. Add beans, broth and beer; mix well. Bring to a boil; reduce heat. Simmer until of desired consistency, stirring occasionally. Add chicken and cheese; stir until cheese melts. Serve with sour cream and salsa.
Yield: 8 to 10 servings.

Jaci S. Stocking, Xi Iota Epsilon
Defiance, Ohio

SOUPER CHOWDER

1 pound flounder filets	1/4 teaspoon garlic powder
1 10-ounce can cream of potato soup	1/4 teaspoon thyme
1 soup can milk	1/4 teaspoon white pepper
1 teaspoon Worcestershire sauce	Chopped parsley

Cut fish into 1/2-inch pieces. Combine with remaining ingredients in large glass bowl; mix well. Microwave on High for 6 to 7 minutes or until fish flakes easily. Top servings with parsley.
Yield: 4 servings.

Janelle Williamson, Xi Phi Sigma
Texarkana, Texas

RAINBOW SOUP

500 grams haddock, turbot or cod filets	10 milliliters chicken bouillon concentrate
25 milliliters melted butter or margarine	75 milliliters water
125 milliliters thinly sliced carrots	15 milliliters finely chopped parsley
250 milliliters thinly sliced celery	Salt and pepper to taste
	500 milliliters milk
50 milliliters chopped green onions	50 milliliters chopped pimento
75 milliliters all-purpose flour	5 milliliters grated lemon rind

Thaw fish filets partially. Cut into 1-inch pieces. Combine butter, carrots, celery and green onions in glass bowl. Microwave on High for 4 minutes, stirring after 2 minutes. Stir in flour. Add bouillon, water, parsley, salt and pepper. Microwave on High for 3 minutes; mix well. Add fish and milk. Microwave for 7 minutes, stirring after 3 1/2 minutes. Let stand, covered, for 2 minutes. Stir in pimento and lemon rind. Yield: 5 servings.

Marilyn Yardley, Xi Delta Upsilon
Simcoe, Ontario, Canada

CORN AND SALMON CHOWDER

2 tablespoons chopped onion	1 10-ounce can Cheddar cheese soup
2 tablespoons margarine	1 cup milk
1 16-ounce can tomatoes, chopped	1 16-ounce can salmon, drained, flaked
1 12-ounce can whole kernel corn	1 tablespoon chopped parsley

Sauté onion in margarine in large saucepan until tender but not brown. Add tomatoes, undrained corn, soup and milk; mix well. Cook until heated through. Stir in salmon and parsley. Cook until heated through. Yield: 5 to 6 servings.

Frances Kucera, Laureate Omicron
Eugene, Oregon

CRAB BISQUE

This soup always reminds me of home and my mother's wonderful dinner parties.

1 onion, chopped	1 bay leaf
2 tablespoons butter or margarine	8 whole cloves
	1 teaspoon dill
1 10-ounce can tomato soup	1 teaspoon dill
	Salt and pepper to taste
½ cup water	2 ounces sherry or 1 ounce brandy
Juice of ¼ lemon	1 7-ounce can crab meat
1 teaspoon sugar	Cream

Sauté onion in butter in saucepan. Stir in soup, water, lemon juice, sugar, bay leaf and seasonings. Simmer for 10 minutes. Stir in sherry. Simmer for 10 minutes. Discard cloves and bay leaf. Add crab meat. Simmer just until heated through. Add enough cream to make of desired consistency and color. Simmer just until heated through. Yield: 4 servings.

Cheryl Cole, Alpha Pi
Pritchard, British Columbia, Canada

CRAB MEAT AND CORN CHOWDER

½ cup chopped onion	1 teaspoon Worcestershire sauce
½ cup margarine	½ teaspoon MSG
2 tablespoons all-purpose flour	Tabasco sauce to taste
1 pound fresh or frozen crab meat	¼ cup shredded Colby cheese
4 cups milk	¼ cup chopped green onions
1 16-ounce can white cream-style corn	¼ cup chopped parsley
1 10-ounce can cream of potato soup	

Sauté onion in margarine in 4-quart saucepan until tender. Stir in flour and crab meat. Add milk gradually, stirring until smooth. Add corn, soup, Worcestershire sauce, MSG and Tabasco sauce. Simmer for 15 minutes, stirring occasionally. Stir in cheese, green onions and parsley. Serve with salad and crescent rolls. Yield: 6 servings.

Kathy Malone, Eta Iota
West Chester, Pennsylvania

QUICK CLAM CHOWDER

4 10-ounce cans New England-style clam chowder	1 teaspoon salt
	½ teaspoon pepper
4 10-ounce cans cream of potato soup	4 ounces bacon, chopped
	1 small onion, chopped
4 6-ounce cans clams with liquid	½ cup butter or margarine
1 quart half and half	1 2-ounce jar chopped pimento
1 quart milk	¼ cup all-purpose flour

Combine first 7 ingredients in large saucepan; mix well. Simmer for several minutes. Fry bacon with onion in skillet until bacon is crisp; drain. Add to soup with butter. Simmer for 30 minutes. Stir in pimento and flour gradually. Simmer until thickened to desired consistency, stirring frequently. Yield: 12 servings.

Janice Rockvam, Xi Gamma Psi
Fort Collins, Colorado

CRAB MEAT AND SHRIMP SOUP

This was served at the Birthday Sorority Picnic at our Cottage and has become a favorite.

1 10-ounce can tomato soup	4 ounces cooked tiny shrimp
1 10-ounce can cream of mushroom soup	4 ounces fresh mushrooms, sliced
1 soup can milk or half and half	½ teaspoon curry powder
8 ounces crab meat	

Combine all ingredients in large saucepan; mix well. Simmer over medium heat until heated through. Yield: 6 servings.

Gladys Dewey, Preceptor Iota
West Hartford, Connecticut

SLANG JANG

This cold oyster soup recipe has been in my husband's family for more than 80 years. It was originally used as the appetizer course for Thanksgiving and Christmas dinners, but we also like it as a light supper on hot summer nights. The secret seems to be the correct amount of pepper sauce to suit your taste.

1 8-ounce can cove oysters, coarsely chopped	½ to ¾ cup finely shredded cabbage
	1 teaspoon Worcestershire sauce
4 16-ounce cans stewed tomatoes, chopped	6 drops of Tabasco sauce
	1 tablespoon vinegar
½ cup chopped celery	1 tablespoon (or more) pepper sauce
1 tablespoon minced onion	Salt and pepper to taste

Combine all ingredients in 2-quart bowl; mix well. Chill until serving time. Oysters may be drained or undrained, depending on taste. Yield: 6 to 8 servings.

Judee Lyon, Xi Beta Xi
Oklahoma City, Oklahoma

CHEESE AND SHRIMP CHOWDER

1 tablespoon chopped onion	1 16-ounce can tomatoes, chopped
2 tablespoons butter or margarine	Chopped parsley, salt and pepper to taste
1 10-ounce can Cheddar cheese soup	8 ounces fresh or frozen small shrimp
½ cup milk	1 tablespoon sherry

Sauté onion in butter in saucepan until tender. Add soup, milk, tomatoes, parsley, salt and pepper. Cook until heated through. Stir in shrimp and sherry. Simmer for 10 minutes. Yield: 4 servings.

Ivogene Ogle, Laureate Beta Delta
Hillsborough, California

GINGER SHRIMP SOUP

4 cups brown clear chicken stock	Salt and pepper to taste
1 teaspoon ground ginger	6 green onions, chopped
	16 large shrimp, peeled, cooked

Heat chicken stock with ginger, salt and pepper in saucepan until bubbly. Add green onions and shrimp; remove from heat. Let stand for 15 minutes. Heat to serving temperature. Yield: 4 servings.

Sheila Anderson, Laureate Alpha Iota
Ottawa, Ontario, Canada

SHRIMP BALL SOUP

3/4 cup minced shrimp	3 cups chicken or duck broth
1 tablespoon cornstarch	1/4 cup julienned ham
1 1/2 teaspoons sherry or rice wine	2 green onions, slivered
1/2 teaspoon soy sauce	1 1/2 teaspoons cornstarch
1 tablespoon sesame oil	1 tablespoon water
3 dried forest mushrooms	

Combine first 4 ingredients in bowl; mix well. Shape into 20 tiny balls. Brown on all sides in oil in skillet; drain. Soak and shred mushrooms using package directions. Combine with broth in saucepan. Simmer for 10 minutes. Add shrimp balls, ham and green onions. Bring to a boil. Stir in mixture of 1 1/2 teaspoons cornstarch and water. Cook until thickened, stirring constantly. Yield: 3 to 4 servings.

Lynda Edith Pellett, Beta Omega
Menomonie, Wisconsin

ARTICHOKE SOUP

1 cup sliced green onions	1 14-ounce can artichoke hearts
1/4 cup chopped onion	1/4 teaspoon white pepper
2 tablespoons melted margarine	2 tablespoons minced fresh parsley
2 tablespoons all-purpose flour	
1 14-ounce can chicken broth	

Sauté green onions and onion in margarine in large saucepan until tender. Add flour. Stir in broth. Cook for 1 minute or until thickened, stirring constantly. Drain artichokes, reserving liquid. Chop coarsely. Add artichokes, reserved liquid and white pepper to onion mixture. Cook over low heat until heated through, stirring frequently. Ladle into soup bowls. Garnish with parsley. Yield: 2 servings.

Sylvia Barham, Xi Pi
Decatur, Alabama

CREAM OF ASPARAGUS SOUP

My daughter shared this recipe with me.

1 pound fresh asparagus	1/4 cup all-purpose flour
1 cup chicken broth	2 1/2 cups chicken broth
1/4 cup butter or margarine	1/2 cup half and half
	Pepper to taste

Trim asparagus; cut into 1-inch pieces. Cook in 1 cup chicken broth in medium saucepan until tender. Melt butter in large deep saucepan. Remove from heat; stir in flour. Add 2 1/2 cups chicken broth gradually, stirring constantly. Cook over medium heat until slightly thickened, stirring constantly. Add half and half, pepper, asparagus and broth. Cook until heated through, stirring frequently. Yield: 4 servings.

Katherine S. Hill, Preceptor Gamma Eta
Denver, Colorado

MAGIC CHILI BEAN SOUP

Members brought these recipe ingredients to a sorority meeting luncheon and put this together there.

1 medium onion, chopped	1/4 teaspoon oregano
1 teaspoon margarine	1 tablespoon parsley flakes
2 cups water	1 10-ounce package frozen mixed vegetables
2 envelopes low-salt beef bouillon	1 14-ounce can stewed tomatoes
1 14-ounce can low-salt beef broth	1 10-ounce can chicken noodle soup
1/8 teaspoon garlic powder	1 15-ounce can chili beans
1/4 teaspoon basil	

Sauté onion in margarine in skillet for 8 to 10 minutes or until tender. Combine with water, bouillon, beef broth, garlic powder, basil, oregano and parsley in large saucepan. Bring to a boil; reduce heat. Simmer for 5 minutes. Add vegetables and tomatoes. Bring to a boil; reduce heat. Simmer for 5 minutes. Add soup and beans. Simmer for 10 minutes longer. Serve with cornmeal muffins and green salad. May substitute 1 tablespoon onion powder for chopped onion. Yield: 6 to 8 servings.

Dorothy A. Grant, Laureate Omicron
Eugene, Oregon

Valdessa Stuempfle, Laureate Alpha Epsilon, Bloomsburg, Pennsylvania, makes Shrimp Delight Soup by combining 2 cans cream of shrimp soup, 1 can milk and 1 tablespoon butter in bowl. Microwave on Medium until heated through. Season with salt and pepper to taste. Serve with assorted crackers and cheese.

HUSKY BEAN SOUP

A great favorite that takes so little time and is so good.

1 cup cooked ham strips
½ cup chopped onion
2 tablespoons vegetable oil
1 16-ounce can tomatoes, drained
1 14-ounce can baked beans in molasses sauce
¼ teaspoon salt
1 bay leaf
⅛ teaspoon crushed thyme

Sauté ham strips and onion in oil in 1½-quart saucepan until onion is tender. Place tomatoes and beans in blender container. Process until smooth. Pour into ham mixture. Add salt, bay leaf and thyme. Bring to a boil; reduce heat. Simmer, covered, for 20 minutes, stirring occasionally. Discard bay leaf before serving. Yield: 4 to 6 servings.

Alice M. Hoelzer, Laureate Alpha Zeta
Sandusky, Ohio

THREE-BEAN AND VEGETABLE SOUP

This soup is healthy and quick.

1 15-ounce can navy beans
1 15-ounce can pinto beans
1 15-ounce can black beans, drained, rinsed
2 onions, chopped
1 28-ounce can tomatoes, chopped
2 carrots, chopped
3 or 4 stalks celery, thinly sliced
2 envelopes vegetable soup mix
6 to 8 cups water
1 teaspoon pepper
2 tablespoons cumin
½ head cabbage, shredded

Mix beans, onions, tomatoes, carrots, celery, soup mix, water, pepper and cumin in 8-quart stockpot. Bring to a boil; reduce heat. Simmer for 10 to 15 minutes or until vegetables are tender-crisp. Add cabbage. Cook for 10 minutes longer. Serve with corn bread. Yield: 15 servings.

Jo Nell V. Noe, Epsilon Epsilon
Brooksville, Florida

WHITE BEAN SOUP WITH HERBS

1 large onion, chopped
2 cloves of garlic, minced
1 carrot, shredded
1 tablespoon canola oil
2 15-ounce cans Great Northern beans
1 14-ounce can chicken broth
Salt and pepper to taste
1 teaspoon dried sage
¼ teaspoon thyme
Oregano to taste

Sauté onion, garlic and carrot in oil in large saucepan until tender. Add undrained beans and chicken broth. Stir in remaining ingredients. Bring to a boil; reduce heat. Simmer for 5 minutes until heated through, stirring occasionally. Yield: 4 servings.

Vienna Eva Curcio, Beta Mu
Vineland, New Jersey

VERY EASY BORSCH

1 envelope onion soup mix
2 16-ounce cans julienne-style beets
1 16-ounce jar sweet and sour red cabbage
1 11-ounce can beef broth
Sour cream

Prepare onion soup in 4-quart saucepan using package directions. Stir in undrained beets, undrained cabbage and beef broth. Simmer until heated through. Ladle into soup bowls. Top with sour cream. Yield: 8 to 10 servings.

Joan L. DiPippa, Beta Zeta
Berwick, Pennsylvania

BROCCOLI AND CHEESE SOUP

1 medium onion, chopped
2 stalks celery, chopped
3 tablespoons margarine
1 10-ounce can cream of mushroom soup
1 10-ounce can cream of celery soup
1½ soup cans milk
1 10-ounce package frozen chopped broccoli, thawed
1 8-ounce jar Cheez Whiz with jalapeños

Sauté onion and celery in margarine in large saucepan until tender. Add soups, milk and broccoli; mix well. Simmer for 15 minutes. Add cheese. Cook over low heat until cheese melts, stirring frequently. Serve hot. Yield: 6 servings.

Pam Dunn, Xi Upsilon Delta
Mt. Pleasant, Texas

BROCCOLI SOUP

1 10-ounce package frozen chopped broccoli, thawed
2 stalks celery, chopped
1 onion, chopped
1 cup unsalted chicken broth
2 cups skim milk
2 tablespoons cornstarch
¼ teaspoon salt
⅛ teaspoon pepper
⅛ teaspoon thyme
1 ounce Swiss cheese, shredded

Bring first 4 ingredients to a boil in large saucepan. Simmer, covered, for 8 minutes or until vegetables are tender. Mix milk, cornstarch, salt, pepper and thyme in medium bowl. Add to vegetable mixture. Cook over high heat for 4 to 5 minutes until mixture thickens, stirring constantly. Remove from heat. Add cheese, stirring until melted. Yield: 4 servings.

Carolyn Sue Lumm, Xi Alpha Mu
Austin, Arkansas

Nelda M. Donahue, Preceptor Beta Theta, Casa Grande, Arizona, heats 1 can each tomatoes, mixed vegetables, chicken broth, drained okra and drained corn together for a Quick Vegetable Soup.

BROCCOLI CHOWDER

1/2 cup water	1 cup milk
1 10-ounce package frozen chopped broccoli	1 10-ounce can cream of chicken soup
1 medium onion, chopped	1 cup shredded Cheddar cheese
	1/8 teaspoon pepper

Bring water to a boil in 2-quart saucepan. Add broccoli and onion. Simmer, covered, for 5 minutes or until tender; do not drain. Add milk, soup, cheese and pepper. Cook until heated through, stirring frequently. Top with additional cheese if desired. Yield: 4 to 6 servings.

Mary Vannoy, Xi Theta Zeta
Gilbert, Iowa

VERMONT CHEDDAR CHEESE SOUP

This was a great success at a recent sorority potluck supper. Everyone fought over the leftovers!

3 tablespoons butter or margarine	1/2 cup chopped green bell pepper
3 tablespoons all-purpose flour	1/2 cup chopped onion
3 cups chicken broth	2 cups milk, warmed
1/2 cup grated carrot	3 cups shredded Cheddar cheese
1/2 cup chopped celery	

Melt butter in 4-quart saucepan. Add flour, stirring to make roux. Stir in chicken broth gradually. Add carrot, celery, green pepper and onion. Simmer over medium-low heat for 30 minutes. Add warmed milk and cheese. Cook until heated through. Serve immediately. Yield: 12 servings.

Mary E. Schindler, Laureate Alpha Theta
Troy, Illinois

CORN CHOWDER

Wonderful served on a fall or winter evening with grilled cheese sandwiches.

5 slices bacon	1 cup cubed potatoes
1 medium onion, thinly sliced	1 10-ounce can mushroom soup
2 cups cooked whole kernel corn	2 1/2 cups milk
	Salt and pepper to taste

Fry bacon in 5-quart saucepan until crisp; crumble and set aside. Drain saucepan, reserving 3 tablespoons drippings. Sauté onion in drippings until light brown. Add corn, potatoes, soup, milk, salt and pepper. Bring to a boil; reduce heat. Simmer for 1 to 2 minutes, stirring frequently. Ladle into soup bowls; sprinkle with crumbled bacon. Yield: 6 servings.

Alison F. Cox, Delta Alpha
Brunswick, Maryland

CHEESE AND CORN SOUP

1/3 cup finely chopped green bell pepper	2 cups chicken stock
1/4 cup finely chopped onion	1 cup milk
	1 8-ounce can cream-style corn
1 tablespoon butter or margarine	8 ounces cream cheese
1 tablespoon canola oil	Salt and pepper to taste

Sauté green pepper and onion in butter and oil in 2-quart saucepan until tender. Add chicken stock, milk, corn and cream cheese. Simmer until cheese melts, stirring frequently. Season with salt and pepper. Serve hot. Yield: 4 servings.

June Webber, Preceptor Tau
Courtenay, British Columbia, Canada

❖ MINESTRONE SOUP

4 slices bacon, chopped	1 20-ounce can chick peas
1 large onion, chopped	
1 cup chopped celery	1 10-ounce package frozen green beans
2 10-ounce cans beef broth	1 cup chopped fresh parsley
4 cups water	
1 cup uncooked ditalini	1 teaspoon salt
1 32-ounce jar spaghetti sauce	1 teaspoon pepper
	Parmesan cheese
1 cup chopped carrot	

Sauté bacon, onion and celery in skillet until brown; drain. Combine with beef broth and water in 5-quart saucepan. Cook for 20 minutes. Cook ditalini using package directions; drain. Add to broth with spaghetti sauce, carrot, chick peas, beans, parsley, salt and pepper. Simmer for 20 minutes, stirring occasionally. Ladle into soup bowls; sprinkle with Parmesan cheese. Yield: 10 servings.

Marg Barton, Laureate Mu
North Bay, Ontario, Canada

GOURMET FRESH MUSHROOM SOUP

6 medium onions, chopped	1/4 cup all-purpose flour
1/2 teaspoon sugar	1 10-ounce can chicken broth
6 tablespoons butter or margarine	1 1/2 cups water
	1 teaspoon salt
1 pound fresh mushrooms	1/3 teaspoon pepper
	1 cup dry vermouth

Sauté onions with sugar in butter in 3-quart saucepan for 10 minutes or until golden brown. Slice mushrooms caps and chop stems; add to onions. Sauté for 3 minutes. Stir in flour. Add chicken broth, water, salt, pepper and 1/2 cup vermouth. Simmer for 10 minutes. Add remaining 1/2 cup vermouth just before serving. Yield: 6 servings.

Linda M. Hagenson, Laureate Alpha Xi
West Vancouver, British Columbia, Canada

NATIONS' FIVE-CAN HOT SOUP

This is a very spicy soup. To make it milder, decrease the amount of Ro-Tel tomatoes.

1 16-ounce can chili
   without beans
1 16-ounce can whole
   kernel corn, drained
1 10-ounce can Ro-Tel
   tomatoes, drained
1 16-ounce can mixed
   vegetables
1 10-ounce can
   vegetable soup

Combine chili, corn, tomatoes, mixed vegetables and vegetable soup in 2 1/2-quart saucepan. Simmer over medium heat until warmed through. Yield: 4 to 6 servings.

Jane A. Baucum, Mu Master
Texas City, Texas

MICROWAVE FRENCH ONION SOUP

3 medium onions,
   thinly sliced
3 tablespoons butter
2 10-ounce cans beef
   broth
1 1/2 cups water
1 teaspoon salt
1/8 teaspoon pepper
4 slices French bread,
   toasted
1 1/2 cups shredded
   Swiss cheese

Place onions and butter in 3-quart microwave-safe dish. Microwave, covered, on High for 10 minutes, stirring after 5 minutes. Add broth, water, salt and pepper. Microwave, covered, for 8 to 10 minutes. Ladle into microwave-safe soup bowls. Top with bread; sprinkle with cheese. Microwave for 45 seconds to 1 minute or until cheese melts. Yield: 4 servings.

Ginny Thomas, Preceptor Gamma Eta
Merritt Island, Florida

PANTRY SOUP

2 10-ounce cans beef
   consommé
6 cups water
2 cups tomato juice
1 1/2 cups chopped
   carrots
1 1/2 cups chopped green
   onions
1/2 cup chopped fresh
   parsley
Salt and pepper to taste
1 tablespoon sugar
3 cups torn fresh
   spinach
2 12-ounce cans ravioli
   Parmesan cheese

Combine consommé and water in large soup pot. Bring to a boil; reduce heat. Add tomato juice, carrots, green onions, parsley, salt, pepper and sugar. Simmer until carrots and green onions are tender. Add spinach and ravioli. Cook until heated through, stirring gently. Ladle into soup bowls; top with grated Parmesan cheese. Yield: 10 servings.

Barbara McDiarmid, Xi Alpha
Beaconsfield, Quebec, Canada

EASY PEANUT SOUP

This has a different taste that reminds me of peanut butter sandwiches from childhood.

1 1/2 cups cream of
   chicken soup
1 1/2 cups cream of celery
   soup
1/4 cup chunky peanut
   butter
1 1/2 cups water

Combine soups, peanut butter and water in 2-quart saucepan; mix well. Simmer over medium heat for 5 minutes, stirring occasionally. Yield: 4 servings.

Nan Bazemore, Xi Beta Mu
Montgomery, Alabama

CHUNKY CHEESY POTATO SOUP

6 slices bacon, chopped
1 cup chopped onion
2 stalks celery, chopped
1 16-ounce can whole
   potatoes, drained,
   chopped
1/2 cup water
1 10-ounce can cream
   of chicken soup
1/4 teaspoon thyme
1/8 teaspoon pepper
1 cup milk
1 8-ounce jar Cheez
   Whiz

Fry bacon in 3-quart saucepan until crisp. Drain, reserving 2 tablespoons pan drippings. Sauté onion and celery in reserved drippings for 6 minutes or until tender. Add potatoes, water, soup, thyme and pepper. Bring to a boil; reduce heat. Simmer, covered, for 10 minutes. Stir in milk and cheese. Heat until cheese melts. Yield: 4 servings.

Joan Ashford, Xi Kappa Sigma
Arroyo Grande, California

EASY POTATO-CHEESE SOUP

I sometimes add more cooked potatoes to this quick and easy soup.

3 carrots, grated
3 stalks celery, chopped
1 small onion, chopped
1/4 cup margarine
2 10-ounce cans
   chicken broth
2 10-ounce cans cream
   of potato soup
16 ounces Velveeta
   cheese, cubed
1 cup sour cream

Sauté carrots, celery and onion in margarine in 3-quart saucepan until tender. Add chicken broth. Simmer until heated through. Add cream of potato soup and cheese. Simmer until cheese melts and mixture is creamy, stirring constantly. Stir in sour cream just before serving. Yield: 6 to 8 servings.

R. Jeanette Beard, Xi Iota Alpha
Adrian, Missouri

CHEESY POTATO SOUP

4 beef bouillon cubes	1/4 teaspoon celery salt
6 cups boiling water	1 16-ounce package
1 6-ounce jar Cheez	frozen hashed brown
Whiz	potatoes
1/4 teaspoon garlic salt	1 carrot, grated

Dissolve bouillon cubes in boiling water in 6-quart saucepan. Add remaining ingredients. Simmer until potatoes are tender. May omit carrot.
Yield: 6 servings.

Melisa Branch, Xi Sigma Omega
Ozona, Texas

POTATO-VEGETABLE SOUP

7 cups water	1 2-pound package
7 chicken bouillon cubes	hashed brown
1 large onion, chopped	potatoes, thawed
1 10-ounce package	2 cups milk
frozen chopped	2 10-ounce cans cream
broccoli, thawed	of chicken soup
1 10-ounce package	16 ounces Velveeta
frozen mixed	cheese, cubed
vegetables, thawed	Pepper to taste

Combine water, bouillon cubes, onion, broccoli, mixed vegetables and potatoes in 6-quart saucepan. Bring to a boil; reduce heat. Simmer for 30 minutes, stirring frequently. Add milk and soup. Simmer until heated through; remove from heat. Add cheese and pepper, stirring until cheese melts.
Yield: 20 servings.

Gladys Clark, Laureate Alpha Mu
Richland, Michigan

SAVORY POTATO SOUP

3 10-ounce cans cream	2 teaspoons thyme
of potato soup	2 cups shredded
3 soup cans low-fat	Cheddar cheese
milk	1 cup frozen chopped
1 teaspoon salt	broccoli
2 teaspoons savory	

Combine soup, milk, salt, savory, thyme, cheese and broccoli in 3-quart saucepan; mix well. Simmer over low heat for 30 minutes, stirring frequently.
Yield: 6 servings.

Darlene Gudgeon, Xi Alpha Sigma
Thermopolis, Wyoming

EASY CHILLED VICHYSSOISE

3 green onions	1 1/3 cups milk
1 10-ounce can cream	1/4 cup sherry
of potato soup	1/8 teaspoon hot pepper
1 10-ounce can chicken	sauce
broth	

Chop white part of green onions; mince tops. Combine potato soup, chicken broth, milk, sherry, pepper sauce and chopped whites of onions in blender container. Process until smooth. Chill, covered, until serving time. Serve in chilled bowls, sprinkled with minced green onion tops. Yield: 4 servings.

Mary Helen Goldberg, Psi Beta
Plattsburg, Missouri

SOUTHERN CHOWDER

This recipe comes from a dude ranch in Wyoming.

2 slices bacon	1 10-ounce can bean
1/2 cup chopped celery	and bacon soup
1 medium onion,	1 10-ounce can pea soup
chopped	1 16-ounce can
1 clove of garlic, minced	tomatoes, drained
1 teaspoon chili powder	1 1/2 soup cans water

Fry bacon in 2-quart saucepan until crisp; drain on paper towels. Sauté celery, onion and garlic with chili powder in pan drippings until tender. Add soups, tomatoes, water and crumbled bacon. Simmer until heated through. Yield: 6 servings.

Margaret Patterson, Xi Iota Rho
Yucca Valley, California

SQUASH SOUP

1 medium butternut	1 apple, chopped
squash, chopped	6 cups chicken broth
1 cup chopped celery	Half and half
1 carrot, chopped	

Combine squash, celery, carrot, and apple with chicken broth in saucepan. Cook until vegetables are tender. Purée in blender. Combine with enough half and half to make of desired consistency in saucepan. Cook just until heated through. Yield: 6 to 8 servings.

Lynne Lavigueur, Lambda Alpha
Welland, Ontario, Canada

TOMATO-VEGETABLE SOUP

1 onion, chopped	1 tablespoon chicken
2 medium carrots,	bouillon
thinly sliced	1 teaspoon sugar
2 stalks celery, thinly	1 teaspoon basil
sliced	1/2 teaspoon thyme
2 tablespoons butter or	1/2 teaspoon salt
margarine	1/8 teaspoon cumin
4 cups water	1/8 teaspoon pepper
1 28-ounce can	Hot pepper sauce to
tomatoes, chopped	taste

Combine onion, carrots, celery and butter in large glass bowl. Microwave on High for 8 minutes. Add remaining ingredients; mix well. Microwave for 18 minutes or until vegetables are tender. May stir in frozen peas or cooked rice at end of cooking time if desired. Yield: 8 servings.

Linda Main, Laureate Beta Delta
Agincourt, Ontario, Canada

SOPA DE TORTILLA

1 medium onion, chopped	12 cups chicken broth
1 large clove of garlic, chopped	3 4-ounce cans green chilies
2 tablespoons vegetable oil	1/2 teaspoon cumin
4 10-count packages corn tortillas, torn	2 tablespoons seasoning salt
	Monterey Jack or Cheddar cheese

Sauté onion and garlic in oil in saucepan. Add tortillas, broth, chilies and seasonings. Simmer for 30 minutes or until tortillas are tender. Serve with grated Monterey Jack or Cheddar cheese. Yield: 10 to 12 servings.

Ann Welch, Xi Beta
Brandon, Mississippi

ZUCCHINI SOUP

1 medium zucchini, sliced	1 12-ounce can evaporated milk
1 medium onion, chopped	Salt and pepper to taste
1 14-ounce can chicken broth	Butter or margarine to taste
2 chicken bouillon cubes	1/2 to 1 teaspoon chili powder

Cook zucchini with onion in chicken broth in saucepan until tender. Process half the zucchini mixture with 1 bouillon cube and 1/2 can evaporated milk in blender container until well blended. Repeat process. Combine with salt, pepper and butter in saucepan. Stir in chili powder. Cook until heated through. Yield: 4 servings.

Wanda E. Dudley, Laureate Alpha
Albuquerque, New Mexico

CURRIED ZUCCHINI SOUP

1 pound zucchini, thickly sliced	1 14-ounce can chicken broth
1 medium onion, chopped	1 teaspoon curry powder

Cook zucchini and onion in chicken broth in medium saucepan until tender. Purée in blender or food processor. Combine with curry powder in saucepan. Cook just until heated through. Yield: 4 servings.

Marjorie Raiche, Preceptor Iota
Eugene, Oregon

VEGETABLE CHOWDER

3/4 cup canned corn	1/2 teaspoon celery salt
1 1/2 cups canned tomatoes	3/4 teaspoon salt
2 tablespoons chopped parsley	1 1/2 cups hot water
1 teaspoon minced onion	1 1/2 cups evaporated milk
	1 cup cracker crumbs

Combine corn, tomatoes, parsley, onion, seasonings and hot water in saucepan. Simmer for 10 minutes. Add evaporated milk. Cook until heated through. Stir in cracker crumbs. May top servings with additional parsley. Yield: 6 servings.

Ronda Jo McLean, Beta Kappa
Meeteetse, Wyoming

EASY VEGETABLE SOUP

2 14-ounce cans chicken broth	1 10-ounce package frozen Italian vegetables
1/3 cup catsup	1/4 cup uncooked small pasta
2 tablespoons celery flakes	Chopped potatoes (optional)
1 tablespoon chopped onion	
1 teaspoon Italian seasoning	

Bring all ingredients to a boil in saucepan; mix well. Simmer for 30 minutes. Yield: 8 servings.

Norma Brubaker, Laureate Alpha Omega
Wakeman, Ohio

VERMICELLI SOUP

1 14-ounce can chicken broth	1 teaspoon dried onion
1 14-ounce can water	2 teaspoons dried parsley
2 chicken bouillon cubes	2 8-ounce packages vermicelli, broken
1/2 14-ounce can chopped tomatoes	

Combine first 6 ingredients in saucepan. Bring to a boil. Add vermicelli. Cook for 8 minutes.
Yield: 3 to 4 servings.

Joyce Terzian, Preceptor Delta Lambda
Sanger, California

CREAM OF WILD RICE SOUP

This is a big hit with our husbands and at sorority Soup Socials.

1 large onion, finely chopped	1/2 cup margarine
1 carrot, finely chopped	1 cup all-purpose flour
1 stalk celery, finely chopped	8 cups chicken broth
3 slices turkey bacon, chopped	Salt and pepper to taste
	3 cups cooked wild rice
	1 cup light cream

Sauté onion, carrot, celery and turkey bacon in margarine in 4-quart saucepan for 3 minutes. Sift in flour gradually, stirring constantly until smooth but not brown. Add broth slowly, stirring constantly. Add salt and pepper. Stir in rice. Simmer for several minutes. Add cream just before serving. Simmer until heated through. Yield: 10 to 12 servings.

Esther H. Krueger, Laureate Gamma
Dover, Delaware

Speedy Salads

As kids, many of us thought of salads as little heaps of iceberg lettuce, tomato slices and perhaps a bit of cucumber, with an occasional scoop of chicken salad added for lunch. But in the past two decades, salads have gone through a virtual revolution, becoming a mainstay of the American diet. Today's salads include appetizers, main dishes and even desserts, served cold, hot and in-between. Probably no other dish is as versatile, or as popular. For the cook on-the-go, salads have even more appeal. We've brought together salads you can assemble and serve on the spot, and salads you can prepare ahead and use when needed. The ingredients are generally simple (we've even found a popcorn salad!). And, best of all, lots of them can be prepared easily by husbands and children—a real time saver.

AMBROSIA

1 20-ounce can
  pineapple chunks,
  drained
1 11-ounce can
  mandarin oranges,
  drained
1 banana, sliced

1½ cups seedless grapes
1 cup miniature
  marshmallows
½ cup flaked coconut
¼ cup chopped almonds
1 cup vanilla yogurt

Combine pineapple, oranges, banana, grapes, marshmallows, coconut and almonds in bowl; mix well. Fold in yogurt gently. Chill until serving time. Yield: 4 to 6 servings.

Kristie Gray, Epsilon Tau
Stafford, Virginia

APPLE SALAD

2 unpeeled Delicious
  apples, cut into
  wedges
¾ cup grapes, cut into
  halves
⅓ cup chopped nuts

1 cup marshmallows
1 cup low-fat pineapple
  yogurt
2 tablespoons
  mayonnaise-type
  salad dressing

Combine all ingredients in bowl; mix well. Yield: 6 to 8 servings.

Jane Happy, Xi Delta Chi
Camden, Missouri

APPLE-PINEAPPLE SALAD

1 20-ounce can crushed
  pineapple
½ cup sugar
3 tablespoons
  cornstarch
1 tablespoon vinegar

4 cups chopped apples
1 cup chopped celery
1 cup miniature
  marshmallows
Grapes

Combine pineapple, sugar and cornstarch in saucepan. Cook over medium heat until thickened, stirring constantly. Stir in vinegar. Let stand until cool. Stir in remaining ingredients. Yield: 8 servings.

Ruth M. Needels, Preceptor Epsilon Beta
Princeton, Missouri

APPLE-PEA SALAD

Everyone enjoys this interesting combination.

1 cup chopped celery
3 medium Delicious
  apples, peeled, chopped
1 20-ounce can peas,
  drained

½ cup chopped walnuts
½ cup mayonnaise-
  type salad dressing
2 tablespoons milk or
  liquid from peas

Layer celery, apples, peas and walnuts in bowl. Spread with mixture of salad dressing and milk. Stir gently before serving. Yield: 6 servings.

Ethel M. Toovey, Laureate Alpha Mu
Buena Vista, Colorado

CHERRY DELIGHT

This recipe may be used as a salad or dessert.

1 14-ounce can
  sweetened condensed
  milk
1 7-ounce can crushed
  pineapple
1 7-ounce can
  mandarin oranges

1 15-ounce can cherry
  pie filling
16 ounces whipped
  topping
1 cup chopped pecans

Combine all ingredients in bowl in order listed, mixing well after each addition. Chill until serving time. Yield: 8 servings.

Lynn White, Rho Mu
Big Lake, Texas

CRANBERRY AMBROSIA

1 16-ounce can whole
  cranberry sauce
1 14-ounce can
  sweetened condensed
  milk
¼ cup lemon juice

1 20-ounce can
  pineapple, drained
¾ cup chopped nuts
8 ounces whipped
  topping

Combine cranberry sauce, condensed milk, lemon juice, pineapple and nuts in bowl; mix well. Fold in whipped topping gently. Freeze until firm. Remove from freezer 5 minutes before serving. Yield: 12 to 14 servings.

Eleanor Jones, Laureate Alpha Rho
Olney, Illinois

❖ DAIQUIRI SALAD

8 ounces cream cheese,
  softened
1 package custard mix
1 6-ounce can frozen
  daiquiri concentrate,
  thawed

1 8-ounce can crushed
  pineapple, drained
1 cup chopped walnuts
12 ounces whipped
  topping

Combine cream cheese, custard mix, daiquiri concentrate and pineapple in bowl; mix well. Fold in walnuts and whipped topping gently. Yield: 6 to 8 servings.

Betty Morley, Preceptor Eta Kappa
West Covina, California

FIVE-CUP SALAD

1 cup crushed pineapple,
  drained
1 11-ounce can
  mandarin oranges,
  drained

1 cup light sour cream
1 cup flaked coconut
1 cup miniature
  marshmallows

Combine all ingredients in bowl; mix well. Yield: 8 servings.

Dottie Gray, Laureate Delta Tau
Amarillo, Texas

FIVE-MINUTE FRUIT SALAD

1 11-ounce can mandarin oranges
1 8-ounce can pineapple tidbits
1 17-ounce can fruit cocktail
2 cups miniature marshmallows
1 21-ounce can lemon pie filling
8 ounces whipped topping

Combine oranges, pineapple, fruit cocktail and marshmallows in bowl; toss lightly. Fold in pie filling and whipped topping gently.
Yield: 6 to 8 servings.

Delores "Chris" Schmidt, Laureate Delta Pi
Susanville, California

FRUITY-COTTA-WHIP

This is my children's favorite salad. May be made with any flavor gelatin and fruit.

2 cups cottage cheese
1 3-ounce package raspberry gelatin
8 ounces whipped topping
1 cup raspberries

Combine cottage cheese and gelatin in bowl; mix well. Fold in whipped topping and raspberries. Chill until set. Yield: 8 to 10 servings.

Lisa M. Peterson, Kappa Gamma
Grand Island, New York

FRUIT AND CREAM SALAD

This is a favorite at our family reunions.

1 4-ounce package vanilla instant pudding mix
8 ounces whipped topping
1 cup sour cream
1 to 2 cups miniature marshmallows
1 16-ounce can fruit cocktail

Blend pudding mix, whipped topping and sour cream in bowl. Stir in remaining ingredients. Spoon into 2-quart dish. Chill until serving time.
Yield: 8 servings.

Glenys Burdett, Xi Alpha Zeta
Pendleton, Oregon

FRUIT SALAD

1 small package sugar-free vanilla instant pudding mix
8 ounces whipped topping
1 20-ounce can pineapple chunks
1 apple, chopped
1 11-ounce can mandarin oranges
1 cup seedless grapes

Blend pudding mix and whipped topping in bowl. Stir in pineapple. Fold in remaining fruit gently.
Yield: 8 to 10 servings.

Carol S. Boyer, Xi Epsilon Tau
Seymour, Indiana

TROPICAL FRUIT SALAD

1 20-ounce can pineapple chunks
1 4-ounce package French vanilla instant pudding mix
3 bananas, sliced
1 11-ounce can mandarin oranges, drained
1 8-ounce jar maraschino cherries, drained

Drain pineapple, reserving juice. Mix reserved juice and pudding mix in bowl. Stir in pineapple, bananas, oranges and cherries. Yield: 8 to 10 servings.

Marilyn Chaussee, Xi Sigma Omicron
Marysville, California

CREAMY FRUIT SALAD

This is a great potluck recipe for working moms.

1 16-ounce can crushed pineapple, drained
1 16-ounce can fruit cocktail, drained
1 21-ounce can strawberry pie filling
1 14-ounce can sweetened condensed milk
1 cup blueberries
8 ounces whipped topping

Combine all ingredients in bowl; mix well. Chill until serving time. Yield: 10 to 12 servings.

Calla Effa, Xi Zeta
Yorkton, Saskatchewan, Canada

FROZEN FRUIT SALAD

This recipe was given to me by my grandmother, who died this year at the age of 106.

1 21-ounce can apricot pie filling
1 15-ounce can crushed pineapple, drained
2 10-ounce packages frozen strawberries thawed
3 bananas, sliced

Combine all ingredients in bowl. Spoon into 9-by-13-inch dish. Freeze until firm. Remove from freezer 15 to 20 minutes before serving. Yield: 10 to 12 servings.

Jean E. Ewing, Zeta Beta
Omaha, Nebraska

GLAZED FRUIT SALAD

1 8-ounce can pineapple tidbits
2 teaspoons Fruit-Fresh
1 large banana, sliced
1 4-ounce jar maraschino cherries, drained
1 16-ounce can peach pie filling
1 to 2 cups seedless green grapes
1 to 2 cups fresh strawberries

Drain pineapple, reserving juice. Dissolve Fruit-Fresh in reserved juice in bowl. Add banana; toss to coat. Drain banana. Add pineapple and remaining fruit; mix well. Chill until serving time.
Yield: 12 to 15 servings.

Faye Williams, Xi Delta Pi
Kennett, Missouri

KEEBLER SALAD

1 package Keebler
  striped fudge cookies
1 cup buttermilk
1 4-ounce package
  butter pecan instant
  pudding mix

8 ounces whipped
  topping
1 11-ounce can
  mandarin oranges,
  drained

Crumble cookies, reserving a small amount for topping. Mix remaining ingredients in bowl. Top with reserved cookie crumbs. Yield: 10 to 12 servings.

Marian Brunsvold, Xi Delta Theta
Spirit Lake, Iowa

FROSTED LEMON SALAD

2 cups lemon yogurt
1 4-ounce package
  lemon instant
  pudding mix

1 cup flaked coconut
1 8-ounce can crushed
  pineapple, partially
  drained

Blend yogurt and pudding mix in bowl until smooth. Stir in coconut and pineapple. Spoon into 9-by-12-inch dish. Freeze until firm. Remove from freezer 20 minutes before serving. Yield: 16 to 20 servings.

Diane Dovel, Xi Alpha Eta
Luray, Virginia

PEACH SALAD

1 21-ounce can peach
  pie filling
2 bananas, sliced

1 11-ounce can
  mandarin oranges,
  drained

Combine all ingredients in bowl. Chill until serving time. Yield: 8 servings.

Charlotte Foreman, Xi Tau Zeta
Orange, Texas

DELIGHTFUL PEAR SALAD

1½ 16-ounce cans
  pears
1 3-ounce package
  lemon gelatin

8 ounces cream cheese,
  softened
9 ounces whipped
  topping

Drain pears, reserving juice. Chop pears. Bring pear juice to a boil in saucepan over medium heat. Stir in gelatin until dissolved. Remove from heat. Beat in cream cheese. Stir in pears and whipped topping. Spoon into serving dish; chill. Yield: 10 to 12 servings.

Betty Faggard, Laureate Delta Xi
High Island, Texas

PINEAPPLE SALAD

3 ounces cream cheese,
  softened
½ cup lemon juice
1 14-ounce can
  sweetened condensed
  milk

1 16-ounce can crushed
  pineapple, drained
8 ounces whipped
  topping
1 cup chopped pecans

Beat cream cheese and lemon juice in bowl until smooth. Add remaining ingredients in order listed, mixing well after each addition. Chill or freeze until serving time. Yield: 10 servings.

Diane Housenga, Xi Gamma Rho
Thomson, Illinois

PISTACHIO SALAD

1 20-ounce can crushed
  pineapple
1 4-ounce package
  pistachio instant
  pudding mix

2 cups small curd
  cottage cheese
12 ounces whipped
  topping

Mix undrained pineapple and pudding mix in bowl. Stir in cottage cheese and whipped topping. Chill until serving time. Yield: 10 to 12 servings.

Donna Carmichael, Preceptor Kappa
North Syracuse, New York

PUDDING FRUIT SALAD

1 16-ounce can juice-
  pack sliced peaches
1 16-ounce can juice-
  pack sliced pears
1 15-ounce can juice-
  pack pineapple
  tidbits, drained
1 11-ounce can
  mandarin oranges,
  drained

4 red apples, chopped
1 4-ounce package
  vanilla instant
  pudding mix
2 to 3 teaspoons
  Fruit-Fresh
2 bananas, sliced

Drain peaches and pears, reserving liquid. Combine peaches, pears, pineapple, oranges and apples in bowl. Sprinkle with pudding mix and Fruit-Fresh; toss gently. Add a small amount of reserved liquid if needed. Chill until serving time. Stir in bananas just before serving. Yield: 10 to 12 servings.

Sharon L. Gulbrandson, Xi Gamma
Minot, North Dakota

SPEEDY FRUIT SALAD

1 16-ounce can fruit
  cocktail
1 8-ounce can chunk
  pineapple
1 11-ounce can
  mandarin oranges,
  drained

3 to 4 bananas, sliced
2 tablespoons lemon
  juice
1 4-ounce package
  lemon instant pudding
  mix

Combine fruit cocktail, pineapple, oranges, bananas, lemon juice and pudding mix in bowl; mix well. Chill until serving time. Yield: 10 to 12 servings.

Kathy Aufman, Xi Omega Psi
Hewitt, Texas

FROZEN STRAWBERRY SALAD

1 21-ounce can strawberry pie filling	1 16-ounce can pineapple chunks, drained
1 14-ounce can sweetened condensed milk	1 cup nuts (optional)
1 teaspoon lemon juice	16 ounces whipped topping

Combine all ingredients in 2-quart bowl; mix well. Freeze until firm. Thaw slightly before serving. Yield: 10 to 12 servings.

Dorothy Starnes, Xi Nu Theta
Dickinson, Texas

STRAWBERRY SALAD

2 3-ounce packages strawberry gelatin	1 4-ounce package vanilla instant pudding mix
2 cups boiling water	1 1/2 cups milk
1 8-ounce can crushed pineapple	8 ounces whipped topping
1 21-ounce can strawberry pie filling	

Dissolve gelatin in water. Add pineapple and pie filling; mix well. Spoon into 9-by-13-inch glass dish. Chill until set. Mix pudding mix and milk in bowl until thickened. Fold in whipped topping. Spread over congealed layer. Chill until serving time. Yield: 12 servings.

Beverly Long, Preceptor Zeta Gamma
Tampa, Florida

TOFU SALAD SPREAD

This is a delicious vegetarian eggless egg salad. It is good as a sandwich spread, as a garnish on green salads or as a spread for crackers.

1 8-ounce package tofu	3 tablespoons (heaping) mayonnaise
10 green olives, chopped	1 teaspoon prepared mustard
1 medium onion, chopped	
2 stalks celery, chopped	

Mash tofu in bowl. Add remaining ingredients; mix well. Store in refrigerator. Yield: 8 servings.

Verna Fogarty, Theta Preceptor
Selinsgrove, Pennsylvania

PICNIC PIE

This is good for summer barbecues or for potluck dinners.

8 hard-cooked eggs, chopped	Pepper to taste
1/2 cup chopped celery	3/4 cup mayonnaise
2 tablespoons sunflower seed	1 baked 9-inch pie shell, chilled
1 tablespoon bacon bits	1/2 cup shredded Colby or Cheddar cheese
1 teaspoon celery salt	1/4 cup sliced black olives
1/2 teaspoon seasoned salt	

Combine first 8 ingredients in bowl; mix well. Spoon into pie shell. Top with cheese and olives. Yield: 4 to 6 servings.

Jan Rucks, Xi Gamma
Coon Rapids, Minnesota

CHILI SALAD

This was always a favorite with my children and all their friends.

1 20-ounce can chili with beans	1 2-ounce can sliced black olives, drained
1 head lettuce, torn	3/4 cup shredded Cheddar cheese
1 large tomato, chopped	3 cups small corn chips
1 4-ounce package sliced pepperoni	

Heat chili in saucepan until bubbly. Combine remaining ingredients in salad bowl; toss to mix well. Spoon chili over top. Yield: 6 servings.

Linda A. McConnell, Preceptor Iota Sigma
Dallas, Texas

EASY TACO SALAD

1 pound ground beef	1 medium package tortilla chips, crushed
1 15-ounce can kidney beans, drained	1 cup shredded Cheddar cheese
1 head lettuce, chopped	1 8-ounce bottle of Catalina salad dressing
1 bunch green onions, chopped	
4 tomatoes, chopped	

Brown ground beef in skillet, stirring until crumbly; drain. Add beans. Simmer for 5 minutes; cool. Combine with lettuce, green onions and tomatoes in salad bowl; mix well. Add chips, cheese and salad dressing; toss lightly. Serve immediately. Yield: 6 to 8 servings.

Sharon Adams, Preceptor Laureate Theta
Estevan, Saskatchewan, Canada

TACO SALAD SUPREME

2 pounds ground beef	15 black olives, chopped
1 envelope taco seasoning mix	2 canned chili peppers, chopped
1/2 head lettuce, torn	1/2 to 1 cup shredded cheese, (optional)
2 tomatoes, chopped	2 avocados, chopped
2 green onions, chopped	4 taco shells or 1/4 package taco chips, crushed
1 stalk celery, chopped	
2 16-ounce cans dark red kidney beans, drained, rinsed	Catalina salad dressing

Brown ground beef in skillet, stirring until crumbly; drain. Stir in taco seasoning mix using package directions. Combine with remaining ingredients in glass bowl; toss lightly. Yield: 6 to 10 servings.

Dorothy Chamberlain, Xi Tau
New Haven, Connecticut

TACO SALAD

1 pound ground beef	1½ cups shredded cheese
1 envelope taco seasoning mix	1 cup mayonnaise-type salad dressing
¾ cup water	½ cup golden Italian salad dressing
½ to ¾ head lettuce, chopped	1 medium package taco chips
1 large tomato, chopped	
1 bunch green onions, chopped	1 16-ounce can kidney beans (optional)

Brown ground beef in skillet, stirring until crumbly; drain. Stir in taco seasoning mix and water. Simmer until liquid is nearly absorbed; cool. Combine lettuce, tomato and green onions in salad bowl; mix well. Layer cheese and ground beef mixture over salad. Mix salad dressings in bowl. Layer chips, dressing mixture and beans over salad at serving time; toss to mix well. Yield: 6 to 8 servings.

S. Heather Abel, Lambda
Minnedosa, Manitoba, Canada

HAM SALAD

8 ounces medium pasta shells, cooked, drained	1 cup sliced cucumber
	½ cup mayonnaise
	½ cup plain yogurt
1½ cups chopped cooked ham	2 teaspoons Dijon mustard
½ cup sliced celery	1 teaspoon garlic salt
½ cup sliced radishes	Crackers

Combine pasta, ham, celery, radishes and cucumber in salad bowl. Mix remaining ingredients in small bowl. Add to salad; toss to mix well. Chill until serving time. Serve with crackers. Yield: 4 servings.

Anne Munro
Buckeye, Arizona

SMITHFIELD HAM SALAD

Leftover Smithfield ham, ground	Lettuce cups
	Sliced tomatoes
Sweet pickle relish	Wedges of sharp cheese
Mayonnaise	

Combine ham with relish and enough mayonnaise to moisten in bowl; mix well. Spoon into lettuce cups. Serve with tomatoes and cheese. Yield: variable.

Kathy Scarberry, Gamma Tau
Smithfield, Virginia

Nellie Kiel, Laureate Epsilon Upsilon, San Leandro, California, makes a Main-Dish Salad by combining 2 cups shredded carrots, 1 cup dried celery, ¼ cup minced onion, mixture of 1 cup mayonnaise-type salad dressing, ½ teaspoon mustard and 2 tablespoons cream. Add 2 cups chopped cooked chicken, turkey, tuna or ham and 2 cans shoestring potatoes just before serving.

BOMBAY CHICKEN SALAD

This is nice for a summer lunch or supper. It can also be made with leftover chicken or turkey.

2 5-ounce cans chunk white chicken	¼ cup mayonnaise
	2 tablespoons orange juice
1 11-ounce can mandarin oranges, drained	½ teaspoon curry powder
	Salad greens
1 banana, sliced	
Lemon juice	

Combine chicken and oranges in bowl. Sprinkle banana with lemon juice. Add bananas and mixture of mayonnaise, orange juice and curry powder to salad; mix gently. Chill until serving time. Serve on crisp salad greens. Yield: 6 to 8 servings.

Barbara Babb
Seattle, Washington

CHICKEN AND RICE SALAD

My granny won first place with this recipe in a senior adult cooking contest when she was 85 years old.

2 cups chopped cooked chicken	¼ cup mayonnaise
	1 envelope ranch salad dressing mix
2 cups cooked rice	
1 cup chopped celery	½ teaspoon seasoned salt
¼ cup chopped green bell pepper	
	Lettuce cups or tomato shells
¼ cup chopped green onions	

Combine chicken and next 7 ingredients in bowl; mix well. Serve in lettuce cups or tomato shells. Yield: 6 servings.

Sharon Givens, Preceptor Alpha Mu
Benton, Arkansas

CHICKEN TACO SALAD

This is always a hit at our annual salad supper.

2 chicken breast filets	3 cups tortilla chips
1 tablespoon corn oil	3 cups shredded lettuce
½ cup salsa	1 15-ounce can kidney beans, drained, rinsed
1 avocado, mashed	
½ cup mayonnaise-type salad dressing	½ cup chopped tomato
	Shredded Cheddar cheese
½ teaspoon hot pepper sauce	

Cut chicken into pieces. Rinse and pat dry. Stir-fry in oil in skillet or wok over medium-high heat for 4 to 5 minutes or until tender; reduce heat to medium. Stir in salsa. Simmer, covered, for 5 minutes. Mix avocado, salad dressing and pepper sauce in bowl. Layer chips, lettuce, beans, chicken mixture, tomato, avocado mixture and cheese in salad bowl; toss to mix well. Yield: 6 servings.

Cheryl Sheat, Lambda Eta
Lamar, Missouri

CHINESE CHICKEN SALAD

3 chicken breasts
1/4 teaspoon MSG
1 teaspoon salt
1 tablespoon butter or
  margarine
1 head lettuce, shredded
4 green onions, chopped
2 tablespoons chopped
  almonds
2 tablespoons sesame
  seed

1 7-ounce can sliced
  water chestnuts,
  drained
1/4 cup vegetable oil
3 tablespoons vinegar
2 tablespoons sugar
1 teaspoon MSG
1 teaspoon salt
1/2 teaspoon pepper
2 ounces rice chow mein
  noodles

Cut chicken into bite-sized pieces. Rinse and pat dry. Brown with 1/4 teaspoon MSG and salt in butter in skillet. Combine with lettuce, green onions, almonds, sesame seed and water chestnuts in salad bowl. Combine next 6 ingredients in jar; shake to mix well. Add to salad with noodles; toss gently. Serve with hot rolls and dessert. Yield: 6 servings.

Trudy Granot, Preceptor Gamma Rho
Kankakee, Illinois

MARGARET'S CHICKEN SALAD

1/2 cup mayonnaise
2 teaspoons mustard
2 cups chopped cooked
  chicken
1/2 cup thinly sliced
  celery
1 tablespoon finely
  chopped onion
1/2 cup sliced
  mushrooms
1/4 cup chopped green
  bell pepper

1/4 cup chopped black
  olives
1 20-ounce can
  pineapple chunks,
  drained
1 11-ounce can
  mandarin oranges,
  drained
1 cup green or red grape
  halves
Lettuce cups
Croutons

Mix mayonnaise and mustard in salad bowl. Add chicken, vegetables and olives; mix well. Chill in refrigerator. Add fruits; mix gently. Serve in lettuce cups; top with croutons. Serve with croissants and dessert. Yield: 6 servings.

Virginia E. Bryant, Laureate Epsilon
Eagle River, Alaska

TEXAS CHICKEN AND RICE SALAD

3 or 4 medium chicken
  breasts, cooked,
  chopped
4 cups cooked rice
1/2 cup mayonnaise
1/2 cup poppy seed salad
  dressing
1 cup raisins

1/2 cup almond halves
1 11-ounce can
  mandarin oranges,
  drained
1 8-ounce can
  pineapple chunks,
  drained
2 large apples, chopped

Combine chicken, rice, mayonnaise and salad dressing in bowl; mix well. Marinate in refrigerator

overnight. Add remaining ingredients; mix gently. Chill until serving time. Yield: 10 to 12 servings.

Lauren Friend, Alpha Epsilon Beta
Houston, Texas

TURKEY AND RICE FIESTA SALAD

1 cup mayonnaise
1 tablespoon lemon juice
1 4-ounce can chopped
  green chilies
1/4 cup sliced black
  olives
1 tablespoon chili
  powder
1/2 teaspoon salt

2 cups chopped cooked
  turkey
3 1/2 cups cooked rice,
  chilled
Lettuce cups
Chopped tomatoes,
  chopped avocados,
  black olives and chips

Mix first 6 ingredients in bowl. Add turkey and rice; mix well. Chill until serving time. Serve in lettuce cups. Top with tomatoes, avocados, additional olives and chips. Yield: 8 to 12 servings.

Roberta Snead, Xi Rho Xi
Visalia, California

❖ TURKEY SALAD

1 small package
  slivered almonds
1/2 tablespoon butter or
  margarine
2 1-pound packages
  chopped cooked turkey
2 cups cooked long
  grain and brown rice
  mix
2 cups chopped celery

2 tablespoons chopped
  onion
2 cups green grape
  halves
2 11-ounce cans
  mandarin oranges,
  drained
2 cups mayonnaise
2 cups ranch salad
  dressing

Sauté almonds in butter in skillet until golden brown. Combine turkey with remaining ingredients in glass bowl; mix well. Top with sautéed almonds. Chill in refrigerator. Yield: 15 to 20 servings.

Lynn Prasher, Laureate Nu
Menasha, Wisconsin

MACARONI-SALMON SALAD

1 7-ounce package
  elbow macaroni,
  cooked, drained
1 6-ounce package
  snow peas, thawed
1 medium red bell
  pepper, chopped
1 medium yellow bell
  pepper, chopped

1 14-ounce can
  salmon, drained,
  flaked
1/2 cup sliced green
  onions
1/2 cup reduced-calorie
  Italian salad dressing
1/2 teaspoon marjoram

Combine all ingredients in bowl; mix well. Chill, covered, until serving time. Yield: 4 to 6 servings.

Ann M. Lobenstein, Xi Sigma
Tomah, Wisconsin

SEAFOOD AND SHELLS SALAD

This is a wonderful and healthy taste of summer you can enjoy any time.

1 10-ounce package frozen baby peas	3/4 cup plain low-fat yogurt
12 ounces tri-color small pasta shells, cooked, drained	2 tablespoons light mayonnaise
1 cup chopped red bell pepper	1 1/2 tablespoons lemon juice
1/3 cup finely chopped red onion	1 tablespoon Dijon mustard
1/2 cup chopped celery	2 teaspoons dried dillweed or 2 tablespoons chopped fresh dill
1/4 cup chopped parsley	
8 ounces chopped cooked shrimp or seafood flakes	Salt and white pepper to taste
	Cherry tomatoes

Cook peas using package directions for 1 minute; rinse and cool. Combine with pasta, bell pepper, onion, celery, parsley and shrimp in bowl; mix well. Chill in refrigerator. Combine next 7 ingredients in small bowl; mix well. Add to salad; toss gently. Top with cherry tomatoes. Yield: 4 to 6 servings.

Valerie Degnan, Xi Alpha Alpha
Brimfield, Massachusetts

MACARONI AND SHRIMP SALAD

Betty Jane Robinson shared this dish and stories about my father when he died, and I always remember her warmth when I prepare it.

1 cup mayonnaise	2 tablespoons chopped onion
1/4 cup French salad dressing	1/2 cup finely chopped celery
2 cups macaroni, cooked	
2 5-ounce cans tiny shrimp, drained	1/4 cup chopped pimento
2 hard-cooked eggs, finely chopped	1/4 teaspoon paprika
	1/2 teaspoon salt

Combine mayonnaise and salad dressing in bowl; mix well. Add remaining ingredients; mix well. Serve warm or chilled. Yield: 6 servings.

Rita F. Scott, Xi Delta Pi
Kennett, Missouri

SHRIMP-STUFFED AVOCADO

Serve this as an appetizer or with hard rolls as a luncheon or light supper entrée.

1 avocado	1/2 cup shredded Cheddar cheese
Lettuce cups or shredded lettuce	French salad dressing
8 ounces cooked salad shrimp, lobster, crab meat or smoked salmon	

Peel avocado and cut into halves lengthwise; discard seed. Place in lettuce cups on serving plates. Spoon shrimp into centers; sprinkle with cheese. Drizzle with salad dressing. Yield: 2 servings.

Debbie Riley, Xi Eta
Walla Walla, Washington

SHRIMP SALAD

This shrimp recipe is originally from Norway.

1 pound large shrimp, cooked	1/2 cup sour cream
2 Granny Smith apples, chopped	1/2 cup mayonnaise
	Dillweed to taste
	Lettuce cups

Peel and devein shrimp. Cut shrimp into bite-sized pieces. Chill in refrigerator. Combine with next 4 ingredients in bowl; mix well. Serve in lettuce cups. Yield: 4 servings.

Bonnie Jean Ryan, Preceptor Omicron
Sioux Falls, South Dakota

SEAFOOD AND RICE SALAD

Twenty minutes before they sat down to her Beef Wellington dinner, my sister learned that her future mother-in-law did not eat red meat. We quickly prepared this recipe using canned tuna, and she liked it so well that it has been served several times since then.

1 pound cooked shrimp, tuna or crab meat	2 tablespoons chopped onion
3 cups cooked instant rice	1 cup mayonnaise
1 10-ounce package green peas, thawed	1/4 teaspoon lemon pepper
1/2 cup chopped red bell pepper	

Combine all ingredients in bowl; mix well. Serve warm or cold with rolls or crackers. Yield: 6 to 8 servings.

Darlene Rzodkiewicz, Preceptor Alpha Chi
Pittsburgh, Pennsylvania

CHINESE NOODLE-TUNA SALAD

Serve this with crusty hard rolls and iced tea on hot summer days. Leftovers make good sandwiches.

1 6-ounce can tuna, drained	1/2 cup mayonnaise
1/4 cup chopped green onions	1/2 cup sour cream
1 cup chopped celery	1 5-ounce can chow mein noodles
1 cup chopped walnuts	Lettuce cups

Combine tuna, green onions, celery, walnuts, mayonnaise and sour cream in bowl; mix well. Fold in noodles. Spoon into lettuce cups. Yield: 4 servings.

Chris Bielke, Xi Delta Nu
Beaverton, Oregon

LINGUINE-TUNA SALAD

1/4 cup lemon juice
1/4 cup vegetable oil
1/4 cup sliced green
onions
2 teaspoons sugar
1/2 teaspoon Tabasco
sauce
1 teaspoon Italian
seasoning
1 teaspoon seasoned salt

1 7-ounce package
linguine, broken,
cooked, drained
1 12-ounce can white
tuna, drained
1 10-ounce package
frozen green peas,
thawed
2 medium tomatoes,
chopped

Mix lemon juice, oil, green onions, sugar, Tabasco sauce and seasonings in large bowl; mix well. Add hot linguine; toss to mix well. Add tuna, peas and tomatoes; mix lightly. Chill until serving time. Yield: 6 servings.

Bonnie Gayda, Laureate Delta Psi
Scranton, Pennsylvania

TUNA-PASTA SALAD

6 ounces small pasta,
cooked, drained
1 6-ounce can tuna,
drained
3/4 cup mayonnaise
1/3 cup sweet pickle
relish

1/4 cup finely chopped
onion
2 tablespoons chopped
pimento
1 tablespoon mustard
1/4 teaspoon pepper

Combine pasta, tuna, mayonnaise, pickle relish, onion, pimento, mustard and pepper in bowl; mix well. Chill until serving time. Yield: 6 servings.

Patti Skelton, Xi Delta Iota
Canton, Georgia

GOLDEN TUNA SALAD

1/4 cup sliced almonds
2 6-ounce cans tuna
1/4 cup thinly sliced
green onions
1 19-ounce can
pineapple chunks,
drained
1/2 cup sliced celery

1/2 cup mayonnaise
1 teaspoon soy sauce
Ginger to taste
1/4 teaspoon salt
Salad greens
Tomato wedges

Preheat oven to 350 degrees. Sprinkle almonds in single layer in baking pan. Toast for 5 minutes or until golden brown. Drain tuna, reserving liquid. Combine tuna, almonds, green onions, pineapple, celery and 2 or 3 drops of reserved tuna liquid; mix well. Blend mayonnaise, soy sauce, ginger and salt in small bowl. Add to salad; mix gently. Chill until serving time. Serve on salad greens. Garnish with tomatoes. Yield: 3 to 4 servings.

Terry Palmer, Epsilon
Saskatoon, Saskatchewan, Canada

TUNA-CHIP SALAD

My memory of this family recipe is that there was never enough, no matter how big the bowl.

1 head lettuce, torn
2 to 4 stalks celery,
chopped
2 to 4 green onions,
chopped
1/2 green bell pepper,
chopped

1/2 cucumber, chopped
6 to 8 radishes, sliced
1 10-ounce can tuna,
drained
1 medium package
potato chips, crushed
Mayonnaise

Combine lettuce, vegetables and tuna in bowl; mix well. Chill if desired. Add chips and enough mayonnaise to moisten just before serving; mix well. Yield: 6 servings.

Melodie VanderWal, Zeta Omega
Clinton, Ontario, Canada

TUNA SALAD

2 6-ounce cans tuna
1/2 4-ounce can sliced
black olives
1/2 7-ounce can sliced
water chestnuts
2 hard-cooked eggs,
chopped
1/2 cup chopped celery

1 tablespoon pickle
relish
1 tablespoon chopped
onion
1 cup mayonnaise
1/4 cup milk
1 3-ounce can chow
mein noodles

Combine tuna, olives, water chestnuts, eggs, celery, relish and onion in bowl. Add mixture of mayonnaise and milk; mix well. Add chow mein noodles at serving time. Yield: 10 servings.

Lela Watson, Laureate Kappa
Beatrice, Nebraska

SUMMER TUNA SALAD

This recipe is from my mother's 1920 cookbook.

1 large crown summer
squash
French salad dressing
1 head lettuce, torn
1 cup flaked tuna,
chilled
1 cup cooked green
beans, peas or carrots,
chilled

1 cup chopped celery
1 green bell pepper,
minced
2 tomatoes, sliced
2 hard-cooked eggs,
sliced
Mayonnaise
Parsley

Boil or steam squash in saucepan until tender. Scoop out seed and center pulp. Drizzle with French salad dressing. Chill in refrigerator. Place squash on bed of lettuce on serving plate. Combine tuna, beans, celery and green pepper in bowl. Add enough French salad dressing to make of desired consistency; mix well. Spoon into squash. Alternate tomato slices and egg slices in overlapping layer around edge. Garnish with mayonnaise and parsley. Yield: 4 servings.

Dolores Lindell, Xi Phi Phi
Oroville, California

VEGETABLE-TUNA SALAD

1 carrot, thinly sliced
1   10-ounce package
   frozen peas
2 tablespoons minced
   onion
1½ cups water
½ teaspoon salt
⅛ teaspoon pepper
1½ cups instant rice
1   6-ounce can tuna,
   drained
1 cup mayonnaise
¼ cup milk

Bring carrot, peas, onion, water, salt and pepper to a boil in saucepan. Stir in rice. Let stand, covered, for 5 minutes. Fluff with fork. Combine with remaining ingredients in bowl; mix well. Serve warm or chilled. Yield: 6 servings.

Mary Jahnsen, Laureate Theta
Stone Mountain, Georgia

CONFETTI PASTA SALAD

My husband, who professes to hate pasta, first tasted this at a friend's house. He had three helpings that day and now requests this dish at every summer barbecue.

12 ounces uncooked
   tiny shell pasta
1½ cups chopped
   radishes
1½ cups drained canned
   corn
1 cup chopped green bell
   pepper
1 clove of garlic, minced
1 cup mayonnaise
⅓ cup sour cream
1 tablespoon Dijon
   mustard
⅓ cup chopped fresh dill
Salt, cayenne pepper
   and paprika to taste

Cook pasta using package directions for 8 minutes; rinse and drain. Combine vegetables, garlic, mayonnaise, sour cream and mustard in salad bowl; mix well. Add pasta, dill, salt and cayenne pepper; mix well. Garnish with paprika. Chill until serving time if desired. Yield: 8 servings.

Laura Burgess, Xi Delta Upsilon
Simcoe, Ontario, Canada

PASTA SALAD

This is the first dish that I ever saw my husband prepare.

1   16-ounce package
   colored curly noodles
1 red bell pepper,
   chopped
1   16-ounce can black
   olives, drained
1 onion, chopped
3 tablespoons pickle
   relish
1   16-ounce bottle of
   Italian salad dressing

Cook noodles using package directions for 20 minutes; rinse until cool and drain. Combine with red pepper, olives, onion and relish in salad bowl. Add salad dressing; mix well. Chill until serving time. Yield: 10 servings.

Helen Presley, Gamma Alpha Iota
Ontario, California

PERKED-UP PASTA SALAD

This is a great salad for a camp-out.

3 cups cooked rotini
2 cups blanched
   chopped vegetables
   such as broccoli,
   zucchini, carrots and
   red onion
⅔ cup light Italian
   salad dressing
⅓ cup mustard
2 tablespoons minced
   fresh basil (optional)

Combine all ingredients in large bowl; mix well. Yield: 8 servings.

Nivia M. Wilson
Galveston, Texas

EASY CHEESY PASTA

8 ounces uncooked
   colored spiral pasta
Shredded Cheddar
   cheese
½ cup ranch salad
   dressing

Cook pasta *al dente* using package directions. Rinse in cold water until cool and drain. Combine with cheese and salad dressing in bowl; mix well. Chill until serving time. May add flaked tuna or use other salad dressing if desired. Yield: 4 servings.

Kathleen R. Pieper, Xi Alpha Rho
Grand Island, Nebraska

RAVIOLI SALAD

1   9-ounce package
   fresh chicken ravioli
½ cup mayonnaise
½ cup corn oil
¼ cup milk or half and
   half
2 or 3 tablespoons
   Dijon mustard
¼ cup chopped celery
¼ cup each chopped
   green, red and yellow
   bell pepper
¼ cup chopped green
   onions
1 tomato, chopped
1 teaspoon capers
Salt and pepper to taste
Lettuce

Cook pasta in water in saucepan for 3 to 5 minutes. Rinse in cold water and drain. Combine mayonnaise, oil, milk and mustard in bowl; mix until smooth. Add pasta, vegetables, capers and seasonings; mix well. Serve on bed of lettuce. Yield: 4 servings.

Betty Erickson, Xi Epsilon Gamma
Walnut, California

SPAGHETTI SALAD

I served this special salad for my first sorority reveuling and my sisters loved it.

1 pound spaghetti,
   cooked, drained
2 large tomatoes,
   chopped
2 medium green bell
   peppers, chopped
1 large onion, chopped
2 medium cucumbers,
   chopped
1 bottle of salad
   seasoning
1   8-ounce bottle of
   Italian salad dressing

Combine pasta and vegetables in large bowl. Sprinkle with salad seasoning. Add salad dressing; mix well. Chill in refrigerator. Yield: 6 to 8 servings.

Kristi Jenkins, Delta Iota
Somerset, Kentucky

AVOCADO SALAD

Excellent salad with steaks or barbecue.

2 tablespoons vinegar	2 cucumbers, sliced
6 tablespoons peanut oil	1 large red onion,
1 teaspoon dry mustard	chopped
Salt and pepper to taste	3 or 4 avocados, cubed

Combine vinegar, oil, mustard, salt and pepper in small bowl; mix well. Combine cucumbers and onion in salad bowl. Toss with dressing; let stand. Add avocados just before serving; toss to coat. Yield: 4 to 6 servings.

Evelyn Agnew, Delta Delta
Grand Forks, British Columbia, Canada

BEAN SALAD TOSTADA

A healthy, low-fat, quick lunch.

1 16-ounce can chili beans, drained	1/2 cup cottage cheese
	1/4 cup chunky salsa
2 5-inch portions pita bread, split	1/4 cup sliced green onions

Mash beans in bowl with fork. Spread on one side of pita bread. Top with cottage cheese, salsa and green onions. Yield: 4 servings.

Rosa M. Frost, Alpha Alpha
Glasgow, Montana

GOOBER BEAN SALAD

1 16-ounce can red kidney beans, drained	1 large red onion, chopped
1 16-ounce yellow wax beans, drained	2 cups shredded red cabbage
1 16-ounce can green beans, drained	1 7-ounce jar chopped pimento, drained
1 16-ounce can garbanzo beans, drained	1/2 cup vegetable oil
	1 teaspoon salt
1 16-ounce can small green peas, drained	1 cup packed light brown sugar
	1/2 cup vinegar

Combine beans, peas, onion, cabbage and pimento in large bowl; mix well. Whisk oil, salt, brown sugar and vinegar in small bowl. Pour over vegetables, stirring to coat. Marinate in refrigerator; drain before serving. Yield: 10 to 12 servings.

Cheryl Jimerson, Preceptor Beta Iota
Colorado Springs, Colorado

SLOPPY BEAN SALAD

This has been popular at functions for more than 20 years. Easy and yummy!

1 16-ounce can pork and beans, drained	6 green onions, sliced
	12 cherry tomatoes, cut into halves
1/2 cup mayonnaise-type salad dressing	Salt and pepper to taste
1/2 cup crumbled crisp-fried bacon	2 dashes of Tabasco sauce

Combine all ingredients in large bowl; mix well. Chill before serving. May double or triple recipe for large functions. Yield: 6 servings.

Sharla Logan, Xi Delta Kappa
Scott City, Kansas

BROCCOLI-CHEESE-RAISIN SALAD

1 bunch broccoli, chopped	3/4 cup mayonnaise
	1/4 cup sugar
1 cup shredded Cheddar cheese	1/4 cup vinegar
	1/2 to 1 cup cashew halves
1 cup golden raisins	

Combine broccoli, cheese and raisins in large bowl. Combine mayonnaise, sugar and vinegar in small bowl; mix well. Pour over broccoli mixture. Toss well to coat. Chill until serving time. Sprinkle with cashew halves. Yield: 6 servings.

Cindy Stanphill, Xi Beta
Boise, Idaho

BROCCOLI AND MANDARIN ORANGE SALAD

1 egg plus 1 egg yolk	6 slices crisp-fried bacon, crumbled
1 1/2 teaspoons cornstarch	1/2 cup slivered almonds, toasted
1/4 cup tarragon vinegar	1/2 cup raisins
1/2 cup sugar	2 cups sliced mushrooms
1 teaspoon dry mustard	1 11-ounce can mandarin oranges, drained
1/4 cup water	
3 tablespoons margarine	
1/2 cup mayonnaise	1/2 large red onion, sliced
4 cups broccoli flowerets	

Combine egg, yolk, cornstarch, vinegar, sugar, mustard and water in saucepan; mix well. Cook over low heat until thickened, stirring constantly. Add margarine and mayonnaise; beat well. Chill in refrigerator. Combine broccoli, bacon, almonds, raisins, mushrooms, oranges and onion in large salad bowl; mix well. Pour dressing over vegetables, tossing well to coat. Yield: 6 to 8 servings.

Jane Wildoner, Beta Master
Wilmington, Ohio

FRESH BROCCOLI SALAD

1 envelope Italian salad
   dressing mix
1 bunch broccoli,
   chopped
1 15-ounce can kidney
   beans, drained

1 cup shredded sharp
   Cheddar cheese
1 small red onion, finely
   chopped

Prepare salad dressing using package instructions. Pour over broccoli, kidney beans, cheese and onion in large bowl; mix well. Chill, covered, in refrigerator until serving time. Yield: 8 servings.

Leanna Tanner, Kappa Nu
Du Quoin, Illinois

WARM BROCCOLI SALAD

Flowerets of 1 bunch
   broccoli
4 slices bacon
1/2 cup sliced green
   onions
1/2 cup vinegar
1 teaspoon sugar
1/2 teaspoon salt

1/4 teaspoon pepper
1 8-ounce can sliced
   water chestnuts,
   drained
1 2-ounce jar sliced
   pimento, drained
1 hard-cooked egg,
   chopped

Blanch broccoli in boiling water for 1 minute. Drain and plunge into ice water. Drain; pat dry. Fry bacon in skillet until crisp. Remove to paper towel to drain; crumble and set aside. Add onions, vinegar, sugar, salt, pepper and water chestnuts to pan drippings. Bring to a boil, stirring constantly. Add broccoli and pimento. Cook until heated through. Spoon into serving bowl; sprinkle with crumbled bacon and egg. Yield: 6 to 8 servings.

Emma Doubet, Laureate Omega
Kirksville, Missouri

CRUNCHY BROCCOLI AND CAULIFLOWER SALAD

3 cups chopped
   cauliflowerets
3 cups chopped broccoli
   flowerets
1 8-ounce can sliced
   water chestnuts,
   drained
8 ounces fresh
   mushrooms, sliced

1 cup mayonnaise
1 cup sour cream
1 envelope Uncle Dan's
   salad dressing mix
1 10-ounce package
   frozen peas, thawed

Combine cauliflowerets, broccoli, water chestnuts and mushrooms in large salad bowl. Combine mayonnaise, sour cream and dressing mix in small bowl; mix well. Pour over vegetables. Add peas; toss gently to coat. Chill, covered, until serving time. Yield: 6 to 8 servings.

Becky Wilkins, Preceptor Omicron
Royal City, Washington

ZESTY SALAD

2 cups cherry tomatoes,
   cut into halves
8 ounces fresh
   mushrooms, sliced
1 small red onion, sliced

3 bunches broccoli,
   chopped
1 8-ounce bottle of
   zesty Italian salad
   dressing

Combine vegetables and salad dressing in large bowl. Cover; shake well. Chill in refrigerator; shake again before serving. Yield: 10 servings.

Jacquelyn M. Dillard, Preceptor Iota
Henderson, Nevada

BARBECUED MARINATED CABBAGE SALAD

1 head green cabbage,
   shredded
1 head red cabbage,
   shredded
1 4-ounce jar chopped
   pimentos, drained

2 green bell peppers,
   chopped
1 small onion, chopped
1/2 cup honey
1/2 cup vegetable oil
1/2 cup vinegar

Combine vegetables in large bowl; mix well. Bring honey, oil and vinegar to a boil in saucepan, stirring constantly. Pour over vegetables; toss well to coat. Serve with barbecue or meats. Yield: 12 servings.

Rita Kincheloe, Alpha Psi Zeta
Lampasas, Texas

BLEU CHEESE COLESLAW

1/3 cup vegetable oil
1/3 cup sugar
1/3 cup vinegar
Celery seed to taste

Onion powder to taste
4 ounces bleu cheese
1 head cabbage,
   shredded

Combine oil, sugar, vinegar, celery seed and onion powder in bowl; mix well. Crumble in bleu cheese. Pour over shredded cabbage in large bowl, tossing well to coat. Yield: 6 servings.

Elizabeth Brennan, Zeta Pi
Iowa City, Iowa

COLESLAW

2 6-ounce packages
   coleslaw mixture
2 4-ounce packages
   slivered almonds,
   toasted
6 green onions, sliced
2 3-ounce packages
   chicken-flavored
   ramen noodles

1/2 cup sugar
1 cup vegetable oil
1/4 cup cider vinegar
1/2 teaspoon each salt
   and pepper

Combine coleslaw mixture, almonds and green onions in large bowl; sprinkle with broken ramen noodles, reserving seasoning packet. Combine sugar, oil, vinegar, salt, pepper and seasoning packets in bowl; mix well. Spoon over coleslaw mixture; toss well to coat. Yield: 8 to 10 servings.

Mary R. Jackson, Xi Delta Theta
West Palm Beach, Florida

SPICY COLESLAW

1 head cabbage, shredded
1 16-ounce can black-eyed peas
½ cup chopped roasted peanuts
1 to 2 pickled jalapeño peppers, seeded, minced
¼ cup white wine vinegar
2 tablespoons soy sauce
1 teaspoon ginger
2 tablespoons olive oil
6 tablespoons peanut oil
Salt and pepper to taste

Combine cabbage, black-eyed peas, peanuts and peppers in salad bowl; mix well. Whip vinegar, soy sauce, ginger and olive oil in small bowl. Add peanut oil in thin stream, whisking until well mixed. Pour over vegetables, tossing to coat. Chill until serving time. Yield: 8 servings.

L. J. Clark, Xi Beta Nu
Albuquerque, New Mexico

LOW-CALORIE CARROT SLAW

½ to ⅔ cup light sour cream
1 teaspoon ground cumin
½ teaspoon ground coriander
Pinch of cayenne pepper
3 cups coarsely grated carrots
¼ cup chopped fresh coriander, parsley or green onions

Combine sour cream, cumin, ground coriander and cayenne pepper in large bowl; mix well. Add carrots, fresh coriander and additional sour cream if needed; mix well. Chill, covered, until serving time. Yield: 4 to 6 servings.

Alice Cardinal, Laureate Mu
North Bay, Ontario, Canada

COCONUT-CARROT SALAD

1⅓ cups flaked coconut
1½ cups shredded carrots
½ cup mayonnaise
¼ cup raisins
2 tablespoons lemon juice
½ teaspoon ground ginger
4 to 8 lettuce leaves

Combine coconut, carrots, mayonnaise, raisins, lemon juice and ginger in large bowl; mix well. Chill until serving time. Serve on crisp lettuce leaves. Yield: 4 servings.

Lettie Loveleen Turner, Preceptor Zeta Tau
Orange Park, Florida

CASHEW SWEET AND SOUR SALAD

⅓ cup sugar
1 teaspoon salt
1 teaspoon dry mustard
1 teaspoon grated onion
¼ cup wine vinegar
1 cup peanut oil
1 bunch romaine lettuce
4 cups fresh spinach
1 6-ounce can cashews
1 tablespoon celery seed

Combine sugar, salt, mustard, onion, vinegar and oil in small bowl; mix well. Pour over mixture of lettuce and spinach in large salad bowl, tossing well to coat. Sprinkle with cashews and celery seed. Yield: 6 to 8 servings.

Adine Kownacky, Xi Alpha
Honolulu, Hawaii

CHILI SALAD

Delicious with broiled chicken or fish.

1 large bottle Burnstein dressing
1 teaspoon (heaping) minced garlic
1 to 2 teaspoons oregano
1 teaspoon cumin
½ teaspoon cayenne pepper
½ to 1 teaspoon chili powder
1 head lettuce, shredded
1 16-ounce can garbanzo beans, drained
1 9-ounce jar artichoke hearts, drained, chopped
1 14-ounce can hearts of palm, drained, chopped
Cheddar cheese, shredded
French-fried onion rings

Combine dressing, garlic, oregano, cumin, cayenne pepper and chili powder in bowl; mix well. Combine lettuce, beans, artichokes and hearts of palm in large salad bowl; mix well. Add dressing, tossing to coat. Garnish with cheese and onion rings. Yield: 6 servings.

Shirley Fitch, Preceptor Rho
Flagstaff, Arizona

MOCK CAESAR SALAD

1 cup low-fat mayonnaise
2 cloves of garlic, crushed
2 tablespoons lemon juice
2 tablespoons grated Parmesan cheese
1 teaspoon Dijon mustard
Salt and pepper to taste
2 bunches romaine lettuce
½ cup Melba toast crumbs
1 cup cauliflowerets

Combine mayonnaise, garlic, lemon juice, cheese, mustard, salt and pepper in small bowl; mix well. Pour over lettuce, tossing to coat. Top with toast crumbs and cauliflowerets. Yield: 6 to 8 servings.

Lynda Sheltmire, Delta Chi
Denver, Colorado

COLD CORN SALAD

This recipe was handed down from my grandmother to my mother to me.

1/4 cup sour cream	1/8 teaspoon pepper
1/4 cup mayonnaise	1/2 cup chopped onion
1 tablespoon prepared mustard	1 2-ounce jar chopped pimento, drained
2 teaspoons white vinegar	1 17-ounce can whole kernel corn, drained
1 teaspoon sugar	2 carrots, grated
1/4 teaspoon salt	

Combine sour cream, mayonnaise, mustard, vinegar, sugar, salt and pepper in large bowl; mix well. Add onion, pimento, corn and carrots; toss to coat. Chill until serving time. May make ahead of time and store for 2 to 3 days. Yield: 8 servings.

Jimi Hadley, Xi Beta Xi
Oklahoma City, Oklahoma

SHOE PEG CORN SALAD

1/2 cup canola oil	1 16-ounce can small green peas, drained
1 tablespoon water	
3/4 cup white vinegar	1 16-ounce can French-style green beans, drained
1 cup sugar	
Salt and pepper to taste	
1 cup chopped celery	1 8-ounce can sliced water chestnuts, drained
1 cup chopped green onions	
1 cup chopped white onion	1 2-ounce jar chopped pimento, drained
1 16-ounce can Shoe Peg corn, drained	

Mix oil, water, vinegar, sugar, salt and pepper in saucepan. Bring to a boil, stirring well; cool slightly. Pour over mixture of vegetables in large salad bowl; mix well. Chill until serving time. Yield: 8 servings.

Mary Jane Avinger, Laureate Beta Omicron
Harlingen, Texas

GARBAGE SALAD

1/2 cup sliced zucchini	1/2 head cauliflower, chopped
1/2 cup chopped artichoke hearts	1 bunch green onions, sliced
1 6-ounce can black olives, drained	1 avocado, chopped
1 4-ounce jar green olives, drained	1 8-ounce can sliced mushrooms, drained
1 bunch broccoli, chopped	4 to 6 carrots, sliced
1 small tomato, chopped	1 8-ounce bottle of Italian dressing

Combine all vegetables in large salad bowl. Pour in dressing; toss well to coat. Chill until serving time. Yield: 6 servings.

Julie K. Boettcher, Beta Iota
Custer, South Dakota

GAZPACHO SALAD

1/2 cup vegetable oil	1 large cucumber, sliced, quartered
1 large clove of garlic, minced	1 small green bell pepper, coarsely chopped
3/4 teaspoon salt	
1/4 teaspoon each cayenne pepper and ground cumin	3 ripe tomatoes, chopped
2 teaspoons minced cilantro	1 large avocado, chopped
1 tablespoon minced onion	1 1/2 cups shredded Monterey Jack cheese
Freshly ground black pepper to taste	1 4-ounce can sliced black olives, drained
Juice of 1 lime	Crushed tortilla chips

Combine oil, garlic, salt, cayenne pepper, cumin, cilantro, onion, black pepper and lime juice in bowl; mix well. Combine cucumber, green pepper, tomatoes, avocado, cheese and olives in salad bowl. Toss with dressing to coat. Garnish with chips. Yield: 4 to 6 servings.

Michelle Young, Alpha Alpha Gamma
Redding, California

INSTANT ITALIAN SUMMER SALAD

This is so easy I can prepare it after work and still arrive at the sorority meeting on time. A big hit at the year-end Sorority Salad Supper.

1 8-ounce can black olives, drained	4 cups cherry tomatoes, cut into halves
2 6-ounce jars marinated artichoke hearts	1 6-ounce jar marinated mushrooms
	1 teaspoon basil

Combine olives, undrained artichoke hearts, tomatoes and undrained mushrooms in large bowl; mix well. Stir in basil. Chill, covered, until serving time. Yield: 6 to 10 servings.

Joanne Rossa, Preceptor Mu Tau
Austin, Texas

JICAMA AND CARROT SALAD

1 jicama, peeled, cut into julienne strips	1/2 cup mayonnaise
1 carrot, grated	1/4 teaspoon salt
Zest and juice of 1 lime	2 tablespoons chopped parsley

Combine jicama, carrot and lime zest in bowl. Stir in lime juice, mayonnaise and salt. Sprinkle parsley over top. Chill until serving time. Yield: 4 servings.

Ann Robinson, Preceptor Laureate Alpha Pi
Arlington, Texas

HOT PEA SALAD

1 10-ounce package
   frozen peas
6 slices crisp-fried
   bacon, crumbled
1/2 cup sliced green
   onions

Pepper and mayonnaise
   to taste
1 hard-cooked egg,
   chopped

Microwave peas in package on High for 4 to 5 minutes; drain. Combine with bacon, green onions, pepper and enough mayonnaise to moisten in bowl; mix well. Garnish with chopped egg. Serve hot or cold. Yield: 4 servings.

Theda Mills, Preceptor Beta Lambda
Springfield, Oregon

SNOW PEA AND MANGO SALAD

An easy, colorful salad that goes well with chicken or barbecued pork.

1 pound snow peas,
   trimmed
2 mangos, peeled,
   thinly sliced
1/2 cup chopped red bell
   pepper

3 tablespoons lemon or
   lime juice
Salt and pepper to taste
1/2 cup vegetable oil

Blanch snow peas for 1 minute. Drain and rinse with cold water. Combine with mangos and red pepper in large salad bowl. Combine lemon juice, salt, pepper and oil in small bowl; whisk until well mixed. Pour over snow pea mixture; toss well to coat. Yield: 6 servings.

Fran J. Green, Laureate Alpha Sigma
Vancouver, British Columbia, Canada

❖ POPCORN SALAD

12 cups popped popcorn
1 1/2 cups chopped green
   onions
1 1/2 cups chopped celery
1 1/2 cups shredded
   longhorn cheese

1 red bell pepper,
   chopped
1 pound bacon, crisp-
   fried, crumbled
1/2 cup mayonnaise

Toss all ingredients together in large bowl. Serve immediately. Yield: 10 servings.

Donna J. Myers, Xi Chi Epsilon
La Habra, California

HOT GERMAN POTATO SALAD

4 to 6 medium potatoes
6 to 8 slices bacon, cut
   into 1-inch pieces
2 tablespoons
   all-purpose flour
1/4 cup sugar

1 1/2 teaspoons salt
1/2 teaspoon celery seed
1/8 teaspoon pepper
1 cup water
1/2 cup vinegar

Pierce potatoes with fork; place on paper towels in microwave. Microwave on High for 10 minutes, turning once. Peel; slice 1/8 inch thick. Place bacon in 2-quart glass casserole; cover with paper towel. Microwave for 6 minutes, stirring once. Remove to paper towels to drain. Stir flour and seasonings into bacon drippings until smooth. Microwave for 1 to 2 minutes or until bubbly, stirring once. Add water and vinegar; mix well. Microwave for 4 minutes or until mixture boils and thickens, stirring once. Add potatoes and bacon; stir gently. Let stand, covered, until serving time. Yield: 4 to 6 servings.

Marilyn A. Reitmeyer, Preceptor Gamma Nu
Pittsburgh, Pennsylvania

POTATO AND BEAN SALAD

4 red potatoes, cooked,
   cut into quarters
8 ounces green beans,
   sliced, cooked

Basil, chives, seasoned
   salt to taste
Ranch salad dressing to
   taste

Combine potatoes, beans, seasonings and enough salad dressing to moisten in large bowl; mix well. Chill until serving time. Yield: 6 servings.

Margo Boles, Preceptor Eta Psi
San Diego, California

ITALIAN POTATO SALAD

This is an original Italian recipe brought from Italy in 1911 by my grandmother.

5 pounds potatoes,
   cooked, peeled, cubed
1 pound fresh green
   beans, cooked, sliced
1 medium onion, thinly
   sliced

1 cup chopped celery
1 cup chopped parsley
2 tomatoes, chopped
1/4 cup vinegar
1/2 cup olive oil
Salt and pepper to taste

Mix potatoes, beans, onion, celery, parsley, tomatoes, vinegar and oil in large bowl. Sprinkle with salt and pepper. Serve hot or cold. Yield: 8 servings.

Angela Theobald, Laureate Alpha Lambda
Bradenton, Florida

SELF-ESTEEM SALAD

The beauty of this recipe is that it can be increased or decreased to adjust serving quantities. People always call me to ask for the details of this "exotic" salad— makes me feel like a great cook!

1 head Iceberg lettuce,
   torn into pieces
1/4 cup chopped onion
1/4 cup grated Parmesan
   cheese

1/4 cup salad olives
1/2 cup croutons
1/4 cup oil-based Italian
   salad dressing

Combine lettuce, onion, cheese, olives and croutons in salad bowl. Add salad dressing; toss to coat. Yield: 4 to 5 servings.

Joan O'Loughlin, Xi Delta Epsilon
St. Peters, Missouri

SWEET AND SOUR SPINACH SALAD

1/2 cup vegetable oil	8 ounces tofu, cubed
1/2 cup cider vinegar	1 pound fresh spinach,
1/4 cup sugar	torn into pieces
3 tablespoons soy sauce	1 cup bean sprouts,
1 teaspoon salt	rinsed and drained
2 teaspoons ground	1 cup thinly sliced celery
ginger	6 slices crisp-fried
1/4 teaspoon pepper	bacon, crumbled
3/4 cup thinly sliced	3 hard-cooked eggs,
onion	sieved

Combine oil, vinegar, sugar, soy sauce, salt, ginger and pepper in small bowl; whisk briskly. Add onion and tofu; stir and set aside. Combine spinach, bean sprouts, celery and bacon in large bowl. Pour in dressing, tossing to coat. Garnish with eggs. Yield: 4 servings.

Daphene D. Miller, Preceptor Epsilon Beta
Princeton, Missouri

TEXAS TREASURE

This interesting recipe is named after a Texas friend who gave us the recipe. I make it up the night before and it's ready to serve instantly.

1 16-ounce can sweet	2 cups finely chopped
potatoes, drained	celery
1 20-ounce can	1 onion, finely chopped
pineapple chunks,	1 cup chopped pecans
drained	1 teaspoon salt
1 11-ounce can	3/4 cup mayonnaise
mandarin oranges,	3/4 cup sour cream
drained	1 to 1 1/2 teaspoons
1 8-ounce can sliced	curry powder
water chestnuts,	Flaked coconut
drained	

Layer sweet potatoes, pineapple, oranges, water chestnuts, celery, onion and pecans in large bowl; sprinkle with salt. Do not stir. Combine mayonnaise, sour cream and curry powder in small bowl; mix well. Chill salad and sauce overnight. Pour sauce over salad just before serving; toss to coat; sprinkle with coconut. Yield: 6 servings.

Lisa Rodger, Delta Xi
Brampton, Ontario, Canada

FRESH TOMATO SALAD

1/4 cup chopped parsley	2 teaspoons sugar
1/4 cup vegetable oil	1/2 teaspoon salt
2 tablespoons cider	Dash of pepper and
vinegar	garlic powder
2 teaspoons prepared	6 tomatoes, sliced
mustard	

Combine parsley, oil, vinegar, mustard, sugar, salt, pepper and garlic powder in small bowl; mix well.

Pour over sliced tomatoes in bowl. Let stand, covered, until serving time. Yield: 8 to 10 servings.

Marlys Montz, Preceptor Alpha Epsilon
Marshalltown, Iowa

MARINATED TOMATOES

3 large tomatoes,	2 tablespoons chopped
thickly sliced	onion
1/3 cup olive oil	1 tablespoon chopped
1/4 cup red wine vinegar	fresh parsley
1 teaspoon salt	1 tablespoon chopped
1/4 teaspoon pepper	fresh basil or 1
1/2 clove of garlic,	teaspoon dried basil
minced	

Arrange tomatoes in large shallow dish. Combine remaining ingredients in covered jar. Shake to mix well. Pour over tomato slices. Chill, covered, until serving time. Yield: 8 servings.

Patricia L. Fondroy, Theta Iota
Cherokee, Iowa

PAUL'S BREW

12 tomatoes, chopped	Olive oil and vinegar
2 cucumbers, chopped	salad dressing
5 scallions, chopped	Salt and pepper to taste

Combine tomatoes, cucumbers, scallions, salad dressing and seasonings in salad bowl; toss well to coat. Yield: 10 servings.

Vivian Humphries-Koser, Epsilon Epsilon
Brooksville, Florida

HIGH-PROTEIN SALAD

This is a fast and easy recipe to serve during the summer, when it's too hot to cook.

4 cups cooked rice	1 teaspoon lemon pepper
1 16-ounce can chick	2 tablespoons chopped
peas or red kidney	parsley
beans, drained	1/4 cup peanut oil
1 16-ounce can whole	2 tablespoons vinegar
kernel corn, drained	or lemon juice
1 tablespoon minced	1/2 teaspoon salt
onion	1 teaspoon turmeric

Combine all ingredients in large bowl; mix well. Chill until serving time. Yield: 6 servings.

Anneliese Bartelt, Xi Beta Delta
Kamloops, British Columbia, Canada

Deborah A. Kapchinske, Eta Mu, Acworth, Georgia, prepares Warehouse Salad Dressing by combining 1 teaspoon each prepared mustard, summer savory, parsley flakes, dillweed and salt, 1/3 cup sugar and 1/3 cup red wine vinegar in blender container. Blend well and add 1 cup salad oil gradually, processing constantly.

Very Rapid Veggies

For generations there have been two main schools of thought on veggies: the cook-'em-slow-with-all-the-trimmings school, and the cook-'em-quick-with-nothing-added proponents. In general, quick meant crisp, healthy and—too often—boring; slow meant delicious, but time-consuming. While frozen and canned vegetables have long been a mainstay of the hurried/harried cook, all of us have a tough time coming up with new ways to dress up those old standbys. Fortunately, there is another alternative to plainly cooked produce: the cook-'em-easy-and-quick-but-still-delicious approach. Mushrooms in-a-minute? Sure. Spinach in-two-shakes? Easy. Zucchini in-a-zip? Rice on-the-run? Broccoli to-beat-the-clock? You bet. And if you think we're talking plain old steamed or straight-off-the-shelf vegetables, you'll be dazzled by what you'll find. There's nothing "garden variety" about *these* veggies.

ARTICHOKE AND SPINACH SOUFFLÉS

We serve these with smoked turkey, honey ham and green chili cheese grits every New Year's for our Open House.

1 16-ounce can
   artichoke bottoms
1 package frozen
   spinach soufflé,
   thawed
1 cup sour cream
1 lemon
1 hard-cooked egg,
   chopped

Preheat oven to 375 degrees. Rinse and drain artichoke bottoms; place on baking sheet. Place 1 scoop of spinach soufflé on each artichoke. Bake for 10 minutes or until soufflé is puffy and golden brown. Place a dollop of sour cream on each; drizzle with lemon juice. Sprinkle chopped egg over top; spoon onto serving plate. Yield: 6 servings.

Shirley Richardson, Preceptor Beta Beta
Albuquerque, New Mexico

ASPARAGUS AND MUSHROOMS

Add some thinly sliced chicken with the asparagus to use as a main course.

1 pound fresh
   mushrooms
1 pound fresh asparagus
8 thin slices fresh
   gingerroot
1/4 cup vegetable oil
Salt and pepper to taste
1/4 teaspoon sugar

Slice mushrooms. Cut asparagus into diagonal slices. Chop gingerroot. Stir-fry asparagus and gingerroot in vegetable oil in wok or skillet over medium heat for 1 minute. Sprinkle with salt. Add mushrooms, pepper and sugar. Stir-fry for 1 minute longer. Yield: 4 servings.

Ethel Armitage, Laureate Gamma
Delta, British Columbia, Canada

BROCCOLI WITH ALMONDS

Flowerets of 2 pounds
   fresh broccoli
1/4 cup sliced almonds
1/4 cup margarine
Salt and pepper to taste

Cook broccoli in 1 inch boiling water in saucepan for 10 minutes; drain. Place in serving bowl. Sauté almonds in margarine in skillet until golden brown. Spoon onto broccoli. Add salt and pepper to taste. May be prepared ahead and placed in microwave-safe dish. Reheat, covered with vented plastic wrap, in microwave just before serving. Yield: 4 to 6 servings.

Myrt Mortimore, Preceptor Epsilon Nu
San Angelo, Texas

BROCCOLI-CHEESE BAKE

My family enjoys this recipe at Thanksgiving. It's good with any meal.

1 10-ounce package
   frozen cut broccoli,
   thawed, drained
1 1/3 cups sliced celery
1 cup sour cream
1 10-ounce can cream
   of mushroom soup
3/4 cup shredded
   Cheddar cheese

Preheat oven to 350 degrees. Combine broccoli and celery in bowl. Add mixture of sour cream and soup. Add half the cheese; mix well. Pour into greased 2-quart casserole; sprinkle with remaining cheese. Bake at 350 degrees for 20 to 25 minutes or until heated through. Yield: 4 to 6 servings.

Monica Burridge, Xi Alpha Gamma
Rock Springs, Wyoming

BROCCOLI-BEAN CASSEROLE

This is one of my favorites and if there are leftovers I can hardly wait for the next day.

1 10-ounce can
   cream of mushroom
   soup
2 cups sour cream
1 envelope onion soup
   mix
1 10-ounce package
   frozen baby lima
   beans, thawed
1 8-ounce can sliced
   water chestnuts,
   drained
1 10-ounce package
   frozen cut broccoli,
   thawed
1/2 cup melted butter or
   margarine
3 cups crisp rice cereal

Preheat oven to 350 degrees. Combine soup, sour cream and onion soup mix in bowl; mix well. Add lima beans, water chestnuts and broccoli; mix well. Pour into greased casserole. Toss melted butter with cereal in bowl. Sprinkle over casserole. Bake at 350 degrees for 30 minutes or until brown. Yield: 15 servings.

Jackie H. Sanders, Xi Gamma Nu
Petersburg, Virginia

GREEN BEAN CASSEROLE

1 10-ounce can
   mushroom soup
1/2 cup sour cream
2 16-ounce cans green
   beans
1 cup shredded Cheddar
   cheese
1 3-ounce can French-
   fried onions

Preheat oven to 350 degrees. Spray 2-quart casserole with nonstick baking spray. Combine soup and sour cream in bowl; mix well. Add green beans; mix well. Pour into prepared casserole. Bake at 350 degrees for 20 minutes. Top with cheese and onions. Bake for 10 minutes longer. Yield: 8 servings.

Pat Tilley, Laureate Nu
Waynesville, North Carolina

GREEN BEANS ORIENTAL

2 16-ounce cans French-style green beans, drained	1/8 teaspoon red pepper flakes, crushed
1 8-ounce can sliced water chestnuts, drained	1/2 cup shredded sharp Cheddar cheese
1 10-ounce can cream of celery soup	1 tablespoon dried minced onion
1 teaspoon caraway seed	1/4 teaspoon savory
	1/2 cup butter cracker crumbs

Preheat oven to 350 degrees. Mix first 8 ingredients in bowl. Pour into greased 1 1/2-quart casserole; sprinkle with cracker crumbs. Bake for 25 to 30 minutes or until hot and bubbly. Yield: 6 servings.

Camilla Lutz, Preceptor Laureate Gamma Alpha
Dallas, Texas

IMPOSSIBLE GREEN BEAN PIE

8 ounces fresh green beans	1 cup shredded Cheddar cheese
1 4-ounce can mushroom stems and pieces, drained	1 1/2 cups milk
	3/4 cup baking mix
1/2 cup chopped onion	3 eggs
2 cloves of garlic, minced	1 teaspoon salt
	1/4 teaspoon pepper

Preheat oven to 400 degrees. Cut green beans into lengthwise strips. Combine green beans and 1 inch salted water in saucepan. Cook, uncovered, for 5 minutes. Cook, covered, for 5 minutes longer or until tender-crisp; drain. Combine green beans, mushrooms, onion, garlic and cheese in bowl; mix well. Spoon into lightly greased 10-inch pie plate. Combine milk, baking mix, eggs, salt and pepper in bowl; beat well. Pour over vegetables. Bake for 30 to 35 minutes or until knife inserted near center comes out clean. Let stand for 5 minutes. Store any leftover pie in refrigerator. Yield: 6 to 8 servings.

Sandra L. Utz, Psi Beta
Plattsburg, Missouri

LEMON GREEN BEANS

2 cups frozen cut green beans	2 teaspoons lemon juice
1 cup water	1 teaspoon grated lemon rind
1/4 cup sliced almonds	1/4 teaspoon salt
2 tablespoons melted butter or margarine	

Cook green beans in water in saucepan until tender-crisp; drain. Spoon into serving dish; keep warm. Sauté almonds in butter in skillet for 2 minutes. Add lemon juice, lemon rind and salt; mix well. Spoon over green beans. Yield: 4 servings.

Maebelle Herczeg, Laureate Gamma
Cloverdale, British Columbia, Canada

SWEET AND SOUR GREEN BEANS

A dear friend who brought a meal when I was ill included this recipe. My family especially loved the green beans.

2 slices bacon	1/4 cup vinegar
3 tablespoons chopped onion	2 tablespoons sugar
1 tablespoon all-purpose flour	1 16-ounce can French-style green beans

Fry bacon in skillet until brown and crisp; drain, reserving pan drippings. Crumble bacon. Sauté onions in pan drippings until tender. Add flour, stirring until well mixed. Add vinegar and sugar; mix well. Drain bean liquid into mixture; mix well. Add green beans and crumbled bacon. Heat to serving temperature. Spoon into serving bowl. Yield: 4 servings.

Glendena Ellis, Xi Alpha Alpha Theta
Snyder, Texas

❖ BARBECUED BLACK BEANS AND RICE

This is a healthy, quick, delicious and inexpensive dish.

2 16-ounce cans black beans, drained	1 4-ounce can chopped green chilies
1 14-ounce can stewed tomatoes	2 tablespoons barbecue sauce
1 11-ounce can vacuum-packed corn or 1 10-ounce package frozen corn	3/4 teaspoons ground cumin
	Salt and pepper to taste
	Cooked rice

Combine beans, tomatoes, corn, green chilies, barbecue sauce, cumin, salt and pepper in saucepan. Simmer for 10 minutes, stirring occasionally. Serve over hot cooked rice. Yield: 4 servings.

Laura Sutherland, Epsilon Psi
Helena, Alabama

CALIFORNIA CAULIFLOWER

1 medium head cauliflower	8 ounces Cheddar cheese, shredded
1/4 cup water	1 teaspoon salad seasoning
8 ounces onion or garlic-flavored chip-style dip	

Discard outer leaves of cauliflower. Wash cauliflower; place in microwave-safe dish. Add water. Microwave, tightly covered with plastic wrap, on High for 10 to 12 minutes or until tender-crisp, turning once. Drain excess liquid. Spread dip over cauliflower; sprinkle with cheese. Sprinkle with salad seasoning. Broil until cheese is melted. Cut into wedges. Yield: 8 servings.

Michelle Bullington, Alpha Alpha Gamma
Redding, California

MICROWAVE CAULIFLOWER AND PEAS

1 head cauliflower	Garlic salt to taste
1/2 cup mayonnaise-style salad dressing	1/2 cup shredded Cheddar cheese
1 teaspoon prepared mustard	1 10-ounce package frozen peas

Wash cauliflower. Cut off enough core end to make cauliflower stand level; place in microwave-safe dish. Microwave, tightly covered with plastic wrap, on High for 8 minutes or until tender-crisp. Mix salad dressing, mustard and garlic salt in bowl. Spread over cauliflower; sprinkle with cheese. Microwave peas using package directions. Spoon onto dish around cauliflower. Microwave until cheese is melted. Yield: 6 to 8 servings.

Katie Disney, Preceptor Alpha Gamma
Ridgway, Illinois

PHYL'S SAVORY CAULIFLOWER

Flowerets of 1 small head cauliflower	4 ounces mushrooms, thinly sliced
2 medium onions, chopped	1/4 cup margarine
	Salt and pepper to taste

Cook cauliflower in small amount of boiling salted water in saucepan until tender-crisp; drain. Keep warm. Sauté onions and mushrooms in margarine in skillet until onion is tender. Add cauliflower, salt and pepper; mix well. Spoon into serving dish. Yield: 4 servings.

Pam Young, Preceptor Alpha
Fairbanks, Alaska

TANGY CAULIFLOWER

1 medium cauliflower	1 teaspoon prepared mustard
2 tablespoons water	
1/2 cup mayonnaise	1/2 cup shredded Cheddar or Monterey Jack cheese
1 teaspoon chopped onion	

Place cauliflower in microwave-safe dish. Add water. Microwave, covered with plastic wrap, on High for 6 minutes. Combine mayonnaise, onion, mustard and cheese in bowl; mix well. Spread on cauliflower. Microwave for 2 to 3 minutes longer or until cheese is melted. Yield: 4 to 5 servings.

Cyndi Sumner, Kappa
Tucson, Arizona

CORN CASSEROLE

1 17-ounce can cream-style corn	2 eggs
1 17-ounce can whole kernel corn	1 7-ounce package corn muffin mix
	1 cup sour cream

Preheat oven to 350 degrees. Combine corn, eggs, muffin mix and sour cream in bowl; mix well. Pour into casserole. Bake for 25 to 30 minutes or until set. Yield: 6 servings.

Janet Failla, Alpha Gamma
Fresno, California

CONFETTI CORN RELISH

This is colorful and tasty at any gathering.

1 cup vinegar	3 cups whole kernel corn
2/3 cup sugar	1 small green bell pepper, chopped
1 teaspoon salt	
1 teaspoon celery seed	2 tablespoons chopped pimento
1 teaspoon mustard seed	
1/2 teaspoon hot pepper sauce	3 green onions, minced

Combine vinegar, sugar, salt, celery seed, mustard seed and hot pepper sauce in saucepan. Bring to a boil. Simmer for 2 minutes, stirring occasionally. Cool to room temperature. Mix corn, green pepper, pimento and green onions in bowl. Pour in vinegar mixture, stirring to mix. Chill in covered container. May store for several weeks in refrigerator. Flavor improves with standing. Yield: 3 1/3 cups.

Paula C. Langton, Xi Mu Eta
Houston, Texas

HOT CORN

8 ounces cream cheese	2 16-ounce cans white shoe peg corn, drained
1/4 cup butter or margarine	
1/4 cup milk	Salt and pepper to taste
1/8 to 1/4 cup chopped jalapeño peppers	

Preheat oven to 350 degrees. Combine cream cheese, butter and milk in microwave-safe casserole. Microwave, covered with plastic wrap, until melted. Add jalapeño peppers, corn, salt and pepper; mix well. Bake for 20 to 30 minutes or until hot and bubbly. Yield: 6 to 8 servings.

Lora Lee Short, Delta Pi
Montgomery, Alabama

❖ MEXICANA CORN

My mother always worked and she fixed this as a fast alternative to plain vegetables.

2 16-ounce cans whole kernel corn, drained	2 tablespoons salsa
8 ounces cream cheese, cubed	8 ounces Cheddar cheese, shredded

Combine corn and cream cheese in saucepan. Cook over medium heat until cream cheese is melted, stirring frequently. Add salsa and Cheddar cheese. Heat to serving temperature. Yield: 6 servings.

Nikki Caldwell, Omega Upsilon
Appleton City, Missouri

RITZY CORN CASSEROLE

This won first prize in a local newspaper's Holiday Recipe Contest last year.

2 17-ounce cans whole kernel corn, drained	1/2 teaspoon salt
1 16-ounce can French-style green beans, drained	1/4 cup chopped onion
	1/4 cup chopped green bell pepper
1 10-ounce can cream of celery soup	1/4 cup chopped celery
1 cup sour cream	1/2 cup melted margarine
	35 butter crackers, crushed

Combine corn, green beans, soup, sour cream, salt, onion, green pepper and celery in bowl; mix well. Spray 9-by-13-inch microwave-safe casserole with nonstick cooking spray. Pour in vegetables. Mix margarine and cracker crumbs together in bowl. Sprinkle over vegetables. Microwave on High for 9 minutes, turning every 3 minutes. Yield: 10 servings.

Mary E. Young, Xi Zeta Iota
Wagoner, Oklahoma

SCALLOPED CARROTS

4 cups sliced carrots, cooked	Salt and pepper to taste
1 medium onion, chopped	1/2 cup crumbled Velveeta cheese
1 1/2 tablespoons melted butter or margarine	3 cups seasoned croutons
1 10-ounce can cream of mushroom soup	Melted butter or margarine

Preheat oven to 350 degrees. Combine carrots, onion, butter, soup, salt, pepper and cheese in bowl; mix well. Spoon into casserole. Toast croutons in melted butter in skillet, tossing to coat. Sprinkle over casserole. Bake for 30 minutes. May vary by substituting 2 cups green beans for half the carrots.
Yield: 6 to 8 servings.

Sally Hofkes, Rho
Chippewa Falls, Wisconsin

BROILED EGGPLANT

Serve this dish plain or with tomato sauce and shredded cheese.

1 eggplant, peeled	Salt and paprika to taste
Butter or margarine, softened	

Preheat oven to 400 degrees. Cut eggplant into 1/2-inch slices. Spread butter on eggplant; sprinkle with salt and paprika. Place on baking sheet. Bake for 6 minutes or until tender. Turn eggplant. Bake for 6 minutes longer or until brown. Yield: 4 to 6 servings.

Frances W. Almany, Preceptor Alpha Epsilon
Hendersonville, Tennessee

SAUTÉED MUSHROOMS WITH BACON

4 ounces bacon, chopped	1 pound small mushrooms
6 tablespoons butter or margarine	Salt and pepper to taste

Stir-fry bacon in butter in wok until fat is transparent. Add mushrooms. Sauté for 4 or 5 minutes. Season with salt and pepper. Spoon into serving dish. Yield: 4 to 6 servings.

Lori Bredehoft, Gamma Phi
Brookfield, Missouri

MUSHROOMS AU GRATIN

2 pounds fresh mushrooms	2 tablespoons lemon juice
1/4 cup butter or margarine	Pepper to taste
2/3 cup sour cream	1 cup shredded Cheddar cheese
2 teaspoons all-purpose flour	1/8 teaspoon cayenne pepper
1/2 teaspoon salt	1/2 cup chopped parsley

Preheat oven to 350 degrees. Sauté mushrooms in butter in large skillet until tender; drain. Stir in remaining ingredients. Heat until bubbly. Spoon into casserole. Bake for 20 minutes. Yield: 8 servings.

Patricia Ellis, Beta Alpha Tau
Ft. Bliss, Texas

FAST-LANE MARINATED MUSHROOMS

1 tablespoon crushed garlic	1/8 cup lemon juice
1/4 cup vegetable oil	8 ounces fresh mushrooms
1/2 cup white or red wine	

Sauté garlic in oil in skillet for 30 seconds. Add wine and lemon juice. Bring to a boil. Add whole mushrooms. Cook until golden brown; drain. Spoon onto serving dish. Yield: 4 servings.

Linda Gizienski, Xi Alpha
Coventry, Rhode Island

MASHED POTATO CASSEROLE

6 cups prepared instant mashed potatoes	2 tablespoons finely chopped green onion
4 ounces whipped cream cheese	1 tablespoon finely chopped parsley
1 egg, beaten	Margarine

Preheat oven to 400 degrees. Combine potatoes with cream cheese in bowl; mix well. Add egg, onion and parsley; mix well. Spoon into greased casserole; dot with margarine. Bake for 30 minutes.
Yield: 10 servings.

Linda Robinson, Beta Alpha
Mt. Vernon, Ohio

CAESAR SCALLOPED POTATOES

1 medium onion, chopped	1/3 cup grated Parmesan cheese
2 large cloves of garlic, minced	2 cups cubed potatoes
1 1/2 tablespoons butter or margarine	1 teaspoon Dijon mustard
1 tablespoon all-purpose flour	1/2 teaspoon pepper
1 cup milk	1/2 teaspoon Worcestershire sauce

Combine onion, garlic and butter in 4-cup microwave-safe casserole. Microwave on High for 1 to 2 minutes or until onions are tender. Stir in flour. Microwave on High for 30 seconds. Whisk in milk. Microwave on High for 2 to 4 minutes or until mixture boils and thickens slightly, stirring twice. Stir in remaining ingredients. Microwave, covered, on High for 6 minutes or until potatoes are tender, stirring twice.
Yield: 2 to 3 servings.

Beverley Lippitz, Laureate Lambda
Scarborough, Ontario, Canada

MELISSA'S MARINATED POTATOES

2 pounds small new potatoes	3 tablespoons minced fresh parsley
2 7-ounce envelopes Italian salad dressing mix	1 2-ounce jar chopped pimento
1/4 cup minced green onions	

Cook potatoes in a small amount of water in saucepan until tender; drain. Cool slightly. Cut into 1/4-inch slices; arrange in shallow dish. Prepare salad dressing mix using package directions. Add green onions, parsley and pimento; mix well. Pour over potatoes. Marinate, covered, in refrigerator for several hours. Spoon potatoes into lettuce-lined bowl using slotted spoon. Yield: 4 to 6 servings.

Doris S. Bame, Xi Gamma Pi
Carolina Beach, North Carolina

QUICK CHEESY HASHED BROWNS

1 12-ounce package frozen hashed brown potatoes	2/3 cup milk
	Pepper to taste
1/2 cup shredded Cheddar cheese	1/2 teaspoon salt
	1 tablespoon melted butter or margarine

Place potatoes in greased 1-quart microwave-safe casserole. Microwave on High for 7 to 8 minutes or until tender, stirring once. Combine cheese, milk, pepper, salt and butter in bowl. Pour over potatoes. Microwave on High for 2 to 3 minutes or until hot and bubbly. Yield: 4 to 6 servings.

Harriett Laws, Preceptor Beta Psi
Cherokee, Iowa

SPINACH-STUFFED POTATOES

This recipe got my teenage daughter to eat spinach. She loves these potatoes and will even pop one into the microwave after school for a snack.

4 large potatoes	2 cloves of garlic, minced
2 tablespoons olive oil, butter or margarine	1/3 cup plain yogurt
2 teaspoons corn oil	1 cup whole wheat bread crumbs
1 10-ounce package frozen chopped spinach, thawed	4 teaspoons melted butter or margarine

Preheat oven to 400 degrees. Microwave potatoes on High for 10 to 15 minutes or until tender. Cut into quarters; scoop out pulp and reserve. Mix olive oil and corn oil in bowl. Brush both sides of potato skins with oil; place cut side up on baking sheet. Bake for 10 minutes. Reduce oven temperature to 350 degrees. Heat remaining oil in skillet. Add spinach and garlic. Cook until most of moisture evaporates, stirring frequently. Remove from heat. Combine potato pulp and yogurt in mixer bowl; beat until smooth. Add spinach and half the bread crumbs; mix well. Combine remaining bread crumbs and melted butter in bowl, tossing to mix. Mound potato mixture into potato skins; sprinkle with buttered crumbs. Place on baking sheet. Bake at 350 degrees for 10 minutes or until light brown. May be frozen before baking.
Yield: 4 to 6 servings.

Tina Donovan, Xi Beta Sigma
Williams Lake, British Columbia, Canada

SNAPPY SPUDS

1 1/2 cups water	4 medium potatoes, cubed
2 tablespoons instant beef or vegetable bouillon	2 tablespoons minced parsley (optional)
1 medium onion, sliced	

Bring water to a boil in 2-quart saucepan. Stir in bouillon until dissolved. Add onion, potatoes and parsley. Simmer, covered, over low heat for 20 minutes or until potatoes are tender. Yield: 6 servings.

Leonora G. Roberson, Xi Beta Beta
Birmingham, Alabama

SPECIAL CREAMED POTATOES

I like to prepare this in the summer at our lake cabin. It's quick, easy and because an oven is not needed, it helps keep the cabin cool.

4 medium potatoes, peeled, cubed	3 ounces sharp Cheddar cheese, shredded
1/2 cup chopped onion	1/2 cup milk
1 cup water	1/8 teaspoon pepper
1 teaspoon salt	

Combine potatoes, onion, water and salt in sauce-pan. Cook, covered, for 10 minutes. Simmer, uncovered, until water is nearly evaporated, turning potatoes occasionally with spoon. Add cheese, milk and pepper. Heat just until cheese is melted, stirring frequently. Yield: 6 servings.

Roxanne Park, Alpha Epsilon
Wenatchee, Washington

BLANCHARD'S SPECIAL POTATOES

My husband always gets lots of compliments on this dish. He also asked me not to use his name.

8 to 10 medium potatoes, sliced lengthwise	1 or 2 onions, sliced
	Garlic salt to taste
	1/2 cup margarine
Chopped green bell pepper to taste	Sour cream

Alternate layers of potatoes, green pepper, onions, garlic salt and dots of margarine in microwave-safe dish. Microwave on High for 15 minutes, turning several times. Serve with sour cream. Yield: 4 servings.

Deborah Marriott, Zeta Nu
Monroeville, Alabama

PARMESAN POTATOES

4 baking potatoes	Grated Parmesan cheese
Salad dressing	

Cut small slits in potatoes. Microwave on High for 10 to 15 minutes or until tender. Cool slightly. Cut into 1/4-inch slices. Brush with salad dressing; sprinkle with Parmesan cheese. Place on rack in broiler pan. Broil until light brown or microwave until cheese is melted. Yield: 4 to 6 servings.

Mary Herndon, Xi Beta Upsilon
Angel Fire, New Mexico

CHEESY SPINACH BAKE

1 15-ounce can spinach	1/2 cup sliced green onions
4 eggs, beaten	
1 cup milk	1/4 cup grated Parmesan cheese
1 cup shredded Swiss cheese	
1 cup cubed firm white bread	

Preheat oven to 375 degrees. Drain spinach, pressing out excess liquid. Combine eggs and milk in bowl; mix well. Add spinach, Swiss cheese, bread cubes, green onions and Parmesan cheese; mix well. Pour into 1-quart casserole. Bake, covered, for 30 minutes or until set. Yield: 6 servings.

Marilyn C. Vollmar, Preceptor Beta Kappa
Bowling Green, Ohio

SPINACH CASSEROLE

1 10-ounce package frozen spinach	Pepper to taste
	1/4 cup grated Parmesan cheese
4 ounces uncooked spaghetti	
1 egg, beaten	2 tablespoons minced onion
1/2 cup sour cream	2 cups shredded Monterey Jack cheese
1/4 cup milk	
1 teaspoon salt	Grated Parmesan cheese

Preheat oven to 350 degrees. Cook spinach using package directions; drain. Break spaghetti into small pieces. Cook using package directions; drain. Mix egg, sour cream, milk, salt, pepper, 1/4 cup Parmesan cheese and onion in bowl. Add spinach, spaghetti and Monterey Jack cheese; mix well. Spoon into ungreased 1-quart casserole. Sprinkle with additional Parmesan cheese. Bake, covered, for 15 minutes. Bake, uncovered, for 15 minutes longer. Serve with Italian bread. Yield: 6 to 8 servings.

Debbie Marshall, Gamma Theta
Lansing, Michigan

SPINACH DELUXE

This recipe has the look and taste of a special dish for company but is easy enough for everyday meals.

2 10-ounce packages frozen spinach, thawed	1 cup sour cream
	1 envelope onion soup mix

Preheat oven to 350 degrees. Drain spinach, squeezing out excess moisture. Combine all ingredients in bowl; mix well. Pour into casserole. Bake at 350 degrees for 30 minutes. Yield: 4 servings.

Barbara Lentz, Preceptor Beta Upsilon
Port Orchard, Washington

❖ SPINACH SOUFFLÉ

The cheese and sausage for this recipe may be prepared ahead and frozen to keep on hand for unexpected company.

1 package frozen spinach soufflé, thawed	1/2 cup sliced mushrooms
	3/4 cup cooked crumbled Italian sausage
2 eggs, beaten	3/4 cup shredded Swiss or Cheddar cheese
3 tablespoons milk	
2 teaspoons chopped onion	1 unbaked 9-inch pie shell

Preheat oven to 400 degrees. Combine spinach soufflé, eggs, milk, onion, mushrooms, Italian sausage and cheese in bowl; mix well. Pour into unbaked pie shell. Bake for 25 to 30 minutes or until set. May bake mixture in casserole instead of pie shell. Yield: 4 to 6 servings.

Carole M. Steen, Xi Iota Rho
Yucca Valley, California

DECADENT SQUASH

1 medium summer squash, chopped	1/4 cup fresh basil, chopped
1 medium crookneck squash, chopped	1/2 teaspoon salt
	Pepper to taste
4 green onions, finely chopped	1/2 cup water
1 medium zucchini, chopped	1 15-ounce can stewed tomatoes
Greek seasoning to taste	8 mushrooms

Combine summer squash, crookneck squash, green onions, zucchini, seasonings and water in saucepan. Cook, covered, until tender-crisp. Add tomatoes and mushrooms. Cook until mushrooms are tender. Spoon into serving bowl. May substitute or add any kind of squash. Yield: 6 to 8 servings.

Charlotte A. Wilson, Preceptor Chi
Hayden Lake, Idaho

SQUASH CASSEROLE

3 medium yellow squash, chopped	1 cup crushed crisp rice cereal
2 tablespoons chopped onion	3/4 cup oats
1 teaspoon salt	1/2 teaspoon salt
1 teaspoon sugar	1/4 cup packed brown sugar
Pepper to taste	
1/3 cup butter-flavored shortening	

Combine squash, onion, 1 teaspoon salt, sugar and pepper in microwave-safe 1 1/2-quart casserole; mix well. Place shortening in microwave-safe bowl. Microwave on High until melted. Add remaining ingredients; mix well. Spread over top of casserole. Microwave on High for 6 minutes. Yield: 6 servings.

Elizabeth Bisanar, Preceptor Alpha Rho
Hickory, North Carolina

SQUASH DRESSING

This is great with pinto beans!

1/2 cup chopped onion	Salt and pepper to taste
1/2 cup chopped celery	2 cups milk
1/2 green bell pepper, chopped	1 small pan cooked corn bread, crumbled
1/2 cup butter or margarine	1 10-ounce can cream of chicken soup
3 cups cooked squash	

Preheat oven to 450 degrees. Sauté onion, celery and green pepper in butter in skillet. Add remaining ingredients; mix well. Pour into 1 1/2-quart casserole. Bake for 30 minutes or until brown. Yield: 6 servings.

Clady L. Beher, Preceptor Gamma
Memphis, Tennessee

XYZ CASSEROLE

This is great for progression meetings.

1 pound zucchini, sliced	2 teaspoons melted margarine or butter
1 pound yellow squash, sliced	
1 2-ounce can chopped pimento	

Alternate layers of zucchini and yellow squash in microwave-safe dish. Top with undrained pimento; drizzle with margarine. Microwave, covered with plastic wrap, on High for 12 to 15 minutes or until tender-crisp. Yield: 6 to 8 servings.

Patsy Pittman, Xi Iota
Texarkana, Texas

YELLOW CROOKNECK SQUASH PATTIES

Squash always produces so abundantly that new and different recipes are needed for variety. This is very quick too.

3 cups grated yellow crookneck squash	1 egg, slightly beaten
	1/2 teaspoon salt
1 green bell pepper, grated	1/4 teaspoon pepper
	1/4 cup all-purpose flour
1 small onion, grated	2 tablespoons corn oil

Combine squash, green pepper, onion, egg, salt, pepper and flour in bowl; mix well. Drop by tablespoonfuls into hot oil in skillet. Cook until brown on both sides. Yield: 4 servings.

Berniece Jones, Xi Omicron Beta
Sutter Creek, California

SCALLOPED TOMATOES

This is a dish my Grandmother made with her home-canned tomatoes and one my children love. It can be made ahead and baked just before serving.

1 18-ounce can whole tomatoes	10 ounces sharp Cheddar cheese, sliced
1 small onion, finely chopped	Butter or margarine
1 1/2 stacks crackers, coarsely crumbled	Paprika to taste

Preheat oven to 350 degrees. Mash tomatoes and juice in bowl. Layer tomatoes, onion, crackers and cheese 1/3 at a time in 1 1/2-quart casserole. Dot with butter; sprinkle with paprika. Bake for 20 to 25 minutes or until hot and bubbly.
Yield: 8 to 10 servings.

Brenda Bullock, Psi Kappa
Plantation, Florida

TOMATOES AND DUMPLINGS

This recipe takes me back to my childhood. My mother always made this for Sunday lunch.

1½ cups all-purpose
  flour
2 teaspoons baking
  powder
¾ teaspoon salt
3 tablespoons
  shortening

¾ cup milk
1 28-ounce can
  tomatoes
Shredded Cheddar
  cheese

Combine flour, baking powder and salt in bowl; mix well. Cut in shortening until crumbly. Add milk; mix well. Bring undrained tomatoes to a boil in saucepan over high heat. Drop dumplings by tablespoonfuls into tomatoes. Reduce heat to medium-high. Cook, covered, for 15 minutes. Spoon into serving dish; top with cheese. Yield: 6 servings.

Betty Smith, Xi Epsilon Iota
Mississauga, Ontario, Canada

TOMATO WEDGES PROVENÇALE

2 tablespoons fine dry
  bread crumbs
¼ cup each finely
  chopped onion and
  fresh parsley
½ clove of garlic,
  minced

2 tablespoons melted
  margarine
½ teaspoon salt
⅛ teaspoon pepper
¼ teaspoon basil
4 tomatoes

Preheat oven to 425 degrees. Mix first 8 ingredients in bowl. Cut each tomato into 8 wedges. Place in greased 7-by-11-inch casserole. Sprinkle with bread crumb mixture. Bake for 8 minutes. Yield: 4 servings.

Joan MacDonald, Laureate Gamma
Delta, British Columbia, Canada

SAUTÉED ZUCCHINI

2 cloves of garlic, minced
⅛ cup chopped onion
2 tablespoons butter or
  margarine

3 zucchini, chopped
2 teaspoons lemon
  pepper
½ teaspoon salt

Sauté garlic and onion in butter in skillet until golden brown. Add zucchini, lemon pepper and salt. Sauté for 7 to 10 minutes or until zucchini is tender-crisp. Yield: 6 servings.

Kelly Welker, Beta Delta Chi
Lancaster, Texas

Eleanor Milne, Laureate Alpha Zeta, Richmond, British Columbia, Canada, makes Speedy Vegetables by adding 2 heaping tablespoons Chicken-in-a-Mug to 2 cups hot water in saucepan. Stir in mixture of 2 rounded tablespoons each butter and flour. Bring to a boil, stirring constantly. Add 1 package cooked frozen mixed vegetables.

ZUCCHINI ON-THE-RUN

3 medium zucchini
Red pepper or cajun
  seasoning
Green onion tops,
  chopped

3 tablespoons grated
  Parmesan cheese

Cut zucchini lengthwise into 3-inch slices. Sprinkle cut side with seasoning; place in microwave-safe dish. Sprinkle with onion tops and Parmesan cheese. Microwave on High for 3 to 5 minutes or until tender-crisp. Yield: 6 servings.

Susan Gros, Omega
Baton Rouge, Louisiana

ZUCCHINI BOATS

3 medium zucchini
2 tablespoons butter or
  margarine
2 tablespoons chopped
  parsley
1 tablespoon olive oil
1 tablespoon finely
  chopped onion
1 clove of garlic, minced
1 large tomato, chopped

½ cup fine dry bread
  crumbs
2 tablespoons grated
  Parmesan cheese
¼ teaspoon salt
Black pepper and
  cayenne pepper to taste
½ cup shredded
  mozzarella cheese

Cut zucchini into halves lengthwise; scoop out pulp, leaving ¼-inch shells. Place shells in 6-by-10-inch microwave-safe casserole. Combine next 5 ingredients in microwave-safe bowl. Microwave on High for 1½ to 2 minutes or until butter is melted. Stir in tomato, bread crumbs, Parmesan cheese, zucchini pulp and seasonings. Spoon into zucchini shells. Microwave, covered with waxed paper, on High for 5 minutes. Sprinkle with mozzarella cheese. Microwave on High for 1 minute longer or until cheese is melted. Yield: 6 servings.

Linda Sproule, Gamma Xi
Peterborough, Ontario, Canada

BARBECUED VEGETABLES

3 or 4 Roma tomatoes,
  cut into quarters
1 large onion, sliced
2 small zucchini, sliced
Flowerets of ½ bunch
  broccoli
Flowerets of ⅓ head
  cauliflower

1 tablespoon brown
  sugar
Sweet basil to taste
1 teaspoon instant beef
  bouillon
2 tablespoons margarine

Combine all vegetables in bowl; mix gently. Sprinkle with brown sugar, basil and bouillon; toss gently to mix. Spread vegetables on large sheet of heavy-duty foil. Dot with margarine. Fold up foil, sealing edges. Grill over hot coals for 12 to 15 minutes or until tender. Serve hot. Yield: 4 to 6 servings.

Mary Pullins, Lambda
Bluefield, West Virginia

CREAMED VEGETABLE DELIGHT

1 cup chopped broccoli
2 cups thinly sliced
  carrots
1 cup sliced fresh
  mushrooms
2 medium onions, cut
  into 8 wedges
½ cup vegetable oil
1 envelope Lipton Bon
  Appétit cream of
  asparagus soup
1 cup water
½ cup sour cream
Hot cooked noodles or
  rice

Stir-fry each vegetable separately in oil in skillet until tender-crisp. Remove to bowl. Keep warm. Combine soup mix and water in saucepan. Bring to a boil. Reduce heat. Simmer for 5 minutes, stirring constantly. Add sour cream and vegetables. Heat to serving temperature. Serve over noodles or rice. Yield: 4 servings.

Carole Jury, Lambda
Minnedosa, Manitoba, Canada

GOOP

2 packages any flavor
  ramen soup mix
3 or 4 cups chopped
  carrots, broccoli,
  mushrooms and/or
  zucchini
Vegetable oil
8 to 12 ounces hot
  pepper cheese,
  shredded

Cook noodles from soup mix in water in saucepan for 3 minutes or until tender; drain. Stir-fry vegetables in hot oil in wok until tender-crisp. Add drained noodles and seasoning from soup mix. Top with shredded cheese. Cook until cheese is melted. Yield: 6 to 8 servings.

Connie Moreland-Bishop, Alpha Alpha Gamma
Redding, California

MIXED VEGGIES CASSEROLE

This is my favorite casserole to take to church and family gatherings. I always get compliments.

1 10-ounce can cream
  of chicken soup
⅓ cup mayonnaise
2 16-ounce cans mixed
  vegetables, drained
1 8-ounce can sliced
  water chestnuts,
  drained
12 butter crackers,
  crushed

Preheat oven to 350 degrees. Combine soup and mayonnaise in bowl; mix well. Add mixed vegetables and water chestnuts; mix well. Pour into 9-by-13-inch casserole; sprinkle with cracker crumbs. Bake for 30 minutes. Yield: 8 to 10 servings.

Evelyn J. Barker, Xi Beta Phi
Alliance, Ohio

QUICK STIR-FRY "CHO-STYLE"

This recipe is fast, simple and quite eye-appealing. It's a favorite after running all day with my two girls. They help chop vegetables while we talk about the day's events.

4 carrots, thinly sliced
3 stalks of celery, thinly
  sliced
2 tablespoons vegetable
  oil
1 onion, coarsely
  chopped
½ teaspoon minced
  garlic
1 red bell pepper, sliced
1 green bell pepper,
  sliced
2 cups bean sprouts
1 tablespoon soy sauce
1 tablespoon oyster or
  curry sauce
1 6-ounce can tuna
  (optional)
Cooked rice

Combine carrots and celery in microwave-safe bowl. Microwave on High for 8 minutes. Heat oil in wok. Add onion and garlic. Stir-fry for 2 minutes. Add red and green peppers. Stir-fry for 2 minutes. Add cooked carrots and celery, bean sprouts and seasoning; mix well. Stir in tuna. Stir-fry until heated through. Serve over hot cooked rice. Yield: 4 to 6 servings.

Elizabeth Cho, Xi Alpha
Kirkland, Quebec, Canada

SWISS VEGETABLE MEDLEY

1 16-ounce package
  frozen mixed broccoli,
  carrots and
  cauliflower
1 10-ounce can cream
  of mushroom soup
⅓ cup sour cream
1 cup shredded Swiss
  cheese
¼ teaspoon pepper
1 4-ounce can chopped
  pimentos
1 3-ounce can French-
  fried onions

Combine mixed vegetables, soup, sour cream, half the cheese, pepper, pimentos and half the onions in 1-quart microwave-safe casserole. Microwave on High for 8 minutes. Top with remaining cheese and onions. Microwave on High for 1 minute or until cheese melts. Yield: 6 servings.

Jackie Wallace, Preceptor Alpha Alpha
Portland, Oregon

VEGETABLES AMANDINE

1 9-ounce package
  frozen Italian green
  beans
3 cups sliced carrots,
  cooked
½ cup melted margarine
1 tablespoon lemon juice
½ teaspoon salt
¼ teaspoon pepper
½ cup sliced almonds

Cook green beans using package directions; drain. Combine green beans and carrots in serving dish. Mix margarine, lemon juice, salt, pepper and almonds in bowl. Drizzle over vegetables. Yield: 6 servings.

Dora Dillon, Preceptor Laureate Alpha Upsilon
Bothell, Washington

CHILI RELLENOS CASSEROLE

My mother used this recipe a lot when I was growing up—it's fast and delicious!

2 7-ounce cans whole chilies, drained	1½ cups milk
12 ounces each sharp Monterey Jack and Cheddar cheese, sliced	½ teaspoon salt
	¼ cup all-purpose flour
	4 eggs, beaten

Preheat oven to 350 degrees. Alternate layers of chilies and cheeses in 3-quart casserole until all ingredients are used. Combine milk, salt, flour and eggs in bowl; mix well. Pour over chilies and cheese. Bake for 50 minutes. May also microwave on High for 10 minutes, turning after 5 minutes. Yield: 8 to 10 servings.

Ann R. Goodman, Alpha Phi
The Dalles, Oregon

HOMINY CASSEROLE

1 12-ounce can cream of mushroom soup	1 4-ounce can chopped green chilies, drained
1 8-ounce jar Cheez Whiz	6 crackers, crumbled
2 16-ounce cans hominy, drained	

Preheat oven to 350 degrees. Heat soup and cheese in 3-quart saucepan, stirring until cheese melts. Stir in hominy and chilies; mix well. Spoon into 9-by-13-inch baking dish. Bake for 20 minutes or until bubbly. Top with crumbled crackers. Yield: 6 servings.

Dana Bryan, Theta Xi
Guthrie, Oklahoma

MACARONI AND CHEESE SUPERB

2 cups medium cream sauce	1 cup large curd cottage cheese
1½ cups shredded Cheddar cheese	2 cups macaroni, cooked
¼ teaspoon Worcestershire sauce	½ cup buttered bread crumbs
⅛ teaspoon dry mustard	

Preheat oven to 350 degrees. Combine cream sauce, Cheddar cheese, Worcestershire sauce and dry mustard in bowl; mix well. Fold in cottage cheese and macaroni. Spoon into 1½-quart baking dish. Sprinkle with buttered bread crumbs. Bake for 40 minutes or until heated through. Yield: 4 to 6 servings.

Evelyn Lantz, Laureate Alpha Zeta
Mt. Jewett, Pennsylvania

POPPY SEED NOODLES

1 8-ounce package egg noodles or fettucini	¾ cup sour cream
1 tablespoon butter or margarine	2 teaspoons poppy seed
	1 scallion, chopped
	Salt and pepper to taste

Cook noodles using package directions; drain. Heat butter, sour cream, poppy seed and scallion in 4-quart saucepan. Add noodles; toss to coat. Season with salt and pepper. Yield: 4 servings.

Lori Tucker, Lambda
Walla Walla, Washington

ARTICHOKE SAUCE AND SPAGHETTI

Friends can't get enough of this!

1 16-ounce package spaghetti	1 2-ounce can sliced black olives, drained
1 6-ounce jar marinated artichoke hearts	2 teaspoons each basil and oregano
8 ounces mushrooms, sliced	1 teaspoon each minced onion, garlic powder and sugar
1 15-ounce can tomato sauce	½ teaspoon each fennel seed and salt
½ cup dry white wine	¼ teaspoon pepper
	Grated Parmesan cheese

Cook spaghetti using package directions; drain. Drain artichokes, reserving marinade. Chop artichokes coarsely; set aside. Sauté mushrooms in reserved marinade in skillet until tender. Add artichokes, tomato sauce, wine, olives, herbs and seasonings. Simmer for 20 minutes, stirring occasionally. Serve over hot spaghetti. Sprinkle with Parmesan cheese before serving. Yield: 4 to 6 servings.

Beverly J. Beaver, Xi Beta Xi
Huntingdon, Pennsylvania

CREAMY BASIL TORTELLINI

1 16-ounce package tortellini	2 cups light cream
2 cloves of garlic, minced	1 tablespoon each basil and parsley
3 tablespoons margarine	¼ cup grated Parmesan cheese
1 envelope vegetable soup mix	

Cook tortellini using package directions; drain. Sauté garlic in margarine in 4-quart saucepan. Add soup mix and cream; mix well. Simmer for 10 minutes, stirring frequently. Add basil, parsley and cheese; mix well. Stir in cooked tortellini. Simmer until heated through. Yield: 4 to 6 servings.

Maureen King, Mu
Greenwood, Nova Scotia, Canada

ANGEL HAIR PASTA PRIMAVERA

1 16-ounce package angel hair pasta
1/2 cup fresh peas
1/2 cup tiny green beans
1/2 cup sliced mushrooms
1/2 cup fresh asparagus
1/4 cup unsalted butter or margarine
1 cup light cream
Freshly ground pepper
Grated Parmesan cheese

Cook pasta using package directions; drain. Sauté peas, beans, mushrooms and asparagus in butter in saucepan until tender-crisp. Add cream and pepper. Simmer until sauce is slightly thickened. Toss pasta with sauce to coat. Sprinkle with grated Parmesan cheese. Yield: 4 to 6 servings.

Mary Ann Parker, Xi Delta Rho
Clearlake, Washington

PASTA PRIMAVERA PRONTO

This is a great way to encourage spaghetti-loving children to eat their vegetables!

1 16-ounce package spaghetti
2 tablespoons butter or margarine
3/4 cup water
1 16-ounce package California-blend mixed vegetables
Grated Parmesan cheese

Cook spaghetti using package directions; drain. Place in covered dish; dot with 1 tablespoon butter. Combine remaining 1 tablespoon butter with water and mixed vegetables in covered microwave-safe dish. Microwave on High for 3 to 4 minutes or until tender-crisp. Add to spaghetti; toss well. Sprinkle with Parmesan cheese before serving. Yield: 4 servings.

Teresa Groff, Zeta Kappa
Emerson, Iowa

PASTA WITH FRESH VEGETABLES

1 16-ounce package spaghetti or other pasta
1 clove of garlic, minced
1 1/2 cups whole kernel corn
8 ounces green beans, cut into thirds
3 tablespoons olive oil
1 tablespoon basil
1/2 teaspoon each oregano and rosemary
3 tomatoes, chopped
1/4 cup chopped parsley
Juice of 1 lemon
Salt and pepper to taste

Cook spaghetti using package directions; drain. Cook garlic, corn and beans in olive oil over medium heat in skillet for 7 minutes or until tender-crisp. Add next 6 ingredients. Simmer until heated through. Toss with cooked spaghetti in bowl. Season with salt and pepper. Yield: 4 servings.

Anna Rozestraten, Xi Alpha
Pierrefonds, Quebec, Canada

SPINACH FETTUCINI CARBONARA

1 16-ounce package spinach fettucini
3 ounces prosciutto, julienned
1/4 cup chopped onion
1 clove of garlic, minced
2 tablespoons olive oil
1/2 cup whipping cream
2 eggs, beaten
3/4 teaspoon salt
1/4 teaspoon pepper
Grated Parmesan cheese
1 medium tomato, chopped
1 3-ounce can French-fried onions (optional)

Cook fettucini using package directions; drain. Sauté prosciutto, onion and garlic in olive oil in skillet for 5 minutes. Add cooked fettucini and cream. Simmer for 3 minutes, stirring frequently; remove from heat. Stir in eggs, salt and pepper, tossing to coat. Sprinkle with grated Parmesan cheese. Garnish with tomato and French-fried onions. Yield: 4 to 6 servings.

Catharine Stackhouse, Epsilon Master
York, Pennsylvania

TERRIFIC TASTY PASTA

1 16-ounce package angel hair pasta
1/2 cup chopped red onion
4 cloves of garlic, minced
1/3 cup chopped sun-dried tomatoes
6 fresh basil leaves, minced
2 tablespoons margarine
Grated Parmesan cheese

Cook pasta using package directions; drain. Sauté onion, garlic, tomatoes and basil in margarine in skillet for 5 to 7 minutes or until onion is transparent. Toss with cooked pasta in bowl. Sprinkle with freshly grated Parmesan cheese. Serve with favorite bread. Yield: 4 servings.

Jacquie L. Brown, Alpha Alpha Gamma
Redding, California

APRICOT AND BROWN RICE PILAF

1 cup shredded carrot
1 tablespoon pine nuts
1 tablespoon margarine
4 ounces quick-cooking brown rice
1 cup apple juice
3/4 cup water
6 dried apricot halves, chopped
2 tablespoons raisins

Combine carrot, pine nuts and margarine in 1-quart glass casserole. Microwave on High for 2 minutes. Add rice, apple juice and water. Microwave, loosely covered, for 5 minutes, stirring once. Mix in apricots and raisins. Microwave, covered, on Medium for 12 to 15 minutes or until liquid is absorbed and rice is tender. Yield: 4 servings.

Juanita Lunn, Laureate Alpha Kappa
Mt. Vernon, Ohio

VEGETABLE-RICE CASSEROLE

1 5-ounce package
  wild rice
1 large green bell
  pepper, chopped
1 pound fresh
  mushrooms, sliced
1 large onion, chopped
1 tablespoon canola oil

1 16-ounce can
  tomatoes, drained,
  chopped
1 8-ounce can tomato
  sauce
16 ounces Cheddar
  cheese, shredded

Preheat oven to 350 degrees. Cook rice using package directions; set aside. Sauté green pepper, mushrooms and onion in oil in skillet until tender. Stir in tomatoes and tomato sauce. Layer rice, vegetables and cheese 1/2 at a time in 9-by-13-inch casserole. Bake for 40 minutes, or microwave on Medium for 15 minutes. May be used as stuffing for green peppers. Yield: 8 servings.

Carolyn Cole, Beta Omicron
Fletcher, North Carolina

CHINESE FRIED RICE

2 tablespoons butter or
  margarine
3 cups cooked rice
1½ tablespoons soy
  sauce

3 large eggs
1 tablespoon water
1/4 teaspoon sugar
1/4 cup sliced green
  onions

Microwave butter in 3-quart microwave-safe casserole on High for 1 minute. Add rice and soy sauce; mix well. Beat eggs, water and sugar in bowl until blended. Pour into center of rice mixture. Microwave, covered, on Medium for 3 minutes. Stir in green onions. Microwave, covered, for 3 minutes longer. Stir before serving. Yield: 4 to 6 servings.

Donna Oden, Xi Alpha Tau
Kemmerer, Wyoming

VEGETARIAN FRIED RICE

4 radishes, sliced
3 cups cooked brown
  rice
1 teaspoon rice wine
  vinegar
3 cloves of garlic,
  minced
1 teaspoon sesame oil

4 scallions, chopped
4 ounces mushrooms,
  thinly sliced
3 ounces frozen peas,
  thawed
2 ounces water
  chestnuts, sliced
1 tablespoon soy sauce

Combine radishes, rice and vinegar in small bowl; set aside. Sauté garlic in oil in 2-quart saucepan until light brown. Add scallions and mushrooms. Sauté until tender. Add rice mixture, peas, water chestnuts and soy sauce; mix well. Simmer until heated through. Serve hot. Yield: 6 servings.

Yolanda Viramontes, Xi Alpha Pi
Albuquerque, New Mexico

FANTASTIC RICE CASSEROLE

2 cups uncooked long
  grain rice
4 cups hot water
1/2 cup soy sauce
1/4 cup onion flakes

1/2 cup sugar
1/2 cup corn oil
2 tablespoons red
  pepper flakes

Preheat oven to 350 degrees. Combine all ingredients in bowl; mix well. Spoon into 3-quart baking dish. Bake, covered, for 45 minutes. Fluff with fork. Yield: 6 servings.

Roberta Walton, Preceptor
Caribou, Maine

GREEN RICE

3 cups cooked rice, no
  salt added
1 cup chopped spinach
1 cup chopped parsley
2 eggs, beaten

1 cup skim milk
1/4 cup canola oil
1 onion, grated
3/4 cup shredded low-fat
  mozzarella cheese

Preheat oven to 350 degrees. Combine rice, spinach, parsley, eggs, milk, oil and onion in large bowl; mix well. Spoon into 9-by-9-inch baking dish sprayed with nonstick cooking spray. Sprinkle with cheese. Bake for 30 minutes. Cut into squares to serve. Serve plain, with low-calorie white sauce or low-sodium mushroom sauce. Yield: 10 servings.

Margaret L. Browning, Preceptor Laureate Gamma
Port Orange, Florida

HERB RICE

This rice is delicious with any kind of meat and is more economical than Rice-A-Roni.

1 cup uncooked rice
3 tablespoons margarine
1/4 teaspoon salt
3 cups chicken broth

1/2 teaspoon each
  savory, thyme,
  rosemary and
  marjoram

Brown rice in margarine in heavy skillet, stirring frequently. Stir in remaining ingredients. Simmer on low for 25 minutes or until liquid is absorbed. Yield: 4 to 6 servings.

Kay Henderson, Xi Sigma Tau
Austin, Texas

JALAPEÑO RICE

This dish is good served with Mexican food.

1 teaspoon chopped
  onion
1/2 cup canola oil
4 cups water
1/4 cup margarine

2 cups uncooked rice
3 whole jalapeño
  peppers
1 pound Velveeta
  cheese, chopped

Mix all ingredients in large saucepan. Simmer for 30 to 40 minutes or until rice is tender. Yield: 8 servings.

Tena Conner, Xi Beta Chi
Pampa, Texas

RED-EYE RICE

1 cup instant rice	1 cup shredded Cheddar
2/3 cup water	Cheese
1 cup picante sauce	1 cup shredded
1 16-ounce can	Monterey Jack cheese
Mexicorn	1/2 cup sour cream

Preheat oven to 350 degrees. Combine rice, water, picante sauce, corn, cheeses and sour cream in 2-quart baking dish. Bake for 30 minutes. Yield: 4 to 6 servings.

Beverly Patriquin, Preceptor Alpha Phi
Altus, Oklahoma

RICE AND NOODLE CASSEROLE

8 ounces uncooked	1 cup water
medium noodles	2 10-ounce cans beef or
1 cup butter or	chicken broth
margarine	1 teaspoon soy sauce
2 cups uncooked instant	1 7-ounce can sliced
rice	water chestnuts,
2 10-ounce cans onion	drained
soup	

Sauté noodles in butter in 3-quart saucepan until golden brown. Add remaining ingredients. Simmer for 5 minutes. Spoon into 3-quart glass dish. Microwave on High for 20 minutes or until tender, stirring after 10 minutes. May bake at 350 degrees for 45 minutes if preferred. Yield: 12 to 18 servings.

Connie R. Lee, Preceptor Alpha Pi
Huron, Ohio

VEGGIE-RICE SAUTÉ

Great with pork or chicken.

1 cup instant rice	1/4 cup chopped carrot
1/2 cup chopped green,	1 tablespoon canola oil
red or yellow bell	2 eggs
pepper	1 to 2 teaspoons soy
1/4 to 1/2 cup chopped	sauce
yellow squash	1/2 teaspoon poultry
1/4 to 1/2 cup chopped	seasoning
zucchini	Salt and pepper to taste

Cook rice using package directions; drain. Sauté vegetables in oil in large skillet until tender. Stir in rice. Beat eggs with soy sauce and seasonings in bowl. Pour into rice mixture. Cook over medium heat, stirring constantly until eggs are firm. Yield: 4 servings.

Peggy Waller
Floral City, Florida

VEGETABLE PILAF

1/2 cup uncooked long	1 1/2 cups frozen mixed
grain rice	vegetables, thawed
2 tablespoons finely	1 1/3 cups water
chopped onion	2 teaspoons instant
2 tablespoons butter or	chicken bouillon
margarine	

Sauté rice and onion in butter in 2-quart saucepan for 5 to 10 minutes or until rice is light brown. Add vegetables, water and bouillon; mix well. Bring to a boil; reduce heat. Simmer, covered, for 20 minutes or until liquid is absorbed and vegetables are tender. Yield: 4 servings.

Julie McKinnon, Xi Phi
Butte, Montana

RICE AND BEAN CASSEROLE

So so easy to make!

2 cups stewed tomatoes	1 15-ounce can
2 cups cooked rice	ranch-style beans

Combine tomatoes, rice and beans in saucepan. Heat to serving temperature. Yield: 4 to 6 servings.

Brandi Ordile-Fleischmann, Xi Upsilon Omicron
Murphys, California

BAKED PINEAPPLE

2 20-ounce cans	1 cup butter cracker
pineapple chunks	crumbs
1 cup sugar	1/2 cup melted butter or
6 tablespoons	margarine
all-purpose flour	
2 cups shredded	
Cheddar cheese	

Preheat oven to 350 degrees. Drain pineapple, reserving juice. Mix reserved juice with sugar and flour in bowl. Spoon into buttered 9-by-13-inch baking dish. Spread pineapple chunks in prepared dish. Sprinkle with cheese and cracker crumbs; drizzle with butter. Bake for 35 to 40 minutes or until heated through. Yield: 9 to 12 servings.

Laquita J. Cadena, Xi Phi Theta
San Antonio, Texas

Delight M. Somers, Mu Master, Redding, California, makes Summer Squash Fritters by sifting 1/2 cup flour, 1 teaspoon baking powder and 1/2 teaspoon salt into mixture of 2 eggs and 2 tablespoons milk in bowl. Fold in 2 cups minced squash and 1/2 teaspoon minced garlic. Fry in hot oil in skillet.

Brisk Breads

Now, everyone has heard of "quick breads,"
which sometimes aren't all that quick. And
almost everyone you know has "whipped" up a
batch of biscuits—direct from the refrigerated
food case. We bring new meaning to "quick"
with our "brisk breads." Brisk breads? They're
just the way they sound—easy and
quick-to-prepare breads, biscuits, rolls, coffee
cakes and special treats that make you appear to
have spent hours over a hot oven. We've
collected favorite recipes for such delicious
goodies as corn bread, cheese bread, muffins,
French toast and breadsticks, in addition to
more familiar loaves of the staff of life. Some
are "from scratch," and some use easy-to-
find, and easy-to-store, ready-made breads
as their base. And all are fabulous and fast!

APPLE CAKES

1 cup baking mix
1 teaspoon sugar
1 egg
1/2 cup sour cream
1 McIntosh apple,
  chopped

1 teaspoon butter or
  margarine
Cinnamon

Preheat griddle. Combine baking mix, sugar, egg and sour cream in bowl; mix well. Add apple; mix well. Drop by tablespoonfuls onto hot griddle spread with butter. Sprinkle with cinnamon. Bake until brown on both sides. Yield: 12 (4-inch) cakes.

Bertha M. Buss, Xi Zeta Eta
Bethlehem, Pennsylvania

BARBECUED BISCUITS

1/4 cup milk
1 teaspoon chopped
  parsley
1 teaspoon
  Worcestershire sauce

1/4 cup chili sauce
1/2 teaspoon instant
  minced onion
2 cups baking mix

Preheat oven to 450 degrees. Combine milk, parsley, Worcestershire sauce, chili sauce and minced onion in bowl; mix well. Let stand for 5 minutes. Stir in baking mix. Shape into ball on floured surface. Knead 5 times. Roll out to 1/2-inch thickness. Cut into 2-inch rounds; place on ungreased baking sheet. Reroll scraps; cut into rounds. Bake for 8 to 10 minutes or until brown. Yield: 10 to 12 servings.

Sharon Timpe, Xi Alpha Theta
Mequon, Wisconsin

CHEESE-GARLIC BISCUITS

2 cups baking mix
2/3 cup milk
1/2 cup shredded
  Cheddar cheese

1/4 cup melted butter
1/4 teaspoon garlic
  powder

Preheat oven to 450 degrees. Combine baking mix, milk and cheese in bowl; mix well. Add butter and garlic powder. Beat for 30 seconds. Drop by spoonfuls onto ungreased baking sheet. Bake for 8 to 10 minutes or until brown. Yield: 10 to 12 servings.

Sandra Matheus, Xi Epsilon Mu
Hobart, Indiana

PARMESAN BISCUITS

Almost without fail, my children shout with glee that we're having the "fancy biscuits!"

2 tablespoons margarine
2 tablespoons grated
  Parmesan cheese

1 10-count can biscuits

Preheat oven to 400 degrees. Melt margarine in baking pan in oven. Sprinkle cheese over margarine. Separate biscuits. Place in pan, turning to coat both sides. Bake for 8 to 9 minutes or until brown. Yield: 10 servings.

Debbi Roberts-McGinnis, Nu Chi
Bolivar, Missouri

YOGURT-DROP BISCUIT LOAF

This originally was a drop biscuit recipe. Making it as a loaf saves time. I love to bake bread and this is very filling and easy to fix.

1 1/2 cups whole-wheat
  flour
1 1/2 cups unbleached
  flour
2 teaspoons baking
  powder

1 tablespoon fresh or 1
  teaspoon dried herbs
1 1/2 cups plain yogurt

Preheat oven to 400 degrees. Combine flours, baking powder and herbs in bowl; mix well. Add yogurt; mix well. Knead lightly. Shape into flat loaf on oiled baking sheet. Draw starfish-like design in top with knife. Bake for 1 hour. Yield: 6 servings.

Linda Smallwood, Xi Gamma Psi
Fort Nelson, British Columbia, Canada

NEW FRUITED SCONES

1 cup raisins
1 cup orange juice
1/2 cup sugar
3 cups all-purpose flour
4 teaspoons baking
  powder

1 teaspoon cream of
  tartar
1/2 teaspoon salt
1/2 cup shortening
1 egg

Preheat oven to 400 degrees. Soak raisins in orange juice in bowl for several minutes. Mix next 5 ingredients in bowl. Cut in shortening until crumbly. Add raisin mixture and egg; mix well. Roll or pat into 10-by-14-inch rectangle on floured surface. Cut into 24 triangles; place on baking sheet. Bake for 12 minutes. Yield: 24 servings.

Sheena Lund, Xi Alpha
Kirkland, Quebec, Canada

ROSEMARY-TOPPED BREADSTICKS

1 10-count can soft
  breadsticks
1 egg white, lightly
  beaten
Salt

1 to 1 1/2 teaspoons dried
  rosemary
1 to 1 1/2 teaspoons dried
  chives

Preheat oven to 350 degrees. Unroll dough; separate at perforations into 10 breadsticks. Twist each breadstick; place on ungreased baking sheet, pressing down ends to keep bread twisted. Brush tops of breadsticks with egg white; salt lightly. Sprinkle rosemary and chives on top. Bake for 15 to 18 minutes or until brown. Yield: 5 to 8 servings.

Ann Poulson, Xi Beta Alpha
Lakeville, Minnesota

❖ ZESTY BREADSTICKS

1 8-count can crescent rolls	1/4 teaspoon onion salt
2 eggs	1/2 teaspoon garlic powder
2 tablespoons melted butter	1/2 teaspoon parsley flakes
1 teaspoon all-purpose flour	2 3-ounce cans French-fried onions, crushed

Preheat oven to 375 degrees. Unroll crescent roll dough. Cut into 32 strips. Combine eggs, butter, flour, onion salt, garlic powder and parsley flakes in bowl; mix well. Dip each dough strip in mixture to coat; roll in crushed onions. Place on baking sheet. Bake for 10 minutes. May twist each strip before baking. Yield: 10 to 15 servings.

Debra Toft, Omicron
Albert Lea, Minnesota

CHEESE-FILLED COFFEE CAKE

1 envelope dry yeast	3/4 cup margarine
1/4 cup lukewarm water	16 ounces cream cheese, softened
1 teaspoon sugar	
1 egg, slightly beaten	1 cup sugar
2 cups all-purpose flour, sifted	1 teaspoon lemon juice
	Confectioners' sugar
1/4 teaspoon salt	

Preheat oven to 375 degrees. Combine first 3 ingredients in bowl. Let stand for 10 minutes. Add egg; mix well. Combine flour and salt in bowl. Cut in margarine until crumbly. Add yeast mixture; mix well. Divide into 2 portions. Roll each into 8-by-10-inch rectangle on floured surface. Combine cream cheese, 1 cup sugar and lemon juice in bowl; mix well. Spread half the filling on each rectangle. Fold long sides over filling, overlapping slightly. Fold ends up 1 1/2 inches. Place on baking sheet. Bake for 25 minutes. Cool slightly. Sprinkle with confectioners' sugar. Yield: 10 to 15 servings.

Jan Bosiljevac, Xi Alpha Pi
Albuquerque, New Mexico

CRANBERRY-NUT COFFEE CAKE

1/4 cup packed light brown sugar	2/3 cup whole cranberry sauce
1/2 cup chopped walnuts	1 cup confectioners' sugar
1/4 teaspoon cinnamon	
2 cups baking mix	1/2 teaspoon vanilla extract
2 tablespoons sugar	
1 egg	1 tablespoon water
2/3 cup water	

Preheat oven to 400 degrees. Combine brown sugar, walnuts and cinnamon in bowl; mix well. Combine baking mix, sugar, egg and 2/3 cup water in mixer bowl; beat for 30 seconds. Spread batter in greased 9-by-9-inch baking pan. Sprinkle with brown sugar mixture. Spoon cranberry sauce over top. Bake for 20 to 25 minutes or until coffee cake tests done. Combine confectioners' sugar, vanilla and 1 tablespoon water in bowl; mix well. Drizzle in zig-zag pattern over top of warm coffee cake. Yield: 9 servings.

Valerie Herriges, Preceptor Alpha Epsilon
The Dalles, Oregon

MONKEY BREAD

3 10-count cans buttermilk biscuits	Nuts or raisins
	1/2 cup margarine
1 cup sugar	1 cup packed light brown sugar
2 teaspoons cinnamon	

Preheat oven to 350 degrees. Separate biscuits; cut each into quarters. Mix sugar and cinnamon in plastic bag. Add 6 or 8 biscuit pieces at a time to sugar mixture, shaking to coat. Layer coated biscuits and nuts or raisins in well greased tube pan. Combine margarine and brown sugar in saucepan. Boil for 1 minute, stirring frequently. Pour over biscuit layers. Bake for 35 minutes. Cool in pan for 10 minutes. Invert onto serving plate. Pull off biscuits to serve. Yield: 30 servings.

Edith Green, Xi Delta Delta
Portland, Indiana

PEACH COFFEE CAKE

I put the bread dough in the refrigerator to thaw overnight for a very quick and easy Sunday brunch recipe.

2 tablespoons light brown sugar	1 21-ounce can peach pie filling
2 tablespoons all-purpose flour	2 tablespoons melted butter or margarine
2 tablespoons oats	1 cup confectioners' sugar
1/2 teaspoon cinnamon	
2 tablespoons butter or margarine	1 teaspoon vanilla extract
1 pound frozen bread dough, thawed	1 tablespoon milk or water

Mix brown sugar, flour, oats and cinnamon in bowl. Cut in 2 tablespoons butter until crumbly. Roll bread dough into 8-by-12-inch rectangle on lightly floured surface. Place dough on greased baking sheet. Cut 2-inch strips at 1-inch intervals toward center with kitchen shears along the 12-inch sides. Spoon peach pie filling lengthwise down center of dough. Fold strips alternately across pie filling for a braided look. Brush top with melted butter; sprinkle with brown sugar mixture. Let rise in warm area until puffy. Bake in preheated 350-degree oven for 30 to 35 minutes or until golden brown. Cool. Combine confectioners' sugar, vanilla and milk in bowl; mix well. Drizzle over coffee cake. Yield: 10 servings.

Donna W. Jones, Preceptor Beta Beta
Pomeroy, Ohio

QUICK SOUR CREAM COFFEE CAKE

1 egg, beaten
1/2 cup sour cream or
  milk
1/2 cup sugar
2 tablespoons melted
  butter or margarine
1 cup all-purpose flour
1/2 teaspoon salt
2 teaspoons baking
  powder

1/4 cup packed light
  brown sugar
1/4 cup chopped nuts
1 tablespoon
  all-purpose flour
1 tablespoon melted
  butter or margarine
1 teaspoon cinnamon

Preheat oven to 350 degrees. Combine egg, sour cream, sugar and butter in bowl; mix well. Mix flour, salt and baking powder together. Add to batter; mix well. Pour into greased 8-by-8-inch cake pan. Combine brown sugar, nuts, flour, 1 tablespoon melted butter and cinnamon in bowl; mix well. Sprinkle over batter. Bake for 20 to 25 minutes or until cake tests done. Yield: 10 servings.

Margaret Frohlick, Psi
Regina, Saskatchewan, Canada

YOGURT-POPPY SEED COFFEE CAKE

1 2-ounce package
  poppy seed
1 cup yogurt
1 cup butter or
  margarine, softened
1 1/2 cups sugar
2 teaspoons vanilla
  extract

4 egg yolks, beaten
2 cups plus 2
  tablespoons sifted
  all-purpose flour
2 teaspoons baking soda
4 egg whites, stiffly
  beaten
Confectioners' sugar

Preheat oven to 350 degrees. Soak poppy seed in yogurt in cup. Cream butter and sugar in bowl until light and fluffy. Add yogurt mixture; mix well. Add vanilla, egg yolks, flour and baking soda, beating well after each addition. Fold in egg whites gently. Pour into greased and floured bundt pan. Bake for 50 to 60 minutes or until coffee cake tests done. Sprinkle with confectioners' sugar. Yield: 15 servings.

Tammy Rice, Zeta Tau
Bagdad, Arizona

BROCCOLI CORN BREAD

The first time I tried this recipe, the family loved it. The second time I used the wrong mix and we had blueberry corn bread. It really wasn't too bad.

1 package frozen
  chopped broccoli,
  thawed
1 small onion, finely
  chopped
6 ounces cottage cheese

1/2 cup melted butter or
  margarine
1 teaspoon salt
4 eggs, beaten
1 8-ounce package corn
  bread mix

Preheat oven to 400 degrees. Drain broccoli. Combine uncooked broccoli, onion, cottage cheese, butter, salt and eggs in bowl; mix well. Stir in corn bread mix. Pour into greased 9-by-13-inch baking pan. Bake for 23 minutes or until light brown. Do not overbake. Serve hot. Yield: 12 servings.

Ruth G. Holder, Preceptor Nu
Fayetteville, North Carolina

GREAT-TOPPER CORN BREAD

1/4 cup grated onion
1 tablespoon butter or
  margarine
1 6-ounce package corn
  muffin or corn bread
  mix

1 cup shredded sharp
  process American
  cheese
1 teaspoon celery seed

Preheat oven to 375 degrees. Sauté onion in butter in skillet until tender. Prepare corn muffin mix using package directions. Spread batter in greased 6-by-10-inch baking dish. Sprinkle with cheese; dot with sautéed onion. Sprinkle with celery seed. Bake for 20 minutes or until brown. Serve hot. Yield: 6 servings.

Phyllis B. Painter, Laureate Alpha Beta
Staunton, Virginia

SUPER CORN BREAD

1 cup butter or
  margarine, softened
1 cup sugar
4 eggs
1 16-ounce can cream-
  style corn
1/2 cup each shredded
  Cheddar and
  Monterey Jack cheese

1 cup yellow cornmeal
1 cup all-purpose flour
1/4 teaspoon salt
4 teaspoons baking
  powder
1 4-ounce can chopped
  green chilies

Preheat oven to 350 degrees. Cream butter and sugar in mixer bowl until light and fluffy. Add eggs 1 at a time, beating well after each addition. Add corn and cheeses; mix well. Mix cornmeal, flour, salt and baking powder together. Add dry ingredients and green chilies to batter; mix well. Spray 9-by-13-inch baking pan with nonstick cooking spray. Pour in batter. Bake for 30 minutes or until light brown. Yield: 12 servings.

Marge Chadderdon, Preceptor Chi
Coeur d'Alene, Idaho

UPSIDE-DOWN SAUSAGE-ONION CORN BREAD

Great for breakfast, brunch, potluck suppers or with stews or soups. I always keep buttermilk powder on hand.

8 ounces pork or turkey
  sausage
2 medium sweet onions,
  chopped
1 cup cornmeal
1 cup all-purpose flour
2 tablespoons sugar

2 teaspoons baking
  powder
1 teaspoon salt
1/2 teaspoon baking soda
1 egg, beaten
1 cup buttermilk
1/3 cup melted margarine

Preheat oven to 350 degrees. Spray skillet with non-stick cooking spray. Brown sausage with onions in skillet, stirring until crumbly. Drain all but 1 tablespoon drippings. Combine dry ingredients in bowl; mix well. Add mixture of egg and buttermilk and melted margarine; mix just until moistened. Pour batter over sausage in skillet. Bake for 25 to 30 minutes or until brown. Cool in pan for several minutes. Invert onto serving plate. Yield: 8 servings.

Mary Lou McGee, Mass Laureate Alpha
Wilbraham, Massachusetts

BLEU CHEESE BREAD

2 ounces bleu cheese	Freshly ground pepper
3 tablespoons butter or	to taste
margarine, softened	3 or 4 slices crisp-fried
1 French bread baguette	bacon, crumbled
Sage to taste	

Combine bleu cheese and butter in bowl; mix well. Split French bread into halves lengthwise. Spread bleu cheese mixture on each half; sprinkle with sage, pepper and crumbled bacon. Place on rack in broiler pan. Broil until cheese is bubbly.
Yield: 4 to 6 servings.

Rebecca Noble, Alpha Zeta
Jemez Springs, New Mexico

CHEESY FRENCH BREAD

This recipe is always a favorite at high school get-togethers, family reunions and picnics. Don't tell anyone how easy it is!

1 16-ounce loaf of	3 cups shredded
French bread	Cheddar cheese
2 tablespoons	1 cup mayonnaise
margarine, softened	

Preheat oven to 350 degrees. Split French bread into halves lengthwise. Spread margarine over each half. Combine cheese and mayonnaise in bowl; mix well. Spread over bread. Place on baking sheet. Bake for 20 minutes or until cheese is light brown. Serve hot. May also add jalapeño peppers or chopped black olives to cheese mixture. Yield: 12 to 16 servings.

Bonnie Thompson, Xi Beta Iota
Viola, Idaho

DILLY CHEESE BREAD

1 loaf French bread	1 cup mayonnaise
Butter or margarine,	2 cups shredded sharp
softened	Cheddar cheese
Garlic salt or powder	Dillweed

Preheat oven to 350 degrees. Cut French bread into halves lengthwise. Spread with butter; sprinkle with garlic salt or powder. Combine mayonnaise and cheese in bowl; mix well. Spread on bread; sprinkle

with dillweed. Place on baking sheet. Bake for 10 to 15 minutes or until cheese is bubbly. Serve hot. Yield: 10 to 15 servings.

Connie Maher, Xi Delta Mu
Hawarden, Iowa

FRENCH BACON BREAD

2 cups shredded Colby	1/2 cup mayonnaise
or Monterey Jack	4 ounces cream cheese,
cheese	softened
1 pound bacon, crisp-	1/4 cup minced onion
fried, crumbled	1 teaspoon
1 6-ounce can pitted	Worcestershire sauce
black olives, sliced	1 loaf French bread

Preheat oven to 375 degrees. Combine first 7 ingredients in bowl; mix well. Split French bread into thirds lengthwise. Spread cheese mixture between layers; place on baking sheet. Bake for 15 minutes. Cut into 2-inch pieces. Serve warm. Yield: 20 servings.

Arlene A. Carper, Iota Nu
Haxtun, Colorado

ITALIAN FRENCH BREAD

1 cup mayonnaise	1 teaspoon
1/2 cup grated Parmesan	Worcestershire sauce
cheese	1 loaf French bread
1 medium onion, finely	
chopped	

Combine first 4 ingredients in bowl; mix well. Cut French bread into halves lengthwise. Spread mixture on bread. Place on rack in broiler pan. Cook under hot broiler until light brown. Yield: 10 to 15 servings.

Pat Williams, Xi Sigma Omicron
Marysville, California

HERBED VEGETABLE-CHEESE BREAD

1 cup shredded	2 green onions, sliced
mozzarella cheese	1/4 cup mayonnaise
1/2 cup grated carrot	8 3/4-inch slices French
1/2 teaspoon dried	bread
Italian herb seasoning	

Preheat oven to 350 degrees. Combine first 5 ingredients in bowl; mix well. Place bread on baking pan. Brown lightly on 1 side. Turn bread; spread with cheese mixture. Bake for 15 minutes or until cheese is melted. Yield: 8 servings.

Georgia Lucas, Xi Delta Alpha
Sandy, Utah

Mildred Mahler, Laureate Nu, Cookeville, Tennessee, makes Party Rolls by creaming 2 sticks butter or margarine and 1 cup sour cream together. Stir in 2 cups self-rising flour or biscuit mix. Spoon into 45 to 50 miniature muffin cups and bake in preheated 425-degree oven for 15 minutes.

OLIVE BREAD

½ cup margarine,
   softened
1 4-ounce can chopped
   black olives
4 green onions, chopped

1 cup shredded Velveeta
   cheese
1 teaspoon garlic salt
2 loaves French bread

Preheat oven to 350 degrees. Combine first 5 ingredients in bowl; mix well. Slice bread into halves lengthwise. Spread mixture on bottom halves of bread; replace tops. Slice bread to, but not through, bottom. Wrap in foil. Bake for 20 to 25 minutes. Yield: 20 servings.

Kay Henderson, Xi Sigma Tau
Austin, Texas

AVOCADO-PECAN BREAD

Originally this bread was included to complement other Hawaiian foods for a chapter Luau. Later it won several ribbons in contests.

1 egg
½ cup buttermilk
⅓ cup vegetable oil
2 tablespoons
   margarine, softened
½ to ¾ cup mashed
   avocado
2 cups all-purpose flour

¾ cup sugar
½ teaspoon baking soda
½ teaspoon baking
   powder
¼ teaspoon non-iodized
   salt
¾ cup chopped pecans

Preheat oven to 350 degrees. Combine egg, buttermilk, oil, margarine and avocado in mixer bowl; beat well. Add flour, sugar, baking soda, baking powder and salt; mix well. Stir in pecans. Pour into 3 greased 3x5-inch loaf pans. Bake for 30 minutes or until loaves test done. Cool in pans for 10 minutes. Remove to serving plate. Serve warm with cream cheese, butter or margarine. Yield: 9 to 12 servings.

Betty Blanchard, Laureate Alpha Delta
Portland, Oregon

BANANA-APPLE BREAD

½ cup butter or
   margarine, softened
1 cup sugar
2 eggs
1½ tablespoons milk
1 banana, mashed
2 cups all-purpose flour
¼ teaspoon salt
2 teaspoons baking
   powder
½ teaspoon baking soda

1 teaspoon vanilla
   extract
1 large apple, finely
   chopped
1 tablespoon oatbran
1 tablespoon wheat
   germ
½ cup raisins (optional)
½ cup semisweet
   chocolate chips
   (optional)

Preheat oven to 350 degrees. Cream butter and sugar in mixer bowl until light and fluffy. Add eggs 1 at a time, beating well after each addition. Mix milk and banana in bowl. Add to batter; mix well. Mix flour, salt, baking powder and baking soda together. Add

to batter; mix well. Stir in remaining ingredients. Fill 14 greased muffin cups ¾ full. Bake for 20 minutes or until muffins test done. Serve warm. Yield: 14 servings.

Kathleen Freeman, Preceptor Iota
Boulder, Colorado

GOOD BREAD-AND-BUTTER BREAD

This is the easiest bread I have ever made and is especially good while still warm.

3 cups self-rising flour
3 tablespoons sugar

1 12-ounce can beer

Preheat oven to 350 degrees. Mix all ingredients in bowl. Pour into greased 5-by-9-inch loaf pan. Bake for 30 minutes. Serve warm. Yield: 12 servings.

Marilyn F. Richmond, Xi Alpha Epsilon
Cincinnati, Ohio

CANTALOUPE BREAD

This is a family favorite during cantaloupe season. We slice it into thin slices, spread with thinned cream cheese and top with bananas, strawberries or kiwifruit. Really delicious sandwiches.

1 cup sugar
½ cup vegetable oil
2 eggs
1½ teaspoons vanilla
   extract
1½ cups all-purpose
   flour
½ teaspoon baking soda

2 teaspoons baking
   powder
½ teaspoon salt
1 teaspoon cinnamon
1 cantaloupe, puréed,
   including juice
½ cup chopped pecans

Preheat oven to 350 degrees. Beat sugar and oil in mixer bowl until smooth. Add eggs 1 at a time, beating well after each addition. Add vanilla; mix well. Mix dry ingredients together. Add to batter; mix well. Stir in cantaloupe purée and pecans. Pour into 3 greased and floured 3-by-5-inch loaf pans. Bake for 25 minutes or until loaves test done. Cool in pans for 10 minutes. Remove to wire racks to cool completely. Yield: 9 to 12 servings.

Ann Doucet, Preceptor Alpha Omicron
Deer Park, Texas

QUICK CHEESE BREAD

2 cups all-purpose flour
4 teaspoons baking
   powder
1 teaspoon sugar
½ teaspoon onion salt
½ teaspoon oregano
¼ teaspoon dry mustard

1½ cups shredded
   Cheddar cheese
1 egg
1 cup milk
1 tablespoon melted
   butter or margarine

Preheat oven to 350 degrees. Combine dry ingredients in bowl; mix well. Add cheese, egg, milk and butter; mix well. Spoon into 3 buttered 3-by-5-inch

loaf pans. Bake for 25 minutes or until loaves test done. Remove to wire racks to cool.
Yield: 9 to 12 servings.

Terry Hewitson, Zeta Delta
Prescott, Ontario, Canada

HERB BREAD

I prepare this when I need quick bread and want something different.

3 tablespoons margarine
1 tablespoon dried
  minced onion
2 teaspoons dillseed
1 teaspoon sesame seed
1/4 teaspoon celery seed
1 10-count can biscuits
1/4 cup grated Parmesan
  cheese

Preheat oven to 400 degrees. Melt margarine in 8-inch baking pan. Sprinkle next 4 ingredients over melted margarine. Separate biscuits; cut into fourths. Coat with Parmesan cheese; arrange in baking pan. Sprinkle with remaining Parmesan cheese. Bake for 15 to 18 minutes or until golden brown. Invert onto serving plate. Yield: 4 to 5 servings.

Sonia Richards, Preceptor Tau
Merritt Island, Florida

LEMON-POPPY SEED BREAD

1 2-layer pudding-
  recipe lemon cake mix
4 eggs
1/2 cup corn oil
1 cup water
1 tablespoon poppy seed

Preheat oven to 350 degrees. Combine cake mix and eggs in bowl; mix well. Add oil and water; mix well. Stir in poppy seed. Pour into 3 greased and floured 3-by-5-inch loaf pans. Bake for 25 minutes or until loaves test done. Yield: 9 to 12 servings.

Jill Elliott, Xi Theta Iota
Sioux City, Iowa

❖ PICANTE-SPICE BREAD

This bread is great with soup and salad suppers, barbecued foods, ham and beans. Its spicy flavor is really unusual.

2 cups all-purpose flour
3/4 cup sugar
1 teaspoon baking soda
1 teaspoon baking
  powder
1/2 teaspoon cumin
1/2 teaspoon cinnamon
1/2 teaspoon allspice
11/2 cups picante sauce
1/2 cup melted margarine
2 eggs, beaten

Preheat oven to 350 degrees. Combine all dry ingredients in mixer bowl; mix well. Add picante sauce, margarine and eggs; beat well. Spoon into 3 greased and floured 3-by-5-inch loaf pans. Bake for 25 minutes or until loaves test done. Remove to wire racks to cool. Yield: 9 to 12 servings.

Kathy Gasper, Nu Mu
Salina, Kansas

GREEN TOMATO-WHEAT BREAD

2 eggs
1/2 cup corn oil
11/3 cups packed light
  brown sugar
2 cups well drained
  chopped green
  tomatoes
1/2 cup crushed
  pineapple
1/2 teaspoon orange
  extract
2 cups all-purpose flour
Cinnamon to taste
11/2 teaspoons salt
1/4 teaspoon allspice
2 teaspoons baking soda
11/2 cups rolled wheat
1 cup chopped nuts

Preheat oven to 350 degrees. Combine first 3 ingredients in mixer bowl; beat until fluffy. Beat in green tomatoes, pineapple and orange extract. Sift flour with cinnamon, salt, allspice and baking soda. Add to batter; mix well. Stir in rolled wheat and nuts. Spoon into 6 greased and floured 3-by-5-inch loaf pans. Bake for 25 minutes or until loaves test done. Remove to wire racks to cool. Yield: 18 to 24 servings.

Juanita Fleming, Xi Alpha Delta
Pleasant Hill, Oregon

CHEESE-GARLIC BREAD

1 package frozen bread
  dough
1 teaspoon minced garlic
1/4 cup chopped green
  onion tops
1/2 cup shredded
  Cheddar cheese
3 tablespoons melted
  butter or margarine

Thaw bread in refrigerator overnight. Let dough rise in warm place. Roll dough into rectangle on floured surface. Sprinkle with garlic, onion tops and cheese. Roll to enclose filling. Turn open ends under; place in buttered 5-by-9-inch loaf pan. Cut 3 or 4 slashes in top. Let rise in warm place for 1 hour. Drizzle with butter. Bake in preheated 375-degree oven for 30 to 40 minutes or until brown. Remove to wire rack to cool. Yield: 8 to 10 servings.

Kathy Cahill, Xi Upsilon Rho
Kilgore, Texas

GARLIC BUBBLE LOAVES

1/4 cup melted butter or
  margarine
1/2 teaspoon garlic
  powder
1 egg, beaten
1/4 teaspoon salt
1 teaspoon dried
  parsley flakes
1 loaf frozen bread
  dough, thawed
Melted butter or
  margarine

Combine first 5 ingredients in bowl; mix well. Cut dough into walnut-sized pieces. Dip in seasoned butter; place in 3 greased 3-by-5-inch loaf pans. Let rise, covered, in warm place until doubled in bulk. Bake in preheated 350-degree oven for 30 minutes. Brush with melted butter. Remove to wire racks to cool. Yield: 12 servings.

Lou Ann Kiemele, Iota
Devils Lake, North Dakota

HAM-CHEESE AND BROCCOLI BREAD

2 loaves frozen honey
  wheat bread dough,
  thawed
1 cup shredded ham
1 cup shredded Cheddar
  cheese
1 cup chopped broccoli,
  blanched, drained

Flatten bread dough on greased baking pan. Sprinkle with ham, cheese and broccoli. Roll to enclose filling. Place in loaf pan. Let rise until doubled in bulk. Bake using bread dough package directions. Slice and serve hot with coarse mustard. Yield: 4 servings.

Shari K. Foster, Alpha Psi Beta
Lockhart, Texas

SAUSAGE BREAD

2 loaves frozen bread
  dough, thawed
1 pound hot sausage
1 cup shredded
  Monterey Jack cheese
1 cup mozzarella cheese

Let dough stand at room temperature overnight to thaw and rise. Preheat oven to 350 degrees. Brown sausage in skillet, stirring until crumbly; drain and cool. Knead loaves; roll each loaf into 9-by-13-inch rectangle on floured surface. Sprinkle sausage and cheeses on bread dough. Roll to enclose filling; place seam-side down on greased baking sheet. Bake for 45 minutes or until brown. Cut into slices. Yield: 20 servings.

Margaret Doherty, Xi Alpha Alpha Omicron
Ennis, Texas

SWISS ONION RING

Microwave dough, wrapped in plastic wrap, on Low for 6 minutes to thaw, turning occasionally.

1 1-pound loaf frozen
  bread dough, thawed
6 tablespoons melted
  butter or margarine
2 cups shredded Swiss
  cheese
3/4 cup finely chopped
  green onions
2 tablespoons poppy
  seed
1/4 teaspoon salt
  (optional)

Cut dough into 20 pieces. Dip 10 pieces in melted butter; arrange in greased tube pan. Combine Swiss cheese, green onions, poppy seed, salt and half the remaining butter in bowl; mix well. Spread half the mixture over dough in pan. Dip remaining 10 pieces dough in remaining melted butter; arrange in pan. Blend any remaining butter into remaining cheese mixture; spread over top of dough. Let rise in warm place until doubled in bulk. Bake in preheated 375-degree oven for 25 to 30 minutes or until golden brown and bread sounds hollow when tapped. Yield: 10 servings.

Janice Vogt, Lambda Sigma
Centralia, Missouri

TEDDY BEAR BREAD

2 1-pound loaves
  frozen bread dough,
  thawed
Raisins
Melted butter or
  margarine
Cinnamon sugar

Let thawed dough rise in warm place until doubled in bulk. Cut 1 loaf into 1/3-loaf size and 2/3-loaf size. Roll each into ball. Spray baking sheet with nonstick cooking spray. Place balls on baking sheet with 1/3-loaf size positioned for head, touching 2/3-loaf size positioned for body of teddy bear. Cut remaining loaf into halves lengthwise. Cut each half into 3 portions. Roll each portion into ball. Place on baking sheet, positioned for ears, arms and legs of teddy bear. Let rise in warm place until doubled in bulk. Press raisins into place for eyes and buttons. Brush with melted butter; sprinkle with cinnamon sugar. Bake in preheated 350-degree oven for 20 minutes or until golden brown. Yield: 8 to 10 servings.

Nancy Davis, Xi Beta Iota
Auburn, Alabama

APPLE BUTTER MUFFINS

1 3/4 cups all-purpose
  flour
1/3 cup sugar
2 teaspoons baking
  powder
1 teaspoon apple or
  pumpkin pie spice
1/4 teaspoon salt
1 egg, beaten
3/4 cup milk
1/4 cup vegetable oil
1/3 cup apple butter
1/3 cup chopped pecans
2 tablespoons sugar

Preheat oven to 400 degrees. Combine flour, 1/3 cup sugar, baking powder, spice and salt in bowl; mix well. Mix egg, milk and oil in bowl. Add to dry ingredients all at once, stirring just until moistened. Drop rounded tablespoonfuls batter into lightly greased muffin cups. Top with rounded teaspoonfuls apple butter; fill 3/4 full with remaining batter. Combine pecans and sugar in bowl; mix well. Sprinkle on top of muffins. Bake for 20 minutes or until brown. Yield: 12 servings.

Shirley Welch, Psi Iota
Theodosia, Missouri

CHUNKY APPLE MUFFINS

1/4 cup vegetable oil
3/4 cup packed light
  brown sugar
1 egg
1 tablespoon cream,
  milk or yogurt
1/2 cup raisins
1 1/2 cups coarsely
  chopped unpeeled
  apples
1 cup all-purpose flour
3/4 teaspoon baking soda
1 teaspoon baking
  powder
3/4 teaspoon salt
1 teaspoon cinnamon
1/2 teaspoon nutmeg
1 teaspoon cinnamon
1 1/2 tablespoons sugar

Preheat oven to 375 degrees. Grease muffin cups or line with paper liners. Beat oil, brown sugar, egg and cream in mixer bowl. Stir in raisins and apples. Mix flour, baking soda, baking powder, salt, 1 teaspoon cinnamon and nutmeg together. Add to batter, stirring just until moistened. Fill muffin cups 3/4 full. Mix remaining 1 teaspoon cinnamon and sugar together. Sprinkle over muffins. Bake for 20 minutes or until muffins test done. Yield: 10 to 12 servings.

Joanne Evans-Daley, Xi Eta Beta
Metcalfe, Ontario, Canada

APRICOT-ORANGE MUFFINS

1/2 cup dried apricots, coarsely chopped	*1/2 cup raisins*
1 cup orange juice	*2 cups all-purpose flour*
2 eggs, lightly beaten	*1/4 cup sugar*
1/4 cup melted butter or margarine	*2 teaspoons baking powder*
1 1/2 teaspoons vanilla extract	*1 teaspoon baking soda*
	Pinch of nutmeg

Preheat oven to 350 degrees. Combine first 6 ingredients in bowl; mix well. Combine flour with remaining ingredients in large bowl; mix well. Stir in orange juice mixture just until moistened. Fill greased muffin cups 3/4 full. Bake for 20 minutes or until golden brown. Yield: 12 servings.

Dorothy L. Crockatt, Laureate Beta Nu
Etobicoke, Ontario, Canada

OAT BRAN MUFFINS

2 cups oat bran cereal	*2 tablespoons grated orange rind*
1/4 cup packed light brown sugar	*1/4 cup honey*
2 teaspoons baking powder	*2 medium bananas, mashed*
1/2 teaspoon salt	*2 tablespoons vegetable oil*
2 eggs, beaten	*1/2 cup chopped walnuts*
1/2 cup orange juice	

Preheat oven to 425 degrees. Combine first 4 ingredients in large bowl; mix well. Beat eggs with remaining ingredients in bowl. Stir into dry ingredients just until moistened. Fill nonstick muffin cups 2/3 full. Bake for 17 minutes. Yield: 12 servings.

Joan Stucey, Preceptor Mu Xi
Cedarville, California

BLUEBERRY-LEMON MUFFINS

1 3/4 cups all-purpose flour	*1 cup lemon yogurt*
1/3 cup sugar	*1/3 cup corn oil*
3/4 teaspoon salt	*2 tablespoons milk*
2 1/2 teaspoons baking powder	*1 teaspoon finely grated lemon rind*
1 egg, beaten	*3/4 cup fresh or frozen blueberries*

Preheat oven to 400 degrees. Combine flour, sugar, salt and baking powder in mixer bowl; mix well. Make a well in center of mixture. Beat egg, yogurt, oil, milk and lemon rind in small bowl. Add to well in dry ingredients; stir just until moistened. Fold in blueberries gently. Fill greased muffin cups 2/3 full. Bake for 20 to 25 minutes or until golden. Serve warm. Yield: 12 servings.

Bonnie Carroll, Xi Nu
Evansville, Indiana

CHERRY-PECAN MUFFINS

1 egg	*1 heaping tablespoon baking powder*
3/4 cup milk	*7 tablespoons corn oil*
2 cups plus 2 tablespoons unbleached flour	*1 cup sour cherries*
1 cup packed light brown sugar	*1/2 cup pecan pieces*

Preheat over to 375 degrees. Mix egg and milk in small bowl. Combine flour, brown sugar and baking powder in mixer bowl; mix well. Add egg mixture. Mix on low speed for 3 minutes. Add oil 1 tablespoon at a time, mixing well after each addition. Stir in cherries and pecans. Spoon into 6 large or 12 regular muffin cups. Bake for 38 to 40 minutes. Yield: 12 servings.

Judy Goeden, Xi Epsilon Epsilon
Topeka, Kansas

CRANBERRY-ORANGE MUFFINS

I freeze several packages of cranberries when they are available in order to have them on hand year-round. No preparation is required- just toss bags in freezer. Muffins can also be frozen and then microwaved when guests appear.

1 cup fresh or frozen whole cranberries	*2 teaspoons cinnamon*
1/4 cup sugar	*1/4 teaspoon allspice*
3/4 cup all-purpose flour	*1 egg, beaten*
3/4 cup whole wheat flour	*1/4 teaspoon grated orange rind*
1/4 cup sugar	*3/4 cup orange juice*
	1/3 cup vegetable oil

Preheat oven to 375 degrees. Combine cranberries and 1/4 cup sugar in bowl; mix well. Set aside. Combine flour, whole wheat flour, sugar, cinnamon and allspice in large bowl; mix well. Make well in center. Beat egg with orange rind, orange juice and oil in bowl. Stir into well in dry ingredients. Mix just until moistened. Fold in cranberry mixture gently. Fill muffin cups 3/4 full. Bake for 20 minutes. Yield: 12 servings.

Joanne Huth, Laureate Omega
Guelph, Ontario, Canada

GRAHAM CRACKER MUFFINS

18 graham crackers,
  finely crushed
2 tablespoons sugar
1 tablespoon
  all-purpose flour
1 tablespoon baking
  powder

1/4 teaspoon salt
1/2 cup raisins, cut into
  halves
3 tablespoons melted
  butter
1/2 cup lukewarm milk
1 egg, beaten

Preheat oven to 400 degrees. Combine graham cracker crumbs, sugar, flour, baking powder, salt and
raisins in bowl; mix well. Stir in melted butter. Pour
milk and egg over mixture; mix lightly. Fill greased
muffin cups 2/3 full. Bake for 20 minutes.
Yield: 12 servings.

Carol Johannigmeier, Laureate Mu
Ft. Collins, Colorado

PUMPKIN MUFFINS

1 cup all-purpose flour
1 1/2 cups nonfat dry
  milk
1 1/2 teaspoons pumpkin
  pie spice
2 teaspoons cinnamon
1/2 teaspoon ground
  cloves
2 teaspoons baking soda
4 eggs

6 packets (about)
  artificial sweetener
2 cups canned pumpkin
2 teaspoons vanilla
  extract
1 cup shredded carrot
1 8-ounce can crushed
  pineapple
1/4 cup raisins

Preheat oven to 350 degrees. Mix dry ingredients in
large bowl. Beat eggs with remaining ingredients in
medium bowl; mix well. Add to dry ingredients; mix
well. Spoon into muffin cups coated with nonstick
cooking spray. Bake for 15 to 20 minutes.
Yield: 24 servings.

Dolores H. Brown, Preceptor Omega
Sheldon, South Carolina

QUICK AND HEALTHY BRAN MUFFINS

1 cup stone-ground
  whole wheat
1/2 cup bran flakes
3/4 cup skim milk
1 egg

3 tablespoons safflower
  oil
1 teaspoon baking soda
1/2 cup honey

Preheat oven to 400 degrees. Combine all ingredients
in bowl; mix well. Fill greased muffin cups 2/3 full.
Bake for 15 minutes. Yield: 12 servings.

Kelly Evanoff, Epsilon Theta
Salem, Oregon

RASPBERRY MUFFINS

1 1/2 cups all-purpose
  flour
1/2 cup sugar
2 teaspoons baking
  powder

1/2 cup milk
1/2 cup melted butter
1 egg, beaten
1 cup fresh or frozen
  raspberries

Preheat oven to 375 degrees. Mix dry ingredients in
bowl. Beat milk, butter and egg in small bowl. Add
to dry ingredients; stir just until mixed. Spoon 1
tablespoon batter into each of 12 greased muffin
cups. Top with half the raspberries. Add remaining
batter. Top with remaining raspberries. Bake for 20
to 25 minutes. Yield: 12 servings.

Peggy Triggs, Nu Mu
Salina, Kansas

SOUR CREAM MUFFINS

2 cups baking mix
1/2 cup melted margarine

1 cup sour cream

Preheat oven to 425 degrees. Combine baking mix,
margarine and sour cream in bowl; stir just until
mixed. Fill greased muffin cups 3/4 full. Bake for 12
to 15 minutes. Yield: 12 servings.

Rose A. Harris, Alpha Master
Nashville, Tennessee

DILLY CHEESE ROLLS

These rolls are great with soup and salad for a light lunch.

6 tablespoons melted
  butter or margarine
1 teaspoon chopped
  parsley
2 teaspoons dillweed

1 teaspoon minced onion
3 tablespoons grated
  Parmesan cheese
1 10-count can
  biscuits, cut into halves

Preheat oven to 425 degrees. Pour butter into 8-inch
round pan. Combine parsley, dillweed, onion and
Parmesan cheese; mix well. Roll biscuit halves in
butter; coat with cheese mixture. Arrange in pan.
Bake for 10 to 15 minutes or until light brown.
Yield: 10 servings.

Carla Kopecky, Xi Epsilon Nu
Emporia, Kansas

BUSY-DAY CHEESE ROLLS

1 envelope dry yeast
1 cup warm water
2 tablespoons sugar
1 teaspoon salt
2 tablespoons
  shortening

1 egg
2 1/4 cups all-purpose
  flour
6 to 8 ounces Cheddar
  cheese, cut into
  1/2-inch cubes

Dissolve yeast in water with sugar and salt in bowl.
Add shortening, egg and half the flour. Beat until
mixed. Add remaining flour. Mix until smooth. Stir
in cheese. Let rise, covered, in warm place until
doubled in bulk. Divide into 12 portions. Place in
greased muffin cups. Bake in preheated 400-degree
oven for 15 minutes or until golden brown.
Yield: 12 servings.

Punky Daniels
White Deer, Texas

MAYONNAISE ROLLS

2 cups self-rising flour   1 cup milk
1/4 cup mayonnaise   1 tablespoon sugar

Preheat oven to 400 degrees. Combine all ingredients in bowl; stir just until mixed. Spoon into greased muffin cups. Bake for 15 to 20 minutes or until golden brown. Yield: 12 servings.

Regina Farris, Alpha Delta
Madisonville, Kentucky

PARMESAN PULL-APARTS

3 tablespoons melted   1/4 teaspoon celery seed
  margarine   1 10-count can large
1 tablespoon minced   biscuits, cut into
  dried onion   quarters
2 teaspoons dillseed   1/4 cup grated Parmesan
1 teaspoon poppy seed   cheese

Preheat oven to 400 degrees. Pour margarine into 8-inch round pan. Combine next 4 ingredients in bowl. Sprinkle over margarine. Place biscuits and cheese in plastic bag; shake to coat. Arrange in prepared pan. Sprinkle any remaining cheese over top. Bake for 15 to 18 minutes or until golden brown. Yield: 6 to 8 servings.

Linda Holland, Sigma Alpha
Buda, Illinois

PARSLEY FANTANS

1 teaspoon lemon juice   2 tablespoons chopped
2 tablespoons melted   parsley
  butter or margarine   2 tablespoons chopped
6 butterflake brown   chives
  and serve rolls,
  partially separated

Preheat oven to 400 degrees. Mix lemon juice and butter in bowl. Brush rolls with half the lemon-butter. Sprinkle with half the parsley and chives. Place in muffin cups. Brush with remaining lemon-butter. Sprinkle with remaining parsley and chives. Bake for 10 minutes or until golden brown. Yield: 6 servings.

Pearl Hoffman, Preceptor Rho
Asheboro, North Carolina

QUICK ROLLS

1 10-count can   1 teaspoon onion salt
  buttermilk biscuits   1 teaspoon dillseed
1 cup crisp rice cereal

Preheat oven to 475 degrees. Cut rolls into halves. Roll each half into log. Dip in mixture of cereal, salt and dillseed. Place on baking sheet. Bake for 10 minutes. Yield: 20 servings.

Audrey Sasse, Xi Gamma
Miles City, Montana

CINNAMON SNAILS

Great to serve for breakfast.

1 can crescent rolls   Cinnamon to taste
Softened margarine   1 egg, lightly beaten
Sugar to taste   (optional)

Preheat oven to 375 degrees. Separate roll dough into triangles. Spread rolls with margarine. Sprinkle with sugar and cinnamon. Roll up from wide end. Cut into 1 1/4-inch pieces. Place cut side up on ungreased baking sheet. Brush tops with egg. Bake for 10 to 12 minutes or until golden brown. Yield: 20 servings.

Jan Pringle, Theta Gamma
Arkansas City, Kansas

LAZY CINNAMON BUNS

These buns are delicious and gooey. The kids will really love them.

2 loaves frozen bread   1 6-ounce package
  dough, thawed   vanilla instant
1/2 cup melted butter   pudding mix
  or margarine   2 tablespoons milk
1 cup packed light   Cinnamon to taste
  brown sugar

Pinch dough into bite-sized pieces. Arrange in greased 9-by-13-inch baking pan. Combine butter, brown sugar, pudding mix, milk and cinnamon in bowl; mix well. Pour over dough. Let rise, covered with plastic wrap, in warm place until doubled in bulk. Bake in preheated 350-degree oven for 25 to 30 minutes or until brown. Yield: 12 servings.

Gloria Chapman, Sigma
Estevan, Saskatchewan, Canada

❖ BREAKFAST ROLLS

These will melt in your mouth. They are great to share with friends over coffee.

1 pint vanilla ice cream,   2 loaves frozen bread
  melted   dough, thawed
1 cup packed light   Cinnamon and sugar to
  brown sugar   taste

Combine ice cream and brown sugar in 9-by-13-inch pan. Cut dough into pieces. Arrange in ice cream mixture. Sprinkle with cinnamon and sugar. Let rise in warm place until doubled in bulk. Bake in preheated 350 degree oven for 30 to 40 minutes or until golden brown. Yield: 24 servings.

Melinda Shannon, Beta Chi
Syracuse, Nebraska

Cut bread-baking time by using several small 3-by-5-inch loaf pans rather than one 5-by-8-inch pan.

ICE CREAM CARAMEL ROLLS

10 to 12 frozen
  cinnamon rolls
1 cup packed light
  brown sugar
1 cup ice cream
1/2 to 3/4 cup butter or
  margarine
Chopped nuts to taste

Arrange rolls in 9-by-13-inch baking pan. Let rise until doubled in bulk. Combine next 3 ingredients in glass bowl. Microwave on High until heated through; mix well. Pour over rolls. Bake in preheated 350-degree oven for 15 to 20 minutes. Invert onto platter; sprinkle with nuts. Yield: 12 servings.

Diane Durham, Alpha Omicron
Williston, North Dakota

PECAN ROLLS

1 loaf frozen bread,
  thawed
1/2 cup margarine,
  softened
1 teaspoon cinnamon
3/4 cup sugar
1/2 cup whipping cream
1 cup packed light
  brown sugar
3/4 teaspoon cinnamon
4 ounces chopped pecans

Pat bread dough into rectangle on floured surface. Spread with margarine. Sprinkle with cinnamon and sugar. Roll lengthwise; slice into 20 rolls. Spread mixture of next 3 ingredients in 9-by-13-inch pan. Sprinkle with pecans. Arrange rolls in pan. Let rise, covered, until doubled in bulk. Bake in preheated 350-degree oven for 15 to 20 minutes or until golden brown. Cool for 2 minutes. Invert onto platter. Yield: 20 servings.

Susan Thompson, Beta Psi
Scottsdale, Arizona

QUICK AND STICKY BUNS

1 cup chopped pecans
1 package frozen dinner
  rolls
3/4 cup packed light
  brown sugar
1 4-ounce package
  butterscotch instant
  pudding mix
1/2 cup melted butter or
  margarine

Sprinkle pecans in 9-by-13-inch pan. Arrange rolls over pecans. Sprinkle with next 2 ingredients. Pour butter over top. Let rise, covered with waxed paper, until doubled in bulk. Bake in preheated 375-degree oven for 20 to 25 minutes. Yield: 24 servings.

Elaine Caldwell, Kappa Delta
Lake Jackson, Texas

STICKY ROLLS

1/4 cup melted butter or
  margarine
1/4 cup packed light
  brown sugar
1 tablespoon corn syrup
1/4 cup chopped pecans
1 11-ounce can soft
  breadsticks
1/2 teaspoon cinnamon
1 tablespoon sugar

Preheat oven to 350 degrees. Mix first 3 ingredients in bowl. Spread in ungreased 8-inch round pan.
Sprinkle with pecans. Separate breadsticks into 8 coils. Mix cinnamon and sugar in bowl. Dip 1 side of each coil in mixture. Arrange cinnamon-sugar side down in prepared pan. Sprinkle with remaining cinnamon-sugar. Bake for 30 minutes or until golden brown. Cool in pan for 1 minute. Invert onto serving plate. Yield: 8 servings.

Cheryl Pickard, Alpha Upsilon Epsilon
Clarendon, Texas

THIS-MORNING CINNAMON ROLLS

1 11-ounce can soft
  breadsticks
1/2 cup melted butter
  or margarine
1 tablespoon cinnamon
1/3 cup sugar
1 cup confectioners' sugar
1 teaspoon vanilla
  extract
1/4 to 1/2 cup water

Preheat oven to 350 degrees. Unroll breadsticks. Brush with butter. Sprinkle with mixture of cinnamon and sugar. Recoil breadsticks. Arrange in greased 8-inch round pan. Sprinkle with remaining cinnamon-sugar. Bake for 15 to 20 minutes or until brown. Spread with glaze of remaining ingredients. Yield: 8 servings.

Tanya Harencak, Beta Beta Mu
Abilene, Texas

FANCY FRENCH TOAST

2 egg whites
1 tablespoon sugar
2 egg yolks
2/3 cup milk
1 cup all-purpose flour
1 teaspoon baking
  powder
1/2 teaspoon salt
1/2 teaspoon cinnamon
5 slices bread, cut into
  halves
2 cups crushed
  cornflakes
Vegetable oil for frying

Beat egg whites until soft peaks form. Add sugar. Beat until stiff peaks form. Beat egg yolks in bowl until light and lemon-colored. Beat in next 5 ingredients. Fold in egg whites gently. Dip bread slices in egg mixture, coating evenly. Dip in cornflake crumbs. Fry in hot oil in skillet until golden. Yield: 5 servings.

Gena Tollis, Beta Phi
Cortez, Colorado

FRENCH TOAST

3 eggs
1 1/4 cups all-purpose
  flour
1 1/2 teaspoons salt
1/4 teaspoon nutmeg
2 teaspoons cinnamon
1 1/2 teaspoons baking
  powder
2 cups milk
Thickly sliced day-old
  bread
Vegetable oil for frying

Beat eggs in bowl. Add next 6 ingredients. Beat until smooth. Dip bread slices into egg batter, coating evenly. Fry in hot oil in skillet until golden brown. Yield: 8 servings.

Dode Thomas, Laureate Gamma
Blackfoot, Idaho

Meats in Minutes

If a quick meal at your house usually means grilled burgers and hot dogs, you'll find this chapter a lifesaver. Today's too-busy cook has several major time-saving appliances to her advantage. The slow cooker and microwave allow us to serve meals that once took hours of stove watching. And the availability of quick-to cook meats such as steak pre-cut into strips for stir-frying, minute steaks, sliced ham and Italian and Polish sausages makes quick cooking even faster. Here you'll find the best recipes for quick meat main dishes, selected for their variety and ease of preparation. We've put crowd-pleasers like hearty Cowboy Stew and Pizza-Pasta Casserole together with quick-fix entrées such as Chili Dogs and Ham in-a-Hurry. And for instant elegance, we've even discovered new recipes for Beef Burgundy and Fast Skillet Veal Parmigiana.

BARBECUED BEEF

This takes longer to cook, but the slow cooker does all the work.

1 3- or 4-pound chuck roast
1 12-ounce can beer
1 16-ounce can barbecue sauce
8 sandwich buns

Combine roast and beer in slow cooker. Cook on Low for 8 to 12 hours. Remove roast and drain slow cooker. Shred roast, discarding fat and bones. Combine shredded beef with barbecue sauce in slow cooker. Cook on Low for 2 hours longer. Serve on sandwich buns. Yield: 8 servings.

Sandra Famuliner, Chi Kappa
Carrollton, Missouri

BEEF BURGUNDY

This is a good recipe for the working woman. The beef doesn't even have to be browned, and only the noodles have to be prepared at dinner time.

1 to 1½ pounds round steak, cubed
1 10-ounce can golden mushroom soup
1 4-ounce can sliced mushrooms, drained (optional)
1 envelope onion soup mix
¼ to ½ cup rosé or Burgundy
1 16-ounce package noodles, cooked

Combine steak and next 4 ingredients in slow cooker. Cook on Low for 6 to 8 hours. Serve over noodles. Yield: 2 to 4 servings.

Teri Bycroft, Xi Delta Chi
Broken Arrow, Oklahoma

BEEF FAJITAS

1 pound flank steak or top round steak, ½ inch thick
¾ cup fresh lime juice
1 to 1½ teaspoons garlic salt
½ teaspoon pepper
2 packages flour tortillas, warmed
1 large tomato, chopped
3 bunches green onions, chopped
3 cups shredded Cheddar cheese
Guacamole
Picante sauce
Sour cream

Place beef in plastic bag. Sprinkle both sides with lime juice, garlic salt and pepper; tie bag securely. Marinate in refrigerator; drain. Broil steak over medium-hot coals for 2 to 3 minutes on each side. Cut cross grain into thin slices. Serve in warmed tortillas with tomato, green onions, cheese, guacamole, picante sauce and sour cream. Yield: 4 servings.

Becky Wachs, Theta Sigma
Hays, Kansas

BEEF STROGANOFF

12 ounces sirloin steak
2 tablespoons corn oil
4 4-ounce cans sliced mushrooms
1 medium onion, chopped
2 cups beef broth
2 tablespoons Worcestershire sauce
½ cup tomato sauce
½ teaspoon paprika
1½ cups instant rice
½ cup sour cream

Cut steak into thin strips. Brown in oil in skillet. Add mushrooms and onion. Sauté for 3 minutes or until onion is tender. Add broth, Worcestershire sauce, tomato sauce and paprika. Bring to a boil. Cook for 3 minutes. Stir in rice. Let stand, covered, for 5 minutes. Stir in sour cream. Yield: 4 servings.

Darlene Fier, Preceptor Gamma Mu
De Witt, Iowa

STEAK STROGANOFF

The quick preparation for this dish can be done the night before. Just place the slow cooker in the refrigerator, ready to plug in and leave the next morning.

2 tablespoons all-purpose flour
½ teaspoon garlic powder
¼ teaspoon paprika
½ teaspoon pepper
1¼ pounds boneless beef round steak
1 10-ounce can cream of mushroom soup
½ cup water
1 envelope onion soup mix
1 9-ounce jar sliced mushrooms, drained
½ cup sour cream

Mix flour, garlic powder, paprika and pepper in slow cooker. Trim beef; cut into 1-inch strips. Add to flour mixture; toss to coat well. Add mushroom soup, water and soup mix; mix well. Cook on Low for 6 to 7 hours or on High for 3 to 3½ hours. Stir in mushrooms and sour cream. Cook on High for 10 to 15 minutes or just until heated through. Serve with beef-flavored rice and a spinach salad. Yield: 6 servings.

Lisa Orbin, Phi Gamma
Macon, Missouri

FLANK STEAK TERIYAKI

1¾ cups soy sauce
2 tablespoons crushed garlic
1 teaspoon ginger
2 pounds flank steak

Combine soy sauce, garlic and ginger in shallow dish. Add steak, coating well. Marinate for 1 hour. Place steak on rack in broiler pan or on grill. Broil or grill for 10 minutes on each side. Yield: 4 servings.

Debbie Imker, Xi Gamma Beta
Burke, Virginia

BEEFED-UP SKILLET DINNER

1 pound sirloin steak
Salt and pepper to taste
Vegetable oil
1 16-ounce package
　frozen mixed broccoli,
　carrots and cauliflower
1 10-ounce can cream
　of mushroom soup

1/3 cup light sour cream
1 4-ounce jar chopped
　pimento
1 teaspoon pepper
1 3-ounce can French-
　fried onions
1 cup shredded Swiss
　cheese

Cut steak into strips or 1-inch cubes; sprinkle with salt and pepper to taste. Brown on all sides in skillet sprayed with oil. Add vegetables, soup, sour cream, pimento, 1 teaspoon pepper, half the onions and half the cheese; mix well. Simmer for 10 minutes. Top with remaining onions and cheese. Cook until cheese melts. Yield: 4 servings.

Merline McCoy, Laureate Beta Psi
Village Mills, Texas

ROUND STEAK ROYALE

1 cup tomato juice
1 tablespoon cornstarch
Sugar substitute to
　equal 1 tablespoon
　sugar
1 teaspoon instant beef
　bouillon
Salt to taste
1/4 teaspoon pepper
1 pound boneless round
　steak, thinly sliced

2 stalks celery, thinly
　sliced
1 onion, thinly sliced
　into rings
2 small white potatoes,
　peeled, thinly sliced
4 carrots, thinly sliced
1 tomato, chopped
　(optional)

Blend tomato juice, cornstarch, sugar substitute, bouillon, salt and pepper in 3-quart glass dish. Add steak, stirring to coat well. Add celery, onion, potatoes and carrots. Microwave, covered, on High for 5 minutes; stir to mix well. Microwave on Medium for 25 to 30 minutes or until tender, rotating dish 1/4 turn. Stir in tomato. Microwave for 5 minutes longer. Let stand, covered, for 5 minutes. May brush with browning sauce if desired. Yield: 4 to 6 servings.

Betsy Clark, Theta Sigma
Hays, Kansas

MUSHROOM-TOPPED TENDERLOINS

4 3/4-inch tenderloin
　steaks
2 tablespoons margarine
Salt and pepper to taste
1 1/2 cups chopped
　mushrooms
1/4 cup sliced green
　onions

1/2 teaspoon minced
　garlic or 1/8 teaspoon
　garlic powder
1/4 teaspoon marjoram
1/8 teaspoon pepper
2 tablespoons dry sherry

Brown steaks in margarine in large skillet over high heat for 6 to 8 minutes or until done to taste, turning once. Remove to warm serving plate; sprinkle with salt and pepper to taste. Add mushrooms, green onions, garlic, marjoram and 1/8 teaspoon pepper to drippings in skillet. Cook over medium heat for 4 minutes or until mushrooms are tender; remove from heat. Stir in sherry. Spoon over steaks. Yield: 4 servings.

Rhonda Sollis, Epsilon Nu
Corning, Arkansas

ORIENTAL BEEF

I sometimes use leftover roast beef for this dish. It is especially quick if you cut up all the vegetables the night before.

1 pound lean beef
2 tablespoons soy sauce
Several drops of corn oil
1 tablespoon cornstarch
1 tablespoon sugar
Pepper to taste
1/2 cup diagonally sliced
　celery

1/2 cup sliced onion
1/2 cup chopped green
　bell pepper
4 tablespoons corn oil
1 clove of garlic, crushed
3/4 cup beef broth
2 tablespoons soy sauce
1 tablespoon cornstarch

Slice beef into 2-inch strips. Combine with 2 tablespoons soy sauce, several drops of oil, 1 tablespoon cornstarch, sugar and pepper in bowl; mix well. Stir-fry vegetables in 2 tablespoons oil in skillet for 5 minutes or until tender-crisp. Steam, covered, for several minutes. Remove vegetables to plate. Add 2 tablespoons oil and garlic. Stir-fry until brown. Stir in beef mixture. Stir-fry until beef is tender. Add mixture of remaining ingredients. Cook until thickened, stirring constantly. Add vegetables. Cook until heated through. Serve over rice. Yield: 4 servings.

Gail Fraser, Zeta Omega
Clinton, Ontario, Canada

EASY POT ROAST

1 3- to 4-pound beef
　roast
4 to 6 potatoes, cut into
　quarters
6 to 8 carrots

1 envelope onion soup
　mix
1 10-ounce can cream
　of mushroom soup

Sprinkle roast with salt and pepper. Combine with potatoes and carrots in slow cooker. Prepare soup mix using package directions. Stir in mushroom soup. Add to slow cooker. Cook on Low all day. Serve with salad and rolls. Yield: 4 to 8 servings.

Gayle Myers, Alpha Psi Zeta
Lampasas, Texas

Shelly Ann Fry, Zeta Phi, Bryan, Ohio, lets the slow cooker do the work with Special Round Steak. Combine 3 pounds round steak and mixture of 1 can cream of mushroom soup and 1 envelope onion soup mix in slow cooker. Cook on Low for 8 hours.

SAVORY MINUTE STEAKS

4 minute steaks	1/4 cup vegetable oil
Seasoned salt and pepper to taste	1 10-ounce can cream of mushroom soup
Italian bread crumbs	1 soup can milk

Preheat electric skillet to 350 degrees. Sprinkle both sides of steaks with seasoned salt and pepper. Coat with bread crumbs. Brown on both sides in oil in electric skillet. Blend soup and milk in glass bowl. Microwave on High for 2 minutes; stir to mix well. Pour over steaks. Simmer for 20 minutes. Yield: 4 servings.

Helen French, Xi Iota Omega
Florissant, Missouri

STIR-FRIED BEEF AND VEGETABLES

8 ounces sirloin steak, partially frozen	1 tablespoon corn oil
1 10-ounce can beef broth	4 green onions, cut into 1-inch pieces
1 tablespoon cornstarch	1 cup chopped broccoli
1 tablespoon soy sauce	1 7-ounce can water chestnuts, drained
2 tablespoons corn oil	Cooked rice
1 clove of garlic, minced	

Cut steak into thin slices. Mix broth, cornstarch and soy sauce in small bowl; set aside. Heat 2 tablespoons oil in skillet or wok over medium-high heat. Add beef and garlic. Stir-fry until light brown. Remove to bowl. Add remaining 1 tablespoon oil, green onions and broccoli to skillet. Stir-fry for 1 minute. Add water chestnuts. Stir-fry for 30 seconds longer. Return beef to skillet. Stir cornstarch mixture. Add to skillet. Cook for 1 minute or until thickened, stirring constantly. Serve over rice. Yield: 2 servings.

Roxanne Schultz, Xi Tau Omicron
Galveston, Texas

MICROWAVE STIR-FRIED BEEF WITH PEA PODS

1 10-ounce package frozen pea pods	1 tablespoon cornstarch
1 pound sirloin steak, partially frozen	1 teaspoon ginger
	Garlic powder to taste
1/4 cup soy sauce	1 to 1 1/2 cups sliced mushrooms
2 tablespoons vegetable oil	Cooked rice

Microwave pea pods in package on High for 1 to 2 minutes or until thawed. Cut steak into 1/4-by-2-inch strips. Combine steak with soy sauce, oil, cornstarch, ginger and garlic powder in bowl; mix well. Marinate for 30 minutes. Preheat 10-inch microwave dish on High for 5 1/2 minutes. Add beef mixture; stir until mixture is no longer sizzling. Add mushrooms and pea pods; mix well. Microwave on High for 5 1/2 to 8

minutes or until vegetables are tender-crisp and beef is done to taste. Serve over rice. May substitute green pepper and onion for mushrooms and pea pods. Yield: 4 servings.

Linda Wilkinson, Preceptor Alpha Omega
Shippensburg, Pennsylvania

MOCK SUKIYAKI

16 ounces round steak, thinly sliced	1/2 cup sliced green onions
2 tablespoons corn oil	1 10-ounce can beef broth
1 1/2 cups sliced celery	
1 medium green bell pepper, sliced	1 tablespoon soy sauce
1 1/2 cups sliced mushrooms or 1 6-ounce can sliced mushrooms	2 tablespoons cornstarch
	1/4 cup water
	4 cups hot cooked rice

Stir-fry steak in oil in skillet. Add vegetables, broth and soy sauce. Cook, covered, over low heat for 10 minutes or until steak is tender and vegetables are tender-crisp, stirring frequently. Stir in mixture of cornstarch and water. Cook until thickened, stirring constantly. Serve over hot rice. Yield: 4 servings.

Marg Smith, Zeta Sigma
Elkford, British Columbia, Canada

CORNED BEEF AND CABBAGE

3 or 4 stalks of celery with heart leaves, chopped	1 medium head cabbage, chopped
	1 teaspoon sugar
1 medium onion, chopped	1 12-ounce can corned beef, chilled

Combine celery and onion with just enough water to cover in saucepan. Add cabbage; sprinkle with sugar. Simmer just until cabbage is tender. Place unopened can of corned beef in hot water. Open can and remove corned beef in 1 piece; cut into 1/4-inch slices. Arrange over top of cabbage. Simmer just until heated through. Yield: 4 to 6 servings.

Joyce Ward, Preceptor Alpha Omicron
Deer Park, Texas

CORNED BEEF HASH

1 medium onion, chopped	1/2 medium green bell pepper, chopped
2 tablespoons vegetable oil	1/2 teaspoon freshly ground pepper
1 cup chopped frozen potatoes, cooked	1/2 12-ounce can corned beef
1 cup chopped frozen carrots, cooked	3 scallions, chopped

Sauté onion in oil in 10-inch skillet until tender. Add potatoes, carrots, green pepper and pepper. Cook over high heat for 5 minutes, stirring frequently. Add corned beef. Cook for 10 minutes longer, stirring frequently. Garnish with scallions. Yield: 4 servings.

Mary E. Larson, Preceptor Sigma
Pecatonica, Illinois

❖ IRISH BEEF BURGERS

1 12-ounce can corned beef, flaked	2 tablespoons prepared mustard
3 tablespoons finely chopped onion	2 teaspoons prepared horseradish
2 tablespoons mayonnaise-type salad dressing	8 sandwich buns 8 slices Colby or Cheddar cheese

Mix first 5 ingredients in bowl. Spread over bottom halves of buns. Arrange on baking sheet. Broil just until heated through. Top with cheese. Broil until cheese melts. Replace tops of buns. Yield: 8 servings.

Virginia M. Korbelik
Grand Island, Nebraska

BARBECUE BEEF BUNS

1 pound ground beef	1 tablespoon sugar
1/2 cup chopped onion	2 tablespoons prepared mustard
1 medium green bell pepper, chopped	1 tablespoon vinegar
1 tablespoon butter or margarine	Salt and pepper to taste
1/4 cup water	1 package hamburger buns
3/4 cup catsup	

Brown ground beef with onion and green pepper in margarine in skillet, stirring frequently; drain. Add remaining ingredients except buns; mix well. Simmer, covered, for 15 minutes. Serve on buns. Yield: 8 servings.

Doris St. Clair, Laureate Beta Nu
El Campo, Texas

BEANS AND BUNS

1 pound ground beef	1/4 cup packed light brown sugar
1/2 sweet onion, chopped	Hamburger buns
1 28-ounce can baked beans	

Brown ground beef with onion in skillet, stirring until ground beef is crumbly; drain. Stir in beans and brown sugar. Simmer for 5 to 10 minutes. Serve on hamburger buns. Yield: 6 servings.

Lavonne Lloyd, Preceptor Chi
Coeur d'Alene, Idaho

WESTERN BURGERS

1 pound ground beef	1/4 cup prepared mustard
12 ounces Velveeta cheese, cut into cubes	6 hamburger buns

Preheat oven to 350 degrees. Brown ground beef in skillet, stirring until crumbly; drain. Add cheese and

mustard, stirring until cheese melts. Spoon on bottom half of bun; replace top half of bun. Bake, wrapped in foil, for 20 minutes or until heated through. Yield: 6 servings.

Kerry Hall, Preceptor Gamma
Kelso, Washington

DEVILED VIENNA BURGERS

1 pound ground chuck	1 teaspoon salt
1/3 cup chili sauce	Dash of pepper
1 1/2 teaspoons prepared mustard	1 loaf Vienna bread
2 teaspoons horseradish	Butter or margarine, softened
1 teaspoon minced onion	4 ounces shredded sharp cheese
1 1/2 teaspoons Worcestershire sauce	Oregano to taste

Preheat broiler. Combine first 8 ingredients in bowl; mix well. Cut bread into halves lengthwise. Spread each half with butter. Spread beef mixture over butter layer. Place in broiler pan. Broil for 6 minutes or until ground beef is browned. Sprinkle with cheese and oregano. Broil until cheese melts. Cut into serving pieces. Yield: 4 to 6 servings.

Betsy Glor, Preceptor Epsilon Lambda
Wellington, Ohio

GRILLED HAMBURGERS ITALIAN-STYLE

1 1/2 pounds ground beef	1/2 teaspoon onion powder
1 1/4 teaspoons Italian seasoning	1/4 teaspoon salt
3/4 teaspoon garlic powder	2 ounces mozzarella cheese, cut into 4 pieces

Combine first 5 ingredients in bowl; mix well. Shape into eight 1/4-inch patties. Place cheese in center of 4 patties; top with remaining patties, sealing edge. Grill over medium-hot coals until done to taste, turning once. Yield: 4 servings.

Grilled Hamburgers French-Style: Prepare as for Italian-style, using ground beef with 1/2 teaspoon onion powder, 1 teaspoon thyme, 1/2 teaspoon garlic powder, 1/4 teaspoon salt, 1/4 teaspoon pepper and 2 ounces Brie or Camembert cheese.

Grilled Hamburgers Mexican-Style: Prepare as for Italian-style, using ground beef with 1 tablespoon chili powder, 1/2 teaspoon ground cumin, 1/2 teaspoon onion powder, 1/4 teaspoon garlic powder, 1/4 teaspoon salt and 2 ounces Monterey Jack cheese.

Grilled Hamburgers Greek-Style: Prepare as for Italian-style, using ground beef with 1 1/2 teaspoons onion powder, 1 teaspoon oregano, 1/2 teaspoon garlic powder, 1/4 teaspoon pepper and 2 ounces feta cheese mixed with 1 tablespoon lemon juice.

Joyce A. Phillips, Alpha Sigma
Beverly, West Virginia

LONG-BOY CHEESEBURGERS

1 pound ground beef	1/2 cup evaporated milk
1 tablespoon	1 teaspoon salt
Worcestershire sauce	1/4 teaspoon pepper
1/4 cup catsup	6 to 8 hamburger buns
1/4 cup finely chopped	6 to 8 slices Velveeta
onions	cheese, cut into strips
1/2 cup bread crumbs	

Preheat oven to 350 degrees. Combine first 8 ingredients in bowl; mix well. Spread mixture on cut sides of buns. Place in baking pan. Bake for 25 minutes or until ground beef is done to taste. Top with strips of cheese during last 5 minutes of baking time. Yield: 6 to 8 servings.

Mary Vitale, Zeta Phi
Bryan, Ohio

SLOPPY JOES

1 pound ground beef	2 tablespoons
1 medium onion,	Worcestershire sauce
chopped	1 small bottle of catsup
1 teaspoon pepper	1/4 cup packed light
Butter-flavored salt to	brown sugar
taste	Hamburger buns

Brown ground beef with onion in large skillet, stirring frequently; drain. Stir in next 5 ingredients. Simmer until of desired consistency. Serve on buns. Yield: 8 to 10 servings.

Linda S. Smith, Zeta Phi
Bryan, Ohio

SOUTHERN BURGERS

1 pound ground beef	3 tablespoons catsup
1 medium onion, finely	1 10-ounce can cream
chopped	of mushroom soup
1 clove of garlic, crushed	4 toasted buns
1 tablespoon prepared	Pickles, carrot curls
mustard	and onion slices

Brown ground beef with onion and garlic in skillet, stirring until ground beef is crumbly; drain. Stir in next 3 ingredients. Simmer until slightly thickened. Spoon onto open-faced buns. Garnish with pickles, carrot curls and onion slices. Yield: 4 servings.

Jerry Olson, Preceptor Alpha Lambda
Memphis, Tennessee

ALBERTA'S "STUFF"

1 pound ground beef	1 16-ounce can whole
1 15-ounce can	kernel corn, drained
tamales, chopped	Shredded cheese and
1 15-ounce can ravioli	sliced olives
1 15-ounce can chili	

Brown ground beef in skillet, stirring until crumbly; drain. Stir in tamales, ravioli, and chili. Simmer for 30 minutes. Stir in corn. Cook until heated through. Serve with shredded cheese and olives. May vary recipe by adding one 8-ounce can tomato sauce and 1/2 envelope chili mix. May also add additional cans of tamales, ravioli or spaghetti. Yield: 4 to 6 servings.

Debra Angel, Preceptor Delta Omega
Victorville, California

BEEF-NOODLE CHOP SUEY

1 pound ground beef	1 16-ounce can mixed
1/2 cup chopped onion	Chinese vegetables,
3 1/4 cups water	drained, sliced
1 8-ounce can water	1 package Hamburger
chestnuts, drained,	Helper beef noodle
sliced	dinner

Brown ground beef with onion in skillet, stirring until ground beef is crumbly; drain. Stir in remaining ingredients. Bring to a boil, stirring constantly. Reduce heat to low. Simmer for 10 to 15 minutes, stirring frequently. Yield: 5 or 6 servings.

Jana Gail Evans, Xi Gamma Chi
Hayes Center, Nebraska

BEEF 'N POTATO BAKE

4 cups frozen hashed	1 teaspoon garlic salt
brown potatoes,	1 10-ounce package
slightly thawed	frozen mixed
3 tablespoons vegetable	vegetables
oil	1 cup shredded Cheddar
1/2 teaspoon pepper	cheese
1 pound ground beef	1 3-ounce can French-
1 envelope gravy mix	fried onions
1 cup water	

Preheat oven to 400 degrees. Combine potatoes, oil and pepper in 9-by-12-inch baking dish; mix well. Press over bottom and sides of pan to form shell. Bake for 15 minutes. Brown ground beef in skillet, stirring until crumbly; drain. Stir in next 3 ingredients. Bring to a boil. Add mixed vegetables; mix well. Reduce heat to low. Cook for 5 minutes. Stir in half the cheese and half the onions. Spoon into potato shell. Reduce oven temperature to 350 degrees. Bake for 15 minutes. Top with remaining cheese and onions. Bake for 5 minutes longer. Yield: 4 servings.

Sharon Kirk, Laureate Alpha Sigma
Vancouver, British Columbia, Canada

CAVATINI

1 pound ground beef	1 16-ounce jar old
1 pound Italian sausage	world-style spaghetti
1 8-ounce jar mild	sauce
taco sauce	4 cups shredded
8 ounces small shell	mozzarella cheese
macaroni, cooked	

Preheat oven to 350 degrees. Brown ground beef and sausage in skillet, stirring until crumbly; drain. Stir in next 3 ingredients. Layer meat sauce and cheese 1/2 at a time in 7-by-11-inch pan sprayed with non-stick cooking spray. Bake for 30 minutes.
Yield: 6 to 8 servings.

Ruth H. Yordy, Xi Epsilon Theta
Marshalltown, Iowa

COMPASSIONATE DINNER

With this recipe, you can have a full meal ready for a neighbor in need in 30 minutes.

2 pounds lean ground beef	4 cups water
2 15-ounce cans chili with beans	2 teaspoons chili powder
4 cups canned tomatoes	1/2 teaspoon garlic powder
1 envelope country vegetable soup mix	1 cup uncooked elbow macaroni

Brown ground beef in electric skillet, stirring until crumbly; drain. Stir in next 6 ingredients. Bring to a boil. Stir in macaroni. Turn off heat. Let stand for 15 to 20 minutes or until macaroni is tender.
Yield: 12 to 15 servings.

June Phillips, Laureate Gamma
Pocatello, Idaho

BEEF AND CHEESE CASSEROLE

1 pound ground beef	6 ounces shredded Cheddar Cheese
1 10-ounce can cream of onion soup	1/4 teaspoon each salt and pepper
6 ounces wide noodles, cooked	2 tablespoons chopped parsley
1/2 cup sour cream	

Preheat oven to 350 degrees. Brown ground beef in skillet, stirring until crumbly; drain. Stir in next 5 ingredients. Spoon into 1 1/2-quart baking dish. Bake for 30 minutes. Garnish with parsley just before serving. Yield: 4 servings.

Tari J. McClung, Alpha Kappa
Hot Springs, South Dakota

BUSY-DAY CASSEROLE

1 pound ground beef	1 1/2 cups uncooked elbow macaroni
1 15-ounce jar spaghetti sauce	1 cup shredded mozzarella cheese
1 cup water	

Brown ground beef in skillet, stirring until crumbly; drain. Mix with remaining ingredients in microwave-safe dish. Microwave, covered, on High for 7 minutes; stir. Microwave for 5 minutes longer or until macaroni is tender. Sprinkle cheese over top. Let stand, covered, for 3 to 5 minutes. Yield: 6 servings.

Cindi Stueck, Theta Chi
Dodge City, Kansas

CHINESE HAMBURGER CASSEROLE

1 pound ground beef	1 10-ounce can golden mushroom soup
1 cup chopped onion	1 10-ounce can cream of chicken soup
1 cup chopped celery	1 3-ounce can Chinese noodles
1 16-ounce can bean sprouts, drained	Soy sauce
1 5-ounce can sliced water chestnuts, drained	

Preheat oven to 350 degrees. Brown ground beef with onion and celery in skillet, stirring until ground beef is crumbly; drain. Stir in next 4 ingredients. Spoon into 9-by-13-inch baking pan. Top with noodles. Bake for 30 minutes. Serve with soy sauce.
Yield: 6 to 8 servings.

Alta Reesy, Laureate Nu
Cody, Wyoming

ENCHILADA CASSEROLE

2 pounds ground beef	1 jar enchilada sauce
1 medium onion, chopped	1 4-ounce can chopped jalapeño peppers (optional)
1 10-ounce can cream of mushroom soup	Corn tortillas
1 10-ounce can cream of chicken soup	2 pounds Mexican Velveeta cheese, chopped
1/2 cup milk	

Preheat oven to 350 degrees. Brown ground beef with onion in skillet, stirring until ground beef is crumbly; drain. Stir in soups, milk, enchilada sauce and peppers. Bring to a boil. Layer tortillas, meat sauce and cheese 1/2 at a time in greased 9-by-13-inch baking dish. Bake for 15 minutes or until cheese melts. Yield: 6 servings.

Linette Walton, Beta Eta
Youngsville, Louisiana

HAMBURGER CASSEROLE

1 to 2 medium onions, sliced	1 pound lean ground beef, shaped into 4 patties
2 teaspoons margarine	4 potatoes, cooked, peeled
2 tablespoons all-purpose flour	1 teaspoon margarine
1 cup hot water	1 tablespoon milk
2 chicken bouillon cubes	

Sauté onions in 2 teaspoons margarine in skillet until transparent. Stir in flour. Add water gradually, stirring constantly. Cook over low heat until thickened, stirring constantly. Stir in bouillon. Arrange patties over sauce, basting with sauce. Simmer for 10 minutes. Turn patties over. Simmer for 10 minutes longer or until done to taste, basting with sauce again. Mash potatoes with remaining margarine and milk. Serve with patties and sauce. Yield: 4 servings.

Frances Judith Cotter, Laureate Lambda
Medina, New York

HAMBURGER-GREEN BEAN CASSEROLE

1 pound ground round
1/4 cup chopped onion
6 to 8 potatoes, peeled
chopped, cooked
1 16-ounce can
French-style green
beans, drained
1 10-ounce can cream
of mushroom soup
1 soup can milk
5 slices American cheese
1 3-ounce can French-
fried onions

Preheat oven to 350 degrees. Brown ground beef with chopped onion in skillet, stirring until ground beef is crumbly; drain. Combine potatoes, ground beef mixture and green beans in 2-quart casserole. Mix soup and milk in bowl. Pour over mixture; mix well. Arrange cheese on top; sprinkle with French-fried onions. Bake for 20 to 25 minutes. Yield: 6 to 8 servings.

Judy Nelson, Iota Delta
Rose Hill, Kansas

INSIDE-OUT RAVIOLI CASSEROLE

1 pound ground beef
1/2 cup chopped onion
1 clove of garlic, minced
1 tablespoon vegetable
oil
1 10-ounce package
frozen chopped spinach
1 16-ounce jar
spaghetti sauce
1 8-ounce can tomato
sauce
1 6-ounce can tomato
paste
Salt and pepper to taste
7 ounces shell
macaroni, cooked
4 ounces American
cheese, shredded
1/2 cup bread crumbs
2 eggs, beaten
1/4 cup vegetable oil

Preheat oven to 350 degrees. Brown ground beef with onion and garlic in 1 tablespoon oil in skillet, stirring until crumbly; drain. Cook spinach using package directions. Drain, reserving liquid. Add enough water to liquid to equal 1 cup. Add to ground beef mixture with spaghetti sauce, tomato sauce, tomato paste, salt and pepper; mix well. Simmer, covered, for 10 minutes. Combine macaroni, cheese, bread crumbs, eggs, remaining oil and spinach; mix well. Spread mixture in 9-by-13-inch baking dish. Top with meat sauce. Bake for 30 minutes. Let stand for 10 minutes before serving. Yield: 6 to 8 servings.

Joyce Borges, Xi Gamma Omega
Gilbert, Arizona

MEXICAN CASSEROLE

1 1/2 pounds ground beef
1/2 onion, chopped
1 16-ounce can ranch-
style beans
1 16-ounce can
Spanish rice
1/3 pound Velveeta
cheese, chopped
2 cups corn chips,
crushed

Brown ground beef with onion in skillet, stirring until ground beef is crumbly; drain. Reduce heat to low. Add beans, rice and cheese. Cook until mixture is heated through and cheese melts. Stir in corn chips gently. Yield: 6 servings.

Terry Cummings, Upsilon Kappa
Denver City, Texas

MEXICAN COWBOY CASSEROLE

1 pound ground beef
1 16-ounce can
Spanish rice
1 16-ounce can ranch-
style beans
Flour tortillas, torn
into strips
Shredded longhorn
cheese

Preheat oven to 350 degrees. Brown ground beef in skillet, stirring until crumbly; drain. Stir in rice and beans. Simmer for several minutes. Line 9-by-9-inch baking dish with tortillas. Layer ground beef mixture, half the cheese and remaining tortillas in prepared dish. Sprinkle with remaining cheese. Bake for 15 minutes or until cheese melts. Yield: 6 servings.

Dorothy Aurouze, Laureate Delta Tau
Amarillo, Texas

TATER TOTS LAYERED CASSEROLE

1 pound ground beef
Velveeta cheese
1 10-ounce can cream
of mushroom soup
1 small package tater
tots

Preheat oven to 350 degrees. Layer ingredients in order listed in 2-quart baking dish. Bake for 45 minutes. May add onions with ground beef. Yield: 6 to 8 servings.

Alice E. Hall, Preceptor Gamma Epsilon
Deltona, Florida

CHEESEBURGER AND FRIES

2 pounds lean ground
beef
1 10-ounce can golden
mushroom soup
1 10-ounce can
Cheddar cheese soup
1 20-ounce package
frozen French fries
Pickles and catsup

Preheat oven to 350 degrees. Brown ground beef in skillet, stirring until crumbly; drain. Spoon into 9-by-13-inch pan. Combine soups in bowl; mix well. Pour over ground beef. Arrange French fries over top. Bake for 45 to 55 minutes or until potatoes are golden brown. Garnish with pickles and catsup. Yield: 6 servings.

Georgia Tenney, Xi Epsilon
Pierceton, Indiana

❖ ENCHILADAS

This recipe was a hit when our sorority had a Mexican dinner to welcome new pledges into our chapter.

1 10-ounce can mild enchilada sauce	2 cups cooked ground beef
1 12-ounce can evaporated milk	Shredded Cheddar cheese
1 10-ounce can cream of mushroom soup	10 flour tortillas
1 4-ounce can chopped green chilies	Lettuce and chopped tomatoes

Preheat oven to 350 degrees. Combine first 4 ingredients in bowl; mix well. Spoon 1 to 2 tablespoons sauce mixture, ground beef and cheese onto each tortilla. Roll up to enclose filling. Place into 9-by-13-inch pan. Top with remaining sauce and cheese. Bake, covered with foil, for 15 to 20 minutes. Top with lettuce and tomatoes. Yield: 10 servings.

Judy Woelk, Alpha Nu
Russell, Kansas

MOCK FILETS

1 pound ground beef	1/8 teaspoon pepper
3/4 cup cracker crumbs	6 slices bacon
2 eggs, lightly beaten	1/2 cup catsup
2 tablespoons chopped onion	2 tablespoons light brown sugar
1 1/2 teaspoons salt	1/4 teaspoon dry mustard

Preheat broiler. Mix ground beef and cracker crumbs in bowl. Add eggs, onion, salt and pepper; mix well. Shape into 6 patties. Wrap bacon around edge; secure with wooden pick. Place on rack in broiler pan. Broil 5 inches from heat source for 10 minutes. Mix catsup, brown sugar and mustard in small bowl. Spoon over patties. Broil for 5 minutes longer. Yield: 6 servings.

Lana Maskus, Alpha Delta
Wright, Kansas

MY FAVORITE GOULASH

1 pound ground beef	Salt to taste
3/4 cup chopped onions	1 teaspoon pepper
2 16-ounce cans whole tomatoes, chopped	1 cup medium macaroni shells, cooked
1 teaspoon garlic powder	Grated Parmesan cheese

Brown ground beef in skillet, stirring until crumbly; drain. Add onions. Sauté for 5 minutes. Add tomatoes, garlic powder, salt and pepper. Bring to a boil over medium-high heat. Cook for 10 minutes. Reduce heat to low. Stir in macaroni. Top with Parmesan cheese. Yield: 6 to 8 servings.

Janie Martinez, Alpha Chi Chi
Pleasanton, Texas

HAMBURGER JAPANESE

1 pound ground beef	1 16-ounce package frozen Oriental vegetables
3 to 5 tablespoons soy sauce	6 servings minute rice

Brown ground beef with soy sauce in skillet, stirring until crumbly; drain, reserving 1 tablespoon drippings. Remove ground beef to warm plate. Stir-fry vegetables in reserved pan drippings until tender. Add ground beef. Stir-fry for 1 to 2 minutes. Serve over rice. Yield: 4 to 6 servings.

Doreen Degenhardt, Xi Beta Zeta
Milwaukee, Wisconsin

HAMBURGER-NOODLE BAKE

1 1/2 pounds ground beef	1 cup sour cream
2 tablespoons butter or margarine	3 ounces cream cheese, softened
1 clove of garlic, crushed	4 or 5 green onions, chopped
1 teaspoon salt	8 ounces egg noodles, cooked
1/4 teaspoon pepper	1/2 cup shredded cheese
1 tablespoon sugar	
2 8-ounce cans tomato sauce	

Brown ground beef with garlic, salt and pepper in butter in skillet, stirring until crumbly; drain. Stir in sugar and tomato sauce. Combine sour cream, cream cheese and green onions in bowl; mix well. Layer noodles, half the meat mixture and sour cream mixture in 9-by-13-inch glass dish. Top with remaining meat mixture; sprinkle with shredded cheese. Microwave on High until cheese melts. Yield: 8 servings.

Cheryl R. Shields, Epsilon Epsilon
Elk City, Oklahoma

HAMBURGER STEAK DIANE

1 tablespoon steak sauce	1 3-ounce can sliced mushrooms
1 teaspoon dry mustard	1 tablespoon chives
1/2 teaspoon salt	1 tablespoon lemon juice
1/4 teaspoon pepper	1/2 teaspoon Worcestershire sauce
1 pound ground beef	
2 teaspoons melted margarine	

Combine steak sauce, dry mustard, salt, pepper and ground beef in bowl; mix well. Shape into 4 patties. Cook in margarine in skillet over medium-high heat for 3 minutes. Turn patties. Cook for 3 minutes longer. Remove to warm plate. Stir in remaining ingredients. Bring to a boil. Spoon sauce over patties. Yield: 4 servings.

Tanya Hunter, Mu Chi
Harker Heights, Texas

HAMBURGER SURPRISE

1½ pounds ground beef	¼ teaspoon each salt
1 egg	and pepper
½ cup seasoned bread	4 ounces mozzarella
crumbs	cheese, cut into cubes

Combine first 5 ingredients in bowl; mix well. Divide into 12 portions; shape into 3-inch patties. Top 6 patties with cheese. Place remaining patties on cheese, pressing edge to seal. Grill over hot coals until done to taste, turning once. May be baked in 350 degree oven for 30 minutes. Yield: 6 servings.

Doris Steiner, Laureate Chi
Toledo, Ohio

EASY LASAGNA

8 to 16 ounces ground	½ teaspoon pepper
beef, crumbled	9 to 11 uncooked
1 48-ounce jar	lasagna noodles
spaghetti sauce	8 ounces mozzarella
½ cup water	cheese, thinly sliced
1¼ cups ricotta cheese	½ cup grated Parmesan
1 egg, slightly beaten	cheese
½ teaspoon salt	

Microwave ground beef in glass bowl on High for 2 to 3 minutes. Add spaghetti sauce and water; mix well. Microwave on High for 4 to 5 minutes or until bubbly. Mix next 4 ingredients in bowl. Spoon ½ cup into 9-by-13-inch glass dish. Layer noodles, egg mixture, mozzarella cheese and meat sauce ⅓ at a time in prepared dish. Microwave, covered with plastic wrap, on High for 10 minutes. Microwave on Medium for 35 minutes or until noodles are tender. Sprinkle with Parmesan cheese. Let stand, covered, for 15 minutes before serving. Yield: 8 servings.

Chris Kelly, Epsilon Kappa
Guelph, Ontario, Canada

MICROWAVE LASAGNA

1 pound ground beef	½ teaspoon salt
1 32-ounce jar	½ teaspoon pepper
spaghetti sauce	8 uncooked lasagna
½ cup water	noodles
1½ cups cottage cheese,	8 ounces mozzarella
drained	cheese, shredded
1 egg, beaten	Grated Parmesan cheese

Crumble ground beef into large glass bowl. Microwave on High for 2 to 3 minutes or until browned; drain. Stir in spaghetti sauce and water. Combine cottage cheese, egg, salt and pepper in bowl; mix well. Spoon ½ cup ground beef mixture in 9-by-13-inch glass baking dish. Alternate layers of noodles, cottage cheese mixture, mozzarella cheese and ground beef mixture in prepared baking dish. Microwave, covered, for 8 minutes. Microwave on

Medium for 30 minutes longer. Sprinkle with Parmesan cheese. Let stand, covered, for 15 minutes before serving. Yield: 6 to 8 servings.

Selma R. Spurgeon, Preceptor Gamma Iota
Overland, Missouri

"IN-A-JIFFY" MEATBALLS IN GRAVY

I have passed this recipe on to many friends who have told me it has become a family favorite.

1¼ pounds lean ground	3 tablespoons
beef	all-purpose flour
2 tablespoons finely	1 beef bouillon cube
chopped onion	1¼ cups boiling water
1 egg, beaten	1 teaspoon salt
1½ cups milk	¼ teaspoon each pepper
2 cups crisp rice cereal,	and MSG
crushed	½ teaspoon each
1 teaspoon vegetable	allspice, nutmeg and
oil	parsley

Combine ground beef, onion, egg, ½ cup milk and crushed cereal in bowl; mix well. Shape into balls. Brown in oil in skillet for 4 to 5 minutes; drain on paper towels. Stir flour into pan drippings until smooth. Dissolve bouillon cube in boiling water. Add to mixture, stirring until smooth. Add remaining milk. Simmer until of desired thickness, stirring constantly. Add seasonings and meatballs. Simmer, covered, for 20 minutes. Yield: 4 to 6 servings.

Mildred L. Johnson, Gamma Chi
Ellensburg, Washington

MINI SAUERBRATEN

This only takes about 45 minutes to prepare instead of 3 or 4 days.

1 pound prepared	1 teaspoon ginger
meatballs	Dash of pepper
1 onion, minced	1 teaspoon
Vegetable oil	Worcestershire sauce
2 cups water	1 bay leaf
1 envelope brown gravy	2 tablespoons wine
mix	vinegar
2 tablespoons light	½ teaspoon salt
brown sugar	

Brown meatballs and onion in oil in skillet; drain. Combine water and gravy mix in large saucepan; mix well. Stir in remaining ingredients. Cook until slightly thickened, stirring frequently. Add meatballs and onion. Simmer for 20 minutes, adding additional water if needed for desired consistency. Discard bay leaf. Serve over egg noodles. Yield: 5 to 6 servings.

Elizabeth Gesner, Beta
Eastern Passage, Nova Scotia, Canada

MUSHROOM MEATBALLS

1 pound ground beef	1/4 cup milk
2 eggs, beaten	1 10-ounce can cream
3 slices bread, torn	of mushroom soup
Salt and pepper to taste	3/4 soup can milk
1/2 teaspoon MSG	

Combine ground beef, eggs, bread, seasonings and milk in large bowl; mix well. Shape into balls. Cook in nonstick skillet until browned; drain. Combine mushroom soup and milk in small bowl; mix well. Pour over meatballs. Simmer for 15 minutes. Serve with mashed potatoes or noodles.
Yield: 6 to 8 servings.

Gerri M. Manke, Xi Delta Chi
Ritzville, Washington

PORCUPINE BALLS IT IS

This has been a favorite recipe at family reunions for years.

1 pound ground round	2 tablespoons vegetable
1/2 cup uncooked rice	oil
1/4 cup chopped onion	2 8-ounce cans tomato
1 teaspoon salt	sauce
1/4 teaspoon pepper	1 cup water

Combine ground round, rice, onion, salt and pepper in large bowl; mix well. Shape into small balls. Sauté in oil in skillet until light brown; drain. Add tomato sauce and water; mix well. Cook, covered, over medium heat for 15 minutes. Yield: 4 servings.

Helen A. Walkden, Preceptor Theta
Columbia Station, Ohio

CHARCOALED MEAT LOAF

2 pounds ground beef	1 teaspoon prepared
1 egg, beaten	mustard
1 onion, chopped	3 tablespoons brown
1/4 cup catsup	sugar
2 tablespoons light	1/4 cup catsup
brown sugar	1 teaspoon dry mustard
1/2 cup cracker crumbs	1/4 teaspoon nutmeg

Combine ground beef, egg, onion, 1/4 cup catsup, 2 tablespoons brown sugar, cracker crumbs and prepared mustard in large bowl; mix well. Shape into loaf; place in lightly greased 10-inch baking pan. Grill over hot coals for 15 minutes. Place double thickness of aluminum foil on grill. Remove loaf to foil. Grill for 10 minutes longer, basting with mixture of 3 tablespoons brown sugar, 1/4 cup catsup, dry mustard and nutmeg. Yield: 4 to 6 servings.

Diana Martinie, Epsilon Pi
Boca Raton, Florida

GROUND BEEF ROLL-UP

A light, tasty and easy to prepare meal when you are short of time, and it's very attractive when sliced.

1 pound ground beef	1/4 cup oats
1/2 cup finely chopped	1/2 teaspoon salt
celery	2 cups baking mix
1/4 cup chopped onion	1 tablespoon chopped
1 tablespoon	parsley
Worcestershire sauce	1 teaspoon dry mustard
1/4 cup catsup	1/2 cup milk
1 egg, beaten	

Preheat oven to 375 degrees. Brown ground beef in skillet, stirring until crumbly; drain. Add celery, onion, Worcestershire sauce, catsup, egg, oats and salt; mix well. Combine baking mix, parsley, mustard and milk in large bowl, stirring to moisten. Knead gently 8 to 10 times on lightly floured surface. Roll to 10-by-12-inch rectangle. Spread ground beef mixture to within 1/2 inch of edges. Roll up as for jelly roll. Seal edge; turn under ends. Place on greased baking sheet. Bake for 20 to 25 minutes or until golden brown. Serve with prepared gravy or chili sauce and salad or vegetables. Yield: 6 to 8 servings.

Betty Chase, Preceptor Gamma Delta
Welland, Ontario, Canada

ROLLED STUFFED MEAT LOAF

This is my family's favorite meat loaf.

1 1/2 pounds lean ground	3 slices boiled ham
beef	2 slices mozzarella
1 egg, slightly beaten	cheese
1 teaspoon salt	1/2 cup chopped green
1/4 teaspoon pepper	olives

Combine ground beef, egg, salt and pepper in large bowl; mix well. Pat into 8-by-11-inch rectangle 1/2 inch thick on waxed paper. Arrange ham slices crosswise on beef mixture; top with cheese slices. Sprinkle with chopped olives. Roll up as for jelly roll, sealing edge. Place seam side down in 5-by-9-inch glass loaf pan. Insert microwave meat thermometer into center of loaf. Microwave on High for 5 minutes or to 105 degrees on thermometer. Microwave on Medium for 16 minutes or to 135 degrees on thermometer. Microwave on Medium-Low for 4 minutes or to 155 degrees on thermometer. Yield: 6 servings.

June M. Brown, Preceptor Sigma
Penticton, British Columbia, Canada

OOH YUCK!

The name comes from my children's reaction the first time I served this—it had "yucky green stuff" in it. We dubbed it "Ooh Yuck."

1 pound ground beef	2 tablespoons soy sauce
2 3-ounce packages ramen noodles	2 cups frozen chopped broccoli, cooked

Brown ground beef in skillet, stirring until crumbly; drain. Stir in seasoning packet from noodles, soy sauce and cooked broccoli. Cook noodles using package directions. Add to ground beef mixture; mix well. Cook until heated through. Serve with additional soy sauce. Yield: 4 to 5 servings.

Karen Younce, Xi Zeta
Anthony, Kansas

CHEESEBURGER PIE

1 unbaked 9-inch pie shell	1 teaspoon instant beef bouillon
1 pound ground beef	3 eggs, well beaten
1/2 cup tomato sauce	2 tablespoons all-purpose flour
1/3 cup chopped green bell pepper	8 slices American cheese
1/3 cup chopped onion	Chopped tomato and shredded lettuce

Preheat oven to 425 degrees. Bake pie shell for 8 minutes. Let stand until cool. Reduce oven temperature to 350 degrees. Brown ground beef in skillet, stirring until crumbly; drain. Add tomato sauce, green pepper, onion and bouillon. Cook over medium heat until bouillon dissolves, stirring constantly. Remove from heat; stir in eggs and flour. Chop 6 slices of cheese; add to mixture. Spoon into prepared pie shell. Bake for 20 to 25 minutes or until heated through. Place remaining 2 cheese slices on top. Bake for 3 to 5 minutes longer or until cheese is melted. Garnish with tomato and lettuce.
Yield: 6 to 8 servings.

Cindy Slavin, Zeta Tau
Whiteman Air Force Base, Missouri

CHEESY SHEPHERD'S PIE

1 pound ground beef	16 ounces Cheddar cheese, shredded
8 cups mashed potatoes	

Preheat oven to 350 degrees. Brown ground beef in skillet, stirring until crumbly; drain. Spread mashed potatoes in greased 3-quart baking dish. Layer with ground beef and cheese. Bake for 10 minutes or until cheese has melted. Yield: 6 servings.

Dayna Carlson, Phi Alpha Sigma
Oakland, California

HAMBURGER PIE

1/2 onion, chopped	3 cups mashed cooked potatoes
1 tablespoon shortening	
2 pounds ground beef	2 eggs, beaten
1 16-ounce can green beans, drained	2 tablespoons margarine
1 10-ounce can tomato soup	

Preheat oven to 325 degrees. Sauté onion in shortening in skillet until brown. Add ground beef. Cook until crumbly; drain. Add beans and soup; mix well. Spoon into 2-quart casserole. Whip mashed potatoes in bowl with eggs and margarine until creamy. Spread over ground beef mixture. Bake for 30 minutes or until light brown. Yield: 8 to 10 servings.

Maxine McGuire, Preceptor Kappa
Clearwater, Florida

SKILLET HAMBURGER PIE

A great last-minute meal—you can even use frozen ground beef if you forget to defrost it!

1 1/2 pounds ground beef	1 16-ounce can tomato sauce
1 onion, chopped	
1 16-ounce can green beans, drained	1/2 teaspoon pepper
1 20-ounce can tomatoes, drained	1 teaspoon garlic powder
1 1/2 teaspoons salt	Mashed potatoes

Brown ground beef and onion in electric skillet, stirring until ground beef is crumbly; drain. Stir in green beans, tomatoes, salt, tomato sauce, pepper and garlic powder. Simmer for 15 to 20 minutes. Spoon into serving dish. Arrange mashed potatoes around edge. Yield: 6 to 8 servings.

Bonnie McDowell, Preceptor Chi
Coeur d'Alene, Idaho

MICROWAVE SPAGHETTI PIE

7 ounces spaghetti, cooked	1 pound lean ground beef
	1/2 cup chopped onion
2 tablespoons butter or margarine	1/4 cup chopped green bell pepper
1/3 cup grated Parmesan cheese	1 15-ounce jar spaghetti sauce
2 eggs, well beaten	1/2 cup shredded mozzarella cheese
1 cup cottage cheese	

Combine spaghetti, butter, Parmesan cheese and eggs in large bowl; mix well. Spoon into 9-by-9-inch microwave-safe baking dish. Microwave on High for 2 minutes. Spread cottage cheese over spaghetti; set aside. Place ground beef in microwave-safe colander; set inside glass bowl. Microwave on High for 5 minutes; drain. Add onion and green pepper to ground beef. Microwave for 2 to 3 minutes longer. Combine with spaghetti sauce in glass bowl. Microwave, covered, for 5 to 7 minutes; stir. Pour over cottage cheese layer. Microwave for 7 minutes, turning once. Sprinkle with mozzarella cheese. Microwave for 1 minute. Yield: 8 servings.

Joy Carlson, Xi Eta Iota
Paxton, Illinois

BAKED SPAGHETTI PIE

7 ounces spaghetti, cooked	1 pound ground beef
2 tablespoons butter or margarine	1/2 cup chopped onion
	1/4 cup chopped green bell pepper
1/3 cup grated Parmesan cheese	1 15-ounce jar spaghetti sauce
2 eggs, well beaten	1/2 cup shredded mozzarella cheese
1 cup cottage cheese	

Preheat oven to 350 degrees. Mix spaghetti, butter, Parmesan cheese and eggs in bowl. Press firmly into 10-inch pie plate. Spread with cottage cheese. Brown ground beef, onion and green pepper in skillet, stirring frequently; drain. Stir in spaghetti sauce; spread over cottage cheese layer. Top with mozzarella cheese. Bake for 20 minutes. May prepare ahead and freeze. Bake for 35 to 40 minutes if frozen. Yield: 8 servings.

Beth Rowse, Xi Delta Epsilon
Norfolk, Nebraska

PIZZA HOT DISH

This quick and easy pizza-flavored casserole always gets compliments.

1 pound ground beef	1 6-ounce can tomato paste
1 small onion, chopped	
1/3 cup chopped green bell pepper	2 cups uncooked noodles
	2 cups water
1 clove of garlic, minced	1 teaspoon salt
1 4-ounce can mushrooms, drained	1/8 teaspoon each pepper, basil and oregano
1/2 cup chopped pepperoni	1/4 cup grated Parmesan cheese
1/2 cup sliced black olives	1 cup shredded mozzarella cheese

Combine ground beef, onion, green pepper and garlic in 2-quart glass baking dish. Microwave on High for 5 to 6 minutes or until ground beef is crumbly; drain. Add mushrooms, pepperoni, olives, tomato paste, noodles, water and seasonings; mix well. Microwave for 20 minutes or until noodles are tender, stirring 2 to 3 times. Sprinkle with cheeses. Microwave until cheeses are melted. Yield: 6 to 8 servings.

LouAnn Rochford, Xi Alpha Sigma
North Platte, Nebraska

FRENCH BREAD PIZZA

8 ounces lean ground beef	1 15-ounce jar spaghetti sauce
1 loaf French bread, sliced lengthwise	Shredded mozzarella cheese
Sliced pepperoni	

Preheat oven to 450 degrees. Crumble uncooked ground beef over cut sides of French bread. Arrange pepperoni slices over top. Spread with sauce; sprinkle with cheese. Place on baking sheet. Bake for 15 to 20 minutes or until cheese is melted. Yield: 4 to 6 servings.

Pat Meyr, Preceptor Epsilon Tau
Jackson, Missouri

PIZZA POTATOES

1 5-ounce package scalloped potatoes	1/2 to 1 pound ground chuck
1 14-ounce can tomato purée	1 4-ounce package sliced pepperoni
1 1/2 cups water	8 ounces mozzarella cheese, shredded
1 teaspoon Italian seasoning	

Preheat oven to 400 degrees. Arrange potatoes in 10-by-10-inch baking dish; sprinkle with sauce mix. Combine tomato purée, water and Italian seasoning in saucepan; mix well. Bring to a boil. Pour over potatoes. Brown ground chuck in skillet, stirring until crumbly; drain. Spoon over tomato sauce. Layer with pepperoni slices; sprinkle with cheese. Bake for 30 to 35 minutes. Yield: 4 to 6 servings.

Ann W. Smith, Beta Rho
Lexington, South Carolina

PRONTO PIZZA

8 ounces ground beef	1/4 cup olive oil
1 teaspoon oregano	8 ounces mozzarella cheese, shredded
1/2 teaspoon garlic powder	
	8 ounces Cheddar cheese, shredded
1 10-ounce can tomato soup	9 English muffins, split

Preheat broiler. Brown ground beef in skillet, stirring until crumbly; drain. Combine with remaining ingredients in medium bowl; mix well. Spoon mixture onto English muffin halves. Place on rack in broiler pan. Broil for 2 minutes or until cheese is melted. Ground beef mixture may be frozen or stored in refrigerator for several days. Yield: 18 servings.

Peggy Hunter, Laureate Beta Kappa
Missouri City, Texas

Substitute tortillas, split pita rounds, English muffins or split French buns for the traditional crust for quick and easy pizza snacks.

UPSIDE-DOWN PIZZA

1 pound ground beef
1 15-ounce jar
spaghetti sauce
1 cup shredded
mozzarella cheese

1   8-count can crescent
rolls
Grated Parmesan cheese

Preheat oven to 350 degrees. Brown ground beef in skillet, stirring until crumbly; drain. Stir in spaghetti sauce. Simmer for 5 minutes. Spread mixture in 11-by-13-inch baking pan. Sprinkle with mozzarella cheese. Place crescent roll dough over top, sealing perforations. Sprinkle with Parmesan cheese. Bake for 8 to 10 minutes or until golden brown.
Yield: 6 servings.

Pam Powell, Xi Eta Kappa
Sterling, Kansas

POPPIN' FRESH BARBECUPS

12 ounces ground beef
1/2 cup barbecue sauce
1 tablespoon minced
onion
2 tablespoons dark
brown sugar

1   10-count can flaky
biscuits
3/4 cup shredded
Cheddar or American
cheese

Preheat oven to 400 degrees. Brown ground beef in skillet, stirring until crumbly; drain. Add barbecue sauce, onion and brown sugar; mix well. Place biscuits in greased muffin cups, pressing dough to cover bottom and side. Spoon ground beef mixture into cups; sprinkle with cheese. Bake for 10 to 12 minutes or until golden brown. Remove from pan and serve immediately. Yield: 10 servings.

Joanna Akers, Xi Eta
Newcastle, Wyoming

SKILLET ITALIANO

Growing up in an Italian family, when we needed a quick meal, the meal had to be Italian! My family loves this dish—it's quick and cleanup is a cinch.

1 pound lean ground beef
2 cloves of garlic,
minced
1 onion, chopped
1/2 green bell pepper,
chopped
1 1/2 to 2 teaspoons each
thyme and Italian
seasoning

Salt and pepper to taste
2   16-ounce cans
tomatoes, crushed
1   8-ounce can tomato
sauce
2 cups red wine
3 1/2 to 4 cups uncooked
rigatoni
2 cups water

Brown ground beef and garlic in electric skillet, stirring until crumbly; drain. Add onion and green pepper. Sauté until tender. Stir in seasonings, tomatoes, tomato sauce, wine and rigatoni. Cook over medium heat for 10 minutes, stirring occasionally. Add water. Cook for 15 to 20 minutes longer or until rigatoni is tender, stirring frequently.
Yield: 6 to 8 servings.

Debra Herr, Preceptor Eta Gamma
Cool, California

RUSSIAN HAMBURGER

A version of this recipe has been in my husband's family for generations.

1 pound ground
chuck
1   10-ounce can
tomato soup

1 tablespoon chili
powder
1 1/2 cups instant rice
1 1/2 cups frozen peas

Brown ground chuck in skillet, stirring until crumbly; drain. Stir in tomato soup and chili powder. Simmer for 10 minutes. Prepare rice using package directions; set aside. Microwave peas in glass bowl on High for 5 minutes; set aside. Place ground beef mixture in center of serving platter. Arrange rice and peas around beef. Yield: 4 servings.

Donna L. Meek, Nu Sigma
Tarkio, Missouri

SOUTHWESTERN BEEF AND RICE

Great cooked over a campfire or on the stovetop.

1 1/2 pounds ground beef
1   15-ounce can stewed
tomatoes
2 1/2 cups tomato sauce
1/4 cup chopped green
bell pepper
2 1/2 cups water
2 envelopes taco sauce
mix

2 tablespoons minced
onion flakes
1/2 teaspoon salt
Dash of pepper
1 1/2 cups instant rice
1/2 cup shredded
Cheddar cheese
(optional)

Brown ground beef in skillet, stirring until crumbly; drain. Stir in next 8 ingredients. Bring to a boil. Add rice; reduce heat. Simmer for 15 minutes or until rice is tender. Sprinkle with cheese before serving.
Yield: 6 servings.

Bobbi Carbaugh, Xi Gamma Lambda
Westminster, Colorado

BEEFY SPANISH RICE

1 pound ground beef
1 large onion, chopped
1/2 green bell pepper,
chopped
1 1/4 cups uncooked
rice

1   29-ounce can tomato
sauce
2 cups hot water
2 teaspoons salt
1 teaspoon prepared
mustard

Brown ground beef with onion and green pepper in skillet, stirring frequently; drain. Add rice. Cook until light brown, stirring frequently. Stir in remaining ingredients. Bring to a boil; reduce heat. Simmer, covered, for 25 minutes. Yield: 6 servings.

Joan Gillig, Xi Kappa
St. Joseph, Missouri

SMOTHERED HAMBURGER STEAK

1 pound lean ground beef	1 green bell pepper,
1/2 cup oats	chopped
1 envelope onion soup	1 10-ounce can cream
mix	of mushroom soup
1/2 cup milk	1/2 cup milk

Combine ground beef, oats, onion soup mix, 1/2 cup milk and green pepper in large bowl; mix well. Shape into patties. Place in 8-by-10-inch microwave-safe baking dish. Pour mixture of mushroom soup and remaining 1/2 cup milk over patties. Microwave, loosely covered, on High for 20 minutes. Serve with potatoes, noodles or rice. Yield: 4 servings.

Anita Chambers, Xi Theta
Pratt, Kansas

SPICY HAMBURGER DISH

2 slices bacon	1 14-ounce can stewed
1 small onion, minced	tomatoes
1 to 2 pounds ground	1 16-ounce can tomato
chuck	sauce
Salt, pepper and	3/4 cup water
barbecue spice to	1/2 cup uncooked
taste	macaroni

Preheat electric skillet to 340 degrees. Fry bacon in electric skillet until crisp; drain. Sauté onion in pan drippings until brown; drain. Add ground beef. Cook until brown and crumbly; drain. Add seasonings, stewed tomatoes, tomato sauce, onion, water and macaroni; mix well. Simmer for 20 minutes or until macaroni is tender. Sprinkle with crumbled bacon. May substitute pork and beans for tomatoes and serve over tostado chips. Yield: 4 servings.

Virginia Black, Delta Master
Pueblo, Colorado

CHILI STEW

1 pound ground beef	1 14-ounce can stewed
2 onions, chopped	tomatoes, chopped
1/4 teaspoon minced	1 15-ounce can tomato
garlic	sauce
1 16-ounce can red	1 teaspoon salt
kidney beans,	2 to 3 tablespoons chili
drained	powder

Crumble ground beef into 3-quart glass baking dish. Stir in onions and garlic. Microwave on High for 6 to 7 minutes, stirring once; drain. Add remaining ingredients. Microwave, covered, for 6 to 7 minutes; stir. Microwave on Medium-Low for 30 minutes, stirring occasionally. Let stand, covered, for 7 minutes before serving. Yield: 8 servings.

Marjorie Lounsbury, Xi Nu
Petitcodiac, New Brunswick, Canada

COWBOY STEW

3 pounds ground beef	3 16-ounce cans whole
3 onions, chopped	kernel corn, drained
3/4 cup chopped celery	3 16-ounce cans
12 green onions, chopped	tomatoes, drained
3/4 cup green bell pepper,	3 32-ounce cans ranch-
chopped	style beans, drained
3 cloves of garlic,	2 cups sliced carrots,
minced	cooked
3 tablespoons chili	18 medium potatoes,
powder	peeled, cubed
3/4 teaspoon sugar	9 cups water

Brown ground beef in large soup kettle, stirring until crumbly; drain. Add onions, celery, green onions, green pepper and garlic. Sauté until onions are transparent. Stir in chili powder and sugar. Add remaining ingredients. Bring to a boil; reduce heat. Simmer, covered, for 30 to 40 minutes or until potatoes are tender. Yield: 25 servings.

Clarice Williford, Preceptor Kappa Psi
Port Neches, Texas

HOBO STEW

2 pounds ground beef	2 16-ounce cans pork
1/4 cup catsup	and beans
1/4 cup prepared mustard	1 16-ounce can whole
1/4 cup barbecue sauce	kernel corn, drained
2 16-ounce cans sliced	2 tablespoons minced
potatoes, drained	onion flakes

Preheat electric skillet to 350 degrees. Brown ground beef in skillet, stirring until crumbly; drain. Add catsup, mustard, barbecue sauce, potatoes, pork and beans, corn and onion flakes. Reduce heat to 200 degrees. Simmer for 15 to 20 minutes or until heated through. Yield: 6 to 8 servings.

Darlene Keck, Alpha Kappa Nu
Mansfield, Texas

HAMBURGER STROGANOFF

1 pound lean ground beef	1 cup sliced mushrooms
1/2 cup chopped onion	1 10-ounce can cream
2 tablespoons	of mushroom soup
all-purpose flour	1 cup sour cream
1 teaspoon each salt	Cooked noodles or rice
and pepper	

Brown ground beef and onion in skillet, stirring until ground beef is crumbly; drain. Stir in flour, salt and pepper. Add mushrooms and soup; mix well. Simmer over low heat for 5 minutes. Stir in sour cream. Cook until warmed through. Serve over noodles or rice. Yield: 4 servings.

Norma Hammett
Trenton, Missouri

FIFTEEN-MINUTE STROGANOFF

1 onion, minced	1/2 teaspoon paprika
1 clove of garlic, minced	1/4 teaspoon pepper
1/4 cup margarine	1 10-ounce can cream
1 1/2 pounds ground beef	of chicken soup
1 pound mushrooms,	1 cup sour cream
sliced	8 ounces egg noodles,
2 tablespoons	cooked
all-purpose flour	Chopped parsley
1 1/2 teaspoons salt	

Sauté onion and garlic in margarine in 12-inch skillet for 3 minutes. Add next 6 ingredients. Cook until ground beef is browned, stirring frequently. Add soup. Bring to a boil; reduce heat to low. Simmer for 5 minutes, stirring often. Stir in sour cream just before serving. Serve over cooked noodles. Garnish with chopped parsley. Yield: 6 servings.

Carol Sassin, Xi Psi Beta
Beeville, Texas

STUFFED GREEN BELL PEPPERS

4 large or 6 small green	1/3 cup quick-cooking
bell peppers	oats
1 1/2 pounds ground beef	1 teaspoon salt
1 egg, beaten	Pepper to taste
1/4 cup finely chopped	2 cups spaghetti sauce
onion	

Cut off tops of peppers; remove seed. Combine ground beef, egg, onion, oats, salt, pepper and 1/2 cup spaghetti sauce in large bowl; mix well. Spoon into peppers, pressing gently. Arrange in 3-quart microwave-safe baking dish. Spoon remaining spaghetti sauce over peppers. Microwave, covered, on High for 20 to 25 minutes. Let stand, covered, for 5 minutes before serving. Yield: 4 to 6 servings.

Loretta F. Hill, Preceptor Beta
Westminster, Maryland

SWEET AND SOUR BEEF

1 4-ounce can	3 tablespoons soy sauce
pineapple chunks	1 pound ground beef
1/3 cup packed light	1 small green or red bell
brown sugar	pepper, chopped
2 tablespoons	1 onion, chopped
cornstarch	Cooked rice or noodles
1/4 cup red wine vinegar	

Drain pineapple, reserving 3/4 cup juice. Combine brown sugar, cornstarch, vinegar, soy sauce and reserved pineapple juice in small bowl, stirring to blend; set aside. Crumble ground beef into 3-quart glass baking dish. Microwave on High for 4 to 5 minutes or until browned. Add bell pepper and onion. Microwave, covered, for 2 minutes. Stir in prepared sauce. Microwave for 4 to 5 minutes or until sauce thickens, stirring twice. Add pineapple.

Microwave for 1 1/2 minutes or until heated through. Serve with hot rice or noodles. Yield: 4 servings.

Diana Kienbaum, Alpha
Rathdrum, Idaho

SEVEN-LAYER TACOS

2 pounds ground beef	1 10-ounce can each
1 or 2 onions, chopped	Cheddar cheese soup
Hot pepper sauce and	and tomato soup
Worcestershire sauce	1 4-ounce can chopped
to taste	green chilies, drained
1/2 cup catsup	Crushed corn chips
Salt and pepper to	Shredded lettuce
taste	Chopped tomatoes
2 15-ounce cans chili	Shredded Cheddar cheese
beans	Sour cream

Brown ground beef and onions in skillet, stirring until ground beef is crumbly; drain. Stir in next 5 ingredients. Simmer for several minutes or until heated through. Heat chili beans in saucepan. Combine soups and chili peppers in saucepan. Cook until heated through, stirring frequently. Layer chips, lettuce, tomatoes, ground beef mixture, chili beans, cheese sauce and shredded cheese in 9-by-13-inch dish. Serve with sour cream. Yield: 8 servings.

Bonnie Stratton, Preceptor Chi
Rapid City, South Dakota

MEXICAN TACO CUPS

8 won ton wrappers	12 ounces Cheddar
1 1/2 pounds ground	cheese, shredded
beef	1/2 head lettuce,
1 7-ounce can chicken	shredded
broth	2 tomatoes, chopped
1 onion, chopped	1 cup guacamole
1 15-ounce can chili	1 6-ounce can black
beans, drained	olives, drained

Place each won ton wrapper at a time over bottom of small greased bowl. Microwave on Medium for 75 seconds; set aside. Brown ground beef in skillet, stirring until crumbly; drain. Add chicken broth, onion and chili beans; mix well. Simmer for 5 to 10 minutes, stirring occasionally. Layer ground beef mixture, cheese, lettuce, tomatoes and guacamole in each prepared shell. Top with olives. Serve immediately. Yield: 8 servings.

Cathi Lynn Iacovetto, Theta
Gillette, Wyoming

Kimberly F. Holden, Theta Rho, Nashville, Tennessee, makes Cheesy Tamale Bake by arranging 1 can tamales in 5-by-9-inch pan. Pour 2 cups kidney beans over top. Bake, covered, in preheated 350-degree oven for 25 minutes. Top with 3/4 cup shredded Cheddar cheese and 1/4 cup chopped green onions.

RUNNING-LATE TACOS

1 to 1½ pounds ground beef	Chopped onion
1 16-ounce jar picante sauce	Chopped tomato
	Shredded Cheddar cheese
Crushed taco chips	Taco sauce
Shredded lettuce	

Brown ground beef in skillet, stirring until crumbly; drain. Add picante sauce. Cook until heated through. Place crushed chips on serving plate. Top with ground beef mixture and remaining ingredients. Yield: 4 to 8 servings.

Gail Frics, Laureate Upsilon
Omaha, Nebraska

TEXAS BEANS

1 pound ground beef	2 16-ounce cans pork and beans, drained
½ onion, chopped	
8 ounces bacon, crisp-fried, crumbled	1 cup catsup
	1 cup packed light brown sugar
1 16-ounce can butter beans, drained	
	1½ teaspoons liquid smoke
1 16-ounce can kidney beans, drained	1½ tablespoons vinegar

Brown ground beef in large skillet, stirring until crumbly; drain. Add remaining ingredients; mix well. Simmer for 30 minutes, stirring frequently. May also cook in slow cooker for 1 hour. Yield: 8 to 10 servings.

Lovelita J. Johnson, Xi Epsilon Tau
Seymour, Indiana

TEXAS HASH

1 pound ground beef	Salt, pepper and Tabasco sauce to taste
1 large onion, chopped	
1 10-ounce can Ro-Tel tomatoes	2 cups cooked rice
	8 ounces Cheddar cheese, shredded
1 teaspoon chili powder	

Preheat oven to 300 degrees. Brown ground beef and onion in skillet, stirring until ground beef is crumbly; drain. Stir in tomatoes, chili powder, salt, pepper and Tabasco sauce. Simmer, covered, until liquid is reduced to desired consistency, stirring frequently. Add rice; mix well. Pour into 9-by-12-inch baking dish. Top with cheese. Bake for 5 minutes or until cheese is bubbly. Yield: 6 servings.

Patricia Lighthall, Xi Alpha Beta Theta
Longview, Texas

Joan Marshall, Beta Iota, Duluth, Minnesota, makes Quick Mock Spaghetti by combining 1 pound browned ground beef, 26 ounces Franco-American spaghetti, ½ cup chopped celery and ¼ cup chopped onion in saucepan. Simmer until desired consistency.

ZUCCHINI BOATS

I remember as a child when my mom made this I thought it looked like mush. It doesn't look very appetizing, but it tastes great.

4 ounces ground beef	½ teaspoon garlic salt
½ cup bread crumbs	½ teaspoon chopped onion
1 egg, beaten	
½ teaspoon thyme	4 zucchini
½ teaspoon salt	½ cup shredded Cheddar cheese
½ teaspoon pepper	

Preheat oven to 350 degrees. Brown ground beef in skillet, stirring until crumbly; drain. Combine with bread crumbs, egg and seasonings in bowl; mix well. Cut zucchini into halves lengthwise. Cook in boiling water in saucepan for 15 minutes. Scoop out pulp leaving thin shell. Stir pulp into ground beef mixture. Spoon mixture into zucchini shells; arrange on baking sheet. Bake for 20 minutes. Sprinkle with cheese. Bake for 5 minutes longer or until cheese is melted. Yield: 6 to 8 servings.

Teri R. Novotny, Alpha
Springfield, Missouri

MULTI-PURPOSE HAMBURGER MIX

This is great to have on hand to fix quick Sloppy Joe's, goulash, etc.

4 onions, chopped	½ teaspoon pepper
3 cloves of garlic, chopped	2 12-ounce bottles of catsup
2 cups chopped celery	3 tablespoons Worcestershire sauce
4 pounds ground beef	
2 teaspoons salt	

Sauté onions, garlic and celery in large kettle. Add ground beef. Cook over medium heat, stirring until crumbly. Add remaining ingredients; mix well. Simmer for 20 minutes. Cool; skim off fat. Store in 1-pint containers in freezer to use as needed. Yield: 3½ quarts.

Marilyn Heinisch, Xi Gamma Alpha
Dubuque, Iowa

BURRITO MIX

3 pounds ground beef	10 ounces Cheddar cheese, cubed
1 large onion, finely chopped	
	5 tablespoons picante sauce
1 10-ounce can cream of mushroom soup	
2 16-ounce cans refried beans	

Brown ground beef and onion in large saucepan, stirring frequently; drain. Add remaining ingredients. Cook over medium heat until cheese is melted, stirring frequently. Yield: 3 quarts.

Sandra Steinmann, Xi Upsilon Psi
Yoakum, Texas

EASY HAMBURGER AND CHEESE MIX

1 pound ground beef	1 tablespoon milk
Velveeta cheese, cubed	

Brown ground beef in skillet, stirring until crumbly; drain. Add cheese and milk. Cook over medium heat until cheese is melted, stirring frequently. Vary amounts to suit individual tastes.
Yield: 4 to 6 servings.

Peggy McRedmond, Xi Alpha Pi
Madison, Wisconsin

AT-HOME MICRO MCMUFFIN BREAKFAST

1 12-ounce can ham patties	6 English muffins Butter, margarine or mayonnaise-type salad dressing
1 tablespoon butter or margarine	
6 eggs	6 slices Velveeta cheese

Microwave ham patties in glass dish on High for 3 minutes. Preheat microwave browning dish using manufacturer's instructions. Melt butter in browning dish. Microwave eggs in browning dish on Medium for 2½ minutes or until done to taste. Place muffins in microwave-safe individual dishes. Microwave on Low for 15 to 20 seconds. Butter both sides of muffins. Place ham patty, cheese and egg on muffin bottoms; replace tops. Microwave each for 20 to 30 seconds. Yield: 6 servings.

Helen Schoenrock, Pi Laureate
Fairbury, Nebraska

BROCCOLI AND HAM DELIGHT

1 bunch broccoli	1/3 cup milk
1 6-ounce package sliced cooked ham	1/4 cup mayonnaise
1 10-ounce can cream of mushroom soup	2 teaspoons lemon juice
	1/4 cup grated Parmesan cheese

Preheat oven to 400 degrees. Steam broccoli in saucepan until tender-crisp; separate into stalks. Roll ham around broccoli stalks. Arrange in shallow 9-by-13-inch casserole. Combine soup, milk, mayonnaise and lemon juice in mixer bowl; beat until smooth. Pour over rolls; sprinkle with cheese. Bake for 20 to 25 minutes or until bubbly. Yield: 4 to 6 servings.

Karen Peter, Preceptor Laureate Theta
Estevan, Saskatchewan, Canada

FUSILLI WITH PROSCIUTTO

1 16-ounce package fusilli or pasta spirals	1 8-ounce can peas, drained
8 slices prosciutto, cut into thin strips	1/2 cup grated Parmesan cheese
9 tablespoons unsalted butter	Salt and coarsely ground pepper to taste
	1/2 cup ricotta cheese

Cook fusilli using package directions; drain. Sauté prosciutto in 1 tablespoon butter until crisp. Add peas. Sauté for 2 minutes, stirring frequently. Add remaining butter, stirring to melt. Add fusilli, Parmesan cheese, salt and pepper, tossing to coat. Add ricotta cheese, tossing until warmed. Serve in individual bowls; sprinkle with dash of pepper.
Yield: 4 to 6 servings.

Mary Ann Pokol, Preceptor Gamma Epsilon
De Land, Florida

HAM CASSEROLE AU GRATIN

1/2 onion, chopped	3 cups cooked rice
1/4 cup margarine	3 10-ounce packages frozen chopped broccoli, thawed
2 10-ounce cans cream of mushroom soup	
1 8-ounce jar Cheez Whiz	2 cups chopped cooked ham

Preheat oven to 350 degrees. Sauté onion in margarine in small saucepan until tender. Combine soup and Cheez Whiz in large bowl; mix well. Stir in onion and margarine. Add rice, broccoli and ham; mix well. Spoon into 3-quart casserole. Bake for 30 minutes. Serve with salad and bread. Yield: 6 to 8 servings.

Cayla Armatti, Rho Beta
Ocala, Florida

HAM IN-A-HURRY

2 8-ounce slices fully cooked ham	2 tablespoons light brown sugar
1 8-ounce can sliced pineapple	2 tablespoons pineapple juice
4 maraschino cherries	

Preheat oven to 350 degrees. Line 9-by-13-inch baking pan with foil. Place ham slices in prepared pan. Drain pineapple, reserving 2 tablespoons juice. Arrange pineapple on ham slices with maraschino cherry in center of each ring. Sprinkle with brown sugar. Drizzle with reserved pineapple juice. Fold foil over to seal. Bake for 25 minutes.
Yield: 3 to 4 servings.

Marilyn R. Buchele, Xi Epsilon Nu
Emporia, Kansas

HAM AND POTATO SKILLET

I needed something quick to do with leftover ham and just started putting things together that sounded good.

1 small onion, chopped	2 to 3 cups cooked cubed ham
2 tablespoons margarine	
1 16-ounce package frozen cottage fries	1/2 cup packed light brown sugar

Sauté onion in margarine in large skillet until tender. Add cottage fries. Cook until light brown, stirring frequently. Add ham and brown sugar. Cook over

medium heat until heated through.
Yield: 4 to 6 servings.

Carol Kay, Xi Zeta Mu
Eldridge, Iowa

HAWAIIAN CRESCENT SANDWICHES

1 8-count can crescent rolls	1/2 cup shredded Monterey Jack cheese
1 6-ounce can chunk ham, drained, flaked	1/4 cup chopped green bell pepper
1/3 cup crushed pineapple	

Preheat oven to 375 degrees. Separate crescent rolls into 4 rectangles, sealing perforations. Place on ungreased baking sheet. Combine ham, pineapple, cheese and green pepper in large bowl; mix well. Spoon mixture on half of each rectangle. Fold in half to enclose filling, sealing edges. Bake for 13 to 18 minutes or until golden brown. Yield: 4 servings.

Tammy Booe, Omicron Mu
Osawatomie, Kansas

HURRY-UP HAM

We first used this recipe 30 years ago on a camping trip. It is easy to make on stove top or over a campfire.

2 cups chopped cooked ham	3 tablespoons chili sauce
1 onion, chopped	1/2 teaspoon prepared mustard
1 10-ounce can whole mushrooms, drained	1 teaspoon salt
2 tablespoons butter, margarine or vegetable oil	Tabasco sauce to taste
	Chopped celery
2 cups water	2 cups quick-cooking rice

Brown ham, onion and mushrooms in butter in large skillet. Add water, chili sauce, mustard, salt, Tabasco sauce and celery. Bring to a boil. Stir in rice; remove from heat. Let stand, covered, for 5 minutes. Yield: 4 servings.

Lorraine Connors, Laureate Alpha Psi
Guelph, Ontario, Canada

HAM AND POTATO CASSEROLE

1 10-ounce package frozen green beans, thawed, drained	2 cups shredded Cheddar cheese
1 10-ounce can cream of celery soup	1 20-ounce package frozen hashed brown potatoes
1 cup sour cream	6 ounces chopped cooked ham
1/8 teaspoon nutmeg	

Preheat oven to 350 degrees. Combine beans, soup, sour cream, nutmeg and 1 1/2 cups cheese in large skillet; mix well. Cook over medium heat until heated through, stirring frequently. Stir in potatoes and ham. Spoon mixture into greased 9-by-13-inch casserole. Sprinkle with remaining 1/2 cup cheese. Bake for 45 minute or until bubbly. Yield: 4 servings.

Beverly A. Lubeski, Preceptor Beta Delta
Merriam, Kansas

QUICHE LORRAINE

Great for a "come as you are" breakfast.

1 unbaked 10-inch deep-dish pie shell	4 ounces mozzarella cheese, shredded
Worcestershire sauce	3 eggs
3 slices crisp-fried bacon, crumbled	1/2 cup whipping cream
	1 3-ounce can French-fried onions

Brush pie shell with Worcestershire sauce. Microwave on High for 2 minutes. Crumble bacon over pie crust; sprinkle with cheese. Beat eggs and cream in small bowl until frothy; pour over cheese. Top with onions. Microwave for 10 minutes, turning twice. Yield: 10 servings.

Rebecca Epps, Xi Iota
Texarkana, Texas

QUICK HAM BARBECUE

5 tablespoons vinegar	3 stalks celery, chopped
1/4 cup catsup	1/2 lemon, thinly sliced
2 tablespoons Worcestershire sauce	1 1/2 cups water
	1/2 cup margarine
3 bay leaves	2 tablespoons dark brown sugar
1 clove of garlic, minced	Cornstarch
1 tablespoon chopped onion	1 pound cooked ham, shredded
1 cup canned tomatoes, chopped	6 buns

Combine first 10 ingredients in large saucepan; mix well. Simmer for 15 to 20 minutes; strain. Add margarine and brown sugar, stirring until margarine is melted. Mix cornstarch with water, stirring to blend; add to mixture. Stir in ham. Serve on buns or open face on bread. Yield: 6 servings.

Karen Whitney, Gamma Tau
Bowie, Maryland

QUICK AND EASY HAM BRUNCH

1 English muffin, split, toasted	2 slices Velveeta cheese
	2 pineapple rings
1 slice cooked ham, cut into halves	2 maraschino cherries

Layer each muffin half with ham, cheese and pineapple slice; top with cherry. Place on glass plate. Microwave on Medium for 1 to 2 minutes or until cheese is melted. Yield: 1 serving.

Brenda Streit, Mu Psi
Sabetha, Kansas

RICE DIANE

*I got this wonderful tasting recipe from a sorority sister.
I make this when we have company or go to potlucks.*

3 cups long grain rice	1½ cups thinly sliced
3 chicken bouillon cubes	kielbasa
1 bunch green onions,	1 cup peeled cooked
chopped	shrimp
1 cup sliced mushrooms	½ cup margarine
1½ cups cubed cooked	Parmesan cheese
ham	

Preheat oven to 325 degrees. Cook rice in large saucepan using package directions, adding bouillon
cubes. Sauté green onions, mushrooms, ham, kiel-
basa and shrimp in margarine in large skillet, stirring
frequently. Add rice. Spoon into 5-quart casserole.
Sprinkle with cheese. Bake for 20 to 30 minutes or
until heated through. Yield: 8 servings.

Diane Slezak, Preceptor Beta Upsilon
Port Orchard, Washington

❖ TEMPTING TORTELLINI AND HAM

¾ cup butter or	½ cup half and half
margarine, softened	1 cup grated Parmesan
1 teaspoon basil	cheese
½ teaspoon garlic	8 ounces cheese
powder	tortellini, cooked
¼ teaspoon pepper	1½ cups chopped
2 tablespoons	cooked ham
mayonnaise	1 cup chopped cooked
4 ounces cream cheese,	broccoli
cubed	1 tomato, chopped

Preheat oven to 350 degrees. Combine butter, seasonings, mayonnaise, cream cheese and half and half in
large bowl; mix well. Fold in Parmesan cheese, tortellini, ham and broccoli. Spoon into 9-by-9-inch
casserole. Bake for 25 minutes. Top with chopped
tomato. Bake for 5 minutes longer. Yield: 8 servings.

Janet Chapman, Delta Lambda
Marshall, Minnesota

LAMB CHOPS

*My Irish grandmother taught my mother to cook this
and my mother taught me.*

8 lamb chops	Sage and rosemary to
Salt, pepper and garlic	taste
salt to taste	

Spray skillet with nonstick cooking spray. Sprinkle
salt, pepper and garlic salt on lamb chops. Brown in
skillet for 10 minutes, turning once. Sprinkle with
sage and rosemary. Cook for 10 to 15 minutes longer
or until done to taste, turning every 5 minutes.
Yield: 8 servings.

Roseann R. Cochcroft, Xi Alpha Phi
West Cola, South Carolina

LAMB CHOPS PARMESAN

8 to 12 lamb chops	2 tablespoons
½ cup grated Parmesan	margarine, softened
cheese	½ teaspoon oregano
1 teaspoon lemon juice	Salt and pepper to taste

Arrange lamb chops on rack in broiler pan. Broil 2
inches from heat source for 3 minutes on each side.
Combine cheese, lemon juice, margarine, oregano,
salt and pepper in small bowl; mix well. Spread mixture on one side of chops. Broil for 4 minutes longer
or until cheese is light brown. Yield: 4 servings.

Arlene Bresciani, Gamma
Regina, Saskatchewan, Canada

PORK CHOPS À L'ORANGE

1 pound thinly sliced	2 teaspoons rosemary
pork chops, fat	Salt and lemon pepper
trimmed	to taste
2 teaspoons butter or	Juice of 1 orange
margarine	Sections of 1 orange

Brown pork chops in butter in skillet for 2 minutes
on each side. Sprinkle with rosemary, salt and lemon
pepper. Cook for 5 minutes on each side. Add orange
juice and sections to pork chops. Simmer for several
minutes longer or until done, stirring to scrape pan.
Arrange on serving platter. Place orange sections on
pork chops; pour pan drippings over top. Serve with
steamed vegetables and buttered fettucini.
Yield: 2 to 4 servings.

Rita McLean, Preceptor Beta Xi
Nanaimo, British Columbia, Canada

QUICK-TO-FIX CHOPS AND APPLES

4 pork chops	¼ cup packed light
2 tablespoons butter or	brown sugar
margarine	¼ teaspoon cinnamon
1 cup chopped apple	4 slices lemon

Cook pork chops in butter in skillet over medium
heat for 2 minutes on each side. Spoon ¼ chopped
apple onto each pork chop. Cook, covered, over low
heat for 20 minutes or until apple is tender. Sprinkle
with mixture of brown sugar and cinnamon; top
with slice of lemon. Cook, covered, for 5 minutes
longer or until sugar is melted. Yield: 4 servings.

Shelly Boren, Delta Lambda
Euless, Texas

*Carol Harper, Preceptor Alpha Epsilon, Nashville, Tennessee,
makes Glazed Ham Steak by layering a 1-inch ham slice and
sliced orange in baking dish. Pour mixture of ¼ cup molasses, 2 tablespoons water, ¼ cup orange juice, 2 tablespoons
sugar, ⅛ teaspoon dry mustard and ginger over ham. Bake
in preheated 375-degree oven for 30 minutes.*

SMOTHERED PORK CHOPS

This is excellent served with steamed rice and a green vegetable.

6 pork chops, boned
1/2 cup chicken broth
1/3 cup honey
1/4 cup soy sauce

2 tablespoons catsup
1/4 teaspoon ground ginger
1 clove of garlic, minced

Preheat electric skillet to 350 degrees. Sear pork chops on both sides. Reduce temperature to 225 or 250 degrees. Combine remaining ingredients in bowl; mix well. Pour over pork chops. Simmer, covered, for 20 minutes until sauce thickens, stirring frequently. Yield: 4 to 6 servings.

Dianne Truss, Preceptor Alpha
Victoria, British Columbia, Canada

SPICY AND SWEET PORK CHOPS

4 thickly sliced pork chops
2 tablespoons vegetable oil
4 slices pineapple
2 maraschino cherries, cut into halves

1/2 cup apricot preserves
1/4 cup soy sauce
1/4 cup white wine
Orange slices and watercress

Preheat oven to 350 degrees. Brown pork chops on both sides in oil in skillet. Arrange in 9-by-9-inch shallow baking dish. Place pineapple slice and cherry half on each pork chop. Combine preserves, soy sauce and wine in small bowl; mix well. Pour over pork chops. Bake, covered, for 45 minutes or until pork chops are cooked through. Arrange on serving platter. Serve with sauce. Garnish with orange slices and watercress. Yield: 4 servings.

Marilyn R. Mulhall, Preceptor Sigma
Nashville, Tennessee

CHILI DOGS

My sister and her children arrived unexpectedly one evening and I needed a quick meal that the kids would eat. They loved this!

2 15-ounce cans hot chili beans
1 8-ounce can tomato sauce
1/4 teaspoon chili powder

1/4 teaspoon cumin
1/8 teaspoon cayenne pepper
12 frankfurters
1 slice American cheese, cut into 36 strips

Preheat oven to 400 degrees. Combine beans, tomato sauce and seasonings in bowl; mix well. Pour into 7-by-11-inch baking pan. Make 3 diagonal 1/2-inch deep slits in each frankfurter. Insert cheese strips into slits. Arrange over bean mixture. Bake for 20 minutes. Yield: 4 to 5 servings.

Linda Naber, Omega Mu
Ridgeway, Missouri

BARBECUED FRANKS

1/4 cup chopped onion
1 tablespoon butter or margarine
1/8 teaspoon pepper
4 teaspoons sugar
1 teaspoon prepared mustard

1 tablespoon Worcestershire sauce
1/2 cup catsup
1/2 cup water
1/4 cup white vinegar
1 pound frankfurters

Preheat oven to 400 degrees. Sauté onion in butter in skillet for 3 minutes or until onion is transparent. Add pepper, sugar, mustard, Worcestershire sauce, catsup, water and vinegar; mix well. Simmer for 5 minutes, stirring frequently. Make diagonal slits in each frankfurter. Arrange in 8-by-8-inch baking dish; cover with sauce. Bake for 20 minutes, basting frequently. Serve with browned potatoes or rice and corn. Yield: 3 to 4 servings.

Irene Speed, Laureate Alpha Pi
Surrey, British Columbia, Canada

FRANKFURTER CASSEROLE

This recipe uses only one skillet. It's great for camping and at home.

1 small onion, chopped
1 pound frankfurters, sliced lengthwise
1/2 cup margarine
1 10-ounce can tomato soup

1 soup can milk
1/2 soup can water
2 cups uncooked egg noodles
Sliced American cheese

Brown onion and frankfurters in margarine in skillet over medium heat. Add soup, milk and water; mix well. Reduce heat; stir in noodles. Simmer until noodles are cooked, stirring occasionally. Place cheese slices over top just before serving. Let stand until melted. Yield: 8 servings.

Becky Strong, Alpha Eta
Green River, Wyoming

FRANKFURTER SPANISH RICE

2 tablespoons chopped onion
2 tablespoons chopped green bell pepper
1 tablespoon olive oil

1 1/3 cups cooked rice
1 16-ounce can crushed tomatoes
4 frankfurters, sliced
3/4 teaspoon salt

Sauté onion and green pepper in oil in skillet until tender. Add rice, tomatoes, frankfurters and salt. Cook, covered, over low heat for 15 minutes. Yield: 4 servings.

Meryl Plummer, Xi Beta Epsilon
Pennsauken, New Jersey

A quick surprise for the kids in your family is a big piece of grilled bologna basted with their favorite barbecue sauce.

LAYERED MEXICAN CASSEROLE

1 6-ounce package corn chips	1 large onion, chopped
1 28-ounce can tamales	1 19-ounce can chili without beans
1 6-ounce package quick-cooking rice, cooked	³/4 cup shredded Cheddar cheese

Preheat oven to 350 degrees. Line 9-by-12-inch baking pan with corn chips. Cut each tamale into 5 portions. Layer tamales, rice and onion over chips. Spread chili over top layer; sprinkle with cheese. Bake, covered with foil, for 35 to 40 minutes or until cheese is melted. Yield: 6 to 8 servings.

Anne Beck, Alpha Rho Alpha
Burleson, Texas

MASHED POTATO DOGS

8 hot dogs	¹/2 cup shredded Cheddar cheese
2 cups mashed cooked potatoes	

Preheat broiler. Slice hot dogs lengthwise. Fill with mashed potatoes; sprinkle with cheese. Place on rack in broiler pan. Broil for 5 minutes or until cheese is melted. Yield: 8 servings.

Doris E. Hannagan, Preceptor Alpha Delta
Sparta, New Jersey

CRESCENT OMELET

This was served at a "come as you are" breakfast at my home along with fresh fruit cups.

1 pound sausage	2 cups hashed brown potatoes, cooked
Chopped onion, green or red bell pepper and mushrooms	6 to 8 eggs, scrambled
2 8-count cans crescent rolls	6 slices cheese

Preheat oven to 350 degrees. Brown sausage in skillet, stirring until crumbly. Drain, reserving 1 tablespoon drippings. Sauté vegetables in pan drippings in skillet until tender; set aside. Press crescent roll dough into 9-by-13-inch baking pan, sealing perforations. Layer sausage, potatoes, sautéed vegetables, eggs and cheese in prepared pan. Bake for 15 to 20 minutes. Yield: 8 to 10 servings.

Ethel Baker, Theta Beta
Tampa, Florida

Mary C. Tedrow, Alpha Nu, Shelby, Ohio, makes Hot Pineapple-Dog Bits by combining 8 hot dogs cut into 1-inch pieces, 16 ounces pork and beans, ¹/3 cup packed brown sugar and 1 cup crushed pineapple in casserole. Top with ¹/3 cup Parmesan cheese and ¹/4 cup croutons. Bake in preheated 350-degree oven for 30 minutes.

KIELBASA AND POTATOES O'BRIEN

4 to 5 potatoes, peeled, sliced	1 package kielbasa sausage, cut into 1-inch pieces
1 large green bell pepper, cut into strips	1 cup shredded Swiss cheese
1 large onion, sliced	Salt and pepper to taste
¹/4 cup vegetable oil	

Cook potatoes, green pepper and onion in oil in covered skillet over medium heat until potatoes are tender, stirring occasionally. Add sausage. Steam for 5 minutes or until heated through; remove from heat. Sprinkle with cheese, salt and pepper. Let stand, covered, until cheese is melted. Serve immediately. Yield: 4 to 5 servings.

Tara Richter, Gamma
Mauldin, South Carolina

PIZZA-PASTA CASSEROLE

4 ounces pepperoni, sliced	1 envelope spaghetti seasoning mix
8 ounces Italian sausage	1³/4 cups water
1 green bell pepper, chopped	1 6-ounce can tomato paste
1 onion, chopped	1 8-ounce can tomato sauce
1 cup sliced mushrooms	1 10-ounce package mostaccioli, cooked
¹/2 cup sliced black olives	1 cup shredded mozzarella cheese
¹/2 teaspoon garlic powder or garlic salt	

Preheat oven to 350 degrees. Brown pepperoni and sausage in skillet; drain. Add green pepper, onion, mushrooms, olives, seasonings, water, tomato paste and tomato sauce; mix well. Bring to a boil; reduce heat. Simmer for 10 minutes, stirring frequently. Add pasta, stirring to coat with sauce. Spoon into 8-by-12-inch casserole. Top with cheese. Bake for 15 minutes or until cheese is melted. Serve with salad and breadsticks. Yield: 6 servings.

Kim Emmendorfer, Alpha Alpha Mu
Lees Summit, Missouri

RED BEANS AND RICE WITH SMOKED SAUSAGE

1 onion, chopped	1 16-ounce can red kidney beans, drained
1 4-ounce can chopped green chilies, drained	¹/2 cup shredded Monterey Jack cheese
2 tablespoons vegetable oil	1 pound smoked link sausage, sliced
³/4 cup uncooked rice	1 teaspoon Tabasco sauce
1 cup water	
1 beef bouillon cube	

Sauté onion and chilies in oil in large saucepan for 3 minutes. Add rice, water and bouillon cube. Bring to a boil; reduce heat. Simmer, covered, for 10 minutes or until liquid is absorbed. Stir in beans, cheese, sausage and Tabasco sauce. Simmer until heated through. Yield: 4 servings.

Cheryl Ottas, Epsilon Kappa
Guelph, Ontario, Canada

TORTELLINI AND SPINACH

3 9-ounce packages
   frozen creamed
   spinach, prepared
1/2 cup milk
2 9-ounce packages
   meat tortellini,
   prepared
1 cup chopped
   tomato
1/2 teaspoon dried basil
1/2 cup grated
   Parmesan cheese

Preheat oven to 350 degrees. Mix creamed spinach with milk in bowl. Spoon half the creamed spinach mixture into shallow 2½-quart casserole. Top with half the tortellini and chopped tomato. Repeat layers with remaining creamed spinach, tortellini and tomato. Sprinkle with basil. Bake, covered with foil, for 40 minutes. Yield: 6 servings.

Billie M. Lepere, Preceptor Theta Xi
San Ramon, California

BREAD-BOTTOM QUICHE

10 slices whole wheat
   bread, cut into
   fourths
3/4 cup shredded sharp
   cheese
2 cups cooked sausage
3 tablespoons chopped
   onion
1 medium zucchini,
   grated
6 eggs
2 cups milk
1 teaspoon salt
1/4 cup melted butter or
   margarine

Line bottom and edges of buttered 9-by-12-inch casserole with bread. Layer cheese, sausage, onion and zucchini over bread. Mix eggs, milk, salt and melted butter in bowl. Pour mixture over top. Chill overnight. Bake in preheated 400-degree oven for 50 minutes. Yield: 6 servings.

Kimberly Weight
Boise, Idaho

SAUSAGE AND EGG CASSEROLE

1 pound sausage
12 eggs
1 pound Cheddar
   cheese, shredded
2 cups whipping
   cream

Preheat oven to 325 degrees. Brown sausage in skillet, stirring until crumbly; drain. Break eggs into 9-by-13-inch baking pan. Prick yolks; do not stir. Layer sausage and cheese over eggs. Pour whipping cream over top. Bake for 45 minutes or until set. Yield: 8 servings.

Barb Olson, Preceptor Alpha
Missoula, Montana

SAUSAGE AND EGG PUFF

6 eggs, slightly beaten
1 pound sausage,
   browned, drained
1 cup buttermilk baking
   mix
1 cup shredded Cheddar
   cheese
2 cups milk
1 teaspoon dry mustard

Preheat oven to 350 degrees. Combine all ingredients in bowl; mix well. Pour into greased 2-quart casserole. Bake for 50 minutes or until knife inserted in center comes out clean. Serve with fresh fruit. Yield: 10 to 14 servings.

Florence M. Owen, Laureate Nu
Waynesville, North Carolina

EASY SAUSAGE CASSOULET

12 ounces cooked Polish
   sausage
1 small onion, chopped
1 clove of garlic, minced
1 tablespoon vegetable
   oil
1/4 cup white wine
1/2 teaspoon thyme
1/8 teaspoon pepper
1 16-ounce can pork
   and beans in tomato
   sauce
1 15-ounce can Great
   Northern beans,
   drained
1 tablespoon chopped
   parsley

Slice sausage lengthwise; cut into 3-inch pieces. Cook with onion and garlic in oil in skillet for 3 to 4 minutes until onion is tender. Add wine. Cook over low heat for 2 to 3 minutes. Stir in thyme, pepper, undrained pork and beans and Great Northern beans. Simmer for 10 minutes. Serve hot, garnished with parsley. Yield: 4 servings.

Patricia McKelvy, Preceptor Theta Sigma
Brackettville, Texas

FAST SKILLET VEAL PARMIGIANA

6 frozen veal patties
2 tablespoons vegetable
   oil or margarine
1 15-ounce can
   tomatoes, drained,
   chopped
1 tablespoon dried
   minced onion
1 teaspoon sugar
1 teaspoon each
   oregano and basil
1/2 teaspoon salt
1/4 teaspoon pepper
6 slices mozzarella
   cheese
3 tablespoons grated
   Parmesan cheese

Brown veal patties in oil in skillet; drain on paper towels. Add tomatoes, onion, sugar, and seasonings to skillet; mix well. Cook for 5 to 10 minutes, stirring frequently. Place mozzarella cheese slice on each veal patty. Place on sauce in skillet. Sprinkle with Parmesan cheese. Cook, covered, over medium heat for 10 minutes or until cheese is melted. Yield: 6 servings.

Rae C. Miller, Xi Eta Rho
Camdenton, Missouri

VEAL MARSALA

4 to 6 veal scallopini
1/2 cup milk
1 cup all-purpose flour
1/4 cup butter or
  margarine
Salt and pepper to taste
8 ounces mushrooms,
  sliced

1 bunch green onions,
  chopped
1 1/4 cups Marsala
  cooking wine
1 to 2 teaspoons
  all-purpose flour

Pound veal between sheets of waxed paper to tenderize. Dip in milk; coat with flour. Brown in 2 tablespoons butter in skillet for 3 minutes on each side. Sprinkle with salt and pepper. Remove to warm platter. Melt remaining 2 tablespoons butter in skillet. Add mushrooms and onions. Sauté for 2 to 3 minutes. Add wine. Bring to a boil; reduce heat. Stir in flour. Cook until thickened, stirring constantly. Return veal to skillet. Cook for 1 minute or until heated through. Arrange on serving platter; pour sauce over top. Yield: 4 to 6 servings.

Tricia Gamm, Xi Gamma Nu
Plano, Texas

VEAL SCALLOPINI

This is super for an elegant dinner with minimum time, minimum mess and maximum flavor.

1 1/2 pounds veal
  scallopini
1/4 cup all-purpose flour
Salt and pepper to taste
1/2 cup butter or
  margarine

2 teaspoons lemon juice
1 cup Marsala or dry
  white wine

Pound veal between sheets of waxed paper to flatten. Coat with mixture of flour, salt and pepper. Brown in butter in skillet over high heat for 2 minutes on each side. Combine lemon juice and wine; mix well. Pour over veal. Cook, covered, over low heat for 2 minutes longer. May substitute 1 cup mild beef broth for wine. Serve with pasta and green vegetable. Yield: 4 servings.

Glori Bardua, Preceptor Beta
Winnipeg, Manitoba, Canada

BAKED EGGS IN TOMATOES

4 large tomatoes
4 eggs

Salt and pepper to taste
Bread crumbs

Preheat oven to 350 degrees. Slice off tops of tomatoes; scoop out pulp. Break 1 egg into each tomato. Season with salt and pepper; sprinkle with bread crumbs. Place in greased 8-by-8-inch baking pan. Bake for 20 minutes or until egg is set. May serve on Holland rusk with thin slice of ham or crumbled bacon and top with Hollandaise sauce. Yield: 4 servings.

Georgia M. Cuneo, Laureate Alpha
Winston-Salem, North Carolina

MUSHROOM STROGANOFF

My family has enjoyed this adaptation of a "classic" while reducing our intake of red meat.

1 onion, sliced
8 ounces mushrooms,
  sliced
1 clove of garlic, minced
1 tablespoon vegetable
  oil
1 tablespoon butter or
  margarine
2 tablespoons catsup

1 teaspoon
  Worcestershire sauce
1 14-ounce can beef
  broth
3 tablespoons
  all-purpose flour
1 cup sour cream
4 cups cooked egg
  noodles

Sauté onion, mushrooms and garlic in oil and butter in skillet for 5 minutes or until tender-crisp. Stir in catsup, Worcestershire sauce and 2/3 of the beef broth. Simmer until heated through. Blend flour with remaining broth; add to mushroom mixture. Bring to a boil. Cook for 1 minute, stirring constantly; reduce heat. Add sour cream. Cook until heated through. Serve over noodles. Yield: 4 servings.

Beth Allman, Chi Phi
Vandenberg Air Force Base, California

QUESADILLAS IN-A-HURRY

My family loves Mexican food. Serve this with corn and a huge tray of nacho chips.

1 28-ounce can
  tomatoes, drained
2 tablespoons lime or
  lemon juice
2 teaspoons chili
  powder
1/2 teaspoon chili
  peppers
2 14-ounce cans kidney
  beans, drained

1 1/2 cups shredded
  Cheddar cheese
1 1/4 cups shredded
  mozzarella cheese
8 to 10 soft flour
  tortillas
2 tablespoons olive oil

Preheat oven to 450 degrees. Combine tomatoes, lime juice, chili powder and chili peppers in large saucepan. Bring to a boil; reduce heat to medium. Simmer for 15 minutes. Stir in beans. Mash mixture with fork or process in blender. Combine Cheddar and mozzarella cheeses in bowl. Arrange 1 layer of tortillas in 9-by-13-inch baking dish brushed with olive oil. Alternate layers of bean mixture, remaining tortillas and cheese mixture until all ingredients are used, ending with cheese. Bake for 10 minutes. Yield: 4 to 5 servings.

Rosalee Power, Alpha Zeta
Halifax, Nova Scotia, Canada

Poultry P.D.Q.

It's hard to imagine a bigger boon to today's
hurried cook than the packaged, boned chicken
breast. Unless it's ground turkey. Or maybe
chicken wings. Or turkey breast. Or perhaps
canned chicken. Or maybe frozen chicken
nuggets. Anyway, you get the point. Poultry is
where quick cooking really comes into its own.
In fact, chicken and turkey are among those
foods that are better when cooked quickly.
And very few foods lend themselves so well to
a wide variety of cooking methods, spices
and herbs, sauces and accompaniments. In this
chapter, you're sure to find recipes galore
to add to your favorite collection of chicken
and turkey dishes while cutting your
time in the kitchen to a minimum.

BROILED CELERY CHICKEN

1 2½ to 3-pound chicken, cut into quarters	½ teaspoon salt
	½ to 1 teaspoon pepper
	4 stalks celery
3 tablespoons lemon juice	

Preheat broiler. Rinse chicken; pat dry. Rub lemon juice on chicken; sprinkle with salt and pepper. Place chicken skin side down on rack in broiler pan. Place 1 stalk celery on each piece of chicken. Broil 6 to 9 inches from heat source for 10 to 12 minutes on each side. Yield: 4 servings.

Sharon Sotvik, Xi Alpha Omega
Story, Wyoming

CHICKEN AND RICE

2 tablespoons melted margarine	¾ soup can of milk
	3 cups uncooked instant rice
1 3½ to 4-pound chicken, cut up	¼ teaspoon poultry seasoning
1 10-ounce can cream of mushroom soup	

Place margarine and chicken in 3½-quart glass dish. Microwave, covered, on High for 16 minutes. Turn chicken. Microwave for 16 minutes longer or until done. Remove chicken to warm plate. Stir in soup, milk, rice and seasoning. Microwave for 6 to 8 minutes or until rice is done. Serve with chicken. Yield: 6 servings.

Ann Stapp, Preceptor Beta Delta
Fort Stockton, Texas

BRAISED CHICKEN WINGS

10 chicken wings	¼ cup sherry
¼ cup soy sauce	2 green onions, cut into 1-inch pieces
½ cup water	
2 tablespoons light brown sugar	1 teaspoon dry mustard

Cut chicken wings into 3 pieces, discarding tips. Rinse chicken; pat dry. Combine all ingredients in large saucepan. Bring to a boil over medium heat. Reduce heat to low. Simmer, covered, for 30 minutes. Uncover pan. Simmer for 15 minutes longer, basting frequently. Serve hot or cold. Yield: 6 servings.

Roxane I. Fort, Xi Gamma Xi
Fairfield Bay, Arkansas

GLAZED GRASSHOPPERS

1½ pounds chicken wings	1 tablespoon cinnamon
1½ teaspoons curry powder	½ teaspoon garlic powder
½ cup honey	1 6-ounce can grapefruit juice
1 cup crushed pineapple	

Cut chicken wings into 3 pieces, discarding tips. Rinse chicken; pat dry. Place chicken in electric skillet. Combine remaining ingredients in bowl; mix well. Pour over chicken. Simmer for 30 minutes or until done. Remove chicken to rack in broiler pan. Broil for 5 minutes. Yield: 6 servings.

Marian Beaty, Mu
Jackson, Tennessee

HONEY-GARLIC CHICKEN WINGS

This fast and easy recipe is the first I taught my four teenagers to prepare. We had so much fun. It's really nutritious as well. I usually serve these with rice, steamed vegetables or a salad.

2 pounds chicken wings	1 tablespoon lemon juice
⅓ cup honey	½ teaspoon garlic powder
2 tablespoons instant chicken bouillon	¼ teaspoon ground ginger
2 tablespoon soy sauce	

Preheat oven to 425 degrees. Cut chicken wings into 3 pieces, discarding tips. Rinse chicken; pat dry. Place chicken in large baking pan. Bake for 10 minutes. Combine remaining ingredients in bowl; mix well. Pour over chicken. Increase oven temperature to 475 degrees. Bake for 25 minutes. Yield: 4 servings.

Linda Cunnington, Epsilon Kappa
Guelph, Ontario, Canada

LEMON WINGS

3 pounds chicken wings	½ teaspoon garlic powder
3 tablespoons vegetable oil	1 tablespoon parsley
¼ cup lemon juice	1 tablespoon chopped chives
1 tablespoon grated lemon rind	Salt and pepper to taste
1 tablespoon oregano	

Preheat oven to 425 degrees. Cut chicken wings into 3 pieces, discarding tips. Rinse chicken; pat dry. Place chicken wings in shallow dish. Set aside. Combine remaining ingredients in saucepan. Simmer over medium heat for 10 minutes. Pour mixture over chicken; toss to coat. Marinate for 30 minutes. Arrange chicken wings in single layer on baking pan. Bake for 20 to 25 minutes. Yield: 4 servings.

Donna Coade, Alpha Zeta
Armdale, Nova Scotia, Canada

Agnes Ann Hanson, Xi Eta, Newcastle, Wyoming, prepares Chicken Coating Like-the-Colonel's at home. Mix 3 cups self-rising flour, 2 envelopes tomato cup-of-soup mix, 1 tablespoon paprika, 1 teaspoon seasoned salt and 2 envelopes Italian salad dressing mix.

CACHE-POT CHICKEN

My husband asked me to perform a gourmet miracle for twelve unexpected house guests so I threw this in a pan PDQ and saved the day.

Sliced onion
Sliced green bell pepper
Sliced fresh mushrooms
1/4 cup polyunsaturated
  vegetable oil
2 whole chicken breasts,
  split

Fresh tomatoes,
  chopped or sliced
Shredded mozzarella
  cheese

Combine onion, green pepper, mushrooms and oil in large skillet. Cook, covered, over medium heat for 4 to 5 minutes. Rinse chicken and pat dry. Place on top of mixture. Cook for 5 minutes on each side or until done. Place chicken on serving plate. Spoon vegetables over top. Top with tomatoes and cheese. Yield: 4 servings.

Fern M. Kolb, Xi Epsilon
Gaylord, Michigan

CASHEW AND MANDARIN ORANGE CHICKEN

2 whole boneless
  chicken breasts, cut
  into strips
1 11-ounce can
  mandarin oranges
1/4 cup stir-fry sauce
2 tablespoons vegetable
  oil

1/3 cup roasted cashews
1 clove of garlic, minced
1 tablespoon vegetable
  oil
1 medium onion, sliced
8 ounces fresh snow
  peas
Hot cooked rice

Rinse chicken and pat dry. Drain oranges, reserving 2 tablespoons liquid. Combine reserved liquid and stir-fry sauce. Heat 2 tablespoons oil in wok over high heat. Add chicken, cashews and garlic. Stir-fry for 3 minutes. Remove mixture to warm plate. Heat remaining 1 tablespoon oil in wok. Add onion and snow peas. Stir-fry for 3 minutes. Return chicken mixture with stir-fry sauce mixture to wok; stir to coat. Remove from heat. Stir in oranges. Serve with rice. Yield: 4 servings.

Sharon Fox, Preceptor Alpha
Missoula, Montana

CHEESY CHICKEN CASSEROLE

4 medium to large
  chicken breasts,
  cooked, chopped
2 cups shredded
  Cheddar cheese

1 8-count can crescent
  rolls
1 10-ounce can cream
  of chicken soup
1 cup milk

Preheat oven to 350 degrees. Rinse chicken and pat dry. Toss with cheese in bowl. Separate rolls into triangles. Place some chicken mixture in center of each triangle. Roll up from wide end. Place in

8-by-8-inch baking pan. Combine soup and milk in saucepan; mix well. Bring to a boil, stirring until smooth. Pour over chicken rolls. Sprinkle with any remaining cheese. Bake for 25 to 30 minutes or until brown. Yield: 4 servings.

Juanita D. Fisher, Xi Kappa Pi
Belleville, Illinois

CHICKEN ALLA ROMANO

1 whole boneless
  chicken breast, cut
  into halves
1 ounce sliced Swiss
  cheese, cut into halves
1 thin slice prosciutto or
  smoked ham, cut into
  halves
1 teaspoon paprika

1/8 teaspoon garlic salt
Tarragon to taste
3 tablespoons fine dry
  bread crumbs
1 tablespoon grated
  Parmesan cheese
2 tablespoons melted
  butter or margarine

Remove skin from chicken. Rinse chicken; pat dry. Flatten between sheets of waxed paper to 1/4 inch thickness with mallet. Place 1 piece of Swiss cheese and prosciutto in center of each piece of chicken. Roll up lengthwise; secure with wooden pick. Combine next 5 ingredients; mix well. Dip chicken in melted butter; coat with bread crumb mixture. Place seam side down in 1-quart glass dish. Microwave, covered, with waxed paper, on High for 4 minutes or until done. Yield: 2 servings.

Dolores Curry, Delta Lambda
Graham, Texas

CHICKEN BREASTS DIANE

4 large or 8 small
  boneless chicken
  breasts
1/2 teaspoon salt
1/4 teaspoon pepper
2 tablespoons melted
  margarine
2 tablespoons vegetable
  oil

Juice of 1/2 lemon
3 tablespoons chopped
  green onions
3 tablespoons chopped
  parsley
2 teaspoons Dijon
  mustard
1/4 cup chicken broth

Rinse chicken; pat dry. Place between sheets of plastic wrap; pound slightly. Sprinkle with salt and pepper. Combine margarine and oil in glass dish. Place chicken in dish, coating each piece with oil mixture. Microwave on High for 3 minutes. Let stand for 1 minute. Turn chicken over. Microwave for 3 minutes longer or until done; do not overcook. Combine lemon juice, green onions, parsley and mustard in glass bowl. Microwave on High for 1 minute. Stir in broth and any chicken pan juices. Pour over chicken. Serve immediately. Yield: 4 servings.

Lucy E. Davis, Xi Gamma Sigma
Toccoa, Georgia

CHEDDAR CHICKEN

8 boneless chicken breasts	3/4 medium package potato chips, crushed
1 cup low-fat milk	16 ounces Cheddar cheese, shredded
1 egg	

Preheat oven to 375 degrees. Rinse chicken; pat dry. Combine milk and egg in bowl; mix well. Combine potato chips and cheese in large bowl; toss. Dip chicken into milk mixture; coat with cheese mixture. Place in 9-by-12-inch baking pan. Top with any remaining cheese mixture. Bake for 30 minutes. Yield: 4 to 6 servings.

Candace L. Wagner, Theta Chi
Chesapeake, Virginia

CHICKEN-ARTICHOKE FETTUCINI

To round out this meal, I serve a tossed green salad and a loaf of French bread. The kids love this and it is so easy. It also provides a quick, delicious meal when unexpected guests drop by.

1 pound whole boneless chicken breasts, cut into strips	1 7-ounce can artichoke bottoms, chopped
1/4 cup butter or margarine	8 ounces spinach fettucini, cooked
3/4 cup milk	Freshly ground pepper
1 1-ounce envelope Alfredo sauce mix	Grated Parmesan cheese

Rinse chicken; pat dry. Brown in 2 tablespoons butter in electric skillet; drain. Stir in remaining butter, milk and Alfredo sauce mix. Simmer until slightly thickened. Stir in artichoke bottoms. Cook until heated through. Serve over pasta. Garnish with pepper and Parmesan cheese. Yield: 4 servings.

Ann M. Lang, Lambda
Boise, Idaho

CHICKEN BREASTS CACCIATORE

1 16-ounce can whole tomatoes, chopped	1 1/2 teaspoons Italian seasoning
1/2 medium green bell pepper, cut into strips	4 chicken breasts
1 medium onion, cut into rings	7 ounces vermicelli, cooked
1/4 cup dry white wine	2 tablespoons grated Romano cheese

Combine first 5 ingredients in glass bowl. Microwave, covered, on High for 5 to 7 minutes, stirring once. Rinse chicken and pat dry. Arrange in 2-quart glass dish with meatier portions toward outer edge. Pour sauce over top. Microwave for 14 to 18 minutes or until chicken is cooked through, spooning sauce over chicken once. Toss vermicelli with Romano cheese. Serve chicken and sauce over vermicelli. Yield: 4 servings.

Robin Holmes, Preceptor Alpha Beta
Wetumpka, Alabama

CHICKEN CATCHA-QUICKIE

4 to 6 chicken breasts, boned, skinned	Grated Parmesan cheese
1/2 15-ounce jar (or more) spaghetti sauce	1 package egg noodles or fettucini, cooked

Rinse chicken; pat dry. Arrange in 2-quart glass dish. Pour desired amount of sauce over chicken. Sprinkle generously with Parmesan cheese. Microwave on High for 5 minutes or until done. Serve chicken with sauce over noodles. Yield: 3 to 4 servings.

Janie Hail, Delta Iota
Somerset, Kentucky

CHICKEN CORDON BLEU

4 chicken breasts, boned, skinned	Bread crumbs mixed with 2 tablespoons Italian seasoning
Salt and pepper to taste	2 tablespoons vegetable oil
4 slices Swiss cheese	
4 slices ham	
1 egg, beaten	2 tablespoons margarine

Rinse chicken; pat dry. Flatten chicken with meat mallet. Salt and pepper each side. Layer cheese and ham on each chicken breast. Fold in half. Dip in beaten egg; coat with bread crumbs. Sauté on both sides in oil and margarine in skillet until cooked through, turning once. Yield: 4 servings.

Sandy Wirkus, Xi Gamma Omega
Tempe, Arizona

CHICKEN DIJON

I used this recipe for the first candlelight dinner I cooked for my husband. It's a quick, but elegant, meal.

4 boneless chicken breasts, cooked	1 cup sour cream
4 fresh mushrooms, sliced	2 tablespoons Dijon mustard
4 fresh spinach leaves	2 tablespoons dry white wine
8 ounces Monterey Jack cheese, shredded	

Preheat oven to 350 degrees. Place chicken in baking pan sprayed with nonstick cooking spray. Layer mushrooms, spinach and cheese on each chicken breast. Bake for 10 minutes or until cheese is bubbly. Combine last 3 ingredients in saucepan. Cook over low heat until heated through, stirring frequently. Place chicken on warm serving platter. Pour sauce over top. Yield: 4 servings.

Amy Crump, Kappa Gamma
Columbia, Missouri

CHICKEN FRITTERS

This recipe is short and sweet and my sorority sisters love it. They think these are difficult to make. Wait until they see this!

2 pounds chicken breasts, boned, skinned	1 cup seasoned coating mix for chicken
2 cups buttermilk	1 tablespoon garlic salt
2 eggs	1 teaspoon pepper
1/2 cup all-purpose flour	Vegetable oil for frying

Rinse chicken; pat dry. Chop into 1-inch pieces. Combine buttermilk and eggs in bowl; mix well. Set aside. Combine next 4 ingredients in plastic bag; shake to mix. Dip chicken into buttermilk mixture; coat with flour mixture. Cook in hot oil in skillet until golden brown. Yield: 4 to 6 servings.

Sue B. Fulcher, Xi Alpha Mu
Fayetteville, North Carolina

CHICKEN IN-A-PACKET

As a single working woman it was a blessing to have such a quick, simple meal. Now that I'm married, my husband and I both enjoy taking turns cooking and sharing recipes.

1 tablespoon butter	1 chicken breast
3/4 cup stuffing mix	Paprika to taste
2 tablespoons water	1/2 apple, sliced

Preheat oven to 450 degrees. Fold 12-by-18-inch piece of foil in half. Unfold carefully. Butter top half. Place 1 tablespoon butter on bottom half. Top with stuffing mix; sprinkle with water. Place chicken breast on top of stuffing mix; sprinkle with paprika. Tuck apple slices around chicken. Fold foil, rolling edges to seal. Place in shallow baking pan. Bake for 25 minutes. Yield: 1 serving.

Catherin Halgerson, Xi Alpha Nu
Rapid City, South Dakota

CHICKEN ON-THE-RUN

4 boneless chicken breasts, cooked, cut into strips	2 10-ounce cans cream of chicken soup
2 6-ounce packages chicken stuffing mix	1 cup milk
1 cup chopped celery	1 cup cornflakes, crushed
1 large onion, chopped	1/4 cup melted butter

Preheat oven to 350 degrees. Arrange chicken in greased 9-by-13-inch pan. Prepare stuffing mix using package directions, adding celery and onion. Spoon over chicken. Combine soup and milk in bowl; mix well. Pour over stuffing layer. Top with mixture of cornflakes and butter. Bake for 30 minutes.
Yield: 6 servings.

Kathy Ryder
Rock Springs, Wyoming

TWENTY-MINUTE CHICKEN PARMESAN

4 boneless chicken breasts, skinned	1/2 cup shredded mozzarella cheese
1 egg, slightly beaten	1 tablespoon grated Parmesan cheese
1/2 cup herb-seasoned bread crumbs	1/4 cup chopped fresh parsley
2 tablespoons margarine	Cooked rice or pasta
1 14-ounce jar spaghetti sauce with mushrooms	

Rinse chicken; pat dry. Dip into beaten egg; coat with bread crumbs. Brown in margarine in skillet over medium heat. Add spaghetti sauce. Reduce heat to low. Simmer, covered, for 10 minutes. Sprinkle with cheeses and parsley. Simmer for 5 minutes longer. Serve over rice or pasta. Yield: 4 servings.

Judith Meier, Xi Gamma Pi
Pocahontas, Arkansas

CHICKEN PICCATA

4 boneless chicken breasts, skinned	3 tablespoons butter or margarine
1/3 cup all-purpose flour	1/3 cup fresh lemon juice
1/2 teaspoon each salt and pepper	1/2 cup white wine
3 tablespoons vegetable oil	1 tablespoon capers

Rinse chicken; pat dry. Coat with mixture of flour, salt and pepper. Sauté in oil in skillet for 5 minutes on each side or until golden brown. Melt butter in saucepan. Add chicken, lemon juice and wine. Stir in capers. Cook for 5 minutes or until sauce thickens. Serve with seasonal vegetables and new potatoes. Yield: 4 servings.

Ginny T. Blum, Preceptor Alpha Psi
Redwood City, California

CHICKEN "QUICKEN"

Enjoy! There is no clean-up!

4 chicken breasts	1/4 cup margarine
1 12-ounce package frozen green beans	1/4 cup Dijon mustard
	1/4 cup mayonnaise

Preheat oven to 375 degrees. Rinse chicken; pat dry. Divide green beans into 4 portions on four 10-inch lengths of foil. Layer margarine and chicken over green beans. Spread chicken with mixture of mustard and mayonnaise. Fold foil to enclose chicken, sealing edges. Bake for 25 minutes. Yield: 4 servings.

Dorothy J. Christiansen, Upsilon Kappa
Inverness, Florida

CHICKEN SARONNO

6 boneless chicken breasts, skinned	8 ounces fresh mushrooms
Garlic powder and curry powder to taste	Juice and grated rind of 1 lemon
Salt and pepper to taste	1½ cups chicken broth
All-purpose flour	1 tablespoon cornstarch
Butter or margarine	Chopped tomato
¼ cup Amaretto	Chopped parsley

Rinse chicken; pat dry. Cut into 1-inch strips. Sprinkle with next 4 ingredients; coat with flour. Brown chicken in butter in skillet. Stir in next 4 ingredients. Simmer for 5 minutes. Stir in mixture of chicken broth and cornstarch. Simmer until thickened. Garnish with tomato and parsley. Yield: 6 servings.

Pam Plourde, Alpha Xi
Spruce Grove, Alberta, Canada

CHICKEN SCALA

4 boneless chicken breasts, skinned	½ cup sour cream
2 tablespoons all-purpose flour	1 teaspoon salt
	½ teaspoon pepper
½ cup butter or margarine	1 tablespoon grated Parmesan cheese
1 12-ounce can beef broth	

Rinse chicken; pat dry. Coat with flour. Brown in butter in skillet. Add broth. Simmer, covered, for 45 minutes. Stir in sour cream, salt and pepper. Simmer for 10 minutes. Remove chicken to 9-by-13-inch baking dish. Strain sauce over chicken. Sprinkle with Parmesan cheese. Broil for 5 minutes or until golden brown. Yield: 6 servings.

Karen H. Mahoney, Theta Rho
Hendersonville, Tennessee

DIJON CHICKEN

5 chicken breasts	2 teaspoons
1 cup mayonnaise	Worcestershire sauce
⅓ cup Dijon mustard	

Preheat broiler. Rinse chicken; pat dry. Mix remaining ingredients in 9-by-13-inch baking dish. Add chicken; stir to coat. Broil for 10 minutes or until cooked through. Yield: 5 servings.

Shauna Smith, Mu Chi
Concord, California

GARLIC CHICKEN

1 pound boneless chicken breasts, skinned	1 cup cracker crumbs
	Garlic powder to taste
1 egg, beaten	¼ cup melted butter or margarine

Rinse chicken; pat dry. Dip chicken into egg; coat with cracker crumbs. Sprinkle with garlic powder.

Fry in butter in skillet for 10 minutes or until golden brown and cooked through. Yield: 3 to 4 servings.

Brenda Engstrom, Mu Gamma
Harcourt, Iowa

GINGERED CHICKEN AND BROCCOLI

1 pound chicken, cut into strips	½ teaspoon ginger
½ teaspoon salt	1½ tablespoons soy sauce
Pepper to taste	1½ tablespoons sherry
¼ cup vegetable oil	1 teaspoon sugar
1 pound broccoli, cut into 2-inch flowerets	1 tablespoon cornstarch
	2 tablespoons water
½ cup sliced celery	1 cup rice, cooked
1 16-ounce can chicken broth	

Rinse chicken; pat dry. Season with salt and pepper. Stir-fry chicken in hot oil in wok for 3 minutes. Add broccoli and celery. Stir-fry for 3 minutes. Combine next 5 ingredients; mix well. Stir into chicken mixture. Blend in mixture of cornstarch and water. Bring to a boil. Cook for 1 minute, stirring constantly. Serve over hot rice. May adjust seasonings to suit personal taste and may add other vegetables such as onions and mushrooms. Yield: 4 to 6 servings.

Teri Allan, Alpha Psi
Scottsdale, Arizona

HEAD-OF-THE-CLASS CHICKEN AND VEGGIES

4 boneless chicken breasts, skinned	1 green bell pepper, cut into thin strips
1 tablespoon olive oil	1 large carrot, cut into thin 3-inch strips
½ teaspoon rosemary	
Salt and pepper to taste	1 medium zucchini, cut into thin 3-inch strips
1 14-ounce can stewed Italian tomatoes	5 medium mushrooms, sliced
½ cup pitted small black olives	

Rinse chicken; pat dry. Brown in olive oil in skillet. Sprinkle with rosemary, salt and pepper. Add remaining ingredients. Bring to a boil over medium heat. Cook, covered, for 3 minutes. Remove cover. Cook over medium-high heat for 5 minutes or until thickened. Yield: 4 servings.

Judy Mehrens, Laureate Epsilon Delta
Oxnard, California

Caroline Ulmer, Laureate Alpha Pi, White Rock, British Columbia, Canada, makes Honey-Mustard Chicken by pouring mixture of ½ cup each dark honey and mustard and 1 teaspoon curry powder over browned chicken pieces. Bake in preheated 350-degree oven until tender.

HERB-NUT CHICKEN

I served this for my mother and her two sisters for whom I had never cooked and hardly knew. They loved it and wanted the recipe. I plan to buy each of them a copy of the cookbook.

2 pounds boneless chicken, skinned	*6 ounces hot pepper cheese, shredded*
1 6-ounce package stuffing mix	*1¹/₂ cups chopped walnuts*

Preheat oven to 350 degrees. Rinse chicken; pat dry. Prepare stuffing mix using package directions. Layer chicken and cheese in buttered 3-quart baking dish. Spoon stuffing mix over top. Sprinkle with walnuts. Bake, covered, for 35 minutes. Bake, uncovered, for 10 minutes longer. Yield: 4 to 6 servings.

Jamie K. Gustafson, Delta Gamma
Jamestown, New York

HONEY-GLAZED CHICKEN

3 to 4 chicken breasts	*1/4 cup finely chopped onion*
2 to 3 tablespoons melted butter or margarine	*2/3 cup honey*
1¹/₂ cups chicken broth	*1/2 cup lemon juice*
	1/3 cup soy sauce

Rinse chicken; pat dry. Brown in butter in skillet. Combine remaining ingredients in 4-cup glass bowl; mix well. Microwave on High until mixture boils. Pour over chicken. Simmer, covered, until chicken is tender, basting 3 or 4 times. Yield: 3 to 4 servings.

Barbara-Jo Clute, Preceptor Beta Lambda
Mississauga, Ontario, Canada

CHICKEN LASAGNA

While visiting relatives in Florida, my husband and I enjoyed a "home-delivered" meal featuring Chicken Lasagna. We were so impressed that once we were home, I was determined to come up with my own version. This is it.

4 cups chopped cooked chicken	*1/2 cup plus 2 tablespoons milk*
1/2 cup chopped celery	*1¹/₂ cups shredded Cheddar cheese*
1/2 cup chopped green bell pepper	*1¹/₂ cups shredded mozzarella cheese*
1/2 cup chopped onion	*12 to 14 uncooked lasagna noodles*
2 cups sliced mushrooms	
2 10-ounce cans cream of mushroom soup	

Preheat oven to 350 degrees. Spray square 4-quart baking dish with nonstick cooking spray. Combine chicken, celery, green pepper, onion, mushrooms, soup and milk in large bowl; mix well. Combine cheeses; toss lightly. Alternate layers of chicken mixture, noodles and cheese in baking dish until all ingredients are used. Bake for 30 to 45 minutes or until noodles are tender. Yield: 9 servings.

Valerie Parker, Beta Alpha
Copalis Beach, Washington

LEMON CHICKEN FILETS

I like to serve this chicken dish with rice and baby carrots. This is a quick dish and low in calories.

4 boneless chicken breasts	*1/8 teaspoon each salt and pepper*
1 egg, beaten	*3 tablespoons butter or margarine*
2 tablespoons milk	
1/3 cup all-purpose flour	*2 tablespoons lemon juice*
1/3 cup crushed cornflakes	*Lemon slices*
1/4 teaspoon garlic powder	*Fresh parsley*

Rinse chicken; pat dry. Mix egg and milk in small bowl. Combine flour, cornflakes, garlic powder, salt and pepper in bowl; mix well. Dip chicken into egg mixture; coat with flour mixture. Sauté in 2 tablespoons butter in saucepan for 2¹/₂ to 3 minutes on each side. Remove chicken to serving dish. Melt remaining butter in pan drippings. Stir in lemon juice. Pour over chicken. Garnish with lemon slices and parsley. Yield: 4 servings.

Elizabeth O'Rourke, Preceptor Gamma Rho
Kemptville, Ontario, Canada

❖ LEMONY PECAN CHICKEN

1¹/₂ pounds boneless chicken breasts, skinned	*1/2 cup pecan pieces*
	3 tablespoons lemon juice
1 cup chopped fresh parsley	*3 tablespoons fresh basil leaves*
1/2 cup grated Parmesan cheese	*2 cloves of garlic, chopped*
1/3 cup canola oil	

Preheat oven to 350 degrees. Rinse chicken; pat dry. Arrange chicken in 8-by-12-inch baking pan. Combine 2/3 cup parsley, 1/3 cup Parmesan cheese, oil, 1/3 cup pecans, lemon juice, basil and garlic in blender container. Process until blended. Spread over chicken. Chop remaining parsley. Combine with remaining Parmesan cheese and pecans in bowl. Sprinkle over casserole. Bake for 30 minutes. May microwave on High for 4 to 6 minutes or until cooked through. Yield: 6 servings.

Peg Baldwin, Laureate Beta Mu
Kenton, Ohio

LEMON CHICKEN

2 large boneless chicken
 breasts, skinned
Salt and pepper to taste
1/3 cup Italian salad
 dressing

1/2 lemon, cut into slices
Paprika to taste

Rinse chicken; pat dry. Sprinkle with salt and pepper. Heat salad dressing in skillet over low heat. Add chicken. Simmer for 15 minutes. Arrange lemon slices on chicken; sprinkle with paprika. Simmer, covered, for 5 minutes longer. Yield: 2 servings.

Carrie Bogle, Gamma Master
Reno, Nevada

MANDARIN GINGER CHICKEN

4 boneless chicken
 breasts, skinned
1 navel orange
2 tablespoons butter
 or margarine

1 cup chopped fresh
 mushrooms
1 jar mandarin ginger
 sauce

Rinse chicken; pat dry. Chop into bite-sized pieces. Peel and chop orange, reserving peel. Slice peel into strips. Brown chicken in butter in skillet. Add mushrooms. Cook over medium heat for 5 minutes. Add orange and orange peel. Stir in ginger sauce. Simmer for 20 minutes. Remove orange peel before serving. Yield: 4 servings.

Geraldine Maxwell, Laureate Delta Tau
Amarillo, Texas

MEXICAN CHICKEN

2 whole boneless
 chicken breasts,
 chopped
1 cup sour cream
10 large black olives,
 sliced
1 4-ounce can chopped
 green chilies

3 green onions, chopped
1 10-ounce can cream
 of chicken soup
1/2 teaspoon curry powder
1 cup shredded
 Cheddar and Monterey
 Jack cheese
Flour tortillas

Preheat oven to 350 degrees. Rinse chicken; pat dry. Place in 9-by-9-inch baking dish. Mix next 6 ingredients in bowl. Pour over chicken. Sprinkle with cheese. Bake, covered, for 1 hour. Serve with warm flour tortillas. Yield: 8 servings.

Pam Sargent, Theta Psi
Ames, Iowa

MICROWAVE CHICKEN BREASTS

1/3 cup butter or
 margarine
1/2 teaspoon garlic
 powder
1/4 teaspoon pepper

1/4 teaspoon oregano
1 teaspoon salt
2 whole chicken breasts,
 split, skinned
1/2 cup dry white wine

Microwave butter in 2-quart glass dish until melted. Add seasonings; mix well. Rinse chicken; pat dry.

Arrange in baking dish with thicker portions to outer edge, coating well with butter. Microwave, loosely covered with plastic wrap, on High for 10 minutes. Turn chicken over; pour in wine. Microwave for 6 to 7 minutes or until tender. Let stand for 5 minutes. Serve over rice or noodles. Yield: 4 servings.

Kay Meyers, Alpha Omega
Sioux Falls, South Dakota

CHICKEN NUGGETS

1/2 cup all-purpose flour
Salt and pepper to taste
4 whole chicken breast
 filets

1/3 cup butter or
 margarine
2/3 cup lemon juice
2 cups cooked rice

Combine flour, salt and pepper in bowl; mix well. Rinse chicken; pat dry. Cut into 1-inch pieces; coat with flour mixture. Sauté in butter in skillet for 3 to 5 minutes or until brown. Sprinkle with lemon juice. Simmer until liquid evaporates, stirring constantly. Serve with cooked rice. Yield: 4 servings.

Shar Guggemos
Saugus, California

QUICK AND SAUCY CHICKEN NUGGETS

1/2 cup low-calorie
 mayonnaise
3 tablespoons milk
1/2 teaspoon each cumin
 and onion powder
1/4 teaspoon each red
 pepper and garlic
 powder

1 pound chicken
 breasts, skinned,
 boned
3/4 cup crushed tortilla
 chips or sesame seed
 crackers
1/2 cup each salsa and
 mayonnaise

Preheat oven to 425 degrees. Combine mayonnaise, milk and seasonings in bowl; mix well. Rinse chicken; pat dry. Cut into 1-inch pieces. Dip into milk mixture; coat with crushed chips. Arrange on baking sheet. Bake for 18 to 20 minutes or until golden brown. Serve with mixture of salsa and mayonnaise. Yield: 4 to 6 servings.

Bette Bragg, Master Theta
Albany, Oregon

TACO CHICKEN NUGGETS

1/4 cup cornmeal
2 1/2 tablespoons taco
 seasoning mix

2 large whole chicken
 breasts, boned,
 skinned

Combine cornmeal and taco seasoning in plastic bag; mix well. Rinse chicken; pat dry. Cut into 1-inch pieces. Shake in cornmeal mixture to coat. Arrange in 7-by-12-inch glass baking dish; cover with paper towel. Microwave on High for 5 to 7 minutes or until tender, turning once. Yield: 12 servings.

Greta Hinson, Epsilon Kappa
Elkin, North Carolina

ZIPPY CHICKY CHUNKS

2 eggs
1/4 cup water
1 envelope chicken
    coating mix
1 teaspoon oregano
1/2 teaspoon garlic
    powder
1 cup crushed butter
    crackers
1 pound chicken breast
    filets
Plum sauce or barbecue
    sauce

Preheat oven to 350 degrees. Beat eggs and water in bowl until frothy. Combine coating mix, oregano, garlic powder and cracker crumbs in plastic bag, shaking to mix. Rinse chicken; pat dry. Cut into 1-inch pieces. Dip in egg; shake in coating mix. Arrange on baking sheet. Bake for 20 to 30 minutes or until golden brown. Serve with sauce for dipping. Yield: 6 servings.

Lynda M. Gibson, Alpha Gamma
Fredericton, New Brunswick, Canada

PARMESAN CHICKEN

1/4 cup herb-seasoned
    bread crumbs
2 tablespoons grated
    Parmesan cheese
1 tablespoon parsley
    flakes
1 teaspoon salt
1/8 teaspoon each lemon
    pepper and thyme
6 chicken breast filets
6 tablespoons melted
    margarine
1 tablespoon lemon juice

Preheat oven to 350 degrees. Combine bread crumbs, cheese and seasonings in shallow dish. Rinse chicken; pat dry. Roll in crumb mixture to coat. Combine margarine and lemon juice in 9-by-13-inch baking dish. Dip chicken in margarine, turning to coat. Bake for 30 minutes. Yield: 6 servings.

Delores Kopec, Laureate Phi
Bay City, Michigan

PEACHY CHICKEN BREASTS

6 whole chicken
    breasts, boned,
    skinned
1/8 teaspoon pepper
1 1/2 teaspoons salt
3 fresh peaches, peeled,
    chopped
1/2 cup chopped
    onion
1/2 cup coarsely
    chopped cashews
1/8 teaspoon ginger
6 wooden picks
1/2 cup melted butter or
    margarine
1 fresh peach, peeled,
    sliced
1 cup sour cream
1/2 cup packed light
    brown sugar
2 teaspoons Dijon
    mustard
1/4 teaspoon salt

Rinse chicken; pat dry. Flatten to 1/4-inch thickness between sheets of waxed paper. Sprinkle with pepper and 1 teaspoon salt; set aside. Combine remaining 1/2 teaspoon salt with chopped peaches, onion, cashews and ginger in bowl; mix well. Spoon 1/4 cup filling into center of each chicken breast. Roll up, securing with wooden picks. Pour melted butter into 9-by-13-inch baking dish. Arrange chicken in dish. Bake for 25 minutes; turn. Bake for 20 minutes longer. Combine sliced peach, sour cream, sugar, mustard and 1/4 teaspoon salt in saucepan; mix well. Cook over low heat until heated through, stirring frequently. Serve with chicken. Yield: 6 servings.

Peggy Davis, Laureate Gamma Alpha
Dallas, Texas

PIQUANT CHICKEN SAUTÉ

1 pound chicken breast
    filets
1/3 cup white wine
    Worcestershire sauce
2 tablespoons
    margarine

Rinse chicken; pat dry. Flatten to 1/2-inch thickness between sheets of waxed paper. Dip in Worcestershire sauce in shallow bowl; drain, reserving sauce. Sauté chicken in margarine in skillet for 3 minutes on each side. Remove to platter. Stir reserved sauce into drippings in skillet. Cook until heated through. Pour over chicken before serving. Yield: 4 servings.

Jean L. Smith, Preceptor Kappa
Cicero, New York

TORTILLAS DE POLLO RAPIDO

Marinate, grill and serve with Margaritas for a true Mexican fiesta.

3 tablespoons lime juice
1/4 teaspoon ground
    chilies
1 clove of garlic, minced
1 teaspoon instant
    chicken bouillon
12 ounces chicken
    breast filets
1 small onion, thinly
    sliced into rings
1 green bell pepper, cut
    into 1/4-inch strips
1 tablespoon vegetable
    oil
1 cup corn, drained
1 15-ounce jar chunky
    salsa, drained
1 15-ounce can refried
    beans
6 flour tortillas
3/4 cup shredded
    Cheddar cheese

Combine lime juice, chilies, garlic and chicken bouillon in shallow dish; mix well. Rinse chicken; pat dry. Marinate in lime juice mixture in refrigerator. Sauté onion rings and green pepper strips in oil in skillet until tender-crisp; drain. Combine corn and salsa in small saucepan. Simmer until heated through. Drain chicken, reserving marinade. Grill over hot coals for 15 minutes, turning and basting frequently with reserved marinade. Cut into strips. Combine with sautéed vegetables. Spread refried beans in center of each tortilla. Top with chicken mixture and cheese. Roll up to enclose filling. Top with salsa-corn mixture. Yield: 6 servings.

Patricia Laning, Xi Gamma Psi
Polk City, Iowa

QUICK CHICKEN GOURMET

2 chicken breast filets	1 bunch fresh asparagus
1/4 cup all-purpose flour	Juice of 2 lemons
2 tablespoons butter or margarine	Salt and pepper to taste
	Cherry tomatoes

Rinse chicken; pat dry. Flatten between sheets of waxed paper; dip in flour. Sauté in butter in skillet until tender. Add asparagus. Sauté with chicken until tender-crisp. Sprinkle with lemon juice, salt and pepper. Arrange on serving platter with cherry tomatoes. Serve with white wine and crusty rolls. Yield: 2 servings.

Jackie Ziehe, Preceptor Alpha
Whitehorse, Yukon, Canada

QUICKIE CHICKEN WITH PASTA

4 chicken breast filets	1 tablespoon olive oil
2 teaspoons seasoned salt	2 16-ounce cans Italian stewed tomatoes
1 teaspoon garlic powder	2 teaspoons oregano
2 cloves of garlic, crushed	Salt and pepper to taste
1 small onion, chopped	3 tablespoons margarine
	3 chicken bouillon cubes
	2 coils of linguine

Rinse chicken; pat dry. Cut into strips. Coat with mixture of seasoned salt and garlic powder; let stand for 10 minutes. Sauté with garlic and onion in olive oil in skillet until tender. Stir in tomatoes, oregano, salt, pepper and margarine. Simmer for 15 minutes. Cook linguine using package directions, adding bouillon cubes to cooking water. Drain, reserving 1/2 cup cooking liquid. Stir reserved liquid into chicken mixture. Serve over cooked linguine. Yield: 4 to 6 servings.

Kathryn Vicat, Alpha Alpha Iota
Springfield, Missouri

RASPBERRY CHICKEN

This is quick and easy and my family loves it.

6 chicken breasts, skinned	2 tablespoons chopped scallions
1/4 cup unsalted butter or margarine	2 tablespoons raspberry vinegar

Rinse chicken; pat dry. Brown in butter in skillet for 4 minutes on each side. Remove to warm platter. Sauté scallions in drippings in skillet until tender. Add vinegar, stirring to deglaze skillet. Return chicken to skillet. Cook until heated through. Serve with rice. Yield: 6 servings.

Kristin H. Kenner, Iota
Devils Lake, North Dakota

SESAME DIJON CHICKEN

8 to 12 chicken tenders	1/4 cup sesame seed
1/3 cup bread crumbs	2 teaspoons lemon pepper
1/3 cup grated Parmesan cheese	Garlic salt to taste
2 tablespoons finely chopped parsley	1/2 cup Dijon mustard

Preheat oven to 350 degrees. Rinse chicken; pat dry. Combine bread crumbs, cheese, parsley, sesame seed, lemon pepper and garlic salt in bowl; mix well. Spread chicken with mustard; coat with crumb mixture. Arrange in shallow 2-quart baking dish sprayed with nonstick vegetable cooking spray. Bake for 20 to 30 minutes or until cooked through. Yield: 4 to 6 servings.

Pat Carson, Mu Tau
Avalon, Texas

CHILI-CHICKEN STEW

6 chicken breast filets	1 15-ounce can pinto beans, drained
1 onion, chopped	2/3 cup picante sauce
1 green bell pepper, chopped	1 teaspoon chili powder
2 cloves of garlic, minced	1 teaspoon ground cumin
2 tablespoons olive oil	1/2 teaspoon salt
2 14-ounce cans stewed tomatoes, chopped	Shredded Cheddar cheese, sour cream, avocado slices and chopped green onions

Rinse chicken; pat dry. Cut into 1-inch pieces. Brown with onion, green pepper and garlic in oil in large saucepan. Add tomatoes, beans, picante sauce, and seasonings; mix well. Simmer, covered, for 20 minutes. Top servings with cheese, sour cream, avocado and green onions. Yield: 6 servings.

Pam Bairrington, Xi Upsilon Epsilon
Hallettsville, Texas

CHICKEN STIR-FRY

1 cup chicken bouillon	3 to 4 tablespoons olive oil
1/4 cup white wine	3 carrots, sliced diagonally
4 teaspoons teriyaki sauce	1 green bell pepper, sliced
1 tablespoon honey	8 ounces mushrooms, sliced
1/4 teaspoon ground ginger	2 tablespoons cornstarch
2 pounds chicken breast filets	Salt and pepper to taste
1 onion, sliced	1/4 cup white wine

Mix first 5 ingredients in bowl; set aside. Rinse chicken; pat dry. Cut into strips. Stir-fry chicken and onion in 2 tablespoons oil in wok for 2 to 3 minutes or until chicken is tender. Remove to warm platter. Add carrots. Stir-fry for 2 to 3 minutes. Add green pepper and remaining oil. Stir-fry for 2 minutes. Add mushrooms. Stir-fry for 3 minutes. Return chicken and onions to wok. Add bouillon mixture. Simmer for 3 minutes. Combine cornstarch, salt and pepper with 1/4 cup wine in bowl. Add to wok. Cook until thickened, stirring constantly. Serve over rice. Yield: 4 to 6 servings.

Susan L. Lynam, Xi Epsilon Gamma
Hatfield, Pennsylvania

CHICKEN ORIENTAL STIR-FRY

8 ounces chicken breast filets	1 10-ounce package frozen broccoli, thawed
3 tablespoons peanut oil	1/4 cup water
1 large onion, sliced	3 tablespoons soy sauce
1 large green bell pepper, thinly sliced	1 teaspoon cornstarch
1 teaspoon garlic powder	1/2 teaspoon ginger

Rinse chicken; pat dry. Cut into 1-inch strips. Stir-fry in hot oil in wok for 2 minutes. Add onion, green pepper and garlic powder. Stir-fry for 2 minutes. Add broccoli. Stir-fry for 1 minute. Cook, covered, over low heat for 5 minutes, stirring occasionally. Stir in mixture of remaining ingredients. Bring to a boil. Cook for 1 minute longer or until thickened, stirring constantly. Serve over rice. Yield: 4 servings.

Cindy Speiser, Xi Gamma Nu
Allen, Texas

ORIENTAL CHICKEN STIR-FRY

2 chicken breast filets	1 teaspoon grated gingerroot
2 tablespoons corn oil	3 tablespoons chicken broth
1 10-ounce package frozen Oriental vegetables, thawed	2 tablespoons soy sauce
2 tablespoons water	1 1/2 teaspoons cornstarch
3 tablespoons dry sherry	

Rinse chicken; pat dry. Cut into 3-inch strips. Stir-fry in hot oil in wok for 1 minute. Add vegetables. Stir-fry for 1 1/2 minutes. Add water. Simmer, covered, for 2 minutes, stirring once. Mix remaining ingredients in small bowl. Add to wok. Cook until sauce thickens, stirring constantly. Yield: 4 to 6 servings.

Viola Leona Kofron, Xi Eta Omega
Janesville, Iowa

QUICK CHICKEN STIR-FRY

4 chicken breast filets	1 red bell pepper, cut in julienne strips
2 to 3 tablespoons peanut oil	1 8-ounce can sliced water chestnuts, drained
1 8-ounce can pineapple chunks, drained	Fried rice
1 scallion, chopped	

Rinse chicken; pat dry. Cut into strips. Stir-fry in hot oil in wok for 1 minute. Add pineapple, scallion, red pepper, and water chestnuts. Stir-fry for 5 to 10 minutes or until chicken is tender. Serve with fried rice. Yield: 4 servings.

Cheryl Feist, Alpha Delta
Chadron, Nebraska

P.D.Q. CHICKEN

6 chicken breast filets	1 1/2 tablespoons lemon pepper
1 teaspoon coarsely ground pepper	1/2 cup margarine

Rinse chicken; pat dry. Sprinkle with seasonings. Brown in margarine in skillet for 30 minutes. Serve hot. Yield: 6 servings.

Katheleen Campbell, Zeta Omega
Leavenworth, Kansas

CHEDDAR CHICKEN

4 chicken breast filets	2 tablespoons grated Parmesan cheese
2 ounces Cheddar cheese	1 tablespoon chopped parsley
3 tablespoons melted butter or margarine	1/4 teaspoon marjoram
1/2 cup crushed cornflakes	1/4 teaspoon basil
1 clove of garlic, minced	

Rinse chicken; pat dry. Flatten between sheets of waxed paper. Cut cheese into 1/4-by-1 1/2-inch strips. Roll up chicken around cheese, securing with wooden picks. Dip in melted butter. Coat with mixture of cornflakes, garlic, Parmesan cheese, parsley, marjoram and basil. Arrange in 9-inch round glass dish with thicker portions toward outside. Drizzle with remaining melted butter; sprinkle with remaining crumb mixture. Cover with waxed paper. Microwave on High for 6 to 8 minutes or until chicken is tender, turning once. Let stand, covered, for 5 minutes. Yield: 4 servings.

Carol Cameron, Laureate Beta Delta
Scarborough, Ontario, Canada

CHICKEN PICCATA

4 chicken breast filets	1/2 cup chopped fresh parsley
1/4 cup all-purpose flour	Salt and pepper to taste
1/2 cup margarine	6 tablespoons capers
1 cup dry vermouth	8 thin lemon slices, peeled
1/2 cup chicken broth	

Rinse chicken; pat dry. Flatten between sheets of waxed paper; cut into halves crosswise. Coat with flour. Brown in margarine in skillet for 1 minute on each side or until tender. Stir in next 5 ingredients. Cook, covered, over low heat for 8 to 10 minutes, stirring occasionally. Arrange on serving platter. Garnish with capers and lemon slices. Yield: 4 servings.

Nancy K. Corn, Laureate Delta Omicron
San Antonio, Texas

SOUTHWESTERN CHICKEN

1/2 cup mayonnaise-type salad dressing	1 tablespoon lime juice
1/2 teaspoon garlic powder	1/4 teaspoon red pepper
	4 chicken breast filets

Combine salad dressing, garlic powder, lime juice and red pepper in shallow bowl; mix well. Rinse chicken; pat dry. Arrange on rack in broiler pan. Brush with sauce. Broil for 8 to 10 minutes. Turn; baste with remaining sauce. Broil for 8 to 10 minutes longer or until chicken is tender. May marinate in sauce before grilling. Yield: 4 servings.

Merline McCoy, Laureate Psi
Village Mills, Texas

STUFFED CHICKEN BREASTS

4 4-ounce chicken breast filets	1 teaspoon each parsley and thyme
1 cup julienned carrots	1 10-ounce can cream of mushroom soup
1 cup chopped broccoli	
1 cup finely sliced green onions	

Rinse chicken; pat dry. Cut horizontal pocket in chicken breast. Stuff with mixture of carrots, broccoli, green onions, parsley and thyme; secure with wooden picks. Brown in skillet sprayed with nonstick butter-flavored cooking spray. Add soup and any remaining vegetable mixture. Simmer for 30 minutes or until chicken is tender. Serve with rice. Yield: 4 servings.

Linda Muth, Xi Zeta Chi
Rolfe, Iowa

❖ SUSAN'S CHICKEN

Delicious served with steamed asparagus in lemon butter, congealed fruit salad and croissants.

2 whole chicken breasts, boned, skinned	1/3 cup champagne or sauterne
1/2 cup all-purpose flour	1/4 cup chopped parsley
Salt and pepper to taste	Freshly ground nutmeg to taste
1/4 cup butter or margarine	1 cup whipping cream
8 ounces mushrooms	

Rinse chicken; pat dry. Cut into bite-sized pieces. Coat with mixture of flour, salt and pepper. Sauté in butter in skillet over high heat until tender. Add mushrooms and champagne, stirring to deglaze skillet. Add parsley, nutmeg and cream. Cook over low heat until thickened, stirring constantly. Serve over rice. Yield: 4 servings.

D'Arline R. Beeson, Zeta Master
San Antonio, Texas

TANGY GRILLED CHICKEN BREASTS

8 chicken breast filets	1 12-ounce can pineapple or orange juice
1 16-ounce bottle of oil-based Italian salad dressing	

Rinse chicken; pat dry. Place in large shallow dish. Pierce with fork. Pour mixture of salad dressing and juice over chicken. Marinate, covered, in refrigerator. Drain, reserving marinade. Wrap chicken in foil. Grill over hot coals for 20 minutes or until tender, basting occasionally with reserved marinade. Serve with seasoned rice. Yield: 8 servings.

Defawyna Maier, Omicron Delta
McPherson, Kansas

ZESTY CHICKEN

1/2 cup chopped onion	1 16-ounce can tomatoes, drained, chopped
1/2 cup chopped green bell pepper	1/2 teaspoon oregano
1 clove of garlic, minced	1/4 teaspoon salt
1 4-ounce can mushroom pieces, drained	1/8 teaspoon pepper
1 8-ounce can tomato sauce	2 teaspoons sugar
	1 pound chicken tenders

Combine first 10 ingredients in bowl; mix well. Pour into 8-by-12-inch glass dish. Rinse chicken and pat dry. Add to mixture in dish. Microwave, covered, on High for 10 minutes; stir. Microwave for 10 minutes longer. Serve over noodles. Yield: 4 servings.

Carol S. Nichols, Xi Nu Delta
Dunnellon, Florida

BIG CHICKEN BURGER

2 slices white bread, cubed	2 teaspoons grated onion
1 6-ounce can chunk chicken, drained, flaked	1 carrot, shredded
	1/2 teaspoon salt
1 egg, beaten	1 tablespoon vegetable oil

Combine bread, chicken, egg, onion, carrot and salt in medium bowl; mix well. Shape into 3-inch round patties. Cook in oil in skillet until browned on both sides. Yield: 2 servings.

Denny Porter, Xi Mu Theta
Coral Springs, Florida

CHICKEN CASSEROLE

1 4-ounce can chunk chicken, drained	1/2 cup milk
1 cup cream of chicken soup	1 tablespoon parsley flakes
1 tablespoon chopped pimento	3 cups cooked macaroni
	Salt to taste
	Buttered bread crumbs

Preheat oven to 350 degrees. Combine chicken, soup, pimento, milk, parsley, macaroni and salt in large bowl; mix well. Pour into greased 1½-quart casserole. Top with bread crumbs. Bake for 20 minutes. Yield: 4 servings.

Linda H. Cupp, Preceptor Beta Pi
Vinton, Virginia

CHICKEN-ALMOND CASSEROLE

4 cups chopped cooked chicken breasts	¼ cup water
1 10-ounce can cream of mushroom soup	¼ to ½ cup slivered almonds
1 10-ounce can Cheddar cheese soup	2 cups rice, cooked
1 14-ounce can chicken broth	1 4-ounce jar chopped pimentos, drained
1 7-ounce can chopped green chilies, drained	¼ cup chopped onion
	½ cup shredded Cheddar cheese

Preheat oven to 325 to 350 degrees. Combine chicken, soups, broth, chilies, water, almonds, rice, pimentos and onion in large bowl; mix well. Pour into 9-by-13-inch baking dish. Top with cheese. Bake until heated through and cheese melts. Yield: 6 to 8 servings.

Stacie Haas, Xi Tau
Havre, Montana

CHICKEN-BROCCOLI DIVAN

Flowerets of 1 pound broccoli, cooked	⅓ cup milk
1½ cups chopped cooked chicken	2 tablespoons dry bread crumbs
1 10-ounce can broccoli-cheese soup	1 tablespoon melted butter or margarine

Preheat oven to 450 degrees. Layer broccoli and chicken in 1½-quart baking dish. Mix soup and milk in bowl. Pour over layers. Toss bread crumbs with butter to coat. Sprinkle over top. Bake for 10 to 15 minutes. May make ahead and freeze. Yield: 4 servings.

Kaye Schramm, Laureate Beta Sigma
Sequim, Washington

CHICKEN ENCHILADAS

3 to 4 cups chopped cooked chicken breasts	¾ cup sour cream
	10 flour tortillas
1 10-ounce can cream of mushroom soup	1 cup shredded Monterey Jack cheese
¼ cup chopped green chilies	1 cup shredded Cheddar cheese

Preheat oven to 350 degrees. Combine chicken, soup, chilies and sour cream in bowl; mix well. Spread in center of tortillas. Roll up to enclose filling. Arrange in 9-by-13-inch baking pan. Sprinkle with cheeses. Bake for 30 minutes or until cheese is bubbly. May

prepare the night before and cook just before serving. Yield: 4 to 6 servings.

Rebecca J. Woods, Xi Omicron Delta
San Antonio, Texas

CHICKEN ENCHILADA CASSEROLE

3 cups chopped cooked chicken	1 cup shredded Cheddar cheese
1 10-ounce can cream of mushroom soup	½ 12-ounce package tortilla chips, crushed
1 4-ounce can chopped green chilies, drained	Sour cream and salsa
½ 6-ounce can whole black olives	

Preheat oven to 375 degrees. Combine first 6 ingredients in large bowl; mix well. Pour into 8-by-8-inch baking pan. Bake for 30 minutes or until heated through. Serve with sour cream and salsa. Yield: 4 to 6 servings.

Judith A. Murrill, Preceptor Sigma
Corvallis, Montana

CHILI-CHICKEN ENCHILADAS

½ cup chopped green bell pepper	1 10-ounce can cream of chicken soup
½ cup chopped onion	1 10-ounce can Ro-Tel tomatoes, drained
1 tablespoon margarine	
2 6-ounce cans chunk chicken, drained	1 12-ounce package tortilla chips
1 10-ounce can cream of mushroom soup	1 cup shredded Cheddar cheese

Preheat oven to 350 degrees. Sauté green pepper and onion in margarine in skillet. Combine with chicken, soups and tomatoes in bowl; mix well. Pour over layer of tortilla chips in greased 10-by-13-inch baking dish. Top with cheese. Bake for 15 minutes. Yield: 8 to 10 servings.

Janice Waltz, Laureate Psi
Houston, Texas

GREEN CHICKEN ENCHILADAS

1 12-ounce package tostado chips	2 10-ounce cans cream of chicken soup
1 onion, chopped	4 to 5 cups chopped cooked chicken
1 clove of garlic, chopped	
10 green chilies, chopped	Shredded longhorn cheese
1 cup milk	

Preheat oven to 350 degrees. Layer chips in 9-by-12-inch baking dish. Combine onion, garlic and chilies in blender container. Process until finely chopped. Mix with milk, soups and chicken in saucepan. Cook over low heat until bubbly, stirring frequently. Pour over chips. Top with cheese. Bake for 30 minutes or until heated through. Yield: 15 servings.

Willie Sloan, Preceptor Omega
La Mesa, New Mexico

CHICKEN WITH HOT PEANUT SAUCE

2 tablespoons minced gingerroot	2 teaspoons sesame oil
2 tablespoons minced garlic	1/3 cup plus 2 tablespoons peanut butter
2 tablespoons canola oil	8 ounces chopped cooked chicken
1 cup chicken broth	
1/2 cup dry sherry	3 cups cooked vermicelli
2 tablespoons soy sauce	2 tablespoons chopped green onions
2 tablespoons vinegar	

Sauté gingerroot and garlic in 2 tablespoons oil in skillet for 30 seconds. Add next 6 ingredients; mix well. Simmer for 3 minutes or until thickened, stirring constantly. Stir in chicken. Cook until heated through. Serve over vermicelli. Top with green onions. Yield: 4 servings.

Joan Ogden, Xi Beta Zeta
Lebanon, Oregon

CHICKEN PILLOWS

2 cups chopped cooked chicken	Garlic powder to taste
8 ounces cream cheese, softened	2 8-count cans crescent rolls
1 bunch green onions, chopped	1 cup butter or margarine
Salt and pepper to taste	2 cups dry bread crumbs

Preheat oven to 350 degrees. Mix chicken, cream cheese, green onions and seasonings in bowl. Separate crescent roll dough into triangles. Spoon 1 tablespoon filling onto each triangle. Roll up, pinching edges to seal. Roll in melted butter; coat with bread crumbs. Arrange in 9-by-13-inch baking pan. Bake for 30 minutes or until golden brown. Yield: 16 servings.

Cristal Kenczka, Gamma Beta
Vernal, Utah

CHICKEN POTPIES

2 6-ounce cans chunk chicken, drained	1 16-ounce can sliced potatoes, drained
Salt and pepper to taste	2 10-ounce cans cream of mushroom soup
1 16-ounce can peas, drained	
1 16-ounce can whole kernel corn, drained	2 unbaked 9-inch deep-dish pie shells
1 16-ounce can sliced carrots, drained	2 unbaked all-ready pie pastries

Preheat oven to 425 degrees. Combine first 8 ingredients in large saucepan; mix well. Cook until heated through. Spoon into frozen pie shells. Top with pie pastries. Seal edges; cut vents. Bake for 30 minutes or until golden brown. Yield: 12 servings.

Morag R. Alexander, Epsilon Pi
Boca Raton, Florida

QUICK CRUNCHY CHICKEN STIR-FRY

1 cup diagonally sliced celery	1 6-ounce can sliced water chestnuts, drained
2 tablespoons peanut oil	
1/4 cup thinly sliced onion	2 cups chopped cooked chicken
1 8-ounce can sliced mushrooms, drained	1/2 to 3/4 cup chopped walnuts
1 tablespoon cornstarch	Hot rice, egg noodles or chow mein noodles
3/4 cup cold water	
1/4 cup soy sauce	

Preheat wok to 350 degrees. Stir-fry celery in oil in wok for 1 minute; set aside. Stir-fry onion for 1 minute; set aside. Stir-fry mushrooms for 1 minute; set aside. Mix cornstarch, water and soy sauce in small bowl until blended. Combine with celery, onion and mushrooms in wok. Cook until thickened, stirring constantly. Reduce heat to 250 degrees. Add water chestnuts and chicken. Cook for 3 minutes, stirring gently. Add walnuts. Cook over low heat until heated through. Serve over hot rice, egg noodles or chow mein noodles. May substitute 8 ounces sliced fresh mushrooms for canned mushrooms. Yield: 6 servings.

Colleen Abar, Laureate Delta
Grand Forks, North Dakota

HOMESTYLE CHICKEN POTPIE

2 unbaked all-ready pie pastries	1 12-ounce can chunk chicken, drained
1 10-ounce package frozen mixed peas, carrots and potatoes, thawed	1 10-ounce can cream of potato soup
	1/3 cup milk
1/2 cup chopped onion	1/2 teaspoon poultry seasoning or thyme

Preheat oven to 375 degrees. Line deep-dish 9-inch pie plate with 1 pie pastry. Combine vegetables, onion, chicken, soup, milk and seasonings in bowl; mix well. Spoon into prepared pie plate. Top with remaining pastry. Seal edges; cut vents. Bake for 45 minutes or until golden brown. Yield: 6 servings.

Belinda Brown, Beta Beta Xi
Willow Park, Texas

CRESCENT CHICKEN

1 8-count can crescent rolls	1 10-ounce can cream of chicken soup
2 6-ounce cans chunk chicken, drained	1 cup milk
1/2 cup shredded Cheddar cheese	

Preheat oven to 375 degrees. Separate crescent roll dough into triangles. Combine chicken with 2 tablespoons cheese. Spoon onto center of each triangle. Roll up to enclose filling; seal edges. Combine remaining cheese with soup and milk in saucepan. Heat until cheese melts, stirring occasionally. Pour half the mixture into ungreased 8-by-8-inch baking pan. Arrange chicken rolls in pan. Pour remaining sauce over top. Bake for 20 to 25 minutes. Yield: 4 servings.

Julie Ross, Lambda Rho
Milford, Kansas

MEXICAN CHICKEN

2 cups chopped cooked chicken	1 10-ounce can cream of mushroom soup
1 teaspoon salt	1 10-ounce can Ro-Tel tomatoes, drained
1 teaspoon pepper	Crushed tortilla chips
1 onion, chopped	Shredded Cheddar cheese
1 green bell pepper, chopped	
8 corn tortillas, torn	
1 10-ounce can cream of chicken soup	

Combine chicken, salt, pepper, onion, green pepper and tortillas in bowl; mix well. Spoon into 9-by-13-inch casserole. Pour soups and tomatoes over top. Bake for 30 minutes. Sprinkle with chips and cheese. Bake for 5 minutes longer or until cheese melts. Yield: 6 to 8 servings.

Rogene Schneider
Nebraska City, Nebraska

❖ MEXICAN CORN BREAD-CHICKEN DRESSING CASSEROLE

A German family living in San Antonio gave me this recipe over 50 years ago.

1 8-ounce package Mexican corn bread mix	1/2 cup chopped onion
1/2 cup melted margarine	1/2 cup chopped celery
	1/2 cup mayonnaise
	2 eggs
1 cup water	1 1/2 cups milk
4 1/2 cups chopped cooked chicken	2 10-ounce cans cream of mushroom soup

Preheat oven to 350 degrees. Combine corn bread mix, margarine and water in large bowl; mix well. Spread half the mixture in greased 11-by-14-inch casserole. Combine chicken, onion, celery and mayonnaise in medium bowl; mix well. Spread over corn bread mixture. Beat eggs and milk in small bowl. Pour over chicken mixture. Spread with remaining corn bread batter. Spoon soup over top. Bake for 1 hour or until bubbly in center. Yield: 6 to 8 servings.

Lottie Sullivan, Iota Mu
Nacogdoches, Texas

POPPY SEED CHICKEN

My son is a picky eater but loves this dish.

1 stack butter crackers, crushed	2 5-ounce cans chunk chicken, drained
1 tablespoon poppy seed	1 10-ounce can cream of chicken soup
7 tablespoons melted butter or margarine	1/2 cup sour cream

Preheat oven to 350 degrees. Combine cracker crumbs, poppy seed and butter in large bowl; mix well. Reserve 1/2 cup mixture. Press remaining mixture in 8-by-8-inch baking dish. Combine chicken, soup and sour cream in medium bowl; mix well. Pour into prepared dish. Top with reserved crumb mixture. Bake for 35 minutes. Yield: 4 servings.

Doris Smith, Xi Gamma Tau
Fairfield Bay, Arkansas

HOT CHICKEN SALAD

2 cups chopped cooked chicken	1/2 teaspoon salt
2 cups chopped celery	2 tablespoons lemon juice
1/4 cup slivered almonds	1/3 cup mayonnaise
2 tablespoons chopped pimentos	1/4 cup shredded Swiss cheese
1/4 cup chopped green bell pepper	2 cups crushed potato chips
1/4 cup chopped onion	

Preheat oven to 350 degrees. Combine chicken, celery, almonds, pimentos, green pepper, onion, salt, lemon juice and mayonnaise in large bowl; mix well. Spoon into 2-quart casserole. Top with cheese and potato chips. Bake for 25 minutes or until cheese is melted. Yield: 6 servings.

Cindy Atwell, Delta Iota
Somerset, Kentucky

SUPER CHICKEN CASSEROLE

3 cups chopped cooked chicken	1/2 cup milk
1 cup sour cream	1 6-ounce package stuffing mix
1 10-ounce can cream of chicken soup	1/2 cup melted butter or margarine

Preheat oven to 350 degrees. Arrange chicken in 2-quart casserole. Combine sour cream, soup and milk in small bowl; mix well. Pour over chicken. Toss stuffing mix with melted butter, adding enough hot water to moisten. Sprinkle over casserole. Bake for 30 minutes or until bubbly. Yield: 6 servings.

LeAnn Mack, Beta Omega
Mobridge, South Dakota

QUICK SWEET AND SOUR CHICKEN

I created this dish one evening when I arrived late from work, had to pick up my daughter from basketball practice and had to go to a sorority meeting that night.

2 6-ounce cans chunk chicken	1 tablespoon soy sauce
1/2 cup packed light brown sugar	1 13-ounce can pineapple chunks
1 tablespoon cornstarch	1 small green bell pepper, chopped
1/3 cup vinegar	4 to 5 cups cooked rice

Drain chicken, reserving juice. Mix juice with brown sugar and cornstarch in large saucepan. Stir in vinegar, soy sauce and undrained pineapple. Bring to a boil, stirring occasionally; reduce heat. Add chicken. Simmer, covered, for 10 minutes. Add green pepper. Simmer for 5 minutes. Serve over cooked rice. Yield: 6 servings.

Patricia A. Hudson, Xi Sigma Psi
Malakoff, Texas

TASTY CHICKEN CASSEROLE

I use this as a unique bridal shower gift. I buy the baking dish and fill it with the dry and canned ingredients, and add a copy of the recipe.

1 envelope sour cream sauce mix	2 tablespoons poppy seed
1 8-ounce package chicken noodles and sauce mix	2 10-ounce cans cream of chicken soup
	1 stack butter crackers, crushed
2 6-ounce cans chunk chicken, drained	1/2 cup melted butter or margarine

Preheat oven to 400 degrees. Prepare sour cream mix using package directions; set aside. Prepare noodles and sauce using package directions. Combine with chicken, poppy seed, soup and sour cream sauce in large bowl; mix well. Spoon into 9-by-11-inch baking dish sprayed with nonstick cooking spray. Top with mixture of crackers and butter. Bake for 20 minutes or until brown and bubbly. Yield: 6 to 8 servings.

Delilah Williams, Preceptor Gamma
Columbus, Mississippi

CORNISH GAME HEN GLAZED WITH ORANGE AND GINGER

1 1 1/2-pound Cornish game hen, skinned	1 tablespoon olive oil
1/4 teaspoon each sage and rosemary, crumbled	1/4 cup orange juice
	1 tablespoon honey
1 clove of garlic, crushed	1 tablespoon red wine vinegar
1 teaspoon minced fresh ginger	2 teaspoons Dijon mustard
1/4 teaspoon pepper	1 teaspoon grated orange rind
1 3-inch strip orange peel	

Preheat oven to 375 degrees. Rinse game hen; pat dry inside and out. Sprinkle cavity with sage, rosemary, garlic, half the ginger and half the pepper; place orange strip inside. Truss hen; place breast-side up in shallow roasting pan. Brush with olive oil; sprinkle with remaining pepper. Roast for 35 to 40 minutes or until hen tests done. Combine orange juice, honey, vinegar, mustard and remaining ginger in small saucepan; mix well. Bring to a boil; reduce heat to medium. Simmer for 5 minutes or until mixture is syrupy, stirring frequently. Split hen lengthwise; baste with syrup. Broil, skinned side up, 5 inches from heat source for 2 to 3 minutes or until golden brown. Sprinkle with grated orange rind. Yield: 2 servings.

Elaine Lavelett, Preceptor Alpha Beta
Colorado Springs, Colorado

PHEASANT STIR-FRY

A family favorite for South Dakota pheasant, served over long grain wild rice.

1 whole pheasant or 2 pheasant breasts	1 tablespoon cooking wine
2 tablespoons soy sauce	1/4 cup walnut halves
1 tablespoon cornstarch	2 to 4 tablespoons peanut oil
1 tablespoon catsup	1 green bell pepper, coarsely chopped
1/2 teaspoon each salt and sugar	1 3-ounce can mushrooms, drained
Pepper and seasoned salt to taste	

Rinse pheasant; pat dry inside and out. Remove from bone; cut into bite-sized pieces. Combine soy sauce, cornstarch, catsup, salt, sugar, pepper, seasoned salt and cooking wine in shallow dish. Toss pheasant in mixture. Marinate, covered, in refrigerator. Sauté walnuts in 2 tablespoons oil in wok; drain. Stir-fry green pepper and mushrooms in wok; drain. Stir-fry pheasant until golden brown, adding additional oil as needed. Add cooked vegetables. Cook until heated through. Serve with hot rice, tossed salad and breadsticks. Yield: 3 servings.

Joy Christoffer, Xi Kappa
Pierre, South Dakota

ARIZONA HASH

1 pound ground turkey	1 8-ounce can tomato sauce
2 onions, chopped	
1 green bell pepper, chopped	2 teaspoons chili powder
1/2 cup uncooked rice	

Preheat oven to 350 degrees. Line glass casserole with paper towels. Place turkey in casserole; cover with paper towels. Microwave on High for 5 minutes; drain and crumble. Microwave onion and green pepper, covered tightly, in small glass bowl for 3 minutes or until tender. Combine with cooked turkey, rice, tomato sauce and chili powder in glass baking dish. Bake for 30 minutes. Yield: 4 servings.

Tracy Doyle, Rho Upsilon
Plantation, Florida

BARBECUED TURKEY

I use all my leftover turkey from holidays for barbecue.

2 tablespoons minced onion
1 green bell pepper, chopped
1/4 cup butter or margarine
4 to 5 cups chopped cooked turkey
1/8 teaspoon Tabasco sauce
2 cups catsup
2/3 cup chicken broth
1/3 cup vinegar
1/3 cup sugar
1/3 teaspoon Worcestershire sauce

Sauté onion and green pepper in butter in large saucepan. Add Tabasco sauce, catsup, broth, vinegar, sugar and Worcestershire sauce; mix well. Simmer for 10 minutes, stirring occasionally. Add turkey. Simmer for 20 minutes longer. May freeze and reheat in double boiler. Yield: 8 servings.

Viola M. McBride, Laureate Iota
Sun City West, Arizona

CHEESY MACARONI CASSEROLE

1 1/2 pounds ground turkey
1 onion, chopped
1 15-ounce jar spaghetti sauce
1 10-ounce can Cheddar cheese soup
1 4-ounce can mushroom pieces, drained
1 8-ounce can tomato sauce
1/4 teaspoon each garlic powder, thyme and pepper
8 ounces macaroni, cooked
2 cups shredded Colby cheese

Preheat oven to 350 degrees. Brown turkey and onion in large skillet, stirring until turkey is crumbly; drain. Add spaghetti sauce, soup, mushrooms, tomato sauce and seasonings; mix well. Simmer for 3 to 4 minutes, stirring occasionally. Add macaroni; mix well. Spoon into 9-by-13-inch casserole. Bake, covered, for 25 minutes or until bubbly. Sprinkle with shredded cheese. Bake, uncovered, for 5 minutes longer or until cheese melts. Yield: 8 to 10 servings.

Maurine Glantz, Preceptor Alpha Chi
Harvard, Nebraska

Amy Ogborn, Gamma Theta, Cedar Rapids, Iowa, makes Quick Chicken Parmesan by baking 4 fully cooked breaded chicken patties on baking sheet in preheated 400-degree oven for 20 minutes. Top each patty with 1/2 cup spaghetti sauce and 1 slice mozzarella cheese. Bake for 5 minutes longer. Sprinkle with Parmesan cheese.

EXOTIC CURRIED TURKEY

3 tablespoons chopped onion
3 tablespoons chopped apple
3 tablespoons chopped celery
1/4 cup butter or margarine
1/2 teaspoon each pepper, sugar and MSG
1/4 teaspoon nutmeg
2 1/2 teaspoons curry powder
1 teaspoon salt
1/4 cup all-purpose flour
1 1/2 cups milk
2 teaspoons lemon juice
3/4 teaspoon Worcestershire sauce
2 to 3 cups chopped cooked turkey
Raisin-almond rice
Chopped tomatoes, peanuts, coconut, eggs and/or green pepper

Brown onion, apple and celery in butter in skillet. Add next 6 ingredients and flour; mix well. Stir in milk. Cook over low heat until thickened, stirring constantly. Add lemon juice, Worcestershire sauce and turkey. Cook until heated through. Serve over almond rice. Garnish with chopped tomatoes, peanuts, coconut, chopped eggs or chopped green pepper. Yield: 6 servings.

Ann J. Pemberton, Epsilon Iota
Blair, Nebraska

PASTA FAGIOLI

1 small onion, chopped
2 cloves of garlic, minced
1 to 2 teaspoons olive oil
2 8-ounce cans tomato sauce
1 15-ounce can white beans
Salt and pepper to taste
1 pound ground turkey, cooked
8 ounces spaghetti, cooked

Sauté onion and garlic in oil in large saucepan until lightly browned. Add tomato sauce, undrained beans, salt and pepper; mix well. Simmer for 30 minutes. Add cooked ground turkey and cooked pasta; mix well. Cook until heated through. Yield: 4 to 5 servings.

Marilyn Silva, Xi Beta Xi
El Cajon, California

GRILLED TURKEY BREAST

3/4 cup red cooking wine
1/4 cup soy sauce
1/2 teaspoon garlic powder
1/2 teaspoon crushed basil
1 tablespoon olive oil
1 pound turkey scallops

Combine wine, soy sauce, garlic, basil and oil in shallow bowl; mix well. Rinse turkey and pat dry. Marinate turkey in sauce in refrigerator. Drain, reserving marinade. Grill turkey over hot coals for 10 minutes or until tender, basting occasionally with reserved marinade. Yield: 6 servings.

Sharon Dear, Tau Xi
Versailles, Missouri

JALAPEÑO TURKEY

1 10-ounce can cream of mushroom soup	1 2-ounce jar chopped pimento, drained
8 ounces Velveeta cheese with jalapeños	2 teaspoons parsley flakes
1 4-ounce can sliced mushrooms, drained	2 cups chopped cooked turkey

Combine soup and cheese in saucepan. Heat until cheese melts, stirring to mix well. Add remaining ingredients; mix well. Cook until heated through. Serve over rice or chow mein noodles.
Yield: 6 servings.

Sarah Stephens, Eta Master
Topeka, Kansas

PASTA-TURKEY MELT

1 cup cooked pasta	1/4 cup shredded Cheddar cheese
1/4 cup chopped cooked turkey	

Layer pasta, turkey and cheese in small microwave-safe dish. Microwave, covered, on High for 2 to 3 minutes or until cheese is melted. Stir and serve.
Yield: 1 serving.

Jeanette T. Case, Preceptor Tau
Erie, Pennsylvania

QUICK TAMALE PIE

1 pound ground turkey	1 28-ounce can tamales, drained, chopped
1/2 onion, chopped	
1 green bell pepper, chopped	1 17-ounce can whole kernel corn, drained
1 red bell pepper, chopped	1/2 teaspoon pepper
1 8-ounce can tomato sauce	1/2 teaspoon minced garlic

Brown ground turkey in large skillet, stirring until crumbly; drain. Add onion and bell peppers. Sauté until tender. Add tomato sauce, chopped tamales, corn, pepper and garlic; mix well. Cook over medium heat until heated through. Yield: 6 servings.

Joy Fujii-Donaldson, Xi Sigma Alpha
Dinuba, California

SKILLET TURKEY

1 pound ground turkey	1 16-ounce can mixed vegetables
1 onion, chopped	
1 envelope brown gravy mix	

Brown ground turkey in large skillet stirring until crumbly; drain. Add onion. Sauté until tender. Stir in gravy mix and undrained mixed vegetables, adding water if needed for desired consistency. Simmer until heated through. Yield: 4 servings.

Wanda F. Masek, Rho Nu
Mims, Florida

TURKEY AND BISCUITS

2 cups chopped cooked turkey	1 soup can milk
1 onion, chopped	1 16-ounce can peas, drained
1 to 2 teaspoons butter or margarine	1 10-count can biscuits
2 10-ounce cans cream of chicken soup	

Preheat oven to 350 degrees. Brown turkey and onion in butter in skillet. Combine soup and milk in small bowl, stirring to blend. Add to turkey with peas; mix well. Pour into 8-by-12-inch baking dish. Arrange biscuits on top. Bake for 12 to 15 minutes or until biscuits are golden brown. Yield: 6 servings.

Lynn Pruitt, Xi Alpha Delta
Siloam Springs, Arkansas

TURKEY-CHEESE BAKE

1 pound ground turkey	8 ounces noodles, cooked
2 16-ounce cans stewed tomatoes	1 cup shredded Monterey Jack cheese
1/2 envelope onion soup mix	

Preheat oven to 350 degrees. Brown ground turkey in skillet, stirring until crumbly; drain. Add tomatoes, soup mix and cooked noodles; mix well. Spoon into 1 1/2-quart casserole. Bake for 25 to 30 minutes or until heated through. Top with shredded cheese. Bake for 5 minutes longer or until cheese is melted. Yield: 4 to 6 servings.

Adrienne Geiss, Xi Beta Epsilon
Rochester, New York

QUICK TURKEY CHILI

This chili is more healthful than regular chili.

1 pound ground turkey	1 15-ounce can kidney beans
2/3 cup chopped onion	
1 10-ounce can low-sodium chicken broth	2 teaspoons chili powder
1 8-ounce can tomato sauce	1/4 teaspoon hot pepper sauce
1 6-ounce can tomato paste	

Brown ground turkey with onions in large saucepan, stirring frequently. Stir in broth, tomato sauce and tomato paste. Add kidney beans and seasonings. Brint to a boil; reduce heat. Simmer for 15 to 20 minutes, stirring occasionally.
Yield: 4 (1 1/2-cup) servings.

Carole E. Bolard, Xi Eta Xi
Edinboro, Pennsylvania

TURKEY GOULASH

1 pound ground turkey
Salt, pepper, onion
  powder and garlic
  powder to taste
1 green bell pepper,
  chopped
1 tablespoon minced
  onion
2 16-ounce cans
  tomatoes, drained,
  chopped
1 4-ounce can
  mushroom pieces
3 ounces elbow
  macaroni, cooked

Brown turkey with seasonings in skillet, stirring until crumbly. Add green pepper, onion, tomatoes and mushrooms; mix well. Bring to a boil. Add cooked macaroni. Simmer until all liquid is absorbed and macaroni is tender. Yield: 3 to 4 servings.

Joyce Hasson, Preceptor Alpha Theta
Jackson, Michigan

TURKEY-NOODLE CASSEROLE

Serve with salad and beverage for quick meal.

1 package noodles and
  cheese
1 cup chopped cooked
  turkey
1/2 cup cooked pea
  or 1/2 cup cooked
  carrots

Prepare noodles and cheese using package directions, adding turkey and vegetables. Microwave, uncovered, on High using package directions, stirring once. Let stand for 2 minutes before serving. May serve with rolls if desired. Yield: 4 servings.

B. Kim Hobbs, Xi Epsilon Theta
Pueblo, Colorado

TURKEY-NOODLE RAMEN

1 pound ground turkey
2 3-ounce packages
  beef-flavored Ramen
  noodles
1 16-ounce can
  French-style green
  beans
1 cup water

Brown turkey in skillet, stirring until crumbly; drain. Sprinkle with crushed Ramen noodles and seasoning packets; mix well. Add undrained green beans and water. Simmer, covered, for 10 minutes or until noodles are tender, stirring occasionally.
Yield: 4 to 6 servings.

Carole Stizza, Chi Phi
Vandenberg Air Force Base, California

TURKEY-REUBEN CASSEROLE

1 11-ounce can
  sauerkraut, drained
2 tablespoons butter or
  margarine
1/2 cup Thousand Island
  salad dressing
3 4-ounce packages
  sliced turkey
8 ounces shredded Swiss
  cheese
1 10-count can flaky
  biscuits
2 crisp rye crackers,
  crushed
1/4 teaspoon caraway
  seed

Preheat oven to 425 degrees. Spread sauerkraut into 8-by-12-inch baking dish. Dot with butter and salad dressing. Cover with turkey slices; sprinkle with cheese. Bake for 15 minutes; remove from oven. Separate each biscuit into 3 layers. Arrange over casserole in 3 overlapping rows. Sprinkle with cracker crumbs and caraway seed. Bake for 15 to 20 minutes longer or until golden brown. Yield: 6 servings.

Judy Kutcher, Xi Zeta Mu
Eldridge, Iowa

HOT TURKEY SALAD

This was served for lunch by a Laureate chapter along with a variety of breads and a creamy vegetable salad.

2 cups chopped turkey
2 cups chopped celery
1/2 cup chopped toasted
  almonds
2 teaspoons grated
  onion
1/2 teaspoon salt
1/2 cup shredded
  Cheddar cheese
1 cup crushed potato
  chips
Parsley to taste

Preheat oven to 450 degrees. Combine turkey, celery, almonds, onion and salt in bowl; toss lightly. Spoon into 8-inch square baking dish. Sprinkle with mixture of shredded cheese and crushed potato chips. Bake for 10 minutes. Garnish with parsley.
Yield: 5 to 6 servings.

Blanche Doernhoefer, Laureate Zeta Tau
San Bruno, California

TURKEY TACO SALAD

This taco salad is very low in calories.

1 pound ground
  turkey
1 clove of garlic
  (optional)
1 tablespoon chili
  powder
1 8-ounce can tomato
  sauce
12 taco shells, heated
2 tomatoes, chopped
2 cups chopped lettuce
1 onion, chopped
1 8-ounce bottle of
  reduced-calorie French
  dressing
1 cup shredded low-fat
  cheese

Brown turkey with garlic and chili powder in skillet, stirring until turkey is crumbly; drain. Add tomato sauce. Simmer for 15 minutes. Spoon turkey mixture into crisp taco shells. Top each with tomatoes, lettuce, onion, salad dressing and cheese.
Yield: 4 to 6 servings.

Gail Miller, Laureate Delta Psi
Clarks Summit, Pennsylvania

Use deli turkey or canned chunk turkey for quick appetizers, casseroles, sandwich spreads and salads.

TURKEY SAUTÉED WITH PEARS AND PECANS

1 pound turkey breast slices	1/3 cup apple juice
2 cloves of garlic, chopped	2 tablespoons whipping cream
1 to 2 tablespoons olive oil	2 pears, sliced 1/4-inch thick
1 teaspoon cracked peppercorns	1/4 to 1/2 cup pecan halves, toasted
	Cooked rice

Rinse turkey and pat dry. Sauté turkey and garlic in hot oil in skillet for 1 to 2 minutes or until brown; reduce heat. Stir in peppercorns, apple juice, cream and pears. Cook for 1 to 2 minutes or until heated through. Arrange on serving platter. Garnish wtih toasted pecans. Serve over rice. Yield: 4 servings.

Diane Polansky Ward, Xi Gamma Psi
Ankeny, Iowa

TURKEY TETRAZZINI

1/4 cup butter or margarine	2 cups turkey or chicken broth
1 4-ounce can sliced mushrooms, drained	1/2 cup half and half
1 small onion, chopped	2 1/2 cups chopped cooked turkey
1 1/2 teaspoons lemon juice	7 ounces spaghetti, cooked
1/3 cup all-purpose flour	1/2 cup grated Parmesan cheese
1 teaspoon salt	Paprika to taste
1/2 teaspoon paprika	
1/8 teaspoon nutmeg	

Combine butter, mushrooms, onion and lemon juice in 2-quart microwave-safe casserole. Microwave on High for 2 to 3 minutes or until tender, stirring after 1 minute. Stir in flour, salt, 1/2 teaspoon paprika and nutmeg until smooth. Microwave for 1 minute. Add broth. Microwave for 6 to 8 minutes until thickened, stirring after 3 minutes. Add cream and turkey; mix well. Place cooked spaghetti in greased 8-by-12-inch baking dish. Pour turkey mixture over. Sprinkle with cheese and additional paprika. Microwave for 7 minutes or until heated through. Yield: 4 to 6 servings.

Carole Pipetti, Xi Xi
Altoona, Pennsylvania

CREAMY TURKEY TETRAZZINI

1/4 cup chopped celery	2 cups sour cream
1/4 cup chopped onion	4 cups chopped cooked turkey
2 4-ounce cans mushroom pieces, drained	8 ounces thin spaghetti, cooked
1/2 cup margarine	Grated Parmesan cheese and paprika to taste
2 10-ounce cans cream of chicken soup	

Preheat oven to 350 degrees. Sauté celery, onion and mushroom pieces in margarine in large skillet. Stir in soup, sour cream and turkey; mix well. Add cooked spaghetti. Spoon into buttered 9-by-13-inch casserole. Sprinkle with cheese and paprika. Bake for 40 minutes or until bubbly. Yield: 8 servings.

Mary Jane Ciullo, Preceptor Beta Eta
Warren, Michigan

TURKEY-SAUCED PASTA

1 cup sliced celery	1 7-ounce can cream of mushroom soup
1 small onion, chopped	2 cups chopped cooked turkey
1 cup sliced carrots	Hot cooked noodles
1/2 teaspoon basil	
3/4 cup water	
1 cup yogurt	

Bring first 5 ingredients to a boil in saucepan; reduce heat. Simmer, covered, for 5 to 7 minutes. Add yogurt, soup and turkey; mix well. Cook until heated through, stirring occasionally. Serve over noodles. Yield: 4 to 6 servings.

Jody Malsam, Xi Kappa
Coeur d'Alene, Idaho

TURKEY TORTELLINI

2 10-ounce cans cream of asparagus soup	1 1/2 to 2 teaspoons poultry seasoning
1 pound fresh asparagus, trimmed, sliced	1 tablespoon lemon juice
2 to 3 cups chopped cooked turkey	4 ounces shredded sharp Cheddar cheese
	1 1/4 pounds cheese tortellini, cooked

Combine soup, asparagus, turkey, seasoning and lemon juice in large saucepan; mix well. Simmer for 20 minutes or until asparagus is tender, stirring frequently. Stir in cheese just before serving. Pour over cooked tortellini. Yield: 4 to 6 servings.

Cynthia Albert, Beta Phi
Clatonia, Nebraska

TURKEY TORTILLAS

1 pound sliced cooked turkey	2 tablespoons sour cream
1 16-ounce jar salsa	1 green onion, sliced
6 8-inch flour tortillas	Jalapeño pepper slices
5 slices Cheddar cheese	

Rinse turkey and pat dry. Cut into long strips. Combine with salsa in bowl. Spoon mixture into center of each tortilla. Roll up to enclose filling. Place seam-side down in 8-by-13-inch baking dish. Arrange cheese slices over top. Microwave on High for 2 to 3 minutes or until cheese is melted. Top each tortilla with sour cream, green onion and pepper slices. Yield: 6 servings.

Gerry Smith, Laureate Delta Tau
Amarillo, Texas

Seafood in Seconds

Like poultry, seafood has long been a
favorite among cooks who find their time in
the kitchen at a premium. Versatile, good
for your health, economical and a good foil for
any number of seasonings and tastes, seafood
has become increasingly popular in recent
years. If you're already a devotee of food from
the deep, you'll find a host of great new ideas
in this chapter, from familiar recipes like
Creamed Salmon on Toast to exotic Prawns
with Feta Cheese and Wine. If seafood isn't yet
a familiar part of your daily menu planning, the
following recipes should help to change your
thinking. Fresh seafood is now easy to find,
even in inland supermarkets. And as these
recipes demonstrate, fish and seafood are not
only quick and easy to work with, but
long on taste when you're short on time.

COD WITH ORANGE-WALNUT TOPPING

2 tablespoons butter or
  margarine
1 small onion, chopped
1 pound cod filets
Salt to taste
Freshly ground black
  pepper to taste
Juice and grated rind of
  1 orange

1/4 cup fresh brown
  bread crumbs
1 cup walnuts, coarsely
  chopped
Orange segments
Watercress or parsley

Place butter in microwave-safe casserole. Microwave on High for 30 seconds or until melted. Add onion. Microwave for 2 1/2 minutes longer. Add fish; season with salt and pepper. Pour orange juice over all. Microwave for 3 1/2 minutes longer, turning once. Sprinkle fish with mixture of orange rind, bread crumbs and walnuts. Microwave for 1 1/2 to 2 minutes longer or until fish flakes easily. Garnish with orange segments and watercress. Yield: 4 servings.

Valerie P. Derks, Preceptor Beta Rho
Nine Mile Falls, Washington

CRUMB-COATED FISH FILETS

This recipe is great for low-fat, low-cholesterol diets. Use haddock, orange roughy, cod or sole filets.

3 tablespoons yellow
  cornmeal
1 tablespoon
  unseasoned dry
  bread crumbs
1 teaspoon dried
  parsley flakes

1/2 teaspoon onion
  powder
1/2 teaspoon paprika
1/8 teaspoon salt
Dash of cayenne pepper
1 pound frozen fish
  filets, thawed

Combine cornmeal, bread crumbs, parsley flakes, onion powder, paprika, salt and cayenne pepper on piece of waxed paper; mix well. Press filets lightly into mixture, coating well. Arrange on microwave-safe platter or roasting rack. Microwave on High for 5 to 7 minutes or until fish flakes easily, rotating dish once. Yield: 3 to 4 servings.

Julia Gatsos, Preceptor Sigma
New Albany, Indiana

FILETS BIENVILLE

Everyone who has eaten this dish says it is so good.

1 1/2 pounds cod,
  haddock or bluefish
Salt and pepper to taste
1 egg, beaten
1/2 cup grated Cheddar
  cheese
2 tablespoons melted
  butter or margarine
1 tablespoon lemon juice

1 teaspoon
  Worcestershire sauce
2 tablespoons each
  chopped green onions
  and chopped parsley
1/2 cup sliced
  mushrooms
7 ounces cooked peeled
  shrimp

Arrange filets in single layer in 8-by-8-inch microwave-safe dish. Season with salt and pepper. Combine egg, cheese, butter, lemon juice, Worcestershire sauce, green onions, parsley, mushrooms and shrimp in bowl; mix well. Spread over filets. Microwave, covered, on High for 8 minutes. Let stand, covered, for 2 minutes. Yield: 6 to 8 servings.

Lynn Dahl, Laureate Alpha
Beaconsfield, Quebec, Canada

STUFFED FLOUNDER

This recipe can also be cooked on a foil-lined gas grill.

2 12-inch whole
   flounder
1 package Stove-Top
  stuffing
1/2 cup chopped onion
1/2 cup chopped celery
2 tablespoons melted
  margarine

1/2 cup chopped crab
  meat or shrimp
2 slices bacon
Salt and pepper to taste

Preheat broiler. Slit dark side of flounder to create pocket for stuffing. Place on broiler pan sprayed with nonstick cooking spray. Prepare stuffing using package directions. Sauté onion and celery in margarine in skillet. Stir into stuffing. Add crab meat; mix well. Stuff into flounder. Top with bacon. Season with salt and pepper. Broil for 20 to 30 minutes or until fish flakes easily. Yield: 4 servings.

Linda F. Smith, Xi Upsilon Epsilon
Hallettsville, Texas

CITRUS RICE AND GROUPER

We are native Florida residents, and this uses some of the best items of Florida fare.

4 6-ounce grouper filets
2 tablespoons olive oil
1 large onion, chopped
1 tablespoon grated
  lemon or lime rind

1 cup orange slices
4 teaspoons lemon or
  lime juice
4 cups hot cooked rice

Preheat oven to 350 degrees. Place filets in shallow baking dish. Heat olive oil in skillet. Add onion. Sauté for 2 minutes or until clear and golden. Add lemon rind, orange slices and 2 teaspoons lemon juice. Cook for 1 minute longer; remove from heat. Spoon over filets. Sprinkle with remaining 2 teaspoons lemon juice. Bake, covered, for 15 to 20 minutes or until fish flakes easily. Flake fish; arrange over hot cooked rice. Yield: 4 servings.

Danna Vaught, Xi Zeta Iota
Bartow, Florida

SIMMERED GROUPER WITH VEGETABLES

While visiting Big Pine Key, Florida, a friend and I created this dish from some leftover rice, fresh grouper and vegetables we had on hand. It was wonderful.

1 package 5-minute long grain and wild rice with chicken stock sauce and vegetables	1 small yellow squash, cut into slices
	1 small onion, chopped
	10 mushrooms, cut into slices
1 red pepper, cut into 1-inch pieces	1/4 to 1/2 cup water
1 green bell pepper, cut into 1-inch pieces	1 1/2 pounds grouper or orange roughy
	Salt and pepper to taste

Prepare rice using package directions. Add bell peppers, squash, onion, mushrooms and water. Simmer, covered, for 10 minutes. Add fish. Simmer, covered, for 10 minutes longer or until fish flakes easily. Season with salt and pepper. Yield: 6 servings.

Sandra S. Kelley, Pi Zeta
Monticello, Illinois

JUST-FOR-THE HALIBUT

To serve two or more, just double the recipe and microwave for one more minute.

1 teaspoon olive oil	4 sprigs of fresh basil, tarragon or parsley
1/2 pound 1-inch thick halibut	2 thin lemon slices
4 medium shrimp, butterflied (optional)	1 tablespoon white wine
	Lemon pepper to taste

Brush microwave-safe platter with oil. Place halibut in center. Surround with shrimp. Sprinkle with basil. Top with lemon slices. Sprinkle with wine and lemon pepper. Cover tightly with plastic wrap. Microwave on High for 3 minutes or until fish flakes easily. Pierce plastic with tip of sharp knife. Let stand for 3 minutes. Yield: 1 serving.

Charleene Lanning Pounder, Alpha Master
Sun City, Arizona

MEXICAN FISH

This makes a great fast supper during Lent!

Frozen pollack filets, thawed	1 large package Cheddar or Monterey Jack cheese, shredded
1 jar Mexican salsa	

Place fish in 9-by-13-inch glass baking dish. Spread with salsa. Microwave on High for 10 minutes. Top with cheese. Microwave for 2 to 3 minutes longer or until cheese is melted. Yield: 4 to 6 servings.

Judy Spath, Preceptor Psi
Vesper, Wisconsin

OVEN CRUNCHY FISH STICKS

15 crackers, finely crushed	1/3 cup low-fat sour cream
1/2 teaspoon seasoned salt	1 tablespoon lemon juice
	1 teaspoon water
1/4 teaspoon chili powder	10 ounces firm white fish

Preheat oven to 475 degrees. Mix cracker crumbs, seasoned salt and chili powder in small bowl. Combine sour cream, lemon juice and water in medium bowl; mix well. Dip fish into sour cream mixture, coating all sides; dip into crumb mixture, rolling to coat evenly. Place on baking sheet sprayed with non-stick cooking spray. Bake for 15 minutes or until golden and crunchy. Yield: 2 servings.

Teresa Anderson, Eta Delta
Mackenzie, British Columbia, Canada

ITALIAN-STYLE FISH AND VEGETABLES

2 tablespoons vegetable oil	1 1/2 pounds fresh or frozen orange roughy
1 onion, cut into slices	1/4 teaspoon salt
1 3-ounce jar sliced mushrooms, drained	1/4 teaspoon pepper
1/2 teaspoon basil leaves	2 tomatoes, cut into slices
2 cups frozen mixed vegetables	1/3 cup grated Parmesan cheese

Heat oil in skillet over medium heat. Add onion, mushrooms and basil. Sauté until onion is tender. Stir in vegetables. Top with fish. Sprinkle with salt and pepper. Arrange tomatoes over fish. Reduce temperature to low. Cook, covered, for 12 to 16 minutes or until fish flakes easily. Remove from heat. Sprinkle with cheese. Let stand, covered, for 3 minutes. Yield: 6 servings.

Becky Linn, Iota Gamma
Kinsley, Kansas

❖ SHRIMP FILETS

This recipe can be prepared with sole, halibut, pike or whitefish filets.

1 1/2 to 2 pounds fish filets	1/2 cup shrimp cocktail sauce
3 ounces cream cheese, softened	1 4-ounce can small shrimp, drained

Place filets in microwave-safe 7-by-12-inch baking dish. Mix cream cheese, cocktail sauce and shrimp in bowl. Spread over filets. Cover tightly with waxed paper. Microwave on High for 10 to 16 minutes or until fish flakes easily. Let stand, covered, for 5 minutes. Yield: 4 servings.

Bette M. Wilkens, Xi Beta Nu
Oconomowoc, Wisconsin

SNAPPER FILETS IN NUT CRUST

2 pounds skinless snapper filets	1 egg yolk
1/4 cup all-purpose flour	2 egg whites
1 cup whole wheat bread crumbs	2 tablespoons water
1 cup chopped pecans	2 tablespoons vegetable oil

Preheat oven to 350 degrees. Cut fish into serving size portions. Dust with flour. Mix crumbs and pecans in flat pan. Beat egg yolk, egg whites and water in flat bowl. Heat oil in skillet. Dredge fish in egg wash; dip into crumb mixture. Add to hot oil. Cook for 2 minutes per side or until golden brown. Place fish on bake-and-serve platter. Bake for 5 minutes. Yield: 5 to 6 servings.

Elaine Smith, Xi Mu Nu
Dunnellon, Florida

SWISS FILET ROLLS

1 pound whitefish filets	1 tablespoon all-purpose flour
Salt and pepper to taste	Salt to taste
2 cups sliced fresh mushrooms	1/2 cup milk
1/2 cup chopped onion	1/4 cup shredded Swiss cheese
2 tablespoons margarine	1 tablespoon dry white wine
1 cup herb-seasoned stuffing mix	Fresh parsley
1 tablespoon margarine	

Sprinkle fish with salt and pepper. Combine mushrooms, onion and 2 tablespoons margarine in glass dish. Microwave on High for 2 to 3 minutes or until margarine is melted. Stir in stuffing mix. Spread over fish; roll up. Place seam side down in glass baking dish. Cover with vented plastic wrap. Microwave on High for 4 to 4 1/2 minutes or until fish flakes easily. Set aside. Microwave remaining 1 tablespoon margarine in glass bowl until melted. Stir in flour, salt and milk. Microwave on High for 1 to 1 1/2 minutes or until boiling and thickened, stirring once. Stir in cheese and wine. Spoon over fish rolls. Garnish with parsley. Yield: 4 servings.

Cindy Zechmann, Preceptor Zeta
Caldwell, Idaho

BACON-STUFFED TROUT

The best part of this recipe is catching the trout!

2 eggs	1/2 teaspoon allspice
1 tablespoon milk	8 medium trout
1 teaspoon parsley flakes	8 to 16 slices grilled bacon
1 clove of garlic, minced	

Preheat grill. Combine eggs, milk, parsley, garlic and allspice in bowl; beat well. Coat fish inside and out with egg mixture. Place 1 or 2 bacon slices in each trout. Place trout on hot greased grill. Grill over hot coals for 20 minutes or until fish flakes easily, turning once. Yield: 8 servings.

Mary A. Shook, Xi Zeta Iota
Wagoner, Oklahoma

FISH FOR FISH HATERS

My children and friends who claim they do not like fish love this recipe.

1 pound whitefish filets, cut into pieces	1 16-ounce can whole tomatoes, drained, chopped
1/2 lemon	2 tablespoons melted butter or margarine
6 ounces fresh mushrooms, sliced	1/4 cup bread crumbs
6 to 8 scallions, chopped or 1/2 onion, chopped	2 tablespoons grated Parmesan cheese
Garlic salt and basil to taste	

Preheat oven to 425 degrees. Arrange fish in single layer in 7-by-12-inch baking dish sprayed with nonstick cooking spray. Squeeze lemon juice over fish. Spread with mushrooms and scallions. Season with garlic salt and basil. Top with tomatoes. Pour butter over tomatoes. Bake, covered with foil, for 15 minutes. Sprinkle with bread crumbs and cheese. Broil for 1 to 2 minutes or until bread crumbs are golden brown. Yield: 6 servings.

JoEllen Brown, Alpha Zeta
Los Alamos, New Mexico

MARINATED FISH

2 tablespoons soy sauce	1 teaspoon oregano
1 clove of garlic, minced	1/2 cup orange juice
1/3 cup catsup	1 tablespoon parsley
2 tablespoons lemon juice	4 pollack or halibut filets

Preheat grill or broiler. Mix first 7 ingredients in sealable bag. Add fish. Marinate for 30 minutes or longer; drain. Grill or broil fish until fish flakes easily. May also use marinade for chicken.
Yield: 4 servings.

Radie Sumner, Kappa Beta
Clifton Park, New York

NUMBER-ONE FISH BATTER

Those who catch the fish at our house clean them, and those who don't catch any fish have to cook and do dishes! This batter is also delicious used on onion rings or mushrooms.

1 pound walleye, crappie or white bass fish filets	6 ice cubes
	1 egg
1 cup all-purpose flour	1 teaspoon salt
1 cup water	1 teaspoon seasoned pepper
1 tablespoon vegetable oil	Oil for deep frying

Cut fish into bite-sized pieces. Combine flour, water, oil, ice cubes, egg, salt and seasoned pepper in bowl; mix well. Dip fish into batter. Deep-fry in hot oil in deep-fryer for 5 minutes. Yield: 4 to 6 servings.

Christina Stafford, Preceptor Alpha Gamma
Sterling, Colorado

CREAMED SALMON ON TOAST

This is great for last minute dinner guests!

1 15-ounce can salmon, crab meat, lobster or shrimp	1 15-ounce can peas, drained
Water or milk	1/4 teaspoon salt
1/4 cup butter	1/8 teaspoon pepper
1/4 cup all-purpose flour	Celery seed to taste
	Toast, English muffins or popovers

Drain salmon, reserving liquid. Chop salmon into chunks. Add enough water or milk to salmon liquid to measure 1 cup. Melt butter in skillet over low heat. Stir in flour. Cook for 1 minute, stirring constantly; do not scorch. Remove from heat. Stir in salmon liquid. Cook over low heat until thickened, stirring constantly. Add salmon and peas. Cook until heated through. Season with salt, pepper and celery seed. Serve over toast, English muffins or popovers. Yield: 8 servings.

Debbie Difilippantonio, Xi Alpha Rho
Danville, Kentucky

LIGHTNING SALMON PIE

1 16-ounce can salmon, drained	2 tablespoons milk
1/2 package instant mashed potatoes	1/2 cup grated cheese
	1 tablespoon butter or margarine

Preheat oven to 450 degrees. Break salmon into pieces with fork. Mound in center of greased pie plate. Prepare potatoes using package directions. Arrange ring of hot potatoes around salmon. Sprinkle milk over salmon; sprinkle cheese over potatoes. Dot with butter. Bake for 15 to 20 minutes or until bubbly and heated through. Yield: 4 to 6 servings.

Kathleen Walker, Xi Beta Mu
Baker City, Oregon

SALMON TOAST CUPS

May substitute leftover chicken or diced ham for salmon if desired.

3/4 cup butter or margarine, softened	1 10-ounce can cream of chicken or cream of mushroom soup
12 slices white bread, crusts trimmed	
1 16-ounce can salmon, drained	Chopped green onions or chopped green bell pepper

Preheat oven to 350 degrees. Butter 1 side of bread slices. Place buttered side down in muffin cups. Fill cups 1/2 full with salmon. Add 1 to 2 tablespoons soup. Sprinkle with green onions or green pepper. Bake for 10 to 12 minutes or until soup is bubbly. Yield: 3 to 4 servings.

Elmira Addie
Estevan, Saskatchewan, Canada

❖ VALENTINE SALMON

My date prepared this for me for Valentine's Day dinner, our first date. I was really impressed; we are now engaged.

1 pound fresh salmon filet	1/8 teaspoon Cajun seasoning
1/2 lemon	1/8 teaspoon cayenne pepper
1/4 teaspoon lemon pepper	12 asparagus spears
1/8 teaspoon garlic salt	3/4 cup mayonnaise

Preheat oven to 350 degrees. Cut piece of foil twice the size of salmon. Place salmon on foil. Squeeze lemon over salmon. Sprinkle with seasonings. Arrange asparagus over salmon. Cover with mayonnaise. Fold foil over salmon; crimp sides to seal. Bake for 20 to 30 minutes or until fish flakes easily. Yield: 2 to 3 servings.

Pamela Smith, Xi Beta Delta
Albuquerque, New Mexico

LAURA'S TUNA BAKE

My daughter created this recipe when she was 13 years old and just learning to cook. She was so proud of it that she served it to all her friends; we all loved it.

3 12-ounce cans water-pack tuna, drained	1 tablespoon extra spicy Mrs. Dash seasoning
2 cups low-calorie mayonnaise	Salt and pepper to taste
2 tablespoons red garlic wine vinegar	2 tomatoes, thinly sliced
1/2 cup chopped onion	4 or 5 slices mozzarella cheese
1/2 cup chopped celery	2 1/2 ounces sour cream and onion chips, crushed (optional)
1 tablespoon parsley flakes	

Preheat oven to 350 degrees. Combine tuna, mayonnaise, vinegar, onion, celery, parsley flakes, seasoning, salt and pepper in bowl; mix well. Spread in 6-by-10-inch baking dish sprayed with nonstick cooking spray. Arrange tomatoes and cheese over tuna mixture. Top with crushed chips. Bake for 45 minutes or until cheese is bubbly. Yield: 5 to 6 servings.

Anita Wilson, Laureate Alpha Mu
Mansfield, Ohio

GOURMET TUNA AND SPAGHETTI

This was introduced to me as, "It doesn't sound like much, but wait until you've tried it!"

8 ounces uncooked spaghetti	2 tablespoons butter or margarine
2 tablespoons butter or margarine	1 cup chicken stock
1 clove of garlic, minced	3 tablespoons white wine
2 tablespoons olive oil	1 8-ounce can tuna, drained
	Salt and pepper to taste

Cook spaghetti using package directions; drain. Toss with 2 tablespoons butter. Sauté garlic in olive oil and remaining 2 tablespoons butter. Add chicken stock, wine and tuna. Bring to a boil. Simmer for several minutes. Stir into hot spaghetti. Season with salt and pepper. Serve with tossed salad and garlic bread. Yield: 4 servings.

Laura Hunter, Psi
Petitcodiac, New Brunswick, Canada

MICROWAVE TUNA-PASTA BAKE

6 uncooked lasagna noodles	1½ cups shredded mozzarella cheese
½ cup chopped onion	1 cup cottage cheese
1 tablespoon vegetable oil	¼ cup grated Parmesan cheese
¼ cup all-purpose flour	1 egg
2 cups frozen vegetables	1 12-ounce can tuna, drained
1 cup milk	
⅓ cup lemon juice	

Place noodles and water to cover in 7-by-12-inch glass dish. Combine onion, oil and flour in glass bowl; mix well. Microwave on High for 1 minute. Stir in vegetables and milk. Microwave for 4 minutes longer, stirring once. Add lemon juice; mix well. Mix cheeses, egg and tuna in bowl. Drain noodles. Layer vegetable mixture and tuna mixture over noodles. Microwave on High for 15 minutes. Yield: 9 servings.

Karen Werner, Beta Upsilon
Dalhart, Texas

STUFFED SHELLS NEAPOLITAN

Our family can seldom get together for Thanksgiving, so my three sisters and I mail recipes to each other and prepare them on Thanksgiving Day. In a way, we are all together.

1 10-ounce can cream of celery soup	½ cup chopped drained canned tomatoes
½ teaspoon lemon juice	1 7-ounce can tuna, drained, flaked
¼ teaspoon crushed oregano	24 jumbo macaroni shells, cooked, drained
1 10-ounce package frozen chopped broccoli, cooked, drained	½ cup shredded Cheddar cheese
	Parsley

Preheat oven to 400 degrees. Mix first 6 ingredients in bowl. Spoon ¼ cup mixture into each macaroni shell. Arrange in 6-by-10-inch baking dish. Bake for 20 minutes or until heated through. Sprinkle with cheese. Bake for 5 minutes longer or until cheese is melted. Garnish with parsley. Yield: 12 servings.

Janet Webster, Xi Theta
Pocatello, Idaho

HOMESTYLE TUNA POTPIE

1 package refrigerator all-ready pie pastries	1 10-ounce package frozen peas and carrots, thawed
1 12-ounce can tuna, drained	⅓ cup milk
½ cup chopped onion	½ teaspoon poultry seasoning or thyme to taste
1 10-ounce can cream of potato soup, cream of mushroom soup or onion soup	Salt and pepper to taste

Preheat oven to 375 degrees. Fit 1 pastry into 9-inch pie plate. Combine tuna, onion, soup, peas and carrots, milk, poultry seasoning, salt and pepper in bowl; mix well. Spoon into prepared pie plate. Top with second pastry, sealing and fluting edge and cutting vents. Bake for 45 to 50 minutes or until golden brown. Yield: 6 servings.

Pearl L. Clarke, Preceptor Beta Lambda
Grand Rapids, Michigan

TUNA AND POTATO PIE

2 cups shredded potatoes	1 6-ounce can water-pack tuna, drained
½ cup shredded Cheddar cheese	1 cup shredded Cheddar cheese
1 4-ounce can mushroom stems and pieces, drained	½ cup frozen peas, thawed
8 egg whites	¼ cup chopped onion
	½ cup milk

Preheat oven to 375 degrees. Cook potatoes in water to cover in saucepan for 3 minutes; drain. Mix cooled potatoes and ½ cup cheese in bowl. Press onto bottom and up side of greased 9-inch pie plate. Combine mushrooms, egg whites, tuna, remaining 1 cup cheese, peas, onion and milk in bowl; mix well. Spoon into prepared pie plate. Bake for 45 minutes or until set. Yield: 4 to 6 servings.

Susan Hershey, Xi Theta
Dover, Delaware

CHEESY TUNA-NOODLE DISH

12 ounces wide egg noodles	2 tablespoons butter or margarine
1 10-ounce can cream of mushroom soup	¼ cup milk
1 6-ounce can tuna, drained and flaked	¾ cup chopped Velveeta cheese

Cook noodles using package directions; drain. Combine soup, tuna, butter, milk and cheese in skillet. Cook until butter and cheese melt, stirring constantly. Add noodles; mix well. Yield: 6 servings.

Tammy Lynn-Storie Parker, Gamma Theta
Lansing, Michigan

TUNAMATO DINNER

1 package macaroni and
  cheese dinner
2 tablespoons minced
  onion
2 tablespoons margarine
1 7-ounce can tuna,
  drained, flaked

1 10-ounce can
  tomatoes, drained,
  chopped
2 tablespoons chopped
  parsley
1/4 teaspoon salt

Prepare macaroni and cheese using package directions. Sauté onion in margarine in saucepan until tender. Add macaroni and cheese, tuna, tomatoes, parsley and salt; mix well. Cook over low heat for 10 minutes, stirring occasionally. Yield: 4 servings.

Don Freed, Preceptor Beta Zeta
Claremore, Oklahoma

TUNA-SHRIMP CASSEROLE

1 10-ounce can cream
  of mushroom soup
1/3 cup mayonnaise
1/3 cup milk
1 6-ounce can shrimp
1 7-ounce can tuna
1 5-ounce can sliced
  water chestnuts

1 cup chopped celery
2 tablespoons chopped
  parsley
2 teaspoons grated
  onion
2 cups cooked macaroni
Paprika to taste

Preheat oven to 350 degrees. Mix soup, mayonnaise and milk in 1/2-quart casserole. Add shrimp, tuna, water chestnuts, celery, parsley, onion and macaroni; mix well. Sprinkle with paprika. Bake for 30 minutes or until heated through. Yield: 4 to 6 servings.

Diana Dorsey, Preceptor Gamma Rho
Carlsbad, California

TUNA BURGERS

These tuna burgers are a quick and easy lunch that children love.

1 7-ounce can tuna,
  drained
2 tablespoons
  mayonnaise
1 teaspoon mustard

1 tablespoon relish
1/2 teaspoon minced
  onion
4 hamburger buns, split
4 slices American cheese

Preheat broiler. Combine tuna, mayonnaise, mustard, relish and onion in bowl; mix well. Spread over bottom halves of buns. Add cheese slices. Place on broiler pan. Broil until cheese is melted. Place bun tops on melted cheese. Yield: 4 servings.

Anne-Marie Landry, Alpha Zeta
Halifax, Nova Scotia, Canada

TUNA SANDWICH SPREAD

1 6-ounce can tuna,
  drained, flaked
2 tablespoons chopped
  onion
2 tablespoons sweet
  pickle relish
1 cup cheese, cut into
  small pieces

3 hard-cooked eggs,
  chopped
2 tablespoons chopped
  green bell pepper
1/2 cup mayonnaise-
  type salad dressing
8 hamburger buns

Preheat oven to 200 degrees. Combine tuna, onion, relish, cheese, eggs, green pepper and salad dressing in bowl; mix well. Spread over bottom halves of buns. Replace tops of buns. Wrap in foil; place on baking sheet. Bake for 30 minutes or until heated through. Yield: 8 servings.

Janet Halm, Laureate Nu
Mesa, Arizona

COLOSSAL CLAM SAUCE

This is one of my husband's favorites. I like it, too; it's quick and easy and makes great leftovers!

1 onion, chopped
4 stalks celery, chopped
2 tablespoons butter or
  margarine
1 chicken bouillon cube
1 cup water
2 6-ounce cans
  chopped clams
2 10-ounce cans cream
  of mushroom soup

1/2 teaspoon marjoram
1/2 teaspoon crushed
  rosemary
1/4 teaspoon garlic
  powder
1/4 teaspoon pepper
1/2 cup Parmesan cheese
Spaghetti, linguine or
  spinach noodles

Sauté onion and celery in butter in skillet. Add bouillon cube and water. Bring to a simmer. Stir in clams, soup, seasonings and cheese. Cook until heated through. May add a small amount of milk for desired consistency. Serve over spaghetti, linguine or spinach noodles. Yield: 4 to 6 servings.

Betty J. Sieckman, Xi Nu
Billings, Montana

QUICK CLAM LINGUINE

2 7-ounce cans minced
  clams
3 tablespoons olive oil
2 large cloves of garlic,
  minced
2 teaspoons oregano

1 1-pound package
  linguine, cooked,
  drained
Parmesan cheese to
  taste

Drain clams, reserving liquid. Heat olive oil in skillet. Add garlic. Sauté lightly. Stir in clams and oregano. Simmer for several minutes. Stir in reserved liquid. Simmer for 8 minutes. Combine linguine and clam mixture in large bowl; toss. Sprinkle with cheese. Yield: 8 servings.

Sue Hartranft, Xi Eta Theta
Jersey Shore, Pennsylvania

LINGUINE WITH WHITE CLAM SAUCE

Whenever we order this dish in a restaurant, my husband always thinks mine is better. It has become a regular dish in our home.

2 7-ounce cans chopped clams	1 tablespoon low-fat yogurt
2 tablespoons olive oil	8 ounces linguine, cooked, drained
2 cloves of garlic, minced	1 tablespoon butter or margarine
Oregano to taste	Grated Parmesan cheese
1 tablespoon chopped fresh parsley	
2 tablespoons lemon juice	

Drain clams, reserving liquid. Heat olive oil in skillet. Add garlic. Sauté for 1 minute. Add clams, oregano and parsley. Sauté for 1 minute longer. Stir in lemon juice and reserved liquid. Simmer for 1 to 2 minutes. Stir in yogurt. Remove from heat. Toss linguine with butter. Top with clam sauce and cheese. Yield: 2 servings.

Susan J. Andrus, Alpha
Coeur d'Alene, Idaho

LINGUINE WITH RED CLAM SAUCE

With a crisp green salad, a loaf of crusty bread, a bottle of red wine and a candle, this recipe makes for a very romantic evening.

2 6-ounce cans minced clams, drained	2 large bay leaves
2 15-ounce cans tomato sauce with tomato bits, celery, onion and green pepper	Oregano to taste
	Garlic chips to taste
	8 ounces linguine, cooked, drained

Combine clams and tomato sauce in 3-quart saucepan; mix well. Add bay leaves. Sprinkle liberally with oregano and garlic chips; mix well. Simmer over medium-low heat for 20 to 25 minutes or until heated through, stirring occasionally. Remove bay leaves. Spoon over linguine. Yield: 2 servings.

Rhonda Simmons-Miles, Beta Kappa
Ermine, Kentucky

CRAB MEAT CHARENTE

6 to 8 green onions, chopped	1 pound lump crab meat
1 green bell pepper, chopped	Salt and pepper to taste
	1 teaspoon tarragon
1/2 red bell pepper, chopped	1/4 cup chopped parsley
	1/3 cup cognac or brandy
1/2 cup butter or margarine	Hot cooked rice

Sauté green onions and peppers in butter in 8-inch skillet until tender. Add crab meat, salt, pepper and tarragon. Cook until heated through. Stir in parsley. Heat cognac and ignite; pour over crab meat. Spoon over hot cooked rice. Yield: 4 servings.

Dorothy Coghlan, Preceptor Gamma Chi
Irvine, California

CRAB MEAT GOODIES

1/2 cup margarine, softened	6 ounces Old English cheese spread, softened
1 1/2 teaspoons mayonnaise	6 ounces frozen crab meat, thawed
1/2 teaspoon garlic powder	6 English muffins, split into halves
1/2 teaspoon seasoned salt	

Preheat broiler. Combine margarine, mayonnaise, garlic powder, seasoned salt, cheese spread and crab meat in bowl; mix well. Spread over muffin halves. Place on broiler pan. Broil until brown. Yield: 6 servings.

Sandra Cox, Alpha Zeta
Brownwood, Texas

❖ FETTUCINI ALFREDO

2 cups butter, softened	1 12-ounce package fettucini, cooked, drained
2 cups whipping cream	
2 cups Parmesan cheese	
6 to 8 ounces crab meat	

Combine butter, whipping cream and cheese in bowl; mix well. Warm crab meat in skillet. Combine cheese mixture, crab meat and hot pasta in large bowl; toss well. Place on warmed serving plate. Do not substitute margarine for butter in this recipe. Yield: 4 servings.

Shelly Price, Zeta Phi
Bryan, Ohio

RAINBOW DELIGHT

3 tablespoons olive oil	1 cup 2-inch carrot strips
1 tablespoon minced garlic	1 zucchini, cut into 2-inch pieces
1 onion, cut into rings	1 small red pepper, cut into 1/2-inch strips
1 tablespoon minced fresh coriander	8 ounces crab meat, cut into 2-inch pieces
2 serrano peppers, minced	Salt to taste
1 cup broccoli flowerets	

Heat oil in skillet. Add garlic and onion. Sauté just until heated through. Add coriander, serrano peppers, broccoli, carrots, zucchini and red pepper. Sauté for 5 to 6 minutes or until coated. Add crab meat; reduce temperature. Cook, covered, until vegetables are tender-crisp, stirring several times. Season with salt. Yield: 4 servings.

Mary Camacho, Preceptor Nu
Waukesha, Wisconsin

CRAWFISH FETTUCINI

1 small onion,
chopped
1/2 cup margarine
1 small jar jalapeño
pepper Cheez Whiz
1   10-ounce can cream
of mushroom soup

1   1-pound package
crawfish tails
1 package spiral
noodles, cooked,
drained
8 ounces Cheddar
cheese, shredded

Preheat oven to 350 degrees. Sauté onion in margarine in skillet. Add Cheez Whiz. Cook until cheese is slightly melted. Stir in soup. Add crawfish tails and noodles; mix well. Top with cheese. Bake for 10 minutes. Yield: 4 servings.

Tracey Yarborough, Omega
Baton Rouge, Louisiana

GRILLED OYSTERS

1 cup all-purpose flour
2 tablespoons Old Bay
seafood seasoning
1 pint oysters, drained

1 tablespoon minced
garlic
1 cup butter or
margarine

Mix flour and seafood seasoning in plastic bag. Add oysters; shake until well coated. Combine garlic and butter in glass dish. Microwave for 1 minute or until butter melts. Coat griddle or large cast-iron skillet with additional butter. Add oysters in single layer; drizzle garlic butter over oysters. Cook over medium heat for 5 minutes per side or until oysters are golden brown, continuing to drizzle garlic butter over oysters. Serve warm with red sauce. Yield: 3 to 4 servings.

Karen Nightingale, Xi Tau Omicron
Galveston, Texas

OYSTERS BROCHETTE

12 slices bacon
12 fresh oysters, drained

4 to 6 slices toast or
English muffins

Preheat oven to 350 degrees. Wrap 1 slice bacon around each oyster, securing with wooden pick. Place in baking pan. Bake for 15 minutes or until bacon is cooked through. Serve on toast or English muffins. Yield: 4 to 6 servings.

Karen K. Loyd, Eta Rho
Covington, Louisiana

BACON-WRAPPED SCALLOPS

24 large sea scallops
12 slices bacon, cut into
halves

Lemon pepper to
taste

Preheat broiler. Rinse scallops; pat dry. Wrap each scallop with 1 piece bacon; secure with wooden pick. Place in baking pan. Sprinkle with lemon pepper. Broil for 8 minutes or until bacon is cooked through. Yield: 4 to 6 servings.

Dawn Ford, Xi Alpha Theta
Kennedyville, Maryland

LOW-CALORIE SCALLOPS AND PASTA

8 ounces scallops
8 ounces mushrooms,
sliced
1 small onion,
chopped
1/2 cup chopped red or
green bell pepper
1 tablespoon butter or
margarine

1 tablespoon vegetable
oil
1/8 teaspoon each
nutmeg, salt and pepper
1 cup plain yogurt
1/4 cup grated Parmesan
cheese
8 ounces spaghetti,
cooked, drained

Sauté scallops, mushrooms, onion and bell pepper in butter and oil in skillet for 5 minutes or until scallops are cooked through and vegetables are tender. Stir in nutmeg, salt, pepper, yogurt and cheese. Spoon over spaghetti. Yield: 2 to 4 servings.

Eileen Sastre, Xi Delta Gamma
Milledgeville, Georgia

BARBECUED SHRIMP

1/2 cup melted butter
or margarine
1/2 cup vegetable oil
2 teaspoons garlic
4 bay leaves
2 teaspoons rosemary
1/2 teaspoon basil
1/2 teaspoon oregano

1/2 teaspoon salt
1/2 teaspoon cayenne
pepper
3/4 teaspoon black
pepper
1 teaspoon lemon pepper
1 tablespoon paprika
2 pounds shrimp

Combine butter, oil, garlic, bay leaves and spices in saucepan. Bring to a boil, stirring constantly. Let stand for 15 minutes. Preheat oven to 450 degrees. Remove bay leaves from sauce. Stir in shrimp. Cook for 5 minutes longer or until shrimp turn pink. Spoon into casserole. Bake for 10 minutes. Yield: 6 servings.

Evelyn Ogilvie, Xi Beta Epsilon
Clanton, Alabama

CURRIED SHRIMP

2 tablespoons chopped
onion
1 tablespoon butter or
margarine
1 to 1 1/2 teaspoons
curry powder
1   10-ounce can cream
of celery soup

3/4 pound cooked shrimp
1/3 cup sour cream
1 apple, peeled, chopped
3 cups cooked minute
rice
2 tablespoons chopped
parsley

Sauté onion in butter in saucepan until transparent. Stir in curry powder, soup and shrimp. Cook until bubbly. Reduce heat. Add sour cream and apple; mix well. Cook until heated through; do not boil. Pour over hot cooked rice. Garnish with parsley. Serve with chutney. Yield: 4 servings.

Patti Ann Zaharis, Xi Alpha
Beaconsfield, Quebec, Canada

DAD'S SPICY SHRIMP

1 teaspoon black pepper	1 tablespoon
1/2 teaspoon salt	Worcestershire sauce
1/2 teaspoon crushed red pepper	1/2 cup unsalted butter or margarine
1/2 teaspoon thyme	1 pound shrimp, heads and shells intact
1/2 teaspoon rosemary	1/4 cup beer
1/8 teaspoon oregano	Cuban bread
1/8 teaspoon red cayenne pepper	
1 1/2 teaspoons minced fresh garlic	

Combine black pepper, salt, red pepper, thyme, rosemary, oregano, cayenne pepper, garlic, Worcestershire sauce and butter in large skillet. Cook over high heat until butter is melted. Add shrimp. Shake skillet for 2 minutes. Stir in beer. Shake skillet for 3 minutes longer or until shrimp turn pink. Pour into shallow serving dish. Serve immediately with Cuban bread for dipping. Yield: 4 servings.

Joan Hickman, Epsilon Epsilon
Brooksville, Florida

EASY SHRIMP AND CHILI BEAN STEW

One of my best friends was moving away. She stayed with me the night before she left, and this was the dinner I served. I still hear from her, but I have not seen her since then.

1 12-ounce package frozen shrimp, thawed	1/2 cup water
1 onion, chopped	1 tablespoon chopped fresh basil
1 or 2 cloves of garlic, minced	1 stalk celery, sliced diagonally
1 tablespoon olive oil	1 green bell pepper, cut into 1/2-inch pieces
1 28-ounce can tomatoes, chopped	1 15-ounce can spicy or extra spicy chili beans
1/2 cup uncooked orzo or very small pasta	

Cook shrimp using package directions; drain. Sauté onion and garlic in oil in heavy skillet until tender but not brown. Add undrained tomatoes, orzo, water, basil, celery, and green pepper; mix well. Bring to a boil; reduce heat. Simmer for 30 minutes or until orzo is tender, stirring occasionally. Stir in undrained beans and shrimp. Cook for 5 minutes longer or until heated through. Yield: 6 servings.

Eithel P. Sech, Laureate Alpha Iota
Ann Arbor, Michigan

Helen Ables, Beta Alpha, Mt. Vernon, Ohio, makes Crab Burgers by mixing 6 ounces canned crab meat, 1/4 cup chopped celery, 2 tablespoons chopped onion and 1/2 cup each shredded sharp Cheddar cheese and mayonnaise. Spread on buttered split buns. Broil until brown.

FIVE-MINUTE SHRIMP DINNER

1 package quick-cooking long grain and wild rice with seasoning packet	1 pound large shrimp, shelled, deveined
2 cups water	2 cloves of garlic, minced
2 tablespoons butter or margarine	1/4 teaspoon salt
2 cups diagonally sliced asparagus	1 tablespoon lemon juice
2 tablespoons butter or margarine	1/2 teaspoon grated lemon rind
	2 tablespoons shredded carrot (optional)

Combine first 3 ingredients in saucepan; mix well. Bring to a boil. Stir in asparagus. Reduce heat. Simmer, covered, for 5 minutes or until all water is absorbed. Melt 2 tablespoons butter in 10-inch skillet over medium-high heat. Stir in shrimp, garlic and salt. Stir-fry for 2 to 3 minutes or until shrimp are pink. Stir in lemon juice. Stir lemon rind into rice; sprinkle with carrot. Spoon rice onto serving plate; spoon shrimp beside rice. Yield: 4 servings.

Mary Barnett
Austin, Texas

GRILLED LEMON PRAWNS

1/2 cup lemon juice	2 teaspoons grated lemon rind
1/2 cup vegetable oil	1/4 teaspoon cayenne pepper
1 tablespoon finely chopped parsley	Black pepper to taste
2 cloves of garlic, minced	24 large prawns, peeled, deveined
2 teaspoons dry mustard	

Preheat grill. Mix first 8 ingredients in bowl. Pour into large plastic bag. Add prawns. Marinate, tightly sealed, in refrigerator for 30 minutes to 4 hours. Remove prawns from bag, reserving marinade. Thread prawns onto skewers. Grill over medium-hot coals for 2 minutes per side or until shrimp turn pink, brushing often with reserved marinade. Yield: 4 servings.

Catherine Mazur, Xi Beta Sigma
Williams Lake, British Columbia, Canada

MING SHRIMP FRIED RICE

4 ounces bacon	2 onions, minced
2 tablespoons vegetable oil	8 ounces shrimp
1 clove of garlic, minced	1 1/2 cups cooked rice
1/2 cup chopped green bell pepper	1 egg, beaten
	2 tablespoons soy sauce

Brown bacon in oil in skillet. Stir in garlic, green pepper and onions. Cook for 2 minutes longer. Add shrimp. Cook until shrimp turn pink. Add rice, egg and soy sauce; mix well. Yield: 3 to 4 servings.

Karen Perrotti, Laureate Delta Psi
Scranton, Pennsylvania

MARDI GRAS SHRIMP

1 teaspoon Tabasco
  sauce
1 teaspoon black pepper
1/2 teaspoon crushed red
  pepper
1/2 teaspoon each dried
  thyme and rosemary
1/8 teaspoon dried
  oregano
1/4 cup butter or
  margarine

1 to 2 cloves of garlic,
  minced
1 teaspoon
  Worcestershire sauce
1 pound small shrimp,
  peeled
1/2 cup chicken bouillon
1/4 cup beer
4 servings cooked rice

Mix Tabasco sauce and spices in small bowl. Combine with next 3 ingredients in large skillet. Cook over high heat until butter is melted. Stir in shrimp. Cook for 2 minutes, stirring and turning shrimp constantly. Add bouillon. Cook for 2 minutes longer. Stir in beer. Cook for 1 minute longer. Serve over hot cooked rice. Yield: 4 servings.

Martha Collins, Xi Upsilon Delta
Mt. Pleasant, Texas

PEPPERED SHRIMP

3 cups butter or
  margarine
1/4 cup cracked black
  pepper
1/4 cup lemon juice
6 cloves of garlic,
  minced
1 teaspoon salt

1/4 teaspoon ground
  nutmeg
1 tablespoon paprika
1/2 teaspoon basil
1/2 teaspoon oregano
1/2 to 3/4 teaspoon red
  pepper flakes
6 pounds shrimp, peeled

Melt butter in skillet. Add black pepper, lemon juice, garlic, salt, nutmeg, paprika, basil, oregano and red pepper; mix well. Stir in shrimp. Cook for 5 minutes or until shrimp turn pink. Serve with potatoes, noodles or garlic bread. Yield: 12 to 20 servings.

Deborah Blaz, Xi Delta Xi
Angola, Indiana

PRAWNS WITH FETA CHEESE AND WINE

2 tablespoons olive
  oil
2 cloves of garlic,
  minced
1/4 cup chopped leeks
1/4 cup chopped fresh
  basil
1/4 cup chopped celery
  leaves and stems

1/4 cup chopped green
  onions
1 pound large prawns
16 to 20 mushroom caps
1 cup chopped tomatoes
1/2 cup white wine
Salt and pepper to taste
1/4 cup crumbled feta
  cheese

Heat oil in large skillet. Add garlic, leeks, basil, celery and green onions. Sauté for 3 minutes. Stir in prawns and mushrooms. Sauté for 3 minutes longer. Stir in tomatoes, wine, salt and pepper. Add cheese. Cook for 1 minute, stirring constantly. Yield: 4 servings.

Frances Nixon, Xi Zeta Gamma
Kincardine, Ontario, Canada

SHRIMP BOILED IN BEER

2 12-ounce cans beer
1 clove of garlic, peeled
1 teaspoon dried
  thyme
2 bay leaves
2 tablespoons celery
  seed
2 tablespoons parsley

1/2 teaspoon Tabasco
  sauce
Juice of 1/2 lemon
3 pounds fresh jumbo
  shrimp, deveined
Melted butter or
  cocktail sauce

Combine beer, garlic, thyme, bay leaves, celery seed, parsley, Tabasco sauce and lemon juice in large saucepan; mix well. Bring to a boil. Stir in shrimp. Return to a boil; reduce heat. Simmer for 2 to 5 minutes or until shrimp turn pink. Remove shrimp. Serve hot with melted butter or cocktail sauce. Yield: 8 to 10 servings.

Jan Bierschbach, Beta Omega
Mobridge, South Dakota

SHRIMP DESTIN

1/4 cup chopped green
  onions
2 teaspoons minced
  garlic
1 cup melted butter or
  margarine
2 pounds large shrimp,
  peeled, deveined
1 teaspoon lemon juice
1 tablespoon white wine

1/2 teaspoon salt
Coarsely ground black
  pepper to taste
1 teaspoon dried whole
  dillweed
1 teaspoon chopped
  fresh parsley
3 French rolls, split
  lengthwise, toasted

Sauté green onions and garlic in butter in skillet until onions are tender. Stir in shrimp, lemon juice, wine, salt and pepper. Cook over medium heat for 5 minutes, stirring occasionally. Stir in dillweed and parsley. Spoon over toasted rolls. Serve immediately. Yield: 6 servings.

JoAnn J. Kresky, Preceptor Chi
Lansing, Michigan

SCAMPI-STYLE SHRIMP

1 pound shrimp, shelled
6 tablespoons butter or
  margarine
1 tablespoon chopped
  green onions
1 tablespoon olive oil
4 cloves of garlic,
  minced

1 tablespoon lemon juice
1/4 teaspoon salt
2 tablespoons minced
  parsley
1/4 teaspoon grated
  lemon rind (optional)
Tabasco sauce to taste
Lemon wedges

Rinse shrimp; pat dry. Melt butter in large skillet over medium heat. Stir in next 5 ingredients. Bring to a boil. Stir in shrimp. Cook for 5 minutes or until shrimp turn pink, stirring occasionally. Stir in parsley, lemon rind and Tabasco sauce. Spoon into serving dish. Garnish with lemon wedges. Yield: 6 servings.

Linda A. Chullino, Pi Chi
Harlingen, Texas

SHRIMP ÉTOUFFÉE

This is my father-in-law's recipe; he knows how I love any kind of shrimp. We always share this dish.

2 pounds shrimp, peeled, boiled	1/4 teaspoon garlic salt
Salt, black pepper and red pepper to taste	1 10-ounce can cream of mushroom soup
1/2 cup margarine	1 10-ounce can cream of celery soup
1 cup chopped onion	1 10-ounce can tomato soup
1/2 cup chopped green bell pepper	Hot cooked rice

Season shrimp with salt, black pepper and red pepper. Melt margarine in nonstick 10-inch skillet. Add onion, green pepper and garlic salt. Cook over low heat until onion is wilted. Stir in shrimp. Simmer for 20 minutes. Add soups; mix well. Cook for 1 minute longer. Serve over hot cooked rice. Yield: 6 servings.

Denise Jones Shadoin, Eta Omicron
Ruston, Louisiana

SCAMPI PRIMAVERA

1 10-ounce package spaghetti	1 1/2 pounds medium shrimp, peeled, deveined
3/4 cup olive oil	2 tablespoons lemon juice
3 large cloves of garlic, minced	3/4 teaspoon salt
1/2 teaspoon finely chopped lemon rind	1/8 teaspoon black pepper
2 carrots, julienned	2 teaspoons dried parsley
1 zucchini, julienned	2 teaspoons dried basil
1 red pepper, julienned	

Cook spaghetti using package directions; drain. Heat oil in large skillet. Add garlic and lemon rind. Cook for 30 seconds, stirring constantly. Add carrots, zucchini, red pepper and shrimp; mix well. Cook over medium heat for 3 to 4 minutes or until shrimp turn pink, stirring frequently. Sprinkle with lemon juice, salt and black pepper. Stir in parsley and basil. Spoon over spaghetti; toss well. Yield: 8 servings.

Verlene Williams, Xi Iota Alpha
Lubbock, Texas

SHRIMP IN GREEN SAUCE

1/2 cup chopped onion	1 tablespoon soy sauce
1/4 cup melted butter or margarine	1/2 cup stuffed olives
2 tablespoons all-purpose flour	8 to 12 ounces cooked shrimp
1 cup chicken broth	1 cup sliced mushrooms (optional)
1/2 cup white wine	Hot cooked rice
1/2 cup chopped parsley	

Sauté onion in butter in skillet until tender. Add flour, chicken broth, wine, parsley, soy sauce and olives; mix well. Stir in shrimp and mushrooms.

Cook until heated through. Serve over hot cooked rice. Yield: 3 to 4 servings.

Bobby Erdrich, Laureate Alpha Lambda
Grants Pass, Oregon

SHRIMP AND RICE WITH SALSA

1 family-size boil-in-bag rice	1/3 cup picante sauce or salsa
1 small onion, coarsely chopped	1 tablespoon lime juice
1 small green bell pepper, coarsely chopped	1 pound medium shrimp, peeled, deveined
1 8-ounce can tomato sauce	1/4 cup coarsely chopped cilantro (optional)

Cook rice using package directions. Combine onion and green pepper in large skillet sprayed with non-stick cooking spary. Cook for 2 minutes, stirring frequently. Stir in tomato sauce, picante sauce and lime juice. Bring to a boil. Simmer for 10 minutes. Stir in shrimp. Cook, covered, for 5 minutes or until shrimp are cooked through. Spoon over hot cooked rice. Sprinkle with cilantro. Yield: 4 servings.

Sally Burns, Xi Gamma Pi
Shawnee, Kansas

SEAFOOD AU GRATIN

This recipe has become a family favorite since we ate a similar dish in a seafood restaurant while vacationing in the Pacific Northwest. I created it using our combined memories of the ingredients.

6 tablespoons margarine	8 ounces fresh sea scallops, cut into halves
1/2 cup all-purpose flour	
2 cups milk	1 teaspoon thyme
8 ounces shredded Cheddar cheese	1 teaspoon parsley flakes
6 ounces Monterey Jack cheese, cubed	1/2 teaspoon dry mustard
1 12-ounce package frozen salad shrimp, thawed, drained	1/2 teaspoon garlic salt
	Salt and pepper to taste
1 6-ounce can crab meat, drained	Parmesan cheese to taste

Preheat broiler. Melt margarine in 6-quart saucepan. Stir in flour and milk. Cook until smooth and thickened, stirring frequently. Add Cheddar and Monterey Jack cheeses. Cook until melted, stirring constantly. Add shrimp, crab meat and scallops gradually. Stir in seasonings. Cook for 10 to 15 minutes or until heated through, stirring frequently. Spoon into individual shells or baking dishes. Sprinkle with Parmesan cheese. Broil for 3 to 5 minutes or until bubbly. Yield: 6 to 8 servings.

Beverly Duffer, Preceptor Alpha Kappa
Indianapolis, Indiana

Quick Cookies & Candies

One of the things we all like to do for family
and friends is shower them with treats. But as
hard as it is to set aside time to cook for
survival, we tend to cut back on scrumptious
extras when every minute counts. Even if
you're short on time, though, there's no reason
for the cookie jar to go empty, or the candy dish
to go unfilled. What's your passion? Chocolate,
butterscotch, marshmallow, lemon, almond,
coconut? Do you long for brownies, fudge,
divinity, caramel corn, bonbons, toffee,
old-fashioned sugar cookies? Well, we've got
you covered (in cinnamon, confectioners' sugar,
whipped topping and ground nuts) on all of
these. Many of these recipes make great holiday
treats or gifts for lucky friends. But even if
there's no particularly noteworthy occasion
coming up, you'll find the stuff of
celebrations—the quick way—
in the recipes that follow.

BOURBON BALLS

3 cups finely crushed
  vanilla wafers
1 cup finely chopped
  walnuts
1/3 cup bourbon or rum

1 14-ounce can
  sweetened condensed
  milk
Confectioners' sugar
Colored sprinkles

Mix vanilla wafer crumbs and walnuts in bowl. Add bourbon and condensed milk; mix well. Chill in refrigerator. Shape by teaspoonfuls into small balls with hands dusted with confectioners' sugar. Roll in additional confectioners' sugar or sprinkles. Store, covered, in refrigerator. Yield: 4 dozen.

Karen Milburn, Xi Sigma Delta
Spring, Texas

FRENCH BUTTER COOKIES

1/2 cup butter or
  margarine, cut into
  6 pieces
1 cup all-purpose flour

1/2 cup sugar
1 egg yolk
1 teaspoon vanilla
  extract

Preheat oven to 350 degrees. Combine butter, flour and sugar in food processor container. Process with steel blade for 15 seconds or until crumbly. Mix egg yolk and vanilla in small bowl. Add to food processor, processing constantly for 2 minutes or until mixture forms ball. Shape into log 2 inches in diameter and 5 inches long on waxed paper. Chill in refrigerator. Cut into halves lengthwise. Cut into 1/8-inch slices. Place 3/4 inch apart on nonstick cookie sheet. Bake for 8 minutes. Remove to wire rack to cool. Yield: 2 2/3 dozen.

Kay Chapman, Xi
Brandon, Mississippi

BUTTERSCOTCH-CHOCOLATE CHIP CHEWIES

2 cups baking mix
1 3/4 cups packed light
  brown sugar
2 eggs

2 tablespoons water
1 cup semisweet
  chocolate chips
1 cup chopped pecans

Preheat oven to 350 degrees. Combine baking mix, brown sugar, eggs and water in bowl; mix well. Stir in chocolate chips and pecans. Spread in greased 9-by-13-inch baking pan. Bake for 25 to 30 minutes or until golden brown. Cool on wire rack. Cut into squares. Yield: 3 dozen.

Diana Linville, Xi Gamma Tau
Kingston, Tennessee

Cynthia L. Thomas, Alpha Tau, Orono, Maine, makes Rocky Road Clusters by adding 16 chopped large marshmallows, 3/4 cup seedless raisins and 1 1/2 cups chopped walnuts or pecans to 2 cups semisweet melted chocolate chips. Drop onto waxed paper.

BUTTERSCOTCH-OAT SQUARES

This is the perfect quick recipe. I started making it less than 30 minutes before a sorority meeting and wasn't even late.

1 cup packed light
  brown sugar
1 teaspoon baking
  powder
2 cups oats

1/2 cup melted butter or
  margarine
1/2 teaspoon vanilla
  extract

Preheat oven to 375 degrees. Combine all ingredients in bowl; mix well. Press into ungreased 8-by-8-inch baking pan. Bake for 10 minutes. Cool slightly. Cut into squares. Yield: 1 1/4 dozen.

Lonnie Lang, Iota
Nelson, British Columbia, Canada

ALMOND BROWNIES

2 cups sugar
4 eggs
1 cup melted light
  margarine
1 teaspoon salt
1 teaspoon almond
  extract
1 1/2 cups all-purpose
  flour
1/2 cup light cream
  cheese, softened

1/2 cup light margarine,
  softened
2 teaspoons water
1/2 teaspoon vanilla
  extract
1/2 teaspoon almond
  extract
2 cups confectioners'
  sugar
Slivered almonds

Preheat oven to 350 degrees. Combine sugar, eggs, 1 cup margarine, salt and 1 teaspoon almond extract in mixer bowl; mix until smooth. Mix in flour. Spread in greased 9-by-13-inch baking dish. Bake for 28 minutes; do not overbake. Blend cream cheese, 1/2 cup margarine, water, vanilla and 1/2 teaspoon almond extract in mixer bowl. Add confectioners' sugar; mix well. Spread over baked layer. Top with almonds. Cut into squares. Yield: 3 dozen.

Vickie Zang
Rifle, Colorado

❖ BROWNIE BITES

1 15-ounce package
  brownie mix
1/3 cup hot water
1/4 cup vegetable oil

1 egg
48 miniature peanut
  butter cups or caramel
  cups

Preheat oven to 350 degrees. Combine brownie mix, water, oil and egg in mixer bowl; mix well. Fill paper-lined miniature muffin cups 1/2 full. Press 1 candy cup into batter in each cup. Bake for 15 to 20 minutes or until brownie is set. Remove to wire rack to cool. Yield: 4 dozen.

Linda Foltz, Nu Kappa
Waukee, Iowa

BUTTERMILK BROWNIES

2 cups sifted
  all-purpose flour
2 cups sugar
1/4 cup baking cocoa
1 cup cold water
1/2 cup margarine
1/2 cup corn oil
1/2 cup buttermilk
1 teaspoon baking soda

2 eggs
1 cup packed light
  brown sugar
1/4 cup milk or cream
3 tablespoons butter or
  margarine
1/2 cup semisweet
  chocolate chips

Preheat oven to 350 degrees. Sift flour, sugar and cocoa into bowl. Bring water, margarine and oil to a boil in saucepan. Pour over dry ingredients; beat until creamy. Add buttermilk, baking soda and eggs; mix well. Spoon into greased 10-by-15-inch baking pan. Bake for 18 minutes. Combine brown sugar, milk and butter in glass bowl. Microwave on High for 2 minutes. Stir in chocolate chips. Spread over brownies. Cut into squares. Yield: 4 dozen.

Sarah A. Collins, Xi Epsilon Xi
New Hampton, Iowa

MICROWAVE BROWNIES

You can mix the dry ingredients for this and store in airtight container in refrigerator.

1 cup sugar
3/4 cup all-purpose flour
1/4 teaspoon baking
  powder
3 tablespoons baking
  cocoa

1/2 cup chopped nuts
2 eggs
1/3 cup melted margarine
1/2 teaspoon vanilla
  extract

Combine ingredients in order listed in 8-by-8-inch glass dish. Microwave on Medium for 5 to 7 minutes or until firm, turning twice. Cool for 5 to 10 minutes. Cut into 2-inch squares. Yield: 1 1/4 dozen.

Rita J. White, Xi Lambda Mu
Richmondale, Ohio

TRIPLE-CHOCOLATE COFFEE BROWNIES

1 egg, beaten
1 21-ounce package
  fudge brownie mix
1/4 cup corn oil
1/4 cup strong coffee
1/4 cup water
3/4 cup milk chocolate
  chips

3/4 cup white baking
  chips
1/2 cup semisweet
  chocolate chips
1/2 cup chopped walnuts
  or pecans

Preheat oven to 350 degrees. Combine all ingredients in large mixer bowl; mix well. Spread in greased 9-by-13-inch baking pan. Bake for 30 minutes. Cool on wire rack. Cut into squares. Yield: 2 dozen.

Helen Plummer, Gamma Delta
Bridgeport, Nebraska

TURTLE BROWNIES

1 14-ounce package
  caramels
2/3 cup evaporated milk
1 2-layer package
  German chocolate cake
  mix

3/4 cup butter or
  margarine, softened
1 cup chopped nuts
2 cups chocolate chips

Preheat oven to 350 degrees. Melt caramels with 1/3 cup evaporated milk in double boiler, stirring to mix well. Combine remaining 1/3 cup evaporated milk with cake mix and butter in bowl; mix well. Stir in nuts. Press half the mixture into greased 9-by-13-inch baking pan. Bake for 6 minutes. Sprinkle with chocolate chips; spread with caramel mixture. Crumble remaining cake mix mixture over top. Bake for 15 to 18 minutes longer or until set. Cool on wire rack. Cut into bars. Yield: 3 dozen.

Kim Rozendaal, Xi Beta
Madison, Wisconsin

UNBAKED BROWNIES

1 14-ounce can
  sweetened condensed
  milk
1 12-ounce package
  vanilla wafers, finely
  crushed

1/2 cup chopped walnuts
1 ounce unsweetened
  chocolate, melted
1/2 cup semisweet
  chocolate chips,
  melted

Combine condensed milk, cookie crumbs, walnuts and melted unsweetened chocolate in mixer bowl; mix at low speed. Spread evenly in greased 9-inch round baking pan. Spread melted chocolate chips over top. Cut into wedges. Yield: 1 dozen.

Ruth Neumann, Preceptor Gamma Epsilon
De Kalb, Illinois

BEST-EVER CHOCOLATE CHIP COOKIES

These cookies are easy enough for my two boys to make while I direct from the recliner in front of the TV.

1/2 cup melted
  margarine, at
  room temperature
1 egg

1 2-layer package
  white, yellow or
  chocolate chip cake mix
Chocolate chips

Preheat oven to 350 degrees. Beat margarine with egg in bowl. Add cake mix; mix well. Stir in chocolate chips. Drop by spoonfuls onto greased cookie sheet. Bake 5 to 8 minutes or until edges are set; centers may appear soft. Remove to wire rack to cool. May bake in baking pan and cut into bars. Yield: 3 dozen.

Sue Harkreader, Preceptor Kappa
Broken Arrow, Oklahoma

CHOCOLATE CHIP CHEWIES

These were my children's favorite cookies and now they are known as "Granny's Chewies."

2/3 cup margarine, softened	1/2 teaspoon salt
1 1-pound package light brown sugar	1 teaspoon vanilla extract
3 eggs	2 cups semisweet chocolate chips
2 cups all-purpose flour	1 cup chopped nuts, (optional)
1 teaspoon baking powder	

Preheat oven to 350 degrees. Cream margarine and brown sugar in mixer bowl until light and fluffy. Blend in eggs. Add flour, baking powder, salt and vanilla; mix well. Stir in chocolate chips and nuts. Spread evenly in greased 10-by-15-inch baking pan. Bake for 20 to 25 minutes or until set. Cool on wire rack. Cut into bars. Yield: 3 dozen.

Jeanne K. Mahoney, Preceptor Laureate Alpha Zeta
Battle Creek, Michigan

CHOCOLATE CHIP-DEVIL'S FOOD COOKIES

1 2-layer package devil's food cake mix	1 cup semisweet chocolate chips
2 eggs	1 cup chopped nuts (optional)
1/2 cup vegetable oil	

Preheat oven to 350 degrees. Combine all ingredients in bowl; mix well with spoon. Drop by heaping teaspoonfuls 1 1/2 inches apart onto ungreased cookie sheet. Bake for 8 to 10 minutes or until set; do not overbake. Remove to wire rack to cool. Yield: 3 dozen.

Rebecca S. Eggleston, Xi Delta Epsilon
Covington, Virginia

CHOCOLATE CRUNCHIES

These are so easy to mix up and chill, and then they are ready to microwave and serve.

9 tablespoons margarine	2 cups all-purpose flour
6 tablespoons baking cocoa	1/4 teaspoon salt
2 eggs	1 teaspoon vanilla extract
1 cup sugar	1/2 cup chopped pecans
1 teaspoon baking powder	Confectioners' sugar

Microwave margarine in glass bowl until melted. Add next 8 ingredients; mix well. Chill for 8 hours or longer. Shape into small balls; coat with confectioners' sugar. Arrange in several batches 2 inches apart on paper plate. Microwave on Medium for 2 minutes. Cool on wire rack. Sprinkle again with confectioners' sugar. Yield: 2 1/2 dozen.

Dixie Elmes, Preceptor Beta
Westminster, Maryland

CHOCOLATE CHIP SQUARES

This recipe is popular at family gatherings, in lunch boxes and in packages sent to children at college.

2 3/4 cups finely crushed honey graham crackers	2 cups semisweet chocolate chips
1 14-ounce can sweetened condensed milk	4 ounces chopped walnuts
	1 teaspoon vanilla extract

Preheat oven to 350 degrees. Combine cracker crumbs and condensed milk in bowl; mix well. Mix in chocolate chips, walnuts and vanilla; mixture will be very stiff. Press into buttered 8- or 9-inch square baking pan. Bake in center of oven for 25 to 30 minutes or until light brown. Cut into squares. Serve warm or cool with ice cream. Yield: 2 dozen.

Carol Clark, Preceptor Alpha Gamma
Madison, Wisconsin

DOUBLE CHOCOLATE CRUMBLE BARS

1/2 cup butter or margarine	1/4 teaspoon baking powder
3/4 cup sugar	1/4 teaspoon salt
2 eggs	2 1/2 cups miniature marshmallows
1 teaspoon vanilla extract	1 cup semisweet chocolate chips
3/4 cup all-purpose flour	1 cup creamy peanut butter
1/2 cup chopped nuts	1 1/2 cups crisp rice cereal
2 tablespoons baking cocoa	

Preheat oven to 350 degrees. Cream butter and sugar in mixer bowl until light and fluffy. Beat in eggs and vanilla. Mix next 5 ingredients together. Add to creamed mixture; mix well. Spread in greased 9-by-13-inch baking pan. Bake for 15 to 20 minutes or until layer tests done. Sprinkle with marshmallows. Bake for 3 minutes longer. Cool on wire rack. Melt chocolate chips with peanut butter in small saucepan, stirring to mix well. Stir in cereal. Spread over cooled layer. Chill in refrigerator. Cut into bars. Yield: 3 to 4 dozen.

Jan Healy, Delta Lambda
Marshall, Minnesota

CHOCODILES

1/2 cup butter or margarine, softened	1/2 teaspoon salt
1/2 cup shortening	1/3 cup crunchy peanut butter
1 1/4 cups packed light brown sugar	1 cup semisweet chocolate chips
1 egg	1/2 cup crunchy peanut butter
1 teaspoon vanilla extract	1 1/2 cups lightly crushed cornflakes
2 1/2 cups all-purpose flour	

Preheat oven to 350 degrees. Cream butter, shortening and brown sugar in mixer bowl until light. Blend in egg and vanilla. Add flour, salt and 1/3 cup peanut butter; mix well. Press into ungreased 10-by-15-inch baking pan. Bake for 20 to 25 minutes or until light brown. Cool slightly. Melt chocolate chips in medium saucepan over low heat. Stir in 1/2 cup peanut butter and cornflakes. Spread over baked layer. Cut into bars. Yield: 3 dozen.

Frances Kucera, Laureate Omicron
Eugene, Oregon

SPEEDY LITTLE DEVILS

1/2 cup melted butter or margarine	*3/4 cup creamy peanut butter*
1 2-layer package cake mix	*1 7-ounce jar marshmallow creme*

Preheat oven to 350 degrees. Mix butter and cake mix in bowl. Reserve 1 1/2 cups mixture. Press remaining mixture into ungreased 9-by-13-inch baking pan. Blend peanut butter and marshmallow creme in bowl. Spread over crumb layer. Sprinkle with reserved crumbs. Bake for 20 minutes. Cool on wire rack. Cut into bars. Yield: 3 dozen.

Brenda L. Howerton, Epsilon Xi
Marshall, Missouri

CAKE MIX COOKIES

1 2-layer package any flavor cake mix	*1/2 to 1 cup semisweet chocolate chips, raisins, nuts, candied fruit, dried fruit, or coconut (optional)*
1 egg, slightly beaten	
1/3 cup milk	
1/4 cup vegetable oil	

Preheat oven to 350 degrees. Combine cake mix, egg, milk and oil in bowl; mix well. Stir in one of optional ingredients. Drop by teaspoonfuls onto greased and floured cookie sheet. Bake for 13 to 14 minutes, or until browned. Remove to wire rack to cool completely. For peanut butter cookies, add 1/2 cup peanut butter in place of oil. Yield: 3 dozen.

Sheryl Wood, Xi Zeta Sigma
Boonville, Missouri

COTTAGE CHEESE PINWHEELS

1 cup margarine	*1 to 1 1/2 cups mincemeat, jam or marmalade*
1 1/2 cups all-purpose flour	
1 cup cottage cheese	*Confectioners' sugar*

Preheat oven to 400 degrees. Cut margarine into flour in bowl. Add cottage cheese; mix well. Roll on floured surface. Cut into 3-inch squares. Spoon 1 tablespoon mincemeat, jam or marmalade onto each square. Fold corners over filling to form pinwheels; pinch to seal. Place on cookie sheet. Bake for 8 to 10 minutes or until light brown. Remove to wire rack to cool. Sprinkle with confectioners' sugar.
Yield: 1 1/2 to 2 dozen.

Laurel Lee Prentiss, Eta Xi
Sterling Heights, Michigan

CREAM CHEESE COOKIES

1/4 cup butter or margarine, softened	*1 2-layer package cherry chip cake mix*
8 ounces cream cheese, softened	*2 cups confectioners' sugar*
1 egg, beaten	*2 tablespoons margarine, softened*
1/4 teaspoon vanilla extract	*Cherry juice*

Preheat oven to 375 degrees. Cream butter and cream cheese in bowl until light and fluffy. Stir in egg and vanilla. Add cake mix gradually, stirring to blend. Chill until dough is firm. Drop by teaspoonfuls onto ungreased cookie sheet. Bake for 8 to 10 minutes or until light brown. Cool completely on cookie sheet. Frost with mixture of confectioners' sugar, margarine and cherry juice. Yield: 5 dozen.

Mary Joyce Fahey, Preceptor Epsilon Alpha
Winter Haven, Florida

DISHPAN COOKIES

4 eggs	*4 cups all-purpose flour*
2 cups packed dark brown sugar	*1 teaspoon vanilla extract*
2 cups sugar	*1/2 cup flaked coconut*
2 cups vegetable oil	*1 1/2 cups semisweet chocolate chips*
1 1/2 cups oats	
1 1/2 teaspoons baking soda	*1 cup nuts (optional)*
	4 cups cornflakes

Preheat oven to 350 degrees. Cream eggs, brown sugar, sugar and oil in large bowl until light and fluffy. Stir in remaining ingredients gradually. Drop by tablespoonfuls onto cookie sheet sprayed with nonstick vegetable cooking spray. Bake for 10 minutes or until light brown. Cool in pan for 2 minutes; remove to wire rack to cool completely.
Yield: 7 dozen.

Mary Ellen Hammontree
Saginaw, Texas

CHOCOLATE-MINT COOKIES

1 1/2 pounds chocolate almond bark	*1 12-ounce package butter crackers*
1/2 teaspoon peppermint extract	

Place chocolate almond bark in glass dish. Microwave on High for 1 to 1 1/2 minutes or until melted, stirring once. Add peppermint; stir well. Dip crackers into mixture. Place on waxed paper to cool.
Yield: 3 dozen.

Kathy Eibes, Epsilon Pi
Exline, Iowa

FUDGE LAYER BARS

6 tablespoons butter or
  margarine, softened
1 2-layer package
  yellow cake mix
1 egg, beaten
1 cup chopped pecans

1 cup semisweet
  chocolate chips
1 14-ounce can
  sweetened condensed
  milk

Preheat oven to 325 degrees. Cut butter into cake mix in bowl until crumbly. Add egg and pecans; mix well. Press into 9-by-13-inch nonstick baking pan, reserving 1 1/2 cups mixture. Combine chocolate chips and condensed milk in saucepan. Cook over low heat, stirring constantly until chocolate melts. Spread over prepared crust. Sprinkle reserved crumb mixture over top. Bake for 25 minutes. Cool; cut into bars. Yield: 2 dozen.

Debra Doyle, Xi Iota
Lafayette, Louisiana

"HELLO DOLLY" SLICE

1/4 cup butter or
  margarine
1 cup graham cracker
  crumbs
1 cup semisweet
  chocolate chips

1 cup butterscotch chips
1 cup flaked coconut
1 cup chopped walnuts
1 14-ounce can
  sweetened condensed
  milk

Preheat oven to 350 degrees. Melt butter in 7-by-10-inch baking pan. Layer crumbs, chocolate chips, butterscotch chips, coconut and walnuts in prepared pan. Pour condensed milk over top. Bake for 30 to 35 minutes. Cool in pan; cut into squares. Yield: 3 dozen.

Margery Rutherford, Laureate Alpha Upsilon
Gloucester, Ontario, Canada

QUICK JELLY ROLLS

1 unbaked pie shell
2 or 3 tablespoons any
  flavor jelly

Confectioners' sugar

Preheat oven to 400 degrees. Place pie shell on nonstick baking sheet. Spread jelly over pastry; roll up as for jelly roll. Bake for 10 to 12 minutes or until light brown. Cool. Slice and sprinkle with confectioners' sugar. Yield: 1 dozen.

Mae Hazzard, Xi
Brandon, Mississippi

LEMON CRUMB BARS

1 2-layer package
  lemon cake mix
1/4 cup vegetable
  oil
1 egg, beaten
1 14-ounce can
  sweetened condensed
  milk

1 6-ounce package lemon
  instant pudding mix
1 1/2 teaspoons lemon
  juice
1 cup sifted
  confectioners' sugar
4 to 5 teaspoons water
1/2 teaspoon lemon juice

Preheat oven to 350 degrees. Combine cake mix, oil and egg in bowl, stirring until crumbly. Press into greased 9-by-13-inch baking pan, reserving 1 1/2 cups mixture. Beat condensed milk and pudding mix in bowl until smooth. Stir in lemon juice. Spread over prepared crust; top with reserved crumb mixture. Bake for 20 to 25 minutes. Cool; drizzle with mixture of confectioners' sugar, water and lemon juice. Cut into bars. Yield: 2 dozen.

Ethel Brunes, Preceptor Omega
Belmond, Iowa

LEMON-FLAVORED CRAZY COOKIES

1 2-layer package
  lemon cake mix

8 ounces whipped
  topping

Preheat oven to 350 degrees. Combine ingredients in large bowl, stirring gently. Drop by teaspoonfuls onto greased cookie sheet. Bake for 10 to 12 minutes or until light brown. Cool on cookie sheet for 1 minute; remove to wire rack to cool completely. Yield: 4 dozen.

Barbara Somerville, Eta Master
Seattle, Washington

MAGIC COOKIE BARS

My favorite recipe because it's so easy to make.

1/2 cup margarine or
  butter
1 1/2 cups graham
  cracker crumbs
1 14-ounce can
  sweetened condensed
  milk

1 cup semisweet
  chocolate chips
1 1/3 cups flaked coconut
1 cup chopped nuts

Preheat oven to 350 degrees. Melt margarine in 9-by-13-inch baking pan. Press graham cracker crumbs into pan; drizzle with condensed milk. Layer with chocolate chips, coconut and nuts; press down firmly. Bake for 25 to 30 minutes. Cool completely; cut into bars. Yield: 2 to 3 dozen.

Alicia P. Castañeda, Preceptor Zeta Delta
Rio Grande City, Texas

NADINE'S BARS

1 cup butter or
  margarine, softened
2 cups pucked dark
  brown sugar
2 eggs, beaten
1 teaspoon vanilla
  extract

2 cups all-purpose flour
1 teaspoon baking soda
1/2 teaspoon salt
2 cups oats
1 cup chopped walnuts
2 cups semisweet
  chocolate chips

Preheat oven to 400 degrees. Cream butter and brown sugar in bowl until light and fluffy. Add eggs, vanilla, flour, baking soda, salt and oats; mix well. Spread in greased baking pan. Sprinkle with walnuts and chocolate chips. Bake for 10 minutes or until golden brown. Cool; cut into bars. Yield: 2 dozen.

DeAnna Straub, Beta Pi
Plevna, Montana

NO-BAKE COOKIE BARS

1 cup melted butter or margarine	*1/2 cup chopped nuts*
1/2 cup sugar	*1/4 cup milk*
2 tablespoons baking cocoa	*1/4 cup vanilla instant pudding mix*
1 egg, beaten	*2 cups confectioners' sugar*
1/2 teaspoon vanilla extract	*2 tablespoons butter or margarine*
2 cups graham cracker crumbs	*1 cup semisweet chocolate chips*
1/2 cup shredded coconut	

Combine 1/2 cup melted butter, sugar, cocoa and egg in saucepan. Cook over medium heat until bubbly, stirring constantly; remove from heat. Add next 4 ingredients; mix well. Pat into 9-by-13-inch nonstick baking pan. Mix milk, pudding mix, confectioners' sugar and remaining 1/2 cup melted butter in bowl. Pour over prepared crust. Chill until firm. Melt 2 tablespoons butter and chocolate chips in saucepan over low heat. Drizzle over top. Cool; cut into bars. Yield: 4 dozen.

Suzanne Hart, Preceptor Tau
Weiser, Idaho

THE "NO DILLY-DALLY" BAR

1/2 cup margarine	*2 cups crisp rice cereal*
1 cup semisweet chocolate chips	*1 cup semisweet chocolate chips*
1 10-ounce package miniature marshmallows	*1/3 cup milk*
	1 teaspoon vanilla extract
1 cup peanut butter	*2 cups confectioners' sugar*
1 cup salted peanuts	

Combine first 4 ingredients in glass bowl. Microwave on High for 2 1/2 to 3 minutes; mix well. Stir in peanuts and cereal. Spread in buttered 9-by-13-inch pan. Combine 1 cup chocolate chips and milk in glass bowl. Microwave for 1 to 1 1/2 minutes. Beat in vanilla and confectioners' sugar until smooth. Spread over top. Chill until firm; cut into bars. Yield: 1 1/2 dozen.

Bonnie Carroll, Xi Nu
Evansville, Indiana

OAT AND WHEAT TREATS

35 stone-ground wheat crackers	*2 tablespoons sesame seed*
1 cup oats	*1 cup margarine*
1/2 cup sliced nuts	*1 cup packed dark brown sugar*
1/2 cup wheat germ	

Preheat oven to 350 degrees. Line 10-by-15-inch baking pan with crackers. Mix oats, nuts, wheat germ and sesame seed in bowl. Melt margarine in saucepan; add brown sugar. Bring to a boil. Cook for 3 minutes, stirring constantly. Fold in oats mixture. Spread over crackers. Bake for 10 minutes; cool slightly. Break into pieces to serve. Yield: 3 dozen.

Donnabelle Gerhardt, Laureate Pi
Fairbury, Nebraska

OLD HENRY BARS

1 cup melted margarine	*3/4 cup chunky peanut butter*
1 cup packed dark brown sugar	*2 cups semisweet chocolate chips*
4 cups quick-cooking oats	

Preheat oven to 350 degrees. Mix margarine, brown sugar and oats in bowl. Press into 9-by-13-inch baking pan. Bake for 15 minutes. Cool for 5 minutes. Spread with peanut butter. Microwave chocolate chips in glass bowl until softened. Spread over peanut butter. Cool; cut into bars. Yield: 2 dozen.

Donna Witte, Xi Delta Omicron
Brampton, Ontario, Canada

ORANGE SLICE BAR COOKIES

1 pound candied orange slices, chopped	*4 eggs, beaten*
2 cups sifted all-purpose flour	*1 cup chopped nuts*
1/2 teaspoon salt	*1 teaspoon vanilla extract*
3 cups packed light brown sugar	*Sugar*

Preheat oven to 350 degrees. Toss orange candy with flour and salt in bowl. Add brown sugar, eggs, nuts and vanilla; mix well. Spread in greased 10-by-15-inch baking pan. Bake for 35 minutes; cool in pan. Cut into 1-by-3-inch bars; roll in sugar. Yield: 4 dozen.

Doris Miller, Preceptor Lambda Xi
Sun City, California

PARTY PUFFS

1 8-ounce can crushed pineapple	*1 cup whipped topping*
3 ounces cream cheese, softened	*1 5-ounce package Stella D'Oro Anginetti cookies*

Drain pineapple partially. Beat cream cheese and whipped topping at low speed in mixer bowl for 1 minute. Stir in pineapple. Slice tops off cookies. Drop creamed filling by teaspoonfuls onto bottom halves of cookies; replace tops. Chill until serving time. Yield: 2 to 3 dozen.

Janice Bethel, Epsilon Tau
Salem, Ohio

PEACH CRISP COOKIES

1 16-ounce can peaches	1 cup flaked coconut
1 2-layer package butter-pecan cake mix	1 cup chopped pecans

Preheat oven to 350 degrees. Chop peaches. Spread with juice in 9-by-13-inch nonstick baking pan. Layer with cake mix, coconut and pecans. Bake for 35 to 40 minutes or until golden brown; cool. Yield: 2 dozen.

Marge Sillanpa, Iota Rho
Painesville, Ohio

CHOCOLATE-PEANUT BUTTER PILE-UPS

2 cups peanut butter	2 cups semisweet chocolate chips
1/2 to 11/2 cups sugar	
2 eggs, beaten	

Preheat oven to 325 degrees. Combine peanut butter, sugar and eggs in bowl; mix well. Press into ungreased 10-by-15-inch baking pan. Bake for 20 minutes. Sprinkle with chocolate chips; cover with aluminum foil. Let stand for 3 to 5 minutes. Spread melted chocolate over surface. Cut into bars; cool. Yield: 3 to 5 dozen.

Agnes Marshall, Xi Xi
Swan River, Manitoba, Canada

FUDGY RITZ

Peanut butter	Chocolate almond bark, melted
Butter crackers	

Spread peanut butter between 2 crackers; dip into melted almond bark. Cool on waxed paper. Yield: variable.

Janet Cross, Alpha Nu
Bunker Hill, Kansas

INCREDIBLE COOKIES

1 egg	1 cup chunky peanut butter
1/2 cup sugar	
1/2 cup packed dark brown sugar	20 to 25 maple buds

Preheat oven to 325 degrees. Beat egg, sugar and brown sugar together in bowl. Stir in peanut butter. Shape by teaspoonfuls into balls; arrange on greased cookie sheet. Press 1 maple bud into center of each cookie, flattening slightly. Bake for 10 minutes. Do not overbake. Cool on cookie sheet for 2 minutes; remove to wire rack to cool completely. Yield: 2 dozen.

Elaine Pettigrew, Preceptor Laureate Theta
Estevan, Saskatchewan, Canada

Jeanne Poll, Laureate Mu, Holland, Michigan, makes White Chocolate Candy by melting 32 ounces white chocolate stars over very low heat and stirring in 32 ounces cocktail peanuts. Drop by spoonfuls onto waxed paper.

ONE-CUP COOKIES

1 tablespoon baking soda	1 cup sugar
3 eggs, beaten	1 cup flaked coconut
1 cup margarine, softened	1 cup chopped walnuts
	1 cup raisins
1 cup peanut butter	1 cup semisweet chocolate chips
1 cup all-purpose flour	
1 cup packed light brown sugar	1 cup quick-cooking oats

Preheat oven to 350 degrees. Combine baking soda, eggs, margarine, peanut butter, flour, brown sugar, sugar, coconut, walnuts, raisins, chocolate chips and oats in large bowl; mix well. Drop by teaspoonfuls onto nonstick cookie sheet. Bake for 10 minutes. Cool on cookie sheet for 2 minutes; remove to wire rack to cool completely. Yield: 8 to 9 dozen.

Sandi van den Heuvel, Sigma
Prince George, British Columbia, Canada

PEANUT BUTTER COOKIES

1 2-layer package yellow cake mix	1/2 cup vegetable oil
	2 tablespoons water
1 cup peanut butter	2 eggs, beaten

Preheat oven to 350 degrees. Combine all ingredients in large bowl; mix well. Drop by teaspoonfuls onto ungreased cookie sheet. Press crisscross design with fork on each cookie. Bake for 10 to 12 minutes or until golden brown. Cool on cookie sheet for 1 minute; remove to wire rack to cool completely. Yield: 3 dozen.

Lavaun Zimmerman, Delta Iota
Somerset, Kentucky

❖ THE QUICKEST PEANUT BUTTER COOKIES

Kids of all ages love these—especially my sorority sisters!

1 7-ounce jar marshmallow creme	1/3 cup confectioners' sugar
1 cup crunchy peanut butter	

Preheat oven to 350 degrees. Combine all ingredients in bowl; mix well. Shape by teaspoonfuls into balls. Arrange on ungreased cookie sheet, pressing slightly to flatten. Bake for 10 minutes. Cool on cookie sheet for 1 minute; remove to wire rack to cool completely. Yield: 1 to 11/2 dozen.

Belinda Strittmatter, Xi Alpha
Wahiawa, Hawaii

SIMPLE P-NUT BUTTER COOKIES

The quickest and simplest cookie recipe for my very impatient little boy!

1 cup peanut butter	1 egg
1 cup sugar	

Preheat oven to 350 degrees. Combine all ingredients in bowl; mix well. Drop by teaspoonfuls onto non-stick cookie sheet. Bake for 8 to 10 minutes or until brown. Cool on cookie sheet for 1 minute; remove to wire rack to cool completely. Yield: 1 to 1½ dozen.

Julie Wright, Gamma Phi
Brookfield, Missouri

CRISPY PLAIN COOKIES

1 cup margarine, softened	3½ cups all-purpose flour
1 cup vegetable oil	1 teaspoon baking soda
1 cup sugar	1 teaspoon cream of tartar
1 cup packed dark brown sugar	1 cup crisp rice cereal
1 egg	1 cup flaked coconut
½ teaspoon vanilla extract	1 cup oats

Preheat oven to 350 degrees. Cream margarine, oil, sugar and brown sugar in bowl until light and fluffy. Add egg; mix well. Stir in remaining ingredients. Shape by teaspoonfuls into balls. Arrange on non-stick cookie sheet; flatten with fork. Bake for 10 minutes. Cool on cookie sheet for 1 minute; remove to wire rack to cool completely. Yield: 6 dozen.

Lil Blasko, Preceptor Pi
Kindersley, Saskatchewan, Canada

PECAN BARS

A quick, caramel-tasting treat.

½ cup melted margarine or butter	1 tablespoon vanilla extract
2¼ cups packed dark brown sugar	1½ cups baking mix
2 eggs, beaten	2 cups chopped pecans

Combine all ingredients in large bowl; mix well. Pour into 8-by-10-inch glass baking dish. Microwave on High for 8 to 10 minutes, turning every 3 minutes. Let stand until firm; cut into bars. Yield: 3 dozen.

Terah Sherer, Xi Beta Delta
Jasper, Alabama

POTATO CHIP COOKIES

¾ cup shortening	2 cups all-purpose flour
1 cup packed light brown sugar	½ teaspoon salt
1 cup sugar	1 teaspoon baking soda
2 eggs, beaten	2 cups crushed potato chips
1 teaspoon vanilla extract	1 cup semisweet chocolate chips

Preheat oven to 350 degrees. Cream shortening, brown sugar and sugar in bowl until light and fluffy. Add eggs and vanilla; beat well. Stir in flour, salt and baking soda. Add potato chips and chocolate chips; stir gently. Drop by teaspoonfuls onto ungreased cookie sheet. Bake for 12 minutes. Cool on cookie sheet for 2 minutes; remove to wire rack to cool. Yield: 3 to 4 dozen.

Pearl L. Clarke, Preceptor Beta Lambda
Grand Rapids, Michigan

QUICK CRISPY COOKIES

1 cup butterscotch chips	1 7-ounce can shoestring potatoes
2 tablespoons peanut butter	

Combine chips and peanut butter in glass bowl. Microwave on High for 2 to 3 minutes or until melted. Stir in potatoes. Drop by teaspoonfuls onto waxed paper. Let stand until firm. Yield: 2 to 3 dozen.

Beverly J. Downey, Preceptor Alpha Gamma
Aztec, New Mexico

RAINY-DAY QUICK COOKIES

¾ cup baking mix	¼ cup vegetable oil
1 6-ounce package vanilla instant pudding mix	1 egg, beaten
	Sugar

Preheat oven to 350 degrees. Combine baking mix, pudding mix, vegetable oil and egg in bowl; mix well. Shape by teaspoonfuls into balls; arrange on ungreased cookie sheet. Dip glass bottom in sugar; flatten dough with glass. Bake for 8 to 10 minutes. Cool on cookie sheet for 2 minutes; remove to wire rack to cool completely. Yield: 2 dozen.

Judith Ann Rogers, Preceptor Eta Pi
Fort Pierce, Florida

CHOCOLATE SHORTBREAD COOKIES

1 cup butter or margarine, softened	Dash of salt
⅔ cup confectioners' sugar	⅓ cup baking cocoa
	1½ cups all-purpose flour

Preheat oven to 300 degrees. Cream butter until light and fluffy. Add confectioners' sugar, salt, cocoa and flour; mix well. Drop by teaspoonfuls onto nonstick cookie sheet. Bake for 20 minutes. Cool on cookie sheet for 2 minutes; remove to wire rack to cool completely. Yield: 4 dozen.

Linda Nicol, Xi Gamma Eta
Fernie, British Columbia, Canada

Cheryl Rasmussen, Mu Gamma, Harcourt, Iowa, makes Toffee-Crispix Mix by boiling 2 cups packed dark brown sugar, 1 cup margarine and ½ cup light corn syrup in saucepan for 2 minutes. Pour over 18 ounces Crispix cereal and 32 ounces dry-roasted peanuts; mix well. Microwave ½ at a time in paper bag on High for 4 minutes, shaking once. Cool on baking sheet.

SCOTCH SHORTBREAD

1 cup butter or margarine, softened	2½ cups sifted all-purpose flour
½ cup sugar	

Preheat oven to 275 degrees. Cream butter and sugar in mixer bowl until light and fluffy. Add flour; mix well. Roll on lightly floured surface to ³⁄₈-inch thickness. Cut with cookie cutter; arrange on nonstick cookie sheet. Bake for 25 minutes. Cool on cookie sheet for 2 minutes; remove to wire rack to cool completely. Yield: 4 dozen.

Sally Retzer, Xi Zeta Phi
Orlando, Florida

SHORTBREAD DROPS

This is a favorite traditional Christmas cookie in our family.

1 cup butter, softened	Red and green candied cherries
½ cup confectioners' sugar	
1½ cups all-purpose flour	

Preheat oven to 325 degrees. Cream butter and confectioners' sugar in mixer bowl for 2 minutes. Add flour. Beat for 5 minutes. Drop by teaspoonfuls onto foil-lined cookie sheet. Top with cherries. Bake for 12 to 15 minutes. Cool on cookie sheet for 2 minutes; remove to wire rack to cool completely. Do not substitute margarine for butter. Yield: 2½ dozen.

Linda Campbell, Preceptor Zeta Nu
Cathedral City, California

SOFT RAISIN COOKIES

3¼ cups all-purpose flour	1 teaspoon baking soda
3 eggs	1 teaspoon vanilla extract
1½ cups sugar	½ teaspoon salt
1 cup butter or margarine, softened	1½ cups dark seedless raisins
1 cup milk	½ cup chopped walnuts
2 teaspoons grated lemon rind	

Preheat oven to 375 degrees. Combine first 9 ingredients in mixer bowl. Beat at low speed until slightly mixed. Beat at medium speed for 2 minutes, scraping bowl. Stir in raisins and walnuts. Drop by heaping tablespoonfuls 2 inches apart onto greased cookie sheet. Bake for 12 to 15 minutes or until light brown. Remove to wire rack to cool completely. Yield: 2½ dozen.

Genevieve M. Woods, Laureate Xi
El Paso, Texas

QUICK-AS-A-WINK SUGAR COOKIES

An easy way never to be caught with an empty cookie jar!

1 2-layer package yellow cake mix	2 tablespoons water
½ cup vegetable oil	2 eggs, beaten
	Sugar

Preheat oven to 350 degrees. Combine cake mix, oil, water and eggs in bowl; mix well. Drop by teaspoonfuls onto ungreased cookie sheet. Dip wet glass bottom in sugar; press down cookies with glass. Bake for 10 to 12 minutes. Cool on cookie sheet for 1 minute; remove to wire rack to cool completely. Yield: 4 to 5 dozen.

Sondra Ferguson, Laureate Delta
Milwaukee, Wisconsin

BREAKFAST COOKIES

½ cup margarine, softened	¼ teaspoon baking soda
¾ cup sugar	2 cups cornflakes
1 egg	8 ounces bacon, crisp-fried, crumbled
1 cup all-purpose flour	

Preheat oven to 350 degrees. Cream margarine, sugar and egg in bowl until light and fluffy. Add flour, baking soda and cornflakes; mix well. Stir in bacon. Drop by tablespoonfuls 2 inches apart onto ungreased cookie sheet. Bake for 13 to 15 minutes until golden brown. Cool on cookie sheet for 1 minute; remove to wire rack to cool completely. Yield: 2½ dozen.

Jean C. Hove, Preceptor Chi
Tallahassee, Florida

QUICK OLD-FASHIONED TEA CAKES

⅔ cup vegetable oil	2 eggs
¾ cup sugar	2 cups self-rising flour
2 teaspoons vanilla extract	Grated lemon rind

Preheat oven to 400 degrees. Cream oil, sugar, vanilla and eggs in bowl until light and fluffy. Add flour and lemon rind; mix well. Drop by teaspoonfuls onto ungreased cookie sheet, 2 inches apart. Bake for 15 minutes or until golden brown. Yield: 2½ dozen.

Karen Jo Smith, Xi Beta
Terry, Mississippi

TOFFEE SQUARES

This was my children's favorite recipe—so quick and easy!

1 cup margarine, softened	1 egg
1 cup packed light brown sugar	2 cups sifted all-purpose flour
1 teaspoon vanilla extract	2 cups semisweet chocolate chips
	½ cup chopped nuts

Preheat oven to 350 degrees. Cream margarine and brown sugar in bowl until light and fluffy. Add vanilla, egg and flour; mix well. Spread on nonstick cookie sheet. Bake for 15 minutes. Sprinkle chocolate chips over top. Top with chopped nuts when chocolate melts. Cool in pan; cut into squares. Yield: 2 dozen.

Gloria E. Flanigan, Laureate Chi
Toledo, Ohio

TOOTSIE ROLL BARS

I make this when I have to serve a lot of people.

1 cup melted margarine
2 cups packed light
   brown sugar
2 eggs
Salt to taste
2 teaspoons vanilla
   extract
2½ cups all-purpose
   flour
1 teaspoon baking soda

3 cups oats
2 cups semisweet
   chocolate chips
1 14-ounce can
   sweetened condensed
   milk
2 tablespoons margarine
2 teaspoons vanilla
   extract

Preheat oven to 350 degrees. Mix 1 cup margarine, brown sugar, eggs, salt, 2 teaspoons vanilla, flour, baking soda and oats in large bowl. Spread ⅔ of the mixture onto large nonstick cookie sheet. Combine chocolate chips, condensed milk, 2 tablespoons margarine, salt and remaining vanilla in glass bowl; mix well. Microwave on High until chocolate begins to melt; stir well. Spread over prepared crust. Sprinkle remaining crust mixture over filling. Bake for 20 to 25 minutes. Cool; cut into bars. Yield: 3 dozen.

Darice Hostetler, Theta Delta
Burlington, Colorado

WAFFLE COOKIES

Good recipes always come from good friends.

½ cup margarine,
   melted
2 eggs
¾ cup sugar
3 tablespoons baking
   cocoa

1 cup all-purpose flour
1 teaspoon vanilla
   extract
Salt to taste
Confectioners' sugar
   and baking cocoa

Preheat waffle iron to medium. Combine first 7 ingredients in large bowl; mix well. Drop by tablespoonfuls onto waffle iron. Bake for 2 to 3 minutes. Cool on wire rack. Dust with confectioners' sugar and baking cocoa. Yield: 2 dozen.

Jan Irwin, Xi Zeta Eta
Cherokee, Iowa

MOCK ALMOND BARK

1 stack salted crackers
1 cup melted margarine
¾ cup packed brown
   sugar

1½ cups semisweet
   chocolate chips,
   melted
½ cup sliced almonds

Preheat oven to 400 degrees. Line baking sheet with foil; butter foil. Cover prepared pan with crackers. Mix margarine and brown sugar in bowl. Pour over crackers. Bake for 5 minutes. Spread melted chocolate over top. Sprinkle with almonds. Chill until serving time. Break into serving pieces. Yield: 24 servings.

Edna Mogk, Laureate Omega
Guelph, Ontario, Canada

ALMOND BARK

My children don't think it's Christmas until I've make this treat.

6 ounces semisweet
   baking chocolate,
   melted

1 teaspoon almond
   extract
½ cup whole almonds

Mix melted chocolate and flavoring in bowl. Stir in almonds. Spread on waxed paper-lined baking sheet. Chill until set. Break into serving pieces. Yield: 20 servings.

Harlene Annett, Preceptor Beta Pi
Peterborough, Ontario, Canada

BACON AND EGGS

These treats are great fun to make; they look like bacon and eggs.

1 8-ounce package
   pretzel sticks
4 ounces white
   chocolate, melted

½ cup yellow
   "M & M's" Chocolate
   Candies

Arrange pretzel sticks in groups of 4 with sides touching. Top each group in the middle with 1 teaspoon melted white chocolate. Place 1 yellow candy in the center of white chocolate. Let stand for 10 minutes or until set. Yield: 50 servings.

Sarah Hinton, Tau
Evansville, Indiana

TEN-MINUTE BRITTLE

1 cup sugar
½ cup light corn syrup
⅛ teaspoon salt
1 to 1½ cups roasted
   peanuts, pecans or
   mixed nuts

1 tablespoon margarine
1 teaspoon vanilla
   extract
1 teaspoon baking soda

Combine first 3 ingredients in 2-quart glass bowl. Microwave on High for 5 minutes. Stir in peanuts. Microwave for 2 to 6 minutes or until syrup is light brown, stirring frequently. Stir in last 3 ingredients until light and foamy. Spread ¼ inch thick on buttered baking sheet. Cool; break into pieces. Yield: 1 pound.

Quinta Scarfo, Laureate Alpha Sigma
Lynn Haven, Florida

CHINESE PORCUPINES

1 cup chow mein
  noodles
1 cup dry-roasted
  peanuts, chopped

1/2 cup semisweet
  chocolate chips, melted
1/2 cup milk chocolate
  chips, melted

Combine all ingredients in bowl; toss just until coated. Drop by teaspoonfuls onto waxed paper. Let stand until set. Yield: 24 servings.

Joanne Giles, Preceptor Iota
Henderson, Nevada

CHOCOLATE BARK CANDY

This candy melts in your mouth and everyone loves it.

16 ounces Wilton's
  chocolate candy melts,
  melted

2 tablespoons (heaping)
  crunchy peanut butter

Mix chocolate and peanut butter in bowl. Spread on waxed paper. Chill until set; cut into squares. Yield: 1 pound.

Betty C. Walsh, Xi Beta Kappa
Houston, Texas

ALMOND TOFFEE

I make this for my husband on Valentine's Day.

1/2 cup almonds
1 1/3 cups packed light
  brown sugar
1 cup butter or
  margarine

3 ounces semisweet
  chocolate, grated
Chopped nuts

Spread almonds in buttered 9-by-9-inch pan. Combine brown sugar and butter in saucepan. Cook over medium heat for 12 minutes, stirring constantly. Pour over almonds. Sprinkle chocolate over top, spreading as it melts. Sprinkle nuts over melted chocolate. Chill until set. Break into serving pieces. Yield: 12 servings.

Pauline M. Howatt, Xi Nu
Petitcodiac, New Brunswick, Canada

CHOCOLATE BONBONS

1 cup margarine
1 1/2 cups chunky peanut
  butter
3 3/4 cups sifted
  confectioners' sugar

3 cups crisp rice cereal
2 cups semisweet
  chocolate chips
1/4 bar paraffin

Combine margarine and peanut butter in saucepan. Bring to a boil over medium heat. Remove from heat. Stir in confectioners' sugar and cereal. Melt chocolate chips and paraffin in double boiler. Shape cereal mixture into small balls. Dip into melted chocolate, coating completely. Place on waxed paper. Let stand until set. Yield: 36 servings.

Mary Lou Stark, Preceptor Lambda Xi
Perris, California

CHOCOLATE DIP BALLS

This is a recipe my grandmother taught me to make; it was always used at holidays in our house.

1/4 cup melted butter or
  margarine
2/3 cup peanut butter
2 cups confectioners'
  sugar
1 cup coconut

1 cup chopped walnuts
13 maraschino cherries,
  chopped
2 cups semisweet
  chocolate chips
2 tablespoons paraffin

Combine butter, peanut butter, confectioners' sugar, coconut, walnuts and cherries in bowl; mix well. Shape into small balls. Melt chocolate chips and paraffin in double boiler. Dip candy into chocolate mixture, coating completely. Place on waxed paper. Let stand until set. Yield: 3 pounds.

Kary Groesbeck, Delta Xi
Dixon, California

CHOCOLATE-MARSHMALLOW SQUARES

Graham crackers
1/2 cup margarine
1/2 cup butterscotch
  chips
1/2 cup semisweet
  chocolate chips

1 egg, beaten
1 cup confectioners'
  sugar
2 cups marshmallows

Line 8-by-8-inch pan with graham crackers. Melt margarine in saucepan over medium heat. Add chips. Cook until melted, stirring constantly. Remove from heat. Stir in egg and confectioners' sugar. Cool slightly. Stir in marshmallows. Pour over graham crackers. Chill until serving time. Yield: 20 servings.

Margaret Gordon, Xi Gamma Mu
Newmarket, Ontario, Canada

❖ CHOCOLATE MOUSSE BALLS

My very favorite dessert is chocolate mousse and when I discovered this easy variation, I was in heaven. This makes a delightful gift at Christmas.

16 ounces milk
  chocolate
8 ounces whipped
  topping

2/3 cup crushed vanilla
  wafers

Melt chocolate in saucepan over low heat, stirring frequently. Cool to room temperature. Beat in whipped topping. Chill, covered, for 1 hour. Shape into 1-inch balls. Roll in wafer crumbs. Place in paper petits fours cups. Chill until serving time. Yield: 66 servings.

Phyllis C. Brueckner, Xi Beta Psi
Tucson, Arizona

CINNAMON NUTS

1 tablespoon melted butter or margarine	1¼ cups sugar
1 pound mixed nuts	1½ teaspoons cinnamon
2 egg whites, beaten to soft peaks	¼ teaspoon salt
	¼ cup butter or margarine

Preheat oven to 275 degrees. Drizzle 1 tablespoon butter over nuts in bowl; toss. Spread on 10-by-15-inch baking sheet. Bake for 10 minutes. Combine next 4 ingredients in bowl; mix well. Add nuts, stirring to coat. Melt remaining butter on baking sheet. Spread nut mixture on sheet. Bake for 30 minutes. Let stand until cool. Break into serving pieces. Yield: 16 servings.

Debbie Wilkes, Xi Alpha Sigma
Oshawa, Ontario, Canada

CHOCOLATE TURKS

4 cups cornflakes	2 8-ounce milk chocolate bars, melted
1 cup chopped pecans	
2 ounces unsweetened chocolate, melted	

Combine cornflakes and pecans in bowl; mix well. Blend chocolates in bowl. Pour over cornflake mixture; toss lightly. Drop by teaspoonfuls onto waxed paper. Let stand until set. Yield: 36 servings.

Betty Sue Stuart, Pi
Brunswick, Missouri

CHOP SUEY-NOODLE CANDY

2 cups semisweet chocolate chips, melted	1 cup shredded coconut
	1 1½-ounce can chow mein noodles
2 cups butterscotch chips, melted	1 cup chopped nuts

Combine all ingredients in bowl; mix well. Drop by teaspoonfuls onto waxed paper. Let stand until set. Yield: 30 servings.

Judy Bespalec, Preceptor Alpha Theta
Crete, Nebraska

CHURCH WINDOWS

½ cup margarine	1 10-ounce package colored miniature marshmallows
2 cups semisweet chocolate chips	
1 cup chopped nuts	1 cup coconut

Combine margarine and chocolate chips in saucepan. Cook over low heat until melted. Cool slightly. Stir in nuts and marshmallows. Shape into log on waxed paper sprinkled with coconut, coating well. Freeze until firm. Cut into slices. Yield: 24 servings.

Kimberly S. Livingston, Xi Delta Psi
McKean, Pennsylvania

COCONUT BONBONS

½ cup light corn syrup	1 cup semisweet chocolate chips, melted
1 7-ounce package coconut	
3 ounces white almond bark, melted	

Place corn syrup in 2-quart glass bowl. Microwave on High for 1 to 2 minutes or until corn syrup boils. Stir in coconut. Let stand until cool. Shape into 1-inch balls. Chill until firm. Blend almond bark and chocolate in bowl. Dip candy into mixture. Place on waxed paper. Yield: 24 servings.

Dee McBride, Xi Eta Lambda
New Strawn, Kansas

COCONUT JOYS

½ cup melted margarine	3 cups coconut
2 cups confectioners' sugar	4 ounces unsweetened chocolate, melted

Combine first 3 ingredients in bowl; mix well. Shape by teaspoonfuls into balls, making an indentation in center of each. Place on waxed paper. Fill centers with melted chocolate. Chill until firm. Yield: 36 servings.

Cheri Friedrich, Xi Zeta Sigma
Boonville, Missouri

EASY DIVINITY

2 cups sugar	1 teaspoon vanilla extract
½ cup water	
1 7-ounce jar marshmallow creme	Pecans to taste

Combine sugar and water in saucepan; mix well. Cook over high heat to 234 to 240 degrees on candy thermometer, soft-ball stage. Pour over marshmallow creme in bowl; beat until thick. Add vanilla and pecans; mix well. Drop by teaspoonfuls onto waxed paper. Yield: 40 servings.

Lorraine Harrelson, Preceptor Laureate Beta Phi
Gilmer, Texas

CHOCOLATE DROP FUDGE

1 teaspoon butter or margarine, softened	1 cup smooth or crunchy peanut butter
1 16-ounce package chocolate cream drops	

Spread butter in 9-by-9-inch pan. Place chocolate drops in glass bowl. Microwave on High for 2 minutes, stirring after 1 minute. Stir in peanut butter. Spread into prepared pan. Let stand until cool. Cut into squares. Yield: 1½ pounds.

Wanda Lillard, Xi Delta Zeta
Delano, Tennessee

MICROWAVE CARAMEL FUDGE

1/2 cup melted margarine	35 caramels
1/3 cup baking cocoa	1 tablespoon water
1/4 cup packed light brown sugar	2 cups unsalted peanuts
1/4 cup milk	1/2 cup milk chocolate chips, melted
3 1/3 cups confectioners' sugar	1/2 cup semisweet chocolate chips, melted
1/2 teaspoon vanilla extract	

Combine first 4 ingredients in 2-quart glass bowl. Microwave, uncovered, on High for 2 1/2 minutes or until mixture boils, stirring once. Microwave for 1 minute longer. Stir in next 2 ingredients. Spread in 9-by-9-inch pan lined with foil. Combine caramels and water in glass bowl. Microwave on Medium for 4 to 5 minutes or until melted. Stir in peanuts. Spread over fudge layer. Spread mixture of melted chocolate chips over caramel layer. Chill until set. Remove from pan. Cut into squares. Yield: 52 servings.

Mary Fake, Gamma Epsilon
Willmar, Minnesota

CHOCOLATE FUDGE

4 ounces unsweetened chocolate, melted	1 egg, lightly beaten
1/3 cup melted margarine	1/4 cup sweetened condensed milk
1 1-pound package confectioners' sugar	1 teaspoon vanilla extract

Combine first 5 ingredients in mixer bowl; beat until smooth. Add vanilla; mix well. Spread into greased 8-by-8-inch pan. Chill until serving time. Cut into squares. Yield: 64 servings.

June C. Hackett, Laureate Omicron
Sunbury, Pennsylvania

EASY FUDGE CANDY

A dear friend gave me this recipe—it's so easy and quick to make.

4 ounces Velveeta cheese, cubed	1 1-pound package confectioners' sugar
1/2 cup margarine	1/4 cup baking cocoa

Place cheese and margarine in glass bowl. Microwave on High for 2 minutes or until cheese melts. Add confectioners' sugar and cocoa, beating until mixture thickens and loses its luster. Pour into buttered 8-by-8-inch pan. Chill until firm. May add chopped nuts. Yield: 2 pounds.

Myrtle Landolt, Laureate Delta Alpha
Silsbee, Texas

FANTASY FUDGE

Our family loves fudge, especially during the holidays. This recipe is great for busy people like me.

3/4 cup margarine	1 7-ounce jar marshmallow creme
3 cups sugar	1 cup chopped nuts
2/3 cup evaporated milk	1 teaspoon vanilla extract
2 cups semisweet chocolate chips	

Microwave margarine in 4-quart microwave-safe bowl on High for 1 minute or until melted. Add sugar and milk; mix well. Microwave for 5 minutes or until mixture begins to boil, stirring after 3 minutes. Mix well, scraping bowl. Microwave for 5 1/4 minutes longer, stirring after 3 minutes. Add chocolate chips, stirring until melted. Add remaining ingredients; mix well. Pour into greased 9-by-13-inch baking pan. Let stand until firm. Yield: 3 pounds.

Lucylee Lively, Preceptor Iota Sigma
Dallas, Texas

QUICK FUDGE

2 pounds semisweet chocolate, chopped	2 pints butter brickle ice cream, melted

Melt chocolate in double boiler. Stir into ice cream in large bowl, mixing well. Pour into 9-by-9-inch pan. Chill until firm. Store in refrigerator. Yield: 4 pounds.

Jane Taylor, Xi Alpha Theta
Milwaukee, Wisconsin

TWO-MINUTE FUDGE

1 1-pound package confectioners' sugar	1 tablespoon vanilla extract
1/2 cup baking cocoa	1/2 cup butter or margarine
1/4 teaspoon salt	1 cup chopped nuts
1/4 cup milk	

Combine confectioners' sugar, cocoa, salt, milk and vanilla in 1 1/2-quart microwave-safe dish, stirring well. Top with butter. Microwave on High for 2 minutes; stir until smooth. Add chopped nuts. Pour into 8-by-8-inch dish lined with waxed paper. Chill until firm. Yield: 1 1/2 pounds.

Jean Zeller, Laureate Theta
New Albany, Indiana

SUE'S EASY FUDGE

1 cup peanut butter	1 1-pound package confectioners' sugar
1 cup butter or margarine	

Melt peanut butter and butter in saucepan; remove from heat. Add confectioners' sugar; beat well. Pour into 8-by-9-inch nonstick pan. Chill until firm. Yield: 2 pounds.

Melody Cook, Xi Beta Epsilon
Rock View, West Virginia

HEAVENLY HASH

We always had this at Christmas when all my children were still at home.

2½ cups semisweet chocolate chips	2 cups pecans
1 14-ounce can sweetened condensed milk	1 10-ounce package miniature marshmallows

Heat chocolate chips and milk in saucepan over low heat, stirring until smooth. Sprinkle pecans and marshmallows into buttered 9-by-13-inch baking pan; cover with chocolate mixture. Let stand until firm. Yield: 3 pounds.

Faye Williams, Xi Delta Pi
Kennett, Missouri

KIBBLES AND BITS

24 ounces almond bark	1 18-ounce package Golden Grahams cereal
¼ to ½ cup peanut butter	

Microwave almond bark in microwave-safe bowl on High for 1½ to 2 minutes. Stir in peanut butter; mix well. Fold in cereal. Drop by teaspoonfuls onto waxed paper. Chill until firm. Yield: 46 servings.

Barbara Word, Preceptor Mu Tau
Round Rock, Texas

CHOCOLATE-COVERED CANDIES

1 1-pound package confectioners' sugar	Food coloring and peppermint or other flavor extract
½ cup melted margarine	
1 cup sweetened condensed milk	2 cups semisweet chocolate chips
	¼ bar paraffin

Mix confectioners' sugar, margarine and milk in bowl. Stir in food coloring and flavoring. Shape by teaspoonfuls into balls. Arrange on baking sheet, pressing down to flatten; freeze. Melt chocolate chips and paraffin in top of double boiler, stirring constantly. Dip frozen candy in chocolate. Place on waxed paper to cool. Yield: 2 pounds.

Marsha Duncan, Xi Phi Beta
Rosenberg, Texas

MICROWAVE MILLIONAIRES

1 14-ounce package caramels	1 teaspoon vanilla extract
2 tablespoons butter or margarine	3 cups pecans
2 tablespoons water	Chocolate almond bark, melted

Microwave caramels, butter, water and vanilla in glass dish on High for 1 to 2 minutes; mix until smooth. Stir in pecans. Drop by teaspoonfuls onto baking sheet; chill until firm. Dip in melted almond bark. Place on waxed paper to cool. Yield: 3 dozen.

Charlotte Barger, Alpha
Ft. Worth, Texas

NUCLEAR CARAMEL CORN

1 cup packed light brown sugar	¼ teaspoon salt
½ cup margarine	½ teaspoon baking soda
¼ cup light corn syrup	5 quarts popped corn
	1 cup peanuts, optional

Combine brown sugar, margarine, corn syrup and salt in microwave-safe dish. Microwave on High for 1 minute; stir. Microwave for 2 minutes longer. Stir in baking soda. Mix popped corn and peanuts in large paper bag. Pour in syrup; shake well. Microwave for 1½ minutes; cool on waxed paper. Yield: 12 servings.

Ava C. Lansbery, Xi Theta Chi
Annapolis, Illinois

NUT GOODY BARS

2 cups peanut butter	½ cup evaporated milk
2 cups semisweet chocolate chips	1 cup butter or margarine
2 cups butterscotch chips	¼ teaspoon vanilla extract
½ cup peanuts	
¼ cup vanilla pudding and pie filling mix	2 1-pound packages confectioners' sugar

Heat peanut butter, chocolate and butterscotch chips in double boiler, stirring until melted. Pour half the mixture into greased 9-by-13-inch baking pan; chill. Stir peanuts into remaining chocolate mixture; set aside. Combine pudding mix, milk and butter in saucepan. Bring to a boil. Cook for 1 minute; remove from heat. Add vanilla and confectioners' sugar; mix well. Pour over chilled chocolate layer. Spoon remaining chocolate and peanut mixture over top. Chill until firm. Cut into bars. Yield: 4 dozen.

Phyllis Elmore, Preceptor Omicron
Roanoke, Virginia

PASTEL PATTIES

These are especially good for showers and at Easter.

⅓ cup light corn syrup	½ teaspoon salt
⅓ cup margarine, softened	1 1-pound package confectioners' sugar
1 teaspoon vanilla extract	Food coloring
	1½ cups pecan halves

Combine corn syrup, margarine, vanilla, salt and confectioners' sugar in bowl; mix well. Divide into 3 portions. Tint each portion with 2 to 3 drops food coloring, kneading to mix color. Shape into 1-inch patties; top with pecan halves. Yield: 4 dozen.

Lynna Fuller Kirkpatrick, Alpha Upsilon Theta
Granbury, Texas

PEANUT CLUSTERS

2½ cups semisweet
  chocolate chips
16 ounces white almond
  bark

2 cups salted peanuts

Microwave chocolate chips in glass dish on Medium for 1 to 2 minutes. Microwave almond bark in separate glass dish for 1 to 2 minutes. Mix together with salted peanuts in large bowl. Drop by teaspoonfuls onto waxed paper. Let stand until firm. Yield: 3 pounds.

Kathryn L. Gardner, Zeta Upsilon
Sugar Creek, Missouri

CRUNCHY PEANUT-MALLOW CANDY

1 cup semisweet
  chocolate chips
½ cup crunchy peanut
  butter

2 cups miniature
  marshmallows

Melt chocolate chips and peanut butter in top of double boiler, stirring constantly. Fold in marshmallows. Press into greased 8-by-8-inch baking pan. Chill until firm; cut into squares. Yield: 12 servings.

Vera J. Preston, Preceptor Laureate
Brockville, Ontario, Canada

PEANUT-MALLOW BARS

2 cups semisweet
  chocolate chips
1 14-ounce can
  sweetened condensed
  milk
2 tablespoons butter or
  margarine

2 cups dry-roasted
  peanuts
1 10-ounce package
  miniature
  marshmallows

Heat chocolate chips, condensed milk and butter in saucepan over low heat, stirring until smooth; remove from heat. Stir in peanuts and marshmallows. Pour into 9-by-13-inch nonstick baking pan. Chill until firm. Yield: 3 dozen.

Naomi E. Golden, Laureate Beta Xi
Van Buren, Ohio

PECAN CRUNCH

¼ cup margarine
¼ cup milk or cream
6 packages Macintosh
  toffee

1 package pecans,
  chopped
6 cups cornflakes

Melt margarine, milk and toffee in glass bowl in microwave on High for 3 minutes. Add chopped pecans and cornflakes; mix well. Spread into 9-by-13-inch baking pan. Chill until firm. Yield: 36 servings.

Gail Jensen, Preceptor Eta
Yorkton, Saskatchewan, Canada

PEPPERMINT CRUNCH

This is always a great fund-raiser at the sorority Christmas auction.

16 ounces white
  chocolate

4 ounces red and green
  mint chips

Microwave white chocolate in glass bowl until melted. Stir in mint chips. Pour mixture onto waxed paper-lined baking sheet. Place in freezer for 5 minutes. Break into bite-sized pieces. Yield: 1 pound.

Kathy Burnett, Xi Delta Lambda
Knoxville, Tennessee

POPPYCOCK

1½ cups sugar
½ cup water
½ cup light corn syrup

4 quarts popped popcorn
1 cup unsalted peanuts

Combine sugar, water and corn syrup in saucepan; bring to a boil. Cook to 300 to 310 degrees on candy thermometer, hard-crack stage. Pour over popcorn and peanuts in buttered pan; mix well. Cool; break apart to serve. Yield: 12 servings.

Debbie Wilkes, Xi Alpha Sigma
Oshawa, Ontario, Canada

MICROWAVE PRALINES

1 1-pound package
  light brown sugar
1 cup whipping cream

2 tablespoons butter
  or margarine
2 cups pecan halves

Combine brown sugar and cream in 3-quart glass bowl; mix well. Microwave on High for 14 minutes, stirring after 7 minutes. Add butter and pecans. Microwave for 1 to 2 minutes or to soft-ball stage. Drop by tablespoonfuls onto waxed paper. Let stand until firm. Yield: 20 servings.

Barbara L. Bowlin, Laureate Nu
Grants, New Mexico

PUPPY CHOW

A great conversation snack at parties, and the kids love it too. Serve it in dog food bowls.

2 cups chunky peanut
  butter
1 cup butterscotch chips
1 cup semisweet
  chocolate chips

½ cup margarine
1 12-ounce package
  Crispix cereal
2 1-pound packages
  confectioners' sugar

Microwave peanut butter, butterscotch chips, chocolate chips and margarine in glass bowl on Medium for 5 to 6 minutes, stirring until smooth. Mix with cereal in large bowl. Shake with confectioners' sugar in paper bag. Yield: 13 small dog food bowls.

Rita J. Mock, Xi Xi Xi
Yorba Linda, California

Desserts on the Dot

If there's one type of food that just doesn't adapt itself to life in the fast lane, it's bound to be dessert, right? After all, how can a busy cook afford the hours needed to whip up glorious baked goodies? If your sweet tooth just won't take no for an answer—no matter how busy your day—this chapter is for you. You won't need hours at the oven to come up with truly spectacular desserts, but just a bit of creativity and, for most of these recipes, just a few minutes. "Desserts on the Dot" includes traditional favorites, like Cherry Crisp and Super Bread Pudding with Rum Sauce (made in a microwave!), to "light" desserts that reflect our concern with healthier eating. But quick doesn't mean ordinary! We've picked a number of special recipes that are sure to wow your guests: try Chocolate Pizza or Coffee Tortoni for a beautiful and delicious company finale—without spending all day in the kitchen.

SPIKED APPLE BETTY

5 cups sliced peeled
  apples
1/2 teaspoon cinnamon-
  sugar
1 teaspoon grated
  lemon rind
1 teaspoon grated
  orange rind
2 tablespoons Grand
  Marnier

2 tablespoons Amaretto
3/4 cup sugar
1/4 cup packed dark
  brown sugar
3/4 cup all-purpose flour
1/4 teaspoon salt
1/2 cup butter or
  margarine, softened

Preheat oven to 350 degrees. Arrange apples in greased 2-quart baking dish. Sprinkle with cinnamon-sugar, lemon and orange rinds and liqueurs. Combine sugar, brown sugar, flour and salt in large bowl. Cut in butter until crumbly. Pat mixture over apples. Bake for 1 hour or until light brown. Serve warm with cream, whipped cream or ice cream. Yield: 8 servings.

Susan Woods, Beta Nu
Chatham, Ontario, Canada

APPLE CRISP

2 21-ounce cans apple
  pie filling
1 2-layer package
  yellow cake mix

1 cup melted
  margarine

Preheat oven to 350 degrees. Spread pie filling into 9-by-12-inch baking pan. Sprinkle cake mix over top. Drizzle with melted margarine. Bake for 20 to 30 minutes or until light brown. Yield: 8 servings.

Robbie F. Huling, Preceptor Alpha Eta
Chattanooga, Tennessee

HOT APPLE SUNDAES

2 tablespoons butter or
  margarine
2 tablespoons light
  brown sugar
1 teaspoon lemon juice

2 large red apples, cut
  into 1/4-inch slices
3 cups vanilla ice cream
  or frozen yogurt
1/3 cup chopped walnuts

Melt butter in skillet over medium heat. Stir in brown sugar and lemon juice; mix well. Add sliced apples. Cook for 10 minutes or until apples are tender. Scoop ice cream into goblets. Top with apples, syrup and walnuts. Yield: 6 servings.

Isobel Burnstad, Preceptor Alpha Lambda
Surrey, British Columbia, Canada

Jan Cox, Xi Iota, Texarkana, Texas, makes Cherries Jubilee by microwaving 1 can cherry pie filling, 1/4 cup currant jelly and 1 teaspoon grated orange rind on High for 3 to 5 minutes. Heat 1/3 cup rum in microwave for 15 to 20 seconds. Pour over cherry mixture; ignite. Serve over vanilla ice cream.

APPLE DIP

A quick and easy dip to serve to friends while watching sports or movies at home.

1 cup butterscotch
  chips
1 14-ounce can
  sweetened condensed
  milk

2 teaspoons apple cider
  vinegar
1/2 teaspoon cinnamon
Sliced apples

Combine butterscotch chips and condensed milk in glass bowl. Microwave on High for 2 minutes; stir. Add vinegar and cinnamon. Microwave for 1 minute longer. Dip sliced apples into warm sauce. Yield: 2 1/2 cups.

LuAnn Bickford, Alpha Omega
Springerville, Arizona

QUICK FRUIT

3 cups sliced unpeeled
  apples
2 tablespoons honey
2 tablespoons water
2 tablespoons light
  brown sugar

1/3 cup quick-cooking
  oats
1/2 teaspoon cinnamon
1 tablespoon margarine,
  softened

Arrange sliced apples in 9-inch microwave-safe pie plate. Pour mixture of honey and water over apples. Microwave, loosely covered, for 5 minutes or until apples are tender. Combine brown sugar, oats and cinnamon in bowl. Cut in margarine until mixture is crumbly. Sprinkle over apples before serving. May substitute pears for apples. Yield: 4 to 6 servings.

Ann-Joy Hardy, Xi Zeta Iota
Auburndale, Florida

MICROWAVE BAKED APPLES

4 apples, cored
2 tablespoons light
  brown sugar
1/2 teaspoon cinnamon

Raisins to taste
1 to 2 teaspoons butter
  or margarine

Fill centers of cored apples with mixture of brown sugar, cinnamon and raisins. Top with pats of butter. Arrange in glass baking dish. Microwave on High for 5 to 8 minutes or until apples are tender, turning once. Yield: 4 servings.

Jill Scott, Xi Gamma Alpha
Sunnyside, Washington

FUN BANANAS

Bananas
Chocolate syrup to taste

Colored sprinkles

Slice bananas into serving bowls. Drizzle with chocolate syrup. Scatter sprinkles over top.
Yield: 1 banana per serving.

Andrea K. Hays, Omicron Xi
Prairie Village, Kansas

BANANAS CALYPSO WITH RUM SAUCE

A delightfully light dessert.

2 egg yolks
1/2 cup confectioners'
  sugar
1/2 cup light cream
1/2 teaspoon salt
1 ounce Jamaican rum
2 egg whites
1 tablespoon butter or
  margarine

1/2 cup packed dark
  brown sugar
1/4 teaspoon ground
  cloves
2 tablespoons grated
  orange rind
3/4 cup orange juice
8 bananas

Beat egg yolks in glass bowl until thick and lemon-colored. Add confectioners' sugar, cream and salt; mix well. Microwave on High for 1 minute and 45 seconds or until thickened, stirring every 30 seconds. Add rum gradually, beating until smooth. Beat egg whites until stiff peaks form. Fold into rum sauce; set aside. Microwave butter in 3-quart glass bowl until melted. Add brown sugar, cloves, orange rind and orange juice; mix well. Microwave on High for 3 minutes. Peel bananas and slice lengthwise into thirds. Add to orange sauce, stirring to coat. Microwave for 3 minutes longer, stirring once. Serve with rum sauce. Yield: 8 servings.

Deborah A. Miller, Gamma Pi
Hutchinson, Kansas

HOT CHOCOLATE BANANAS

1 tablespoon butter or
  margarine
1 large banana, peeled,
  split lengthwise

Cinnamon
4 to 6 small pieces milk
  chocolate or
  semisweet chocolate

Melt butter in skillet. Place banana halves, flat side down in butter; sprinkle with cinnamon. Sauté for 1 to 2 minutes; turn bananas. Place chocolate pieces on each banana half. Cook, covered, for 2 to 3 minutes longer or until chocolate is melted. Spread evenly over bananas. Cool slightly. Yield: 2 servings.

Isabelle Henry, Xi Beta Omicron
Springfield, New Jersey

BANANA SPLIT CAKE

1 pound cake
12 ounces whipped
  topping
2 bananas, sliced

1 quart Neapolitan ice
  cream
Chocolate syrup

Slice cake lengthwise into 3 layers. Spread each layer with whipped topping and banana slices; reassemble cake. Cut into slices. Top each slice with scoop of ice cream; drizzle with chocolate syrup. Yield: 6 to 8 servings.

Elma V. Hill, Xi Pi
Las Vegas, Nevada

SINFUL BANANA PUDDING

1 6-ounce package
  vanilla instant
  pudding mix
2 cups milk
1 14-ounce can
  sweetened condensed
  milk
1 tablespoon lemon juice

1/2 cup Amaretto
Vanilla extract to taste
16 ounces whipped
  topping
3 bananas, sliced
1 8-ounce package
  vanilla wafers

Combine pudding mix, milk and condensed milk in bowl; mix well. Stir in lemon juice, Amaretto and vanilla. Fold in whipped topping. Alternate layers of pudding, bananas and vanilla wafers in large bowl. Chill until serving time. Yield: 6 servings.

Marilyn Borras, Epsilon Tau
Stafford, Virginia

BLUEBERRY DELIGHT

It's fast and serves a lot of people.

1 21-ounce can
  blueberry pie filling
1 3-ounce package
  vanilla instant
  pudding mix

1 cup miniature
  marshmallows
12 ounces whipped
  topping

Combine pie filling and pudding mix in large bowl; mix well. Add marshmallows; fold in whipped topping. Chill in refrigerator until serving time. Yield: 12 to 15 servings.

Evelyn J. Barker, Xi Beta Phi
Alliance, Ohio

CHERRY CRISP

I am always surprised to receive so many compliments on this at sorority functions because it's so easy to make.

2 21-ounce cans cherry
  pie filling
1 2-layer package
  white or yellow cake
  mix

1 cup oats
1/2 cup melted
  margarine

Preheat oven to 350 degrees. Spread pie filling into greased 9-by-13-inch baking pan. Combine cake mix and oats in small bowl, stirring to mix. Sprinkle over pie filling; drizzle with melted margarine. Bake for 35 minutes or until golden brown. May substitute any flavor pie filling for cherry filling. Yield: 15 servings.

Kathy Celmer, Xi Beta Chi
Grand Island, Nebraska

FROZEN FRUIT DESSERT

1 14-ounce can sweetened condensed milk	1 8-ounce can crushed pineapple, drained
8 ounces whipped topping	1 21-ounce can blueberry or cherry pie filling
1 2-ounce package chopped walnuts	

Combine all ingredients in large bowl; mix well. Spread in 9-by-13-inch pan. Freeze until firm. Cut into squares to serve. Yield: 16 to 20 servings.

Joy Sellers, Xi Epsilon
Newport News, Virginia

NECTARINE-BERRY SHORTCAKE

1 10-count can flaky biscuits	3 or 4 sliced nectarines
2 tablespoons melted butter or margarine	1 cup fresh blueberries
¼ cup sugar	½ cup sugar
1 teaspoon cinnamon	8 ounces whipped topping

Preheat oven to 375 degrees. Separate each biscuit into 2 sections. Dip 1 side into butter, then into mixture of ¼ cup sugar and cinnamon. Arrange 9 biscuit halves on greased baking sheet sugar side up with edges overlapping to form 8-inch ring. Place 1 biscuit in center. Repeat to form second ring. Bake for 11 to 14 minutes or until light brown; cool. Combine nectarines, blueberries and remaining ½ cup sugar in bowl; mix well. Arrange 1 biscuit ring on serving plate with single biscuit layer in center. Layer with ½ of the fruit mixture, ½ of the whipped topping, second biscuit ring, remaining ½ fruit and ½ whipped topping. Slice to serve. May substitute peaches for nectarines. Yield: 10 servings.

Nancy Luse, Lambda
Belle Fourche, South Dakota

PEACH FLAMBÉ

This recipe was passed on to me by my beloved grandmother, a gracious hostess and wonderful cook.

¾ cup currant jelly	Vanilla ice cream
1 16-ounce can peach halves, drained	½ cup peach or apricot brandy

Melt jelly in chafing dish or double boiler. Add peach halves cut side up. Cook until bubbly, stirring frequently. Spoon ice cream into dessert glasses. Top with peach halves, cut side up. Fill centers with brandy. Ignite and serve immediately. Yield: 6 to 8 servings.

Sharon Dunham, Zeta Nu
Monroeville, Alabama

QUICK AND EASY COBBLER

My mom used to make this when we had company and everyone thought she made it from scratch. The first time I made this for a sorority meeting everyone thought it was made with fresh peaches!

3 frozen peach pies, slightly thawed	Cinnamon to taste
1 cup sugar	¼ cup butter or margarine

Preheat oven to 350 degrees. Break pies into large chunks. Place in buttered 3-quart baking dish. Sprinkle with mixture of sugar and cinnamon; dot with butter. Bake for 1 hour or until golden brown and bubbly. Serve warm with ice cream. Yield: 8 to 12 servings.

Donna Hendrix, Beta Beta Pi
Stephenville, Texas

FLAMBÉED PEACHES AND CREAM

3 tablespoons butter or margarine	8 peach halves, drained
2 tablespoons light brown sugar	5 tablespoons Grand Marnier
	Vanilla ice cream

Heat butter and brown sugar in large skillet until bubbly, stirring frequently. Add peach halves, turning to coat. Stir in Grand Marnier. Cook over low heat until warmed through. Place peach halves over ice cream in dessert glasses. Pour sauce over top; ignite. Yield: 4 servings.

Bev Taylor, Preceptor Alpha Alpha
Burlington, Ontario, Canada

PEACH MELBA

A gourmet-tasting quick recipe.

1 prepared pound cake, cut into 6 or 8 slices	Vanilla ice cream
1 10-ounce package frozen raspberries, thawed	1 10-ounce package frozen peaches, thawed
	Whipped cream

Arrange cake slices on dessert plates. Top with raspberries, ice cream, peaches and whipped cream. Yield: 6 to 8 servings.

Janet Dills, Xi Alpha Pi
Arvada, Colorado

CRAN-PEAR SHORTCAKE

I created this when I needed a last-minute dessert and only had these ingredients on hand.

6 pears, peeled, chopped	1 recipe shortcake dough from baking mix box
1 16-ounce can whole cranberry sauce	Vanilla ice cream

Preheat oven to 350 degrees. Combine pears and cranberry sauce in bowl; mix well. Spread in

9-by-13-inch baking pan. Top with shortcake dough mixture. Bake for 30 minutes or until light brown. Serve in bowls with vanilla ice cream. Yield: 8 servings.

Virginia R. Matlock, Preceptor Beta Kappa
Indianapolis, Indiana

PINEAPPLE-YOGURT DELIGHT

4 cups low-fat plain yogurt	8 packets artificial sweetener
1 4-ounce package pistachio instant pudding mix	2 cups crushed unsweetened pineapple, drained

Combine yogurt, pudding mix and sweetener in bowl; mix well. Fold in pineapple. Spoon into 2-quart serving bowl. Chill in refrigerator until serving time. Yield: 4 servings.

Sally A. Conaway, Beta Rho
Independence, Missouri

PUNCH BOWL CAKE

1 prepared angel food cake	1 pint fresh strawberries, sliced
3 or 4 bananas, sliced	1/2 cup coconut
1 16-ounce can crushed pineapple	2/3 cup chopped pecans
	12 ounces whipped topping

Crumble cake into large clear glass bowl. Layer with bananas, undrained pineapple, strawberries, coconut, half the pecans, and whipped topping. Garnish with remaining pecans and strawberry slices. Yield: 12 servings.

Marie J. Davis, Preceptor Pi
Baton Rouge, Louisiana

PUNCH BOWL-PUDDING CAKE

1 prepared angel food cake	12 ounces whipped topping
2 4-ounce packages French vanilla instant pudding mix	1 4-ounce jar maraschino cherries, drained
3 bananas, sliced	1 6-ounce jar peanuts
1 10-ounce package frozen sliced strawberries, thawed	

Tear cake into bite-sized pieces. Prepare pudding mix using package directions. Layer cake, pudding, bananas and strawberries 1/3 at a time, in glass punch bowl. Top with whipped topping, cherries and peanuts. Yield: 12 to 15 servings.

Trish Liles, Xi Xi Rho
Fort Worth, Texas

RASPBERRY SERENDIPITY

1 1/2 pounds fresh raspberries	2 cups whipping cream, whipped
Sugar to taste	Light brown sugar

Place raspberries in large shallow glass baking dish. Sprinkle with sugar. Spread with whipped cream, sealing to edges. Chill in refrigerator or freezer until firm. Cover with thin layer of brown sugar. Place under broiler until sugar melts and bubbles. Chill until serving time. Yield. 10 to 12 servings.

Shirley Andrist, Preceptor Laureate Theta
Estevan, Saskatchewan, Canada

STRAWBERRY MOUSSE

1 cup crushed strawberries	20 marshmallows
1/4 cup sugar	1/4 cup water
1 tablespoon lemon juice	1 cup whipping cream, whipped

Combine strawberries, sugar and lemon juice in large bowl, stirring to coat. Place marshmallows and water in top of double boiler. Cook until melted, stirring constantly; cool. Stir into strawberries. Fold in whipped cream. Spoon into 1-quart mold. Freeze until firm. Invert onto serving plate. Yield: 6 servings.

Joanne Veverka Tauber, Laureate Omega
Tampa, Florida

BAKED-IN STRAWBERRY SHORTCAKE

1 1/2 cups all-purpose flour	2 tablespoons melted butter or margarine
3/4 cup sugar	2 1/2 cups chopped strawberries
2 teaspoons baking powder	1/4 cup butter or margarine, softened
1/2 teaspoon salt	Whipped cream
1/2 cup milk	
1 egg	

Preheat oven to 350 degrees. Sift 1 cup flour, 1/2 cup sugar, baking powder and salt into mixer bowl. Add milk, egg and melted butter. Beat at low speed for 2 minutes. Spoon into greased 8-by-8-inch baking pan. Top with strawberries. Combine remaining 1/2 cup flour, 1/4 cup sugar and 1/4 cup softened butter in small bowl, stirring until crumbly. Sprinkle over strawberries. Bake for 35 to 40 minutes or until light brown. Garnish with whipped cream. Yield: 9 servings.

Barbara Ball, Preceptor Alpha Zeta
Grand Junction, Colorado

QUICK APPLE DESSERT

3 cups sliced apples
1 3-ounce package
  raspberry gelatin
1 cup all-purpose flour
½ cup sugar
½ cup margarine,
  softened
Whipped topping

Preheat oven to 350 degrees. Arrange sliced apples in buttered 6-by-10-inch baking dish. Sprinkle with gelatin. Combine flour, sugar and margarine in small bowl, stirring until crumbly. Sprinkle over apples. Bake for 30 minutes or until golden brown; cool. Top with whipped topping. Yield: 6 to 8 servings.

Vera Wilson, Laureate Beta
Claremont, New Hampshire

SURPRISE—IT'S YOGURT

1 cup strawberry yogurt
  with strawberries
1 cup sliced strawberries
12 ounces whipped
  topping
Strawberry halves

Mix yogurt and sliced strawberries in bowl. Fold in whipped topping. Spoon into serving bowl. Garnish with strawberry halves. Yield: 6 to 8 servings.

Diana Suplita, Preceptor Iota
Fairmont, West Virginia

KIWI KWICKIE

1 1-layer package
  yellow cake mix
1 egg, beaten
½ cup water
1 9-ounce can vanilla
  pudding
Sliced strawberries
Sliced kiwifruit
Chopped pecans

Preheat oven to 350 degrees. Combine cake mix, egg and water in bowl; mix well. Pour into greased and floured Marion pan. Bake for 10 minutes or until golden brown. Invert onto cake plate while warm; cool. Fill center with vanilla pudding. Layer with strawberries, kiwifruit and pecans. Chill before serving. May substitute cherry or blueberry pie filling for pudding and fruits or brownie mix for cake mix. May fill with ice cream and drizzle with chocolate syrup. Yield: 8 to 10 servings.

Gale Carlson, Preceptor Kappa
Liverpool, New York

SUMMER ZINFANDEL DESSERT

1 3-ounce package
  vanilla instant
  pudding mix
3 cups milk
3 ounces white
  Zinfandel wine
1 cup whipped topping
30 fresh strawberries
15 slices fresh or canned
  pineapple
2 large bananas, sliced
1 11-ounce can
  mandarin oranges,
  drained

Combine pudding mix, milk and wine in mixer bowl. Beat at medium speed for 2 minutes until smooth. Fold in whipped topping. Spoon mixture of fruits into champagne or large wine glasses. Spoon pudding sauce over fruits. Chill for 10 minutes. Sauce may also be used over fruit crêpes. Yield: 15 servings.

Walda Weaver, Xi Gamma Omicron
Pryor, Oklahoma

ALMOND BAR DESSERT

30 marshmallows
½ cup milk
1 cup whipping cream,
  whipped
1 teaspoon vanilla
  extract
1 8-ounce chocolate
  bar with almonds,
  grated
1½ cups graham
  cracker crumbs

Melt marshmallows in milk in saucepan. Cool to room temperature. Fold in whipped cream, vanilla and chocolate. Layer half the cracker crumbs, chocolate mixture and remaining crumbs in 9-by-11-inch dish. Chill until serving time. Yield: 12 servings.

Dee Dee Patrick, Delta Iota
St. Cloud, Minnesota

ALMOND TARTS

1 egg
¼ cup sugar
1 tablespoon almond
  flavoring
½ cup rice flour
2 tablespoons melted
  butter or margarine
12 unbaked tart shells

Preheat oven to 400 degrees. Beat egg in bowl. Beat in sugar. Fold in flavoring, flour and butter. Spoon into tart shells on baking sheet. Bake for 10 minutes. May frost with thin layer of butter frosting if desired. Yield: 12 servings.

Anne Anderson
Sudbury, Ontario, Canada

CHERRY BROWNIE TORTE

1 large package brownie
  mix
1 14-ounce can
  sweetened condensed
  milk
½ cup cold water
1 4-ounce package
  vanilla instant
  pudding mix
8 ounces whipped topping
1 21-ounce can cherry
  pie filling

Preheat oven to 350 degrees. Line bottoms and sides of two 8-inch baking pans with waxed paper; grease waxed paper. Prepare brownie mix using directions for cake-like brownies. Spoon into prepared pans. Bake for 20 minutes. Mix condensed milk, water and pudding mix in bowl. Chill for 10 to 15 minutes. Fold in whipped topping. Layer brownie layers, pudding mixture and pie filling ½ at a time on serving plate, allowing pudding mixture to dribble down side. Yield: 16 servings.

Michelle Bradley, Preceptor Iota
Leawood, Kansas

FABULOUS CHOCOLATE FONDUE

2 or 3 16-ounce chocolate bars	Cinnamon to taste
1 or 2 tablespoons water	Banana slices, pineapple chunks or raisins
2 or 3 tablespoons heavy cream	Almonds or pecans
1 or 2 tablespoons cherry brandy	Marshmallows
1½ teaspoons instant coffee granules	Angel food cake or brownie cubes

Melt chocolate with water in fondue pot over low heat. Stir in cream, brandy, instant coffee and cinnamon. Serve with fondue forks to dip fruit, nuts, marshmallows or cake pieces into chocolate mixture. Yield: 4 to 6 servings.

Ann Rupprecht, Xi Alpha Rho
Grand Island, Nebraska

HONEY-FRUIT FONDUE

½ cup butter or margarine	¼ cup thawed frozen orange juice concentrate
¼ cup apricot-pineapple preserves	Fresh fruit, marshmallows, angel food cake cubes or pretzels
1 cup whipping cream	
¼ cup honey	
1½ tablespoons cornstarch	

Melt butter and preserves with whipping cream and honey in fondue pot over medium temperature; mix well. Reduce heat to low. Blend cornstarch and orange juice concentrate in small bowl. Add to fondue pot; mix well. Cook until thickened, stirring constantly. Serve with fresh fruit, marshmallows, angel food cake cubes or pretzels. Yield: 10 servings.

Lynne Sullivan, Preceptor Iota Beta
Santa Paula, California

CHOCOLATE PIZZA

2 cups semisweet chocolate chips	1 6-ounce jar red maraschino cherries, drained, cut into halves
1 pound white almond bark	3 tablespoons chopped green maraschino cherries
2 cups miniature marshmallows	⅓ cup flaked coconut
1 cup crisp rice cereal	1 teaspoon oil
1 cup peanuts	

Combine chocolate chips and 14 ounces almond bark in 2-quart glass bowl. Microwave on High for 2 minutes; stir. Microwave for 1 to 2 minutes longer or until smooth, stirring every 30 seconds. Stir in marshmallows, cereal and peanuts. Spoon into greased 12-inch pizza pan. Top with cherries; sprinkle with coconut. Microwave remaining 2 ounces almond bark with oil in 1-cup measure for 1 minute; stir. Microwave for 30 seconds to 1 minute longer or until smooth, stirring every 15 seconds. Drizzle over pizza. Chill until firm. Store at room temperature. Cut into wedges to serve. May shape into four 6-inch rounds or twelve 4-inch rounds on waxed paper-lined baking sheets if preferred. May substitute pecans or walnuts for peanuts or red and green "M & M's" candies for cherries. Yield: 12 servings.

Cinda Rodgers, Zeta
Oklahoma City, Oklahoma

JELLY ROLL DESSERT

1 small package jelly rolls	1 4-ounce package vanilla instant pudding mix
1 package lemon pie filling mix	1½ cups milk
1 envelope whipped topping mix	1 teaspoon vanilla extract

Slice jelly rolls ¼ inch thick. Arrange in 9-by-13-inch dish. Prepare lemon pie filling mix using package directions. Let stand for several minutes. Spoon over jelly rolls. Chill in refrigerator. Combine whipped topping mix, pudding mix and milk in mixer bowl. Beat for 8 to 10 minutes or until thickened. Mix in vanilla. Spoon over lemon layer. Chill until serving time. Yield: 15 servings.

Debbie Wilkes, Xi Alpha Sigma
Oshawa, Ontario, Canada

CREAM CHEESE CUPCAKE DESSERT

16 ounces cream cheese, softened	½ cup sugar
2 eggs	12 vanilla wafers
1 teaspoon vanilla or almond extract	1 21-ounce can cherry pie filling

Preheat oven to 375 degrees. Beat cream cheese, eggs, vanilla and sugar in mixer bowl for 5 minutes. Place 1 vanilla wafer in each paper-lined muffin cup. Top with cream cheese mixture. Bake for 15 minutes. Cool to room temperature. Top with pie filling. May substitute blueberries, strawberries or other fruit for pie filling. Yield: 12 servings.

Joan Craighead, Xi Iota Omega
Dellwood, Missouri

Susan A. Fortino, Xi Lambda Delta, Hudson, Florida, makes Fruit Roll-Ups by rolling mixture of 2 cups baking mix and ⅔ cup milk into 12-by-15-inch rectangle. Sprinkle with 2 cups chopped fresh fruit and cinnamon. Rollup; cut into 12 slices. Place in greased baking pan. Pour mixture of 1 cup sugar and 2 cups water over top. Bake in preheated 400-degree oven for 15 minutes; reduce oven temperature. Bake at 350 degrees for 10 minutes longer.

BUTTER BRICKLE

1 cup melted margarine
2 cups all-purpose flour
1/2 cup oats
1/2 cup packed light
  brown sugar
1 cup chopped pecans
1 16-ounce jar caramel
  or butterscotch sauce
1 pint vanilla ice cream,
  softened

Preheat oven to 400 degrees. Combine margarine, flour, oats, brown sugar and pecans in bowl; mix well. Pat into thin layer on baking sheet. Bake for 15 minutes. Crumble while still hot. Sprinkle half the crumbs into 9-by-13-inch dish. Drizzle with half the caramel sauce. Spoon ice cream over sauce. Top with remaining crumbs and caramel sauce. Freeze until serving time. Yield: 15 servings.

Veronica McKinnon, Gamma Zeta
Kirkland Lake, Ontario, Canada

BUTTERFINGER DELIGHT

2 cups graham cracker
  crumbs
6 tablespoons butter or
  margarine, softened
2 4-ounce packages
  vanilla instant
  pudding mix
2 cups milk
1/2 gallon vanilla ice
  cream, softened
2 large Butterfinger
  candy bars, crushed
8 ounces whipped
  topping
1 large Butterfinger
  candy bar, crushed

Mix cracker crumbs and butter in 9-by-13-inch dish; press evenly into dish. Combine pudding mix and milk in bowl; mix until smooth. Let stand for 5 minutes. Blend in ice cream. Fold in 2 crushed candy bars. Spoon into prepared dish. Freeze for 30 minutes. Top with whipped topping and remaining crushed candy bar. Store in refrigerator.
Yield: 12 to 16 servings.

Brenda Stephens, Theta Sigma
Hays, Kansas

BISCUIT TORTONI

This was the dessert served with an Italian dinner at a recent rush party.

1 1/2 cups whipping
  cream, chilled
1/3 cup sugar
24 vanilla wafers,
  crushed
1/2 cup chopped almonds
1/4 cup drained chopped
  maraschino cherries
1 tablespoon rum
1 teaspoon vanilla
  extract

Beat whipping cream and sugar in chilled mixer bowl until soft peaks form. Reserve 1/4 cup cookie crumbs. Fold remaining cookie crumbs into whipped cream. Fold in almonds, cherries, rum and vanilla. Spoon into 12 paper-lined medium muffin cups. Sprinkle with reserved crumbs. Freeze until firm.
Yield: 12 servings.

Cindy Layton, Xi Epsilon Nu
Cape Girardeau, Missouri

COFFEE TORTONI

1 egg white
2 tablespoons sugar
1 tablespoon instant
  coffee granules
1 cup whipping cream
1/4 cup sugar
1 teaspoon vanilla
  extract
1/8 teaspoon almond
  extract
2 tablespoons toasted
  chopped almonds
2 tablespoons toasted
  finely chopped coconut

Beat egg white in mixer bowl until frothy. Beat in 2 tablespoons sugar and coffee granules gradually, beating until stiff peaks form. Beat whipping cream in mixer bowl. Add 1/4 cup sugar gradually, beating until soft peaks form. Fold in flavorings and half the almonds and coconut. Fold in egg whites. Spoon into paper-lined muffin cups. Sprinkle with remaining almonds and coconut. Freeze until firm.
Yield: 8 servings.

Pat Conrath, Alpha Lambda
Cheney, Washington
Deborah Vanderhoek, Alpha Gamma
Port Alberni, British Columbia, Canada

CHOCOLATE-CHERRY ICE CREAM DESSERT

This is an easy make-ahead dessert to keep in the freezer for unexpected company.

30 creme-filled
  chocolate sandwich
  cookies, crumbled
1/4 cup melted margarine
1/2 gallon vanilla ice
  cream, softened
1 21-ounce can cherry
  pie filling

Reserve 1/4 cup cookie crumbs. Combine remaining cookie crumbs with margarine in large bowl; mix well. Press over bottom of 9-by-13-inch dish. Chill for 10 to 15 minutes. Layer half the ice cream, pie filling, remaining ice cream and reserved crumbs in prepared dish. Chill, covered, for 2 hours. Cut into squares. Yield: 12 to 15 servings.

Carla Pearson, Omicron Delta
McPherson, Kansas

CRISPY ICE CREAM DESSERT

3 cups crisp rice cereal
1 cup packed light
  brown sugar
1 cup coconut
1/2 cup chopped nuts
1/2 cup butter or
  margarine
1/2 gallon vanilla ice
  cream

Preheat oven to 300 degrees. Combine cereal, brown sugar, coconut, nuts and butter in bowl; mix well. Spread on baking sheet. Bake for 20 minutes. Slice ice cream. Arrange slices in buttered dish. Top with cereal mixture. Freeze until serving time.
Yield: 8 servings.

Shirley Ruth Balasko, Preceptor Beta Phi
Englewood, Colorado

QUICK CHOCOLATE MOUSSE

This is quick, delicious and delights the palate.

1 14-ounce can
  sweetened condensed
  milk
1 4-ounce package
  chocolate instant
  pudding mix

1 cup water
1 to 1 1/2 cups whipping
  cream, whipped
  Maraschino cherries
  and mint leaves or
  nuts

Combine milk, pudding mix and water in mixer bowl. Beat at medium speed until smooth. Chill for 5 minutes. Fold in whipped cream, reserving some for topping. Spoon into individual dessert dishes. Garnish with reserved whipped topping, cherries, mint leaves or nuts. Yield: 4 to 6 servings.

Nancy Tosetti, Omicron Delta
Nokomis, Illinois

CREAM CHEESE MOUSSE

Vary the pudding flavor and the toppings for a quick dessert.

1 4-ounce package any
  flavor instant pudding
  mix
8 ounces whipped
  topping

8 ounces cream cheese,
  softened
  Slivered almonds or
  shaved chocolate

Prepare pudding using package directions. Fold in whipped topping. Add cream cheese, beating until light and fluffy. Pour into glass dish. Chill until firm. Garnish vanilla mousse with slivered almonds and chocolate mousse with shaved chocolate.
Yield: 6 to 8 servings.

Angie Kay Kidd, Xi Epsilon Kappa
Ligonier, Indiana

MUCHO MOCHA MOUSSE

1 1/2 cups low-fat milk
2 teaspoons instant
  coffee powder
1 envelope whipped
  topping mix

1 3-ounce package
  chocolate instant
  pudding mix

Combine milk and coffee powder in mixer bowl. Let stand for 5 minutes or until coffee is dissolved. Add topping mix and pudding mix. Beat at low speed for 30 seconds. Beat at high speed for 4 minutes or until light and fluffy. Spoon into individual dessert dishes. May substitute sugar-free pudding mix for regular pudding mix and skim milk for low-fat milk to reduce calories. Yield: 6 servings.

Pat McAtee, Xi Alpha Pi
Carrollton, Missouri

SLOW-COOKER BREAD PUDDING

8 slices white bread, cut
  into 1/2-inch cubes
4 eggs, beaten
1/4 cup sugar
1/4 cup melted butter or
  margarine
2 cups milk
1/4 teaspoon nutmeg
1 teaspoon cinnamon

1 cup raisins
1/2 cup sugar
2 tablespoons (heaping)
  all-purpose flour
2 tablespoons butter or
  margarine
1 cup water
1 teaspoon vanilla
  extract

Place bread cubes in greased 1 1/2-quart slow cooker. Combine eggs, 1/4 cup sugar, melted butter, milk, nutmeg and cinnamon in medium bowl, stirring until smooth. Add raisins. Pour mixture over bread cubes. Cook on High, covered loosely to allow steam to escape, for 1 hour. Combine 1/2 cup sugar, flour, butter, water and vanilla in saucepan; mix well. Cook over medium heat until thickened, stirring frequently. Serve over pudding. Yield: 4 to 6 servings.

Tammela Sibert, Beta Lambda
Kendallville, Indiana

SUPER BREAD PUDDING WITH RUM SAUCE

5 or 6 slices bread, cubed
1 1/2 cups evaporated
  milk
1 cup sugar
3 eggs, slightly beaten
1 teaspoon vanilla
  extract
1/8 teaspoon salt
1 teaspoon cinnamon
1/4 cup melted butter or
  margarine

1/4 to 1/2 cup raisins
1/2 cup sugar
2 tablespoons
  cornstarch
1/2 teaspoon cinnamon
1 cup evaporated milk
1/2 cup milk
3 tablespoons
  margarine
1 1/2 tablespoons dark
  rum

Soak bread cubes in 1 1/2 cups evaporated milk in bowl for 10 minutes. Add 1 cup sugar, eggs, vanilla, salt, 1 teaspoon cinnamon, melted butter and raisins; mix well. Pour into 8-inch glass ring mold. Microwave on Medium for 10 to 12 minutes or until knife inserted in center comes out clean. Let stand for 5 minutes. Combine 1/2 cup sugar, cornstarch and 1/2 teaspoon cinnamon in glass bowl; mix well. Stir in 1 cup evaporated milk and 1/2 cup milk. Microwave on High for 2 1/2 minutes; stir. Microwave for 1 1/2 to 2 minutes longer or until thickened. Stir in 3 tablespoons margarine and rum. Pour sauce over sliced bread pudding before serving.
Yield: 8 to 10 servings.

June Williams, Laureate Rho
Woodstock, Georgia

FROZEN CHERRY CHEESECAKE CUPS

It's great to have these on hand in the freezer to pull out and serve to that special unexpected company!

8 ounces cream cheese, softened	1/4 cup sugar
1/2 cup black cherry yogurt	1 egg white, stiffly beaten
1 egg yolk	1 21-ounce can cherry pie filling

Beat cream cheese, yogurt, egg yolk and sugar in mixer bowl until light and fluffy. Fold in egg white. Stir in half the pie filling. Spoon into paper-lined muffin cups. Freeze, covered, until firm. Remove paper liners. Heat remaining pie filling in saucepan. Spoon over cheesecakes. Yield: 12 servings.

Barb Hacking, Gamma Phi
Stratford, Ontario, Canada

GHETTO CHEESECAKE

I work in a nursing home where we periodically treat ourselves to an employee buffet. This is a dish made by one of my male co-workers.

2 cups all-purpose flour	16 ounces whipped topping
1 cup chopped walnuts	
1 cup butter or margarine, softened	2 4-ounce packages chocolate instant pudding mix
8 ounces cream cheese, softened	3 cups milk
1 cup confectioners' sugar	

Preheat oven to 350 degrees. Mix flour, walnuts and butter in bowl. Press into 9-by-13-inch baking pan. Bake for 10 minutes or until golden brown. Combine cream cheese, confectioners' sugar and whipped topping; beat until blended and smooth. Spread over cooled crust. Combine pudding mixes and milk in bowl; beat well. Spoon over cream cheese layer. Yield: 10 to 12 servings.

Donna R. Donnell, Alpha Iota
Oneonta, New York

IRRESISTIBLE CHEESECAKE

Add 1 cup of toffee, Heath bar, butterscotch or chocolate chips to the cream cheese mixture if you desire.

1 1/2 cups graham cracker crumbs	1/2 cup sugar
1/4 cup sugar	1 teaspoon vanilla extract
5 tablespoons melted margarine	1 cup sour cream
16 ounces cream cheese, softened	1/4 cup sugar
2 eggs	1 teaspoon vanilla extract

Preheat oven to 375 degrees. Mix crumbs, 1/4 cup sugar and melted margarine in bowl. Press into 9-inch springform pan. Combine cream cheese, eggs,

1/2 cup sugar and 1 teaspoon vanilla in mixer bowl; beat until smooth. Spread over crumb mixture. Bake for 30 to 35 minutes or until center is set. Let stand for 15 minutes. Increase oven temperature to 475 degrees. Mix sour cream, remaining 1/4 cup sugar and 1 teaspoon vanilla in bowl. Spoon over cheesecake. Bake for 5 to 10 minutes or until light brown. Loosen cake from side of pan with knife. Place on serving plate; remove side of pan. Chill until serving time. Yield: 16 servings.

Judi F. Oliva, Gamma Kappa
Wilber, Nebraska

KAHLUA CHEESECAKE

1 1/3 cups chocolate wafer crumbs	1/4 cup Kahlua
1/3 cup sugar	6 ounces cream cheese, softened
1 tablespoon melted butter or margarine	1/3 cup sugar
1 ounce semisweet chocolate, melted	2 eggs
	2 cups sour cream
2 tablespoons melted butter or margarine	1 ounce semisweet chocolate, melted
	1 teaspoon Kahlua

Mix crumbs, 1/3 cup sugar and 1 tablespoon butter in bowl. Press into 9-inch springform pan; chill. Combine 1 ounce chocolate, 2 tablespoons butter and 1/4 cup Kahlua in bowl; mix well. Beat cream cheese and remaining 1/3 cup sugar in mixer bowl until light and fluffy. Add eggs 1 at a time, beating well after each addition. Stir in chocolate mixture and half the sour cream. Pour into crust. Bake for 10 minutes. Reduce oven temperature to 250 degrees. Bake for 35 to 40 minutes longer or until center is set. Cool completely. Spread with remaining 1 cup sour cream. Spoon or pipe mixture of 1 ounce chocolate and 1 teaspoon Kahlua in circular pattern over cheesecake. Yield: 12 servings.

Marilyn Mercier, Alpha Xi
Spruce Grove, Alberta, Canada

CARLA'S PISTACHIO CHEESECAKE

1 1/2 cups all-purpose flour	16 ounces whipped topping
3/4 cup butter or margarine	2 4-ounce packages pistachio instant pudding mix
1/3 cup ground almonds	2 1/2 to 3 cups milk
2/3 cup sugar	Chopped nuts
8 ounces cream cheese, softened	Cherries

Preheat oven to 350 degrees. Mix flour, butter and almonds in bowl. Pat into greased 9-by-13-inch baking pan. Bake for 25 minutes. Cream sugar and cream cheese in mixer bowl until light. Stir in 1 cup whipped topping. Spread over crust. Chill in refrigerator. Combine pudding mixes and milk in bowl; mix well. Spread over cream cheese mixture. Chill until set. Spread with remaining whipped topping. Decorate with nuts and cherries. Yield: 12 servings.

Emily Maude Wright, Laureate Alpha Psi
Guelph, Ontario, Canada

RASPBERRY ANGEL FOOD CAKE

1 12-ounce package frozen raspberries, thawed	2 tablespoons sour cream
1 9-inch angel food cake	2 tablespoons Crème de Cassis
8 ounces cream cheese, softened	Red food coloring (optional)
2 cups confectioners' sugar	Whole fresh raspberries

Drain thawed raspberries, reserving juice. Cut cake into halves horizontally; remove top layer. Spoon raspberries over bottom layer. Pour all but 2 table-spoons raspberry juice over raspberries. Replace top layer. Beat cream cheese in mixer bowl until light and fluffy. Add remaining 2 tablespoons raspberry juice, confectioners' sugar, sour cream and liqueur; beat well. Stir in food coloring. Spread over top and side of cake. Garnish with whole raspberries. Store in airtight container in refrigerator. Yield: 16 servings.

Sjaan Protulipac, Alpha
Winnipeg, Manitoba, Canada

STRAWBERRY ANGEL FOOD CAKE

1/2 angel food cake loaf	1 16-ounce package frozen strawberries
1 3-ounce package strawberry gelatin	1 cup whipped cream or whipped topping
1 1/2 cups hot water	

Tear cake into small pieces. Place in 9-by-12-inch serving dish. Dissolve gelatin in hot water. Stir in strawberries. Fold in whipped cream. Spoon over cake. Chill until serving time. Yield: 12 servings.

Carla J. Andrews, Delta Theta
Great Bend, Kansas

OLD-FASHIONED APPLE CAKE

This was my grandmother's recipe; she used green Granny Smith apples. It is a very moist cake that keeps well in the refrigerator.

2 cups chopped peeled apples	1/4 cup margarine
1 cup sugar	1/2 cup sugar
1 egg, well beaten	1/2 cup packed light brown sugar
1 cup all-purpose flour	1/4 cup water
1 teaspoon baking soda	3 tablespoons all-purpose flour
1 teaspoon cinnamon	1 teaspoon vanilla extract
1 cup finely chopped walnuts	

Preheat oven to 350 degrees. Mix apples and 1 cup sugar in bowl. Let stand until mixture becomes juicy.

Add egg, 1 cup flour, baking soda, cinnamon and walnuts; mix well. Pour into greased 9-by-12-inch cake pan. Bake for 25 to 30 minutes or until cake tests done. Combine margarine, remaining 1/2 cup sugar, brown sugar, water, 3 tablespoons flour and vanilla in saucepan. Cook until sugar is dissolved and mixture is thickened, stirring frequently. Spread over cooled cake. Yield: 8 to 10 servings.

Shirley Jones, Laureate Beta Mu
Shingletown, California

APPLE 'N CUSTARD SPICE CAKE

1 2-layer package spice cake mix	1 cup sour cream
1 14-ounce can sweetened condensed milk	1/4 cup lemon juice
	2 apples, finely chopped
	Cinnamon to taste

Preheat oven to 350 degrees. Prepare and bake cake mix using package directions for 9-by-13-inch cake pan. Mix condensed milk, sour cream and lemon juice in bowl. Stir in apples. Spread over cake. Bake at 350 degrees for 10 minutes. Sprinkle with cinnamon. Cool in pan. Yield: 15 servings.

Doris McCabe, Laureate Upsilon
Slatington, Pennsylvania

APPLESAUCE-NUT CAKE

2 cups all-purpose flour	2 eggs, well beaten
2 cups sugar	1 tablespoon vanilla extract
2 teaspoons baking soda	2/3 cup chopped walnuts
2 teaspoons nutmeg	
2 2/3 cups applesauce	

Preheat oven to 350 degrees. Sift flour, sugar, baking soda and nutmeg together. Add applesauce, eggs and vanilla; mix well. Stir in walnuts. Pour into un-greased 9-by-12-inch cake pan. Bake for 30 minutes or until cake tests done. Yield: 8 to 10 servings.

Eleanor M. Anderson, Preceptor Gamma Theta
Arkansas City, Kansas

SWEET-TOOTH CHOCOLATE CAKE

1 2-layer package devil's food cake mix	1 8-ounce jar caramel ice cream topping
1 14-ounce can sweetened condensed milk	12 ounces whipped topping

Preheat oven to 350 degrees. Prepare and bake cake mix using package directions for 9-by-12-inch cake pan. Cool in pan. Pierce cake several times with fork. Pour condensed milk over cake. Pour topping over milk. Chill until serving time. Spread with whipped topping. Yield: 15 servings.

Linda Groom Hyde, Alpha Upsilon Theta
Granbury, Texas

CINNAMON SUPPER CAKE

When the cupboard is nearly bare, there always seems to be just enough on hand to bake this moist and tender cake. It can be ready to remove from the oven just as you have finished eating dinner!

1 cup all-purpose flour	1 teaspoon vanilla
1½ teaspoons baking	extract
powder	1 tablespoon butter or
¼ teaspoon salt	margarine, softened
¾ cup sugar	3 tablespoons
¼ cup shortening	confectioners' sugar
1 egg	1 tablespoon cinnamon
½ cup milk	

Preheat oven to 375 degrees. Sift flour, baking powder and salt together. Cream sugar and shortening in mixer bowl until light. Beat in egg. Add milk and vanilla; beat well. Stir in flour mixture. Pour into nonstick 8-by-8-inch cake pan. Bake for 20 to 25 minutes or until cake tests done. Spread butter over hot cake. Sift confectioners' sugar and cinnamon over top. Yield: 6 to 9 servings.

Kay Goodroad, Xi Epsilon Iota
Bristow, Oklahoma

CRÈME DE MENTHE CAKE

1 2-layer package	8 ounces whipped
white cake mix	topping
2 tablespoons green	2 tablespoons green
Crème de Menthe	Crème de Menthe
1 12-ounce can	Chocolate sprinkles
chocolate fudge sauce	

Preheat oven to 350 degrees. Prepare and bake cake mix using package directions for 9-by-13-inch cake pan, adding 2 tablespoons Crème de Menthe to batter. Cool in pan. Spread with fudge sauce. Beat whipped topping and 2 tablespoons Crème de Menthe in bowl. Spread over cake. Garnish with chocolate sprinkles. Yield: 15 servings.

Betsy Kohan, Gamma Mu
Kennewick, Washington

CURIOUS CAKE

1 2-layer package	1 cup chopped pecans
German chocolate or	1 cup milk chocolate
Swiss chocolate cake	chips
mix	1 8-ounce package
¾ cup melted margarine	caramels
⅓ cup evaporated milk	⅓ cup evaporated milk

Preheat oven to 350 degrees. Combine cake mix, margarine and ⅓ cup evaporated milk in bowl; mix well. Press half the mixture into 9-by-13-inch cake pan. Bake for 5 minutes. Let stand for several minutes. Sprinkle with pecans and chocolate chips. Combine caramels and remaining ⅓ cup evaporated milk in saucepan. Cook until caramels are melted,

stirring frequently. Drizzle over pecans. Top with remaining batter. Bake for 20 minutes longer. Yield: 15 servings.

Tommie May, Xi Rho Zeta
Houston, Texas

EGGNOGGING CHOCOLATE CAKE

1¼ cups water	2 cups eggnog
⅓ cup vegetable oil	1 cup packed light
¾ cup egg substitute	brown sugar
1 2-layer package	1 cup sugar
German chocolate	1 cup chopped pecans
cake mix	

Preheat oven to 350 degrees. Beat first 4 ingredients in mixer bowl at medium speed for 2 minutes. Pour into 10-by-15-inch cake pan sprayed with nonstick cooking spray. Bake for 28 minutes. Mix eggnog, brown sugar and sugar in microwave-safe bowl. Microwave on Medium for 10 minutes. Pour into 2-quart saucepan. Stir in pecans. Cook over medium heat, stirring frequently. Punch several holes in cake with wooden spoon. Pour hot eggnog mixture over cake. Chill in refrigerator for 10 to 15 minutes. Serve warm. Yield: 35 servings.

Eula Keegan, Phi
Gulfport, Mississippi

FASTEST CAKE IN-THE-WEST

2 cups all-purpose flour	1 21-ounce can cherry
1½ cups sugar	pie filling
½ teaspoon baking soda	¾ cup vegetable oil
1 teaspoon cinnamon	2 eggs, beaten
½ teaspoon salt	

Preheat oven to 350 degrees. Sift flour, sugar, baking soda, cinnamon and salt into ungreased 9-by-13-inch cake pan. Add pie filling, oil and eggs; mix well. Bake for 40 to 45 minutes or until cake tests done. Serve warm with ice cream or cool and spread with cream cheese frosting. Yield: 12 servings.

Anne Wright, Beta Zeta
Greensburg, Kansas

MAMA'S GRAPEFRUIT CAKE

3 cups cake flour	1 cup unsalted butter or
3½ teaspoons baking	margarine
powder	1½ cups sugar
¾ teaspoon salt	3 eggs
¼ teaspoon baking soda	1 cup grapefruit juice

Preheat oven to 375 degrees. Sift flour, baking powder, salt and baking soda together. Cream butter and sugar in mixer bowl until light and fluffy. Add eggs 1 at a time, beating well after each addition. Add flour mixture and grapefruit juice alternately to creamed mixture, beating well at low speed after each addition. Pour into 2 greased and floured 9-inch round cake pans. Bake for 30 minutes. Cool in pans for several minutes. Remove to wire racks to cool completely. Spread between layers and over top and side of cake with favorite sour cream or cream cheese frosting. Yield: 12 servings.

Patricia Coody, Delta Xi
Crossett, Arkansas

HEATH DELIGHT

1 2-layer package German chocolate cake mix	1 16-ounce jar caramel ice cream topping
6 Heath bars, crushed	8 ounces whipped topping

Preheat oven to 350 degrees. Prepare and bake cake mix using package directions for 11-by-13-inch cake pan. Make holes 3 to 4 inches apart in hot cake with wooden spoon. Sprinkle with half the crushed candy. Pour caramel topping over cake. Cool in pan. Spread with whipped topping. Sprinkle with remaining candy. Chill until serving time. Yield: 16 servings.

Lavon Rose, Preceptor Delta Tau
Kansas City, Missouri

IN-A-JIFFY CAKE

Sometimes I add raisins, sliced apples or cinnamon to this cake to change the taste. This is just as fast as any cake mix you can buy at the store.

1½ cups sifted cake flour	¾ cup milk
¾ cup sugar	1 teaspoon vanilla extract
¼ teaspoon salt	¼ cup melted shortening
2 teaspoons baking powder	1 egg, beaten

Preheat oven to 350 degrees. Sift flour, sugar, salt and baking powder together 3 times. Combine milk, vanilla, shortening and egg in small bowl; mix well. Stir into flour mixture. Pour into greased 8-by-8-inch cake pan. Bake for 30 minutes. Yield: 10 servings.

Irene A. Fritz, Xi Zeta Omicron
Trenton, Ontario, Canada

JIFFY CAKE

This was my first cooking project, at age seven. I made it for a backyard "club" meeting.

1¾ cups all-purpose flour	1 tablespoon baking powder
⅓ cup shortening	½ teaspoon salt
1⅓ cups packed light brown sugar	1 teaspoon cinnamon
2 eggs	¼ teaspoon nutmeg
½ cup milk	¼ teaspoon ginger
½ teaspoon lemon extract	½ teaspoon cloves
	1 cup raisins
	Confectioners' sugar

Preheat oven to 350 degrees. Combine flour, shortening, brown sugar, eggs, milk, flavoring, baking powder, salt, cinnamon, nutmeg, ginger and cloves

in mixer bowl. Beat at low speed until well mixed. Stir in raisins. Pour into greased and floured 8-by-10-inch cake pan. Bake for 25 to 30 minutes or until cake tests done. Sprinkle with confectioners' sugar. Yield: 10 to 12 servings.

Carolyn Colburn, Preceptor Zeta Mu
Citrus Heights, California

LAST-TIME-EVER-I-SAW-MY-WAIST CAKE

1 1-layer package devil's food cake mix	1 6-ounce package chocolate instant pudding mix
8 ounces cream cheese, softened	1 cup milk
8 ounces whipped topping	8 ounces whipped topping

Preheat oven to 350 degrees. Prepare and bake cake mix using package directions for 9-by-13-inch cake pan. Mix cream cheese and 8 ounces whipped topping in bowl. Spread over cooled cake. Combine pudding mix and milk in bowl; mix well. Spread over cream cheese mixture. Top with remaining 8 ounces whipped topping. Chill until serving time. Yield: 18 to 20 servings.

Terri Kippley, Delta Omega
St. Cloud, Minnesota

❖ MANDARIN CAKE

This cake is low fat and low cholesterol. It is very moist and will keep, uncovered, for 3 to 4 days.

2 11-ounce cans mandarin oranges	2 eggs
2 cups all-purpose flour	1 teaspoon salt
2 cups sugar	1 cup chopped walnuts
2 teaspoons vanilla extract	¾ cup packed light brown sugar
2 teaspoons baking soda	3 tablespoons milk
	3 tablespoons butter or margarine

Preheat oven to 350 degrees. Combine undrained oranges, flour, sugar, vanilla, baking soda, eggs, salt and walnuts in mixer bowl; beat until well mixed. Pour into ungreased 9-by-13-inch cake pan. Bake for 30 to 35 minutes or until cake tests done. Cool in pan. Pierce with fork or toothpick. Combine brown sugar, milk and butter in saucepan. Bring to a boil, stirring occasionally. Pour over cake. Yield: 15 servings.

Paula M. Seeley, Xi Beta Beta
Vancouver, Washington

Fern Desjardin, Preceptor, Lewiston, Maine, makes Pineapple Angel Cake by splitting a baked angel food cake and spreading a mixture of 2 cups whipping cream, whipped, and a large can drained crushed pinapple between layers and over top and side of cake.

ORANGE CHIFFON SURPRISE

1 orange chiffon cake
1 4-ounce package
vanilla instant
pudding mix
1 20-ounce can crushed
pineapple, drained

16 ounces whipped
topping
1 2-ounce package
toasted slivered
almonds

Cut cake horizontally into 3 layers. Combine pudding mix, pineapple and whipped topping in bowl; mix well. Spread between layers and over top and side of cake. Sprinkle with almonds. Chill until serving time. Yield: 6 to 8 servings.

Linda Lentz, Iota Mu
Highlands Ranch, Colorado

PEACHY CINNAMON CAKE

1 2-layer package
yellow or spice cake
mix
1 21-ounce can peach
or apple pie filling

3 eggs
3 tablespoons sugar
1 teaspoon cinnamon

Preheat oven to 350 degrees. Combine cake mix, pie filling and eggs in mixer bowl; beat at medium speed for 2 minutes. Spread batter and mixture of sugar and cinnamon 1/2 at a time in greased 9-by-13-inch cake pan. Bake for 30 to 35 minutes or until cake tests done. Yield: 12 servings.

Judy Sommerfelt-Brinker, Beta Zeta
Jefferson, Iowa

PIG PICKIN' CAKE

I took this cake 1200 miles in an ice chest to a family reunion. It was the first dessert eaten, and everyone wanted the recipe.

1 20-ounce can crushed
pineapple
1 2-layer package
yellow cake mix
4 eggs
1 11-ounce can
mandarin oranges

3/4 cup corn oil
1 6-ounce package
banana instant
pudding mix
16 ounces whipped
topping

Preheat oven to 325 degrees. Drain pineapple, reserving juice. Combine cake mix, eggs, oranges and corn oil in bowl; mix well. Pour into 4 greased and floured 8-inch cake pans. Bake for 15 to 20 minutes or until layers test done. Cool in pans for several minutes. Remove to wire racks to cool completely. Spoon reserved pineapple juice over layers. Combine pineapple and pudding mix in bowl; mix well. Stir in whipped topping. Spread between layers and over top and side of cake. Chill until serving time. Yield: 16 servings.

Tracy Sutton, Eta Delta
Farmville, North Carolina

COCONUT-FROSTED PINEAPPLE CAKE

Do not substitute margarine for butter in this recipe.

2 cups all-purpose flour
1 1/4 cups sugar
2 teaspoons baking
soda
1 20-ounce can
crushed pineapple
2 eggs
1/2 cup vegetable oil

3/4 cup shredded coconut
3/4 cup chopped pecans
1/2 cup unsalted butter
1 5-ounce can
evaporated milk
1 1/4 cups sugar
1/2 cup shredded coconut
1/2 cup chopped pecans

Preheat oven to 350 degrees. Mix flour, 1 1/4 cups sugar and baking soda in bowl. Add undrained pineapple, eggs and oil; mix well. Stir in 3/4 cup coconut and 3/4 cup pecans. Pour into lightly greased 9-by-13-inch cake pan. Bake for 30 to 45 minutes or until cake tests done. Combine butter, evaporated milk and remaining 1 1/4 cups sugar in large saucepan. Bring to a boil over medium heat. Simmer for 3 to 4 minutes. Cool slightly. Stir in remaining 1/2 cup coconut and 1/2 cup pecans. Spread over hot cake. Serve warm or at room temperature.
Yield: 15 servings.

Ginny Spann, Preceptor Laureate Gamma Theta
Katy, Texas

FROSTED PINEAPPLE SURPRISE CAKE

This very moist cake was brought to a ladies' golf outing that I attended.

2 cups all-purpose flour
2 cups sugar
2 teaspoons baking soda
2 eggs
1 teaspoon almond
extract
1 20-ounce can crushed
pineapple

1 cup chopped nuts
1/2 cup melted margarine
8 ounces cream cheese,
softened
3 cups confectioners'
sugar
1 teaspoon almond
extract

Preheat oven to 350 degrees. Combine flour, sugar, baking soda, eggs and 1 teaspoon flavoring in bowl; mix well. Stir in pineapple and nuts. Pour into greased and floured 11-by-14-inch cake pan. Bake for 25 minutes. Combine margarine, cream cheese and confectioners' sugar in bowl; mix well. Beat in remaining 1 teaspoon flavoring. Spread over cooled cake. Yield: 30 servings.

Levenia Daniels, Laureate Omega
Kirksville, Missouri

Daphne Barfield, Iota Mu, Grayson, Georgia, makes Frozen Brandy Alexander Pie by combining 1 quart softened vanilla ice cream, 3 tablespoons Brandy and 2 tablespoons creme de cocoa in bowl. Spoon into 9-inch graham cracker pie shell. Freeze until firm.

PINEAPPLE SURPRISE CAKE

I always get compliments on this cake; no one suspects it is a store-bought cake!

1 16-ounce frozen pound cake, thawed	1 4-ounce package vanilla instant pudding mix
1/2 cup pineapple juice	8 ounces whipped topping
1 teaspoon almond extract	Toasted slivered almonds
1 20-ounce can crushed pineapple	

Cut cake horizontally into 3 layers. Drizzle with mixture of pineapple juice and almond flavoring. Combine pineapple and pudding mix in bowl; mix well. Fold in whipped topping. Spread between layers and over top and side of cake. Sprinkle with almonds. Yield: 16 servings.

Barbara Sullivan, Laureate Delta Xi
High Island, Texas

POPCORN CAKE

4 quarts popped popcorn	1 cup chopped nuts
2 2-ounce packages "M & M's" Plain Chocolate Candies	1 1/2 pounds marshmallows
2 2-ounce packages "M & M's" Peanut Chocolate Candies	1/4 cup vegetable oil
	1/2 cup margarine

Combine popcorn, candies and nuts in large bowl; mix well. Combine marshmallows, oil and margarine in saucepan. Cook until marshmallows and margarine are melted, stirring frequently. Pour over popcorn mixture. Press into angel food cake pan to mold. Invert onto serving plate. Yield: 12 servings.

Lisa Rohr, Iota Kappa
Kanopolis, Kansas

SPICY PUMPKIN SHEET CAKE

I make pumpkin rolls every year and everyone loves them. Now they like my cake just as much. It's really moist and delicious.

4 eggs	1 teaspoon cinnamon
1 3/4 cups solid-pack pumpkin	1/2 teaspoon ginger
1 cup sugar	1/2 teaspoon nutmeg
3/4 cup packed light brown sugar	8 ounces cream cheese, softened
1 cup vegetable oil	1/2 cup confectioners' sugar
2 cups all-purpose flour	1/2 teaspoon vanilla extract
2 teaspoons baking powder	2 tablespoons butter or margarine, softened
1 teaspoon baking soda	
1/2 teaspoon salt	

Preheat oven to 350 degrees. Beat eggs in large bowl. Add pumpkin, sugar, brown sugar and oil; mix well. Stir in flour, baking powder, baking soda, salt and spices. Spread in greased and floured 10-by-15-inch cake pan. Bake for 25 minutes or until cake tests done. Cool in pan. Combine cream cheese, confectioners' sugar, vanilla and butter in bowl; mix well. Spread over cooled cake. Yield: 16 servings.

Sheri Burnett, Zeta Phi
Bryan, Ohio

❖ APPLE-PEACHESSY PIE

My mother made this pie; she always made great desserts. It was my favorite dessert when I was growing up, and now it's my children's favorite.

1 recipe 2-crust pie pastry	2 eggs
1 21-ounce can apple pie filling	2 tablespoons lemon juice
1 15-ounce can sliced cling peaches, drained	1/3 cup sugar
1/2 teaspoon apple pie spice	4 ounces cream cheese, softened

Preheat oven to 350 degrees. Fit half the pastry into deep-dish pie plate. Spoon mixture of pie filling, peaches and apple pie spice into prepared pie plate. Combine eggs, lemon juice and sugar in 1-quart saucepan; mix well. Cook over medium heat until thickened. Stir in cream cheese. Pour over fruit. Top with remaining pastry. Bake for 45 to 50 minutes or until golden brown. Yield: 8 to 10 servings.

Carol Gaudiano, Xi Gamma Nu
Dallas, Texas

BACKYARD PIE

I've also used this filling in turnovers and it's great!

2 Granny Smith apples, sliced	2 tablespoons honey
1 1/2 cups blackberries	1 teaspoon cloves
1 1/2 cups raspberries	1 teaspoon grated lemon rind
1 1/2 cups rhubarb	3 tablespoons cornstarch
1 1/3 cups unsweetened apple juice	1 unbaked 9-inch pie shell
1/2 cup packed light brown sugar	

Preheat oven to 375 degrees. Combine apples, blackberries, raspberries, rhubarb, apple juice, brown sugar, honey, cloves and lemon rind in saucepan. Cook until apples are tender, stirring frequently. Stir in mixture of cornstarch and a small amount of water. Cook until thickened. Pour into pie shell. Bake for 35 minutes. Yield: 6 servings.

Beth Booth, Xi Beta Zeta
Challis, Idaho

BANANA CREAM PIE

1 9-inch graham cracker pie shell	1 4-ounce package banana cream instant
1 or 2 bananas, sliced	pudding mix
1/2 pint strawberries	Whole strawberries

Line pie shell with bananas and strawberries. Prepare pudding mix using package directions. Spoon over fruit. Garnish with whole strawberries. Yield: 8 servings.

June Gautreau, Omega
Baton Rouge, Louisiana

MOST DELICIOUS BANANA CREAM PIE

You can use skim milk, light sour cream and light whipped topping for fewer calories and less fat.

1 baked 9-inch pie shell	2 4-ounce packages vanilla instant
1 or 2 bananas, sliced	pudding mix
2 cups milk	1 1/2 cups sour cream
	Whipped topping

Line pie shell with bananas. Combine milk and pudding mix in bowl; mix well. Fold in sour cream. Spoon over bananas. Chill until serving time. Top with whipped topping. Yield: 8 servings.

Anne Marie Owens, Xi Theta Delta
Independence, Missouri

QUICK PIE

8 ounces cream cheese, softened	1 teaspoon almond extract
1 14-ounce can sweetened condensed milk	1 9-inch graham cracker pie shell
1/3 cup lemon juice from concentrate	1 21-ounce can cherry pie filling

Beat cream cheese in mixer bowl until light. Beat in condensed milk gradually. Stir in lemon juice and flavoring. Pour into pie shell. Top with pie filling. Chill for 3 hours. Yield: 8 servings.

Louann Pronk, Xi Phi
Montgomery, Alabama

PIES STRAIGHT-FROM HEAVEN

1 cup chopped pecans	8 ounces whipped topping
2 unbaked 9-inch pie shells	1 teaspoon almond extract
8 ounces cream cheese, softened	2 bananas, sliced
3 cups confectioners' sugar	1 21-ounce can blueberry pie filling

Preheat oven to 350 degrees. Sprinkle pecans into pie shells. Bake using pie shell package directions.

Combine cream cheese, confectioners' sugar, whipped topping and flavoring in mixer bowl; beat until fluffy. Spoon into pie shells. Top with banana slices and pie filling. Chill until serving time. Yield: 12 servings.

Mary Bradshaw, Xi Alpha
Omaha, Nebraska

SOUR CREAM-BLUEBERRY PIE

My daughter won first prize at the county fair with this recipe.

1 cup sour cream	1 unbaked deep-dish pie shell
2 tablespoons all-purpose flour	3 tablespoons all-purpose flour
3/4 cup sugar	3 tablespoons chopped pecans or walnuts
1 teaspoon vanilla extract	1 1/2 tablespoons butter or margarine
1/4 teaspoon salt	
1 egg, beaten	
2 1/2 cups fresh blueberries	

Preheat oven to 400 degrees. Combine sour cream, 2 tablespoons flour, sugar, vanilla, salt and egg in mixer bowl; beat at medium speed until smooth. Fold in blueberries. Spoon into pie shell. Bake for 25 minutes. Combine remaining 3 tablespoons flour, pecans and butter in bowl; mix well. Sprinkle over pie. Bake for 10 minutes longer or until brown. Chill until serving time. Yield: 8 servings.

Margaret Simmons, Alpha Beta
Bedford, Indiana

CRÈME DE MENTHE PIE

This recipe was given to me by a dear neighbor who helped watch my children when they were young.

18 Oreo cookies, crumbled	1 teaspoon peppermint extract
3 tablespoons melted butter or margarine	3 tablespoons Crème de Menthe
20 large marshmallows	1 cup whipping cream, whipped
1/2 cup milk	

Mix cookie crumbs and melted butter in bowl. Pat 3/4 of mixture into 9-inch pie plate. Combine marshmallows and milk in saucepan. Cook until marshmallows are melted, stirring frequently. Stir in flavoring and liqueur. Chill thoroughly. Fold in whipped cream. Spoon into prepared pie plate. Sprinkle with remaining crumbs. Freeze until firm. Let stand for 15 to 20 minutes. Serve with additional whipped cream. Yield: 8 servings.

Jan Lantz, Preceptor Zeta
Caldwell, Idaho

GRASSHOPPER PIE

This recipe was given to me by my mother, who had received it from a special friend.

1 16-ounce package chocolate wafers, crushed	1 cup whipping cream, whipped
1/4 cup melted butter or margarine	1 7-ounce jar marshmallow topping
	1/4 cup Crème de Menthe

Preheat oven to 350 degrees. Mix crumbs and melted butter in bowl. Press into 9-inch pie plate. Bake for 15 minutes or until brown. Combine whipped cream, marshmallow topping and liqueur in bowl; mix well. Spoon into pie shell. Chill for 1 hour. Yield: 8 servings.

Debbie Wilkes, Xi Alpha Sigma
Oshawa, Ontario, Canada

CHIPS AHOY BROWNIE PIE

I saw this recipe on the back of a Chips Ahoy cookie box, and my grandkids wanted it. However, it called for making the pudding from scratch. I tried my variation, and the kids loved it!

25 Chips Ahoy chocolate chip cookies	2 4-ounce packages chocolate instant pudding mix
1/2 cup melted margarine	Whipped cream Chocolate curls

Cut 5 cookies into halves; reserve. Crush remaining cookies. Mix cookie crumbs and melted margarine in bowl. Press onto bottom and up side of 9-inch pie plate. Prepare pudding mix using package directions. Spoon into crust. Insert cookie halves around edge of pie. Chill until set. Garnish with whipped cream and chocolate curls. Yield: 8 servings.

Flo Gordon, Chi Phi
Vandenberg Air Force Base, California

PAULA'S CHOCOLATE FUDGE PIE

1/2 cup melted butter or margarine	1/2 cup sifted all-purpose flour
1 cup sugar	1 tablespoon vanilla extract
2 eggs	
1 ounce baking chocolate, melted	

Preheat oven to 325 degrees. Combine melted butter and sugar in bowl; mix well. Add eggs 1 at a time, beating well after each addition. Add melted chocolate, flour and vanilla; beat well. Pour into well greased 9-inch pie plate. Bake for 25 minutes. Serve with ice cream. Yield: 6 to 8 servings.

Carolyn Dunwoody, Xi Alpha Kappa
La Fayette, Georgia

CHOCOLATE ICE CREAM PIES

This is so quick and convenient when you find out last minute guests are coming.

2 4-ounce packages chocolate instant pudding mix	11/2 cups milk
2 cups softened chocolate ice cream	2 9-inch graham cracker pie shells
	Whipped topping Chocolate shavings

Combine pudding mix, ice cream and milk in bowl; mix well. Spoon into pie shells. Chill until serving time. Garnish with whipped topping and chocolate shavings. Yield: 16 servings.

Sandra Johnson, Laureate Alpha Omega
Stanberry, Missouri

CHOCOLATE-AMARETTO MOUSSE PIE

This is an easy dessert that tastes like you've spent hours preparing it. I'm always asked for the recipe whenever I serve it!

2 envelopes whipped topping mix	1/4 cup Amaretto
11/2 cups milk	1 baked 9-inch pie shell
2 4-ounce packages chocolate instant pudding mix	8 ounces whipped topping Chocolate shavings

Prepare topping mix using package directions. Add milk, pudding mix and Amaretto. Beat at high speed for 2 minutes. Spoon into pie shell. Top with whipped topping. Garnish with chocolate shavings. Chill thoroughly. Yield: 8 servings.

Jean A. Wiyatt, Xi Alpha
Fargo, North Dakota

QUICK HERSHEY PIE

This is great for a quick dessert. It tastes like a chocolate cream pie.

6 11/2-ounce chocolate bars with almonds	1 9-inch chocolate crumb pie shell
8 ounces whipped topping	8 ounces whipped topping
1/4 cup slivered almonds	1/4 cup sliced almonds Chocolate shavings

Melt candy in glass bowl in microwave. Let stand for 5 minutes. Stir in 8 ounces whipped topping and slivered almonds. Spoon into pie shell. Top with remaining 8 ounces whipped topping. Garnish with sliced almonds and chocolate shavings. Yield: 8 servings.

Mandy Scarborough, Beta Epsilon Gamma
Willis, Texas

QUICK ICE CREAM PIE

My elderly aunt made this easy and simple pie.

2 cups crisp rice cereal	Vanilla ice cream
1/3 cup light corn syrup	Chocolate syrup
1/3 cup peanut butter	

Combine cereal, corn syrup and peanut butter in bowl; mix well. Press into 9-inch pie plate. Add enough ice cream to fill. Drizzle with chocolate syrup. Freeze until serving time. Yield: 6 servings.

Jessie B. Duff, Laureate Chi
Toledo, Ohio

QUICK LEMON PIE

1 14-ounce can sweetened condensed milk	1 6-ounce can frozen lemon or lime juice concentrate, thawed
8 ounces whipped topping or softened cream cheese	1 baked 9-inch pie shell or graham cracker pie shell

Combine condensed milk and whipped topping in blender container. Process until smooth. Stir in concentrate. Process until smooth. Pour into pie shell. Chill until set. Yield: 6 to 8 servings.

Betty L. Benson, Preceptor Alpha Gamma
Union, Michigan

HOT LEMON PIE

One evening when guests dropped in unexpectedly, I needed a quick, easy, yet appealing dessert on short notice. This was it!

1 large lemon and rind, chopped	1/2 cup butter or margarine, softened
1 1/2 cups sugar	1 unbaked 9-inch pie shell
4 eggs	

Preheat oven to 350 degrees. Combine lemon, lemon rind, sugar, eggs and butter in food processor container. Process until blended. Pour into pie shell. Bake for 40 minutes. Serve warm with whipped cream. Yield: 6 servings.

Thelma B. Ward, Laureate Iota
Sun City, Arizona

SOUR CREAM-LEMON PIE

My daughter always says she makes a better pie than I do. This recipe is great for kids to make.

1 4-ounce package lemon pudding and pie filling mix	1 cup sour cream
2 tablespoons lemon juice (optional)	1 baked 9-inch pie shell or graham cracker pie shell
2 teaspoons grated lemon rind (optional)	8 ounces whipped topping

Prepare pudding using package directions. Stir in lemon juice, lemon rind and sour cream; mix well. Spoon into pie shell. Let stand until cool. Cover with whipped topping. Yield: 8 to 10 servings.

Patty Ruddell-Willbanks, Xi Gamma Omega
Chandler, Arizona

LEMONADE PIE

My daughter likes to use pink lemonade for a "pretty pink pie."

1 14-ounce can sweetened condensed milk	9 or 10 ounces whipped topping
1 6-ounce can frozen lemonade concentrate, partially thawed	1 9-inch graham cracker pie shell
	1 tablespoon graham cracker crumbs

Mix condensed milk and lemonade concentrate in bowl. Stir in whipped topping. Pour into pie shell. Sprinkle with crumbs. Chill overnight or until serving time. Yield: 6 to 8 servings.

Dolores Payne, Laureate Alpha Zeta
Wichita, Kansas

LEMONADE-ICE CREAM PIE

1 6-ounce can frozen lemonade concentrate, thawed	1 8-inch vanilla, graham cracker or chocolate crumb pie shell
8 ounces whipped topping	
1 1/2 pints vanilla ice cream, softened	

Combine lemonade concentrate, whipped topping and ice cream in bowl; mix well. Pour into pie shell. Freeze until serving time. Yield: 6 to 8 servings.

Lynda Hockett, Preceptor Lambda
Buffalo, Wyoming

PEACH PETAL PIE

1 package refrigerator sugar cookie dough	1 teaspoon sugar
1 20-ounce can peach pie filling	Dash of cinnamon

Preheat oven to 350 degrees. Cut dough into ten 1/4-inch slices. Heat pie filling in saucepan. Spoon into 8-inch pie plate. Arrange dough slices over pie filling, overlapping slices around edge. Sprinkle with mixture of sugar and cinnamon. Bake for 35 to 40 minutes or until cookie dough is brown. Serve warm with ice cream. Yield: 5 to 6 servings.

Mary F. Hessler, Preceptor Alpha Mu
Lincoln, Nebraska

PUMPKIN MOUSSE PIE

1 4-ounce package vanilla instant pudding mix	3/4 teaspoon pumpkin pie spice
3/4 cup milk	1 10-inch graham cracker pie shell
1/2 cup solid-pack pumpkin	1 1/2 cups whipped topping
2 cups whipped topping	

Prepare pudding mix using package directions reducing milk to 3/4 cup. Add pumpkin, 2 cups whipped topping and pumpkin pie spice; mix well. Spoon into pie shell. Top with remaining 1 1/2 cups whipped topping. Chill until serving time. Yield: 6 to 8 servings.

Marion Louise Craig, Omega Mu
Ridgeway, Missouri

❖ SENSATIONAL DOUBLE-LAYER PUMPKIN PIE

3 ounces cream cheese, softened	2 4-ounce packages vanilla instant pudding mix
1 tablespoon cold milk	1 16-ounce can pumpkin
1 tablespoon sugar	1 teaspoon cinnamon
1 1/2 cups whipped topping	1/2 teaspoon ginger
1 9-inch graham cracker pie shell	1/4 teaspoon cloves
1 cup cold milk	Whipped topping
	Finely chopped nuts

Combine cream cheese, 1 tablespoon milk and sugar in bowl; beat with wire whisk until smooth. Fold in 1 1/2 cups whipped topping. Spread in pie shell. Combine remaining 1 cup milk and pudding mix in bowl; beat with wire whisk for 1 to 2 minutes or until well blended. Let stand for 3 minutes. Beat in pumpkin, cinnamon, ginger and cloves. Spread over cream cheese mixture. Chill for 2 hours. Garnish with additional whipped topping and nuts. Yield: 8 servings.

Karen Spence, Xi Epsilon Theta
Pueblo, Colorado

WHITE CHOCOLATE RASPBERRY PIE

I have served this dessert many times as it is so delicious and so simple. It is wonderful for Christmas and Valentine's Day.

12 ounces white chocolate	1 pint fresh raspberries
1/2 cup whipping cream	1 baked 10-inch tart shell
1/4 cup butter or margarine	1 10-ounce package frozen raspberries in heavy syrup, thawed
2 teaspoons light corn syrup	

Cut chocolate into small pieces. Microwave in bowl until softened. Combine whipping cream, butter and corn syrup in saucepan. Bring to a boil, stirring fre-

quently. Pour over chocolate; stir until blended and smooth. Stir in fresh raspberries. Spoon into tart shell. Chill until firm. Serve with thawed raspberries. Yield: 12 servings.

Beverley Matthewson, Alpha Zeta Theta
Richmond, Texas

EASY STRAWBERRY-BANANA PIES

Every time I serve this at chapter meetings, everyone says it is delicious. They think it's hard to make.

8 ounces cream cheese, softened	8 ounces whipped topping
1 cup sugar	1 20-ounce can strawberry pie filling
2 baked 9-inch pie shells	
6 bananas, sliced	

Combine cream cheese and sugar in bowl; beat well. Spread over bottom and sides of pie shells. Add banana slices. Cover with whipped topping. Make indentation in center of each pie. Fill with pie filling. Chill until serving time. Yield: 20 servings.

Connie Leetsch, Laureate Delta Eta
Abilene, Texas

STRAWBERRY PARFAIT PIE

1 3-ounce package strawberry gelatin	1 to 2 cups sliced strawberries
1 cup boiling water	1 baked 9-inch pie shell
2 cups vanilla ice cream	

Combine gelatin and boiling water in bowl; mix well. Add ice cream, stirring until well blended. Fold in strawberries. Pour into pie shell. Chill until set. Yield: 6 servings.

Cheryl Clark, Xi Nu
Watertown, New York

RASPBERRY-SOUR CREAM PIE

A special restaurant served a pie similar to this, but the recipe was not available. This pie tastes almost identical to the one served in the restaurant and is quick and easy.

1/3 cup sugar	2 cups whipped topping
8 ounces cream cheese, softened	1 10-ounce package frozen whole raspberries, thawed, drained
1 teaspoon milk	
1 cup sour cream	
1 teaspoon lemon juice	1 9-inch graham cracker pie shell
1 teaspoon vanilla extract	

Cream sugar, cream cheese and milk in mixer bowl until light and fluffy. Add next 3 ingredients; beat well. Fold in whipped topping. Stir in raspberries. Spoon into pie shell. Chill until serving time. Yield: 8 servings.

Jeanette A. Tims, Xi Gamma Alpha
Norfolk, Nebraska

Metric Equivalents

Although the United States has opted to postpone converting to metric measurements, most other countries, including England and Canada, use the metric system. The following chart provides convenient approximate equivalents for allowing use of regular kitchen measures when cooking from foreign recipes.

Volume

These metric measures are approximate benchmarks for purposes of home food preparation.
1 milliliter = 1 cubic centimeter = 1 gram

Liquid	Dry
1 teaspoon = 5 milliliters	1 quart = 1 liter
1 tablespoon = 15 milliliters	1 ounce = 30 grams
1 fluid ounce = 30 milliliters	1 pound = 450 grams
1 cup = 250 milliliters	2.2 pounds = 1 kilogram
1 pint = 500 milliliters	

Weight

1 ounce = 28 grams
1 pound = 450 grams

Length

1 inch = 2½ centimeters
1/16 inch = 1 millimeter

Formulas Using Conversion Factors

When approximate conversions are not accurate enough, use these formulas to convert measures from one system to another.

Measurements	Formulas
ounces to grams:	# ounces x 28.3 = # grams
grams to ounces:	# grams x 0.035 = # ounces
pounds to grams:	# pounds x 453.6 = # grams
pounds to kilograms:	# pounds x 0.45 = # kilograms
ounces to milliliters:	# ounces x 30 = # milliliters
cups to liters:	# cups x 0.24 = # liters
inches to centimeters:	# inches x 2.54 = # centimeters
centimeters to inches:	# centimeters x 0.39 = # inches

Approximate Weight to Volume

Some ingredients which we commonly measure by volume are measured by weight in foreign recipes. Here are a few examples for easy reference.

flour, all-purpose, unsifted	1 pound = 450 grams = 3½ cups
flour, all-purpose, sifted	1 pound = 450 grams = 4 cups
sugar, granulated	1 pound = 450 grams = 2 cups
sugar, brown, packed	1 pound = 450 grams = 2¼ cups
sugar, confectioners'	1 pound = 450 grams = 4 cups
sugar, confectioners', sifted	1 pound = 450 grams = 4½ cups
butter	1 pound = 450 grams = 2 cups

Temperature

Remember that foreign recipes frequently express temperatures in Centigrade rather than Fahrenheit.

Temperatures	Fahrenheit	Centigrade
room temperature	68°	20°
water boils	212°	100°
baking temperature	350°	177°
baking temperature	375°	190.5°
baking temperature	400°	204.4°
baking temperature	425°	218.3°
baking temperature	450°	232°

Use the following formulas when temperature conversions are necessary.

Centigrade degrees x $\frac{9}{5}$ + 32 = Fahrenheit degrees
Fahrenheit degrees - 32 x $\frac{5}{9}$ = Centigrade degrees

American Measurement Equivalents

1 tablespoon = 3 teaspoons	12 tablespoons = ¾ cup
2 tablespoons = 1 ounce	16 tablespoons = 1 cup
4 tablespoons = ¼ cup	1 cup = 8 ounces
5 tablespoons + 1 teaspoon = ⅓ cup	2 cups = 1 pint
	4 cups = 1 quart
8 tablespoons = ½ cup	4 quarts = 1 gallon

Merit Winners

SNACKS IN A SNAP
First Place
Fraser, Donna, page 48
Second Place
Mansell, Suzanne, page 50
Third Place
Braun, Debbie, page 47
SWIFT SOUPS
First Place
Wilkinson, Karla, page 72
Second Place
Barton, Marg, page 77
Third Place
Osborn, Barbara, page 70
SPEEDY SALADS
First Place
Prasher, Lynn, page 87
Second Place
Myers, Donna J., page 95
Third Place
Morley, Betty, page 82
VERY RAPID VEGGIES
First Place
Sutherland, Laura, page 99
Second Place
Steen, Carole M., page 103
Third Place
Caldwell, Nikki, page 100
BRISK BREADS
First Place
Gasper, Kathy, page 117
Second Place
Shannon, Melinda, page 121
Third Place
Toft, Debra, page 113
MEATS IN MINUTES
First Place
Chapman, Janet, page 142
Second Place
Woelk, Judy, page 131
Third Place
Korbelik, Virginia M., page 127
POULTRY P.D.Q.
First Place
Sullivan, Lottie, page 161
Second Place
Baldwin, Peg, page 153
Third Place
Beeson, D'Arline R., page 158
SEAFOOD IN SECONDS
First Place
Price, Shelly, page 174
Second Place
Wilkens, Bette M., page 169
Third Place
Smith, Pamela, page 171

QUICK COOKIES AND CANDIES
First Place
Foltz, Linda, page 180
Second Place
Brueckner, Phyllis C., page 190
Third Place
Strittmatter, Belinda, page 186
DESSERTS ON THE DOT
First Place
Seeley, Paula M., page 207
Second Place
Spence, Karen, page 213
Third Place
Gaudiano, Carol, page 209
HONORABLE MENTION
Adams, Dorothy W., page 16
Agnew, Evelyn, page 91
Albert, Cynthia, page 166
Alexander, Lou, page 10
Alexander, Morag R., page 160
Anderson, Sheila, page 75
Anderson, Teresa, page 169
Andrist, Shirley, page 199
Andrus, Susan J., page 174
Armitage, Ethel, page 98
Atha, Melinda, page 66
Babb, Barbara, page 86
Bairrington, Pam, page 156
Baker, Ethel, page 144
Barham, Sylvia, page 75
Barker, Evelyn J., page 197
Bartelt, Anneliese, page 96
Baucum, Jane A., page 78
Bazemore, Nan, page 78
Beaty, Marian, page 148
Beaver, Beverly J., page 107
Beher, Clady L., page 104
Bellamy, Heather, page 56
Bent, Mary Jo, page 44
Bethel, Janice, page 185
Bird, Donna, page 8
Blaz, Deborah, page 177
Borges, Joyce, page 130
Borton, Devon, page 47
Bowlin, Barbara L., page 194
Bradley, Michelle, page 200
Brainard, Muriel, page 9
Brennan, Elizabeth, page 92
Brice, Eileen B., page 51
Brown, Becky, page 73
Brown, JoEllen, page 170
Brown, June M., page 133
Browning, Margaret L., page 109
Brunes, Ethel, page 184
Bruns, Noreen, page 10
Bryan, Holly, page 68

Bryant, Virginia E., page 87
Buchele, Marilyn R., page 140
Burns, Sally, page 178
Burnstad, Isobel, page 196
Buss, Bertha M., page 112
Carlsen, Juanita, pages 8, 9
Carlson, Joy, page 135
Carper, Arlene A., page 115
Carroll, Bonnie, page 185
Carson, Pat, page 156
Case, Pat, page 49
Chambers, Anita, page 137
Chitty, Catherine McLeod, page 52
Christiansen, Dorothy J., page 151
Clark, L. J., page 93
Clarke, Pearl L., page 187
Clay, Hazel, page 8
Conner, Tena, page 109
Conrath, Pat, page 202
Cooper, Konda, page 68
Crowell, Holly, page 51
Crump, Amy, page 150
Culkowski, Priscilla, page 69
Cummings, Terry, page 130
Cunningham, Marsha, page 72
Cunnington, Linda, page 148
Curcio, Vienna Eva, page 76
Curle, Vivian, page 49
Curry, Dolores, page 149
Dahl, Lynn, page 168
Davis, Lucy E., page 149
Davis, Marie J., page 199
Davis, Peggy, page 155
Dear, Sharon, page 163
Derks, Valerie P., page 168
Desmond, Lynn Marie, page 63
Dillon, Dora, page 106
Dills, Janet, page 198
DiPippa, Joan L., page 76
Doucet, Ann, page 116
Dovel, Diane, page 84
Effa, Calla, page 83
Eibes, Kathy, page 183
Erickson, Betty, page 90
Ewing, Jean E., page 83
Fahey, Mary Joyce, page 183
Fitch, Shirley, page 93
Foster, Shari K., page 118
French, Helen, page 126
Friend, Lauren, page 87
Fulcher, Sue B., page 151
Funk, Marianne, page 11
Gautreau, June, page 210
Gayda, Bonnie, page 89
Gesner, Elizabeth, page 132
Gibeson, Robin, page 43

Index

Beta Sigma Phi Cookbooks

available from *Favorite Recipes® Press* are chock-full of home-tested recipes from Beta Sigma Phi members that earn you the best compliment of all... "More Please!"

Every cookbook includes:

- ☆ color photos or black-and-white photos
- ☆ delicious, family-pleasing recipes
- ☆ lay-flat binding
- ☆ wipe-clean color covers
- ☆ easy-to-read format
- ☆ comprehensive index

To place your order, call our **toll free** number
1-800-251-1520
or clip and mail the convenient form below.

BETA SIGMA PHI COOKBOOKS	Item #	Qty.	U.S. Retail Price	Canadian Retail Price	Total
The Best of Beta Sigma Phi Cookbook	88285		$9.95	$12.95	
All-Occasion Casseroles Cookbook with Menus	28037		$4.50	$4.50	
The Dining Room	83151		$5.95	$5.95	
Save & Win	70017		$5.95	$5.95	
Shipping and Handling		1	$1.95	$2.95	
TOTAL AMOUNT					

☐ Payment Enclosed
☐ Please Charge My ☐ MasterCard ☐ Visa
☐ Discover

Signature _____

Account Number _____

Name _____

Address _____

City _____ State ____ Zip _____

No COD orders please.
Call our toll free number for faster ordering.
Prices subject to change.
Books offered subject to availability.
Please allow 30 days for delivery.

Mail completed order form to:

Favorite Recipes® Press
P.O. Box 305141
Nashville, TN 37230